Conducting Choral Music

Conducting Choral Music
Fifth Edition

Robert L. Garretson
Colorado State University
Fort Collins

Allyn and Bacon, Inc.
Boston London Sydney Toronto

Library of Congress Cataloging in Publication Data

Garretson, Robert L
    Conducting choral music.
    Bibliography: p.
    Includes index.
    1. Conducting, Choral. I. Title.
MT85.G175C6   1981   784.9′63   80-16281
ISBN 0-205-07145-7

Printed in the United States of America.

Contents

Appendix: Source Information

Preface

In this fifth edition of *Conducting Choral Music*, the book begins with the aspiring conductor's most immediate concerns dealing with conducting techniques, progresses through specific and practical matters dealing with the rehearsal of choirs and choruses, and ends with topics pertaining to various planning and managerial procedures.

Portions of all chapters have been revised and elaborated upon and illustrated with additional examples. In particular, additional information has been added on controlling tempo and dymanics, vocal pedagogy, style and interpretation, and the evaluation of chorus members. The chapter, "The Jazz/Show Choir," however, has been completely revised and expanded to take into account the needs of directors and the diversity of expectations placed upon them, as jazz and show choirs are undeniably an integral part of secondary school music curricula throughout the United States.

Additionally, the list of references at the end of each chapter has been updated. The source information in the Appendix has also been revised and updated, with special attention being given to the inclusion of new choral octavo publications and extended choral works, current addresses of music publishers, educational films relating to choral music, and sources for obtaining various types of musical equipment.

Results of a study by the author focus attention upon the inadequacy with which many choral conductors regard their professional training. It was the consensus of a large group of conductors, whose views were sought, that their training should have been of a more practical nature. With this guiding thought in mind, the author has endeavored to present an approach to the solution of particular problems that the conductor is likely to meet, especially during his first few years of conducting experience. Specific practices and techniques have been presented to give the reader the utmost assistance. Since few teaching situations are identical, the inclusion of basic principles will be found helpful in increasing the conductor's insight and in providing a general approach for meeting and solving problems as they arise.

This book is addressed to conductors of school choirs and choruses, to church choir directors, to leaders of community choral groups, and to students who wish to improve their understanding of the art of choral singing. It may also be of interest and help to administrators and other individuals seeking a knowledge of the aims and problems of the choral conductor. Its design and content are intended to deal with the principles and techniques studied in college and university courses in choral conducting, choral methods and materials, and secondary school music.

Areas of particular concern to the choral conductor and necessary in his professional training are: conducting techniques, tone and diction, style and interpretation, rehearsal techniques, the jazz/show choir, programs and concerts, and planning and organization. A chapter, therefore, is devoted to each of these areas. It is hoped that this book, based upon the teaching needs of numerous choral conductors, will contribute to the betterment of choral singing.

The author is well aware that many women are active today as choral conductors, and their contributions to choral music education in schools, churches, and community groups is well known. Throughout the book, however, the reader will note the use of the words "he," "his," and "him" when reference is made to "the director." No denigration of women conductors is meant; the style was adopted because the words appear so frequently that use of "he and she" or "him and her" throughout would have resulted in awkward writing and difficult reading.

Many persons have contributed to the author's concepts as presented in this book. Some of the ideas have been formulated through observation and discussion with choral conductors throughout the country. The techniques suggested have crystallized during the author's application of them while working with various groups: with school choirs and choruses, church choirs, and choral groups on the university level. To all concerned—conductors and singers—I express my gratitude.

For permission to use excerpts from their choral publications, I am indebted to the following music publishers: AMSI, Associated Music Publishers, Inc., Augsburg Publishing House, Belwin-Mills Publishing Corp., Boosey & Hawkes, Inc., Broude Brothers, Ltd., Galaxy Music Corp., Famous Music Corp., Neil A. Kjos Music Co., Edward B. Marks Music Corp., MCA Music, Inc., Nordiska Muskiforlaget (Stockholm, Sweden), Otto Heinrich Noetzel Verlag (Wilhelmshaven BRD), Plymouth Music Co., Theodore Presser Co., E. C. Schirmer Music Co., G. Schirmer, Inc., Shapiro Bernstein & Co., Shawnee Press, Inc., Walton Music Corp., and World Library Publications.

For permission to quote from their publications, I express appreciation to Oxford University Press, W. W. Norton & Co., *The NATS Bulletin*, Harcourt Brace Jovanovich, Inc., Macmillan (London and Basingstoke), and Collegiate Cap and Gown Company.

To friends and colleagues Ippocrates Pappoutsakis, R. Robert Hornyak, Ira Singleton, Simon V. Anderson, Scott Huston, Mary Swift, Robert Shewan, Edward D. Anderson, Michael Weiker, and Ron Revier for their helpful suggestions in various editions I am especially indebted, and to my wife Aretha, who typed the original manuscript and has offered continual encouragement, I am particularly grateful.

Introduction

During the twentieth century, particularly since World War
I, choral singing has assumed a position of increasing importance and popularity in our society. School and college choirs
and choruses, church choirs, community choruses, and choruses
sponsored by industrial and commercial firms have increased in
size and in quality. Individuals are quite naturally drawn to
activities that they enjoy. Let us, however, examine some of
the underlying reasons for this increase and development of
choral singing.

Considerable credit should be given schools and colleges
for this phenomenal growth. In the past several decades choral
music has progressed from a largely extracurricular activity to
an integral part of the school curriculum. This would not have
occurred without at least some degree of recognition of the values of music participation. Without attempting an exhaustive
consideration of these values, for our purpose they may be
summarized as follows.

Although the benefits of choral singing are many, the *aesthetic* and *expressive* values of music are considered to be the
most important. All persons need to develop a sensitivity to
beauty in music and other art forms, as understanding and appreciation of them may serve to refine and humanize their entire

1

existence. As music is a significant and integral part of man's culture, it is the school's responsibility to help students become more intelligent consumers of music. Participation in musical activities can serve as a means through which individual musical taste may be improved. Through a study of the vast wealth of music literature, students may learn to discriminate between the musically trite and the rich musical heritage that is the right and privilege of every individual. All people have a need for individual self-expression in as many varied ways as possible. Although many concepts and ideas may be expressed through language, other aspects of one's experience can be best expressed through various other art forms. The aesthetic and expressive values of music are, therefore, the principal justifications for its inclusion in the school curriculum.

The *personal-social* values of choral singing also deserve consideration. All individuals need opportunity to engage in activities that promote physical development and that feeling of well-being which is characteristic of good mental health. Music participation can contribute to these ends. Correct posture and proper breathing techniques are emphasized as an adjunct of choral singing and are a necessary attainment of the well-trained choral group. Music also serves as a wholesome outlet and expression of individual emotions. Through music, individuals not only can express themselves, but also can release pent-up feelings of frustration so common in our present-day society.

By contributing time and talent to various social organizations, and through being accepted by other members of such groups, people fulfill their need "to belong": their social beings find expression. A characteristic of the adolescent, as he or she strives to become a social being, is the strong desire to belong to the "gang," inasmuch as membership in various groups usually results in satisfaction and acceptance by members of the peer group. Through cooperative group endeavor, the chorus or choir provides additional opportunity for the development of democratic attitudes and a wholesome channeling of interests toward members of the opposite sex. Students in music activities develop pride in being identified with a fine musical organization and make many social adjustments through the close association with their peers. Certain critics of present-day society say that it has become too individually oriented and that what we need are activities necessitating more group effort. Choral singing certainly fulfills this need. Finally, and not to be overlooked, are the *avocational* and *vocational* values that accrue from music participation. Changes in the attitudes of our society, coupled with many modern living improvements, have resulted in a greater amount of leisure time for most individuals. These changes are highly desirable and offer increased opportunity for individuals to explore many possible areas. As a result of improved educational programs, many persons have discovered music to be an area from which they may derive great personal enjoyment and satisfaction. If continuing programs of music instruction are to be maintained in our society, vocational needs must also be met. In addition to pursuing a teaching career, opportunities also exist in the area of professional music. If one is to be eminently successful in these areas of endeavor, knowledge and skills must be developed at a reasonably early age.

Many institutions in our society other than schools have also contributed to influencing the status of choral music. Increasing awareness of the importance of music as a force in religious worship has resulted in a resurgence of emphasis upon church music programs. An increasing number of churches have employed full-time persons to assume responsibility for the development of the music program. Often these individuals carry the title of Minister of Music, and in effect their duties reflect this title. Choirs for children of elementary school age, for junior and senior high school youth, and for adults are maintained to meet the musical and social needs of all age groups.

Industry's increasing awareness of the importance of rapport in a cohesive, closely knit organization has prompted the establishment of numerous company choruses and other related music activities. Under capable leadership, these organizations have improved employees' morale, developed a feeling of belonging, improved labor and management relationships, and through periodic concerts have strengthened community ties.

The media of radio, television, motion pictures, and recordings have considerably influenced the tastes of the listening public in recent years. Radio has promoted greater understanding and has brought various sections of the country closer together. Remote and isolated areas have reaped a particular benefit. Music of many types has been made available to interested listeners at a minimum cost. Many FM stations, in particular, continue to present music of a high quality. The impact of television has been overwhelming but its cumulative effects have not been fully evaluated. Although an increase in the quality and quantity of musical programs seems desirable, a limited number of excellent programs are being presented. Forward-looking teachers have brought these programs to their students' attention and have utilized them as a valuable educational tool.

Some choirs and choruses have been fortunate enough to make periodic appearances on television. Such experiences, by motivating a choral organization toward maximum group effort, can contribute substantially to the attainment of higher musical standards. The increased use of video tape for such programs also provides a choral group with opportunities to observe and to evaluate the visual as well as the musical aspects of their performance. Educational television especially has utilized the talents of amateur choral groups, and has presented a number of other programs designed to promote musical understanding and appreciation. Since choral music programs may be televised with a minimum of staging and production costs, further possibilities will undoubtedly be explored in the future.

Music has served effectively to heighten the intensity of dramatic situations in motion pictures; and the public is currently experiencing a barrage of tonal sounds and effects associated with theatrical and television productions and the modern dance. Although choral music per se has been too infrequently featured, this background music has perhaps to some extent developed a general tonal awareness of a variety of vocal tone qualities and instrumental tone colors.

Recorded music, especially since the advent of the long-playing record, has made available to the listening public more

music of a high quality than ever before. Numerous recordings of college and university choirs, church choirs, and professional choruses from the United States and Europe are presently
available. Previously produced recordings of choral organizations number in the hundreds, and new recordings are being
released periodically. Especially strong interest was developed
with the advent of high-fidelity and stereophonic recordings.
Although some of this interest may stem from mechanical or
engineering factors, rather than musical aspects, this development has been generally beneficial to the improvement of musical tastes. Inherent in choral recordings are tremendous educational possibilities which, if effectively utilized in educational
programs, may further improve the quality of choral singing in
America.

Choral music has grown considerably and is still growing
in America. However, the previously discussed influences are
bound to reap a desirable cumulative harvest. Capable and
inspired leadership—emphasizing wide participation and high
musical standards—will ultimately place choral music in its
proper sphere as a social and aesthetic art.

Conducting Techniques

The basic function of the conductor is to interpret the music for the singers. Through varied means he endeavors to instill life and vitality into the music—the end result of which can be a truly thrilling and genuinely aesthetic experience for both the participants and the listening audience.

The conductor must be more than a mere time beater. His musical knowledge and interpretative wishes should be conveyed through his conducting technique. Of course, the value and importance of demonstrations and verbal explanations should not be minimized. During rehearsals, however, lengthy verbal explanations should be kept to a minimum, for through his technique[1] the experienced conductor can more quickly help the group achieve the desired interpretation.

Fundamental Conducting Patterns

Each conductor is likely to have his own methods, but the fundamental patterns are the same. Time should be devoted to

[1] *Technique* in this context refers to the multitude of devices used by a conductor to convey the intent of the music and to achieve musical and artistic results. Fundamental conducting patterns, important as they are, are really subservient to the bodily and facial expressions that reflect the mood of the music. Nevertheless, they provide a necessary basis from which to start.

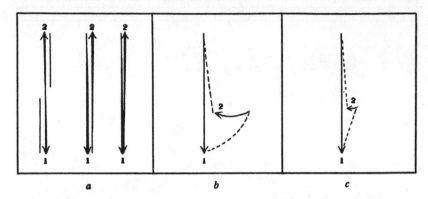

FIGURE 1 *Duple meter (2/4, 2/2, 2/8): (a) the general direction of the pattern (i.e., down, up), (b) the pattern for slower tempi, and (c) the pattern for faster tempi.*

practicing the basic movements until they become automatic. For the purpose of clarification, each of the basic meter patterns, as illustrated in Figures 1–5, is presented in at least two ways. The first diagram indicates the basic direction of the beats within the pattern. The subsequent patterns illustrate the manner in which the conductor may apply them in the interpretation of music. The dotted lines in these conducting diagrams are called *rebounds* or *afterstrokes*. Although they should be considered subordinate to the basic movements within the pattern, they serve as connecting motions between the various beats and as preparatory motions to each subsequent beat. A degree of tension should occur toward the end or point of each beat, which is followed by a degree of relaxation during the rebound. Combined, these factors serve to give the conducting movements definition, clarity, and smoothness or flow—all of which are essential to artistic conducting.

In conducting fast tempi in triple meter (Figure 2c), the second and third beats are negated or omitted, and only the first or primary beat is utilized. In such instances, a slight pause generally occurs at the bottom of this beat; however, the faster the tempo, the less opportunity for pause.

The pattern for conducting quadruple meter is illustrated in Figure 3. Diagram (a) illustrates only the general direc-

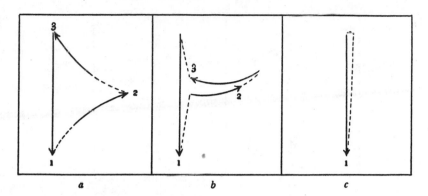

FIGURE 2   Triple meter (3/4, 3/8, 3/2: (a) the basic directions of the pattern, (b) application of the pattern for moderately slow and medium tempi, and (c) pattern for fast 3/4 or 3/8 tempi.

tions of the beats (down, left, right, up), whereas (b) illustrates how the pattern may be utilized with music of a moderate tempo in a legato style.   Note that, following the downbeat and the initial rebound, beats two, three, and four are conducted on a horizontal plane, with the rebound of the fourth beat returning to one.   A pitfall into which the young conductor often falls is utilizing a beat that is too "rounded" in style, with the third beat sometimes rebounding too high, so as to appear as an additional downbeat in the measure.   Thus the conducting

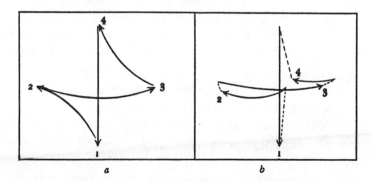

FIGURE 3   Quadruple meter (4/4, 4/2): (a) the basic directions of the pattern, and (b) application of the pattern to music of a moderate tempo.

FIGURE 4   *Sextuple meter (6/8, 6/4): (a) the basic directions of the pattern, and (b) application of the pattern to music of a moderate tempo.*

pattern is often unclear and confusing to the singers.   In summary, keep beats two, three, and four on a horizontal plane.

Three different patterns for conducting sextuple meter are presented in Figures 4–6.   In Figure 4, diagram (a) illustrates the general directions of the pattern, and diagram (b) illustrates how the pattern may be applied in the conducting of actual music.   Many conductors prefer such a pattern, as the fourth beat is clearly defined with a movement in a direction opposite from the first three beats and from the gradual stepwise return to the next downbeat.

Figure 5, however, illustrates an alternative pattern with one clear downbeat and the other beats indicated on a somewhat horizontal plane.   Pattern (a) illustrates the general directions of the beats, whereas pattern (b) illustrates how the movements might be applied in the conducting of actual music.   The advantage of this pattern is simply that there can be no doubt that there is only one downbeat in the measure.

Still another alternative is illustrated in Figure 6.   The advantage of this pattern is the similarity in the direction of the fourth beat.   In pattern (a), six beats are indicated; in pattern (b), the secondary beats—that is, two, three, five, and six—are negated or omitted so that the pattern may be adapted for use with faster tempi.   Because of the similar direction of the primary beats (one and four), the conductor may more easily

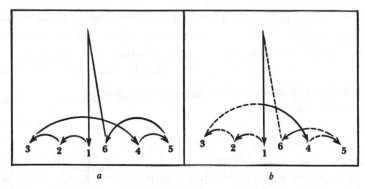

FIGURE 5 *Sextuple meter (6/8, 6/4): (a) the basic directions of the pattern, and (b) application of the pattern to music of a moderate tempo. Note that all beats, with the exception of the downbeat, are on about the same plane and the pattern may be used as an alternative to Figure 4.*

FIGURE 6 *Sextuple meter (6/8, 6/4): (a) for slower tempi, and (b) for faster tempi.*

alternate from one pattern to the other. This flexibility allows the movements in Figure 6 to be used with music involving irregular or changing tempi.

Irregular Meter

Music in irregular meter—that is, 5/4, 7/4, and so on—may be analyzed in combinations of two and three, or three and two;

and three and four, or four and three, depending on the strong and weak syllables of the text structure. Irregular meter occurs rather infrequently in choral music; when it is encountered, however, it is suggested that the conductor generally utilize combinations of the duple, triple, and quadruple meters previously presented. For example, "Nächtens" ("Nightly") by Johannes Brahms (G. Schirmer, No. 10133), written in 5/4 meter, should be conducted throughout by combining duple- and triple-meter patterns (Figure 7). The second downbeat, however, should be conducted on a slightly lower plane so as not to elicit any undue stress on the third beat of the measure. (Actually, the movement should not even be considered as a downbeat, since the gesture for this beat is very small and implies or evokes no particular stress. In contrast, a real downbeat begins from a higher plane, the movement has greater length, and through supporting facial expressions and bodily gestures elicits a particular degree of stress and intensity).

In "To Agni" (from the *Rig Veda*) by Gustav Holst, also written in 5/4 meter, every other measure should be conducted with a triple- and a duple-meter pattern, and alternate measures with a duple and a triple pattern.[2]

Occasional exceptions, however, to the use of such patterns may be encountered. For example, in measure 19 of "Walking on the Green Grass" by Michael Hennagin (Boosey & Hawkes, No. 5443) the rhythmic notation is $\frac{5}{4}$ ♪ ♪ ♩. ♪ | and should be analyzed not as 2 + 3, or 3 + 2, but 1 + 4. This becomes apparent in examining the score and one should be guided by the dictates of the music. Thus the conductor should employ a downbeat, followed by another downbeat on a lower plane and a regular 4/4 pattern.

---

[2] To develop alertness and the flexibility to move from one meter pattern to another, practice conducting the following sequence of changing meters:

2/4, 3/4, 4/4, 5/4, 6/4, 7/4

Devise various other combinations of patterns to conduct and write them on the chalkboard. Another alternative is for one person, through various hand signals, to indicate a changing and varying sequence of patterns.

FIGURE 7 *Excerpt from "Nächtens" by Johannes Brahms (Op. 112, No. 2) in 5/4 meter which may be conducted by combining duple- and triple-meter patterns. Copyright G. Schirmer, Inc., 1953. Used by permission.*

Music in Free Rhythm

Occasionally the conductor will encounter music without a time signature, measure bars, and seemingly without any regular or systematic rhythmic accent or pulsation. In such instances it is

FIGURE 8 *The final measures of Gretchaninov's "Our Father"—
with all but the last beat in the phrase conducted downward. Copyright 1916, Oliver Ditson Company. Used by permission.*

desirable to conduct all the beats downward with the exception
of the last beat in the phrase, which generally should be upward. The beginning of the phrase should receive a regular
precise downbeat; the subsequent words should be treated with
a slight downward movement, varying in length according to
the relative importance of the words. In determining the frequency and the appropriate size of the downward movements,
the conductor should carefully analyze the text of the music.
The final measures of "Our Father" by Alexander Gretchaninov
(Presser, No. 332-13000) necessitates this type of conducting
treatment (Figure 8).[3] The downward movements are indicated under the music.

3 Other examples of music in free rhythm are "Glory Be to God" by Rachmaninoff

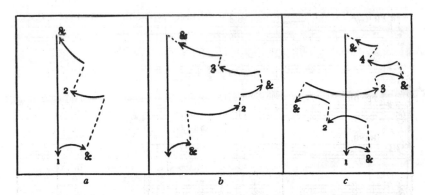

FIGURE 9 *(a) Divided duple meter, (b) divided triple meter, and (c) divided quadruple meter.*

Divided Beats

In conducting music of a moderate tempo, the conductor may utilize effectively the patterns previously illustrated. However, as these patterns are applied to slower tempi, there comes a point where the precision of the beat may become lost and the pattern becomes relatively ineffective. The solution to this problem, therefore, is not simply to slow the beat down further, but to subdivide the beats within the pattern so that in effect they *consume more time by moving through more space.* Through this means, the rhythmic pulsations of the conductor's patterns become more marked and are distinguished by greater clarity, and as a result he is able to obtain a higher degree of precision from the group. When the music is of an exceptionally slow tempo, often indicated by the musical markings *largo* and *grave*, the conductor generally should employ the divided beat to clarify his intentions.

Two well-known examples of choral music that necessitate use of the divided beat, as illustrated in Figure 9, are "Crucifixus" (from the *B Minor Mass*) by Johann S. Bach (E. C. Schir-

---

(Kjos; H. W. Gray), "Gladsome Radiance" by Gretchaninov (H. W. Gray), and "To Thee We Sing," Russian liturgy, arr. Tkach (Kjos).

FIGURE 10 *Excerpt from "Crucifixus" (from the* B Minor Mass) *by J. S. Bach, which should be conducted with a divided triple-meter pattern.*

mer, No. 1174), and "Surely He Hath Borne Our Griefs" (from *Messiah*) by George F. Handel (G. Schirmer, No. 6598). Excerpts from these selections are shown in Figures 10 and 11.

A subdivision of the conducting beat may also be desirable when the rhythmic movement of a particular passage needs to be emphasized or brought out, and during a *ritardando*, when the rhythmic precision of the group needs to be stabilized. Such

FIGURE 11 *From the introduction to "Surely He Hath Borne Our Griefs" (from* Messiah*) by G. F. Handel—in which the divided quadruple-meter pattern should be used.*

instances are likely to occur at the ends of phrases and in the final few measures of a composition. However, any of the beats within a given measure may be subdivided if the tempo of the selection allows sufficient time for the additional movements. The divided beat should not be utilized unless there is adequate time for the rebound of the divided or second half of the beat, as well as for the rebound for the principal beat strokes. Figure 12 offers a case in point, and the correct treatment depends upon the tempo being utilized. Thus, if the tempo were approximately M.M. $\downarrow = 54$, the use of the divided beat as illustrated in Figure 12a would be most appropriate. On the other hand, if the music were being conducted at approximately M.M. $\downarrow = 70$, the added motion of the divided beat would undoubtedly detract from the clarity of the conductor's movements. In this and similar cases involving moderate tempi, it is suggested that the conductor avoid the divided beat pattern and simply accentuate the rebound of beats one and two, as illustrated in Figure 12b. In this treatment a slight pause

FIGURE 12 "Volga Boatmen" (folk song). In conducting the final measure, shown here, pattern (a) is utilized with very slow tempi; pattern (b), with moderate tempi.

should occur at the end of each rebound prior to the stroke of the subsequent beat. This serves to accentuate the rhythmic movement of the divided beat.

Where he has a choice of the preceding alternatives, the conductor should thoughtfully consider the tempo of the music and the conducting pattern appropriate to the music's most effective interpretation.[4]

Attacks and Releases

To be effective, attacks and releases must be executed by the entire ensemble at precisely the same time. To achieve this precision, the group must be alert, it must respond to the rhythmic pulsation of the music, and the conductor must give a clear and precise preparatory beat or movement for each attack or release.

The preparatory beat should always be given at the same rate of speed as that desired in the subsequent measures. Prior to beginning a selection, the conductor should thoughtfully consider his desired tempo and the appropriate preparatory movement. This is especially important to the beginning conductor; later, as one gains experience, this process becomes somewhat automatic in nature. In general, the preparatory beat should approximate the direction of the movement preceding the beat upon which the music begins. For example, if the music begins on the first beat of a measure in quadruple meter, the preparatory movement should occur in the fourth beat preceding, and should be made in the same general direction of the beat utilized for the standard conducting pattern for quadruple meter. Of course, when the music begins on the first beat of a measure in triple meter, the preparatory movement will occur on the third beat preceding the downbeat or actual attack (Figure 13).

---

[4] For further discussion of tempo, see section titled "Determining the Tempo" later in this chapter.

My coun-try, 'tis   of thee, sweet land of   lib - er - ty,   Of thee I   sing.

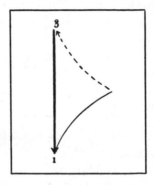

FIGURE 13   *"America" by Carey. The preparatory beat for the attack is indicated by the dotted line preceding the first beat.*

Effective and precise attacks depend not only on adequate preparatory movements executed by the hand and arm, but upon an alert physical stance of the body and appropriate facial expressions.   The attack is facilitated if the conductor is alert to the readiness of the singers, breathes with the group during the preparatory movement, and "mouths" the words in the first measure or so of the text.

One must also prepare adequately for releases if any degree of precision is to be achieved.   A slight upward movement is usually sufficient as a preparatory motion to the actual release, which is generally a precise downward or sideways movement. The size of these movements (the preparation and the actual release) should coincide with the mood of the music and the general size of the conducting pattern being utilized.   That is, the preparation and release of music of a soft, subdued nature will demand a shorter upward preparation and downstroke, whereas the release of a dramatic *fortissimo* passage will necessitate a larger upward movement and a longer, deeper downstroke for an effective and precise release.

The preceding general rules are particularly appropriate for a release at the end of a selection, for phrases with some degree of finality, or for those followed by a slight pause. The conductor should use a modified technique, however, for many of the phrases within the "heart" of a choral selection—particularly when the last note or chord in a phrase needs to be extended to its maximum value and quickly released, with the group "grabbing" a quick catch breath before the attack of the subsequent phrase. A suggested movement to utilize in such cases is to simply turn the palm of the hand over and close it. This movement has been likened to "turning off a water faucet." In certain musical selections one or more of the parts may need to be "cut off" while the others are sustained. When these voice parts are to the conductor's right, this subtle release may be utilized with the right hand; when they are to his left, the left hand may be used for the release, while the basic conducting pattern is continued with the right hand.

Attacks on Incomplete Measures

Problems in achieving precise, accurate attacks most frequently occur when dealing with *incomplete measures*. Following are several variants and suggested techniques for dealing with each.

1 When a composition begins on a full or complete beat, the conductor should prepare the group by conducting the preceding beat as a preparatory movement. For example, when in quadruple meter the music begins on the fourth beat, the conductor should utilize the third beat as the preparatory movement (Figure 14).
2 When a composition begins on the second half of the beat, the first half of the beat is given as the preparation (Figure 15).
3 When a composition begins after the second half of the beat and is closer to the following than to the preceding beat, then use a full or complete beat as the preparatory movement according to rule 1 (Figure 16).

It will be noted that no special treatment is utilized in Figure 16 for the sixteenth note preceding the fourth beat. As this note falls more closely to the following (fourth) beat than to the preceding (third) beat, the same preparatory movement is utilized as that for any music beginning on a full or complete

Oh beau - ti - ful for spa - cious skies for am - ber waves of grain,

FIGURE 14   *"America, the Beautiful" by Samuel A. Ward.   The preparatory beat is indicated by the dotted line preceding the fourth beat.*

beat [compare the diagram in Figure 16 with that suggested for use with "America, the Beautiful" (Figure 14)].

An exception to the treatment of a sixteenth note occurs with the note following the *fermata* in Figure 17.

I __ wish   I   was __ in de land ob   cot - ton.

FIGURE 15   *"Dixie" by Daniel Emmett.   The preparatory beat is indicated by the dotted line.*

Ye sons of France, a - wake to glo - ry!

FIGURE 16 *"La Marseillaise" (French national anthem) by Rouget de Lisle. The preparatory beat is indicated by the dotted line preceding the fourth beat.*

De __ sun so hot I froze to death, Su- san-na don't you cry.

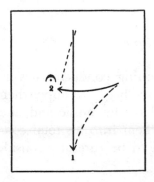

FIGURE 17 *Excerpt from "Oh! Susanna" by Stephen Foster. The preparatory movement (following the fermata) is the upward motion that precedes the first beat of the following measure.*

Fermatas

One should prepare for all *fermatas*, or holds, if precision in performance is to be expected; that is, the movements preceding the *fermata* should be especially clear, concise, and definite in character. When a slight *ritardando* precedes the *fermata*, as is often the case, the conductor should slightly enlarge the pattern of his beat as a means of gaining attention and preparing the group for the *fermata*. Raising the plane or height of the beat on which the *fermata* occurs is often helpful when the group is sustaining a *forte* passage. This is not always necessary, however, when the group is singing *piano*.[5]

During the hold, the conductor should continue a slow, steady movement of the beat and avoid a stationary position in midair. Musical tone is continuing—not static—and this suggested slight movement will assist the singers in maintaining an even, steady flow of breath necessary for adequate tonal support.

The release of the *fermata*, or hold, is as important as the preparation, and either of two procedures may be utilized, depending upon the interpretative effect desired. One procedure is to cut off completely the tone following the hold; the alternative is to carry over the tone to the succeeding phrase without a break in the flow of the breath. The conducting patterns for these two procedures are illustrated in Figure 18.

Unifying the Technique

As soon as the beginning conductor has a knowledge of the basic patterns, he must begin to apply them in ways that are meaningfully related to the music and at the same time endeavor to integrate them into his total conducting technique. Various factors need to be carefully considered at this point,

---

[5] When singing softly there is a tendency for singers to lessen the breath support, thus causing intonation problems. To avoid this difficulty, singers should have the illusion of using more and not less energy when singing softly.

Figure 18 *"Flow Gently, Sweet Afton." Two procedures for releasing the* fermata: *(a) complete release, and (b) carryover.*

including correct posture, surety of beat patterns, facial expressions that reflect the mood of the music, coordination of the movements of the wrist, elbow, and hand, and even whether or not to use a baton.

Bodily Attitudes

The correct posture of a choral conductor can be described as "a bodily position that enables the conductor to most effectively achieve his task." In this sense, the posture resembles somewhat the "correct" posture of the singer (see Figure 39 in Chapter 2: one foot is placed several inches ahead of the other and the feet are spread apart so as to provide a solid foundation; this position allows the conductor to remain alert and responsive to the musical situation.[6] Conducting gestures or movements should occur only in the upper body. From the waistline down, the body should generally be stationary. This

---

[6] When the feet are in this position, the conductor should be careful not to rock back and forth, or to bend the upper body too far forward. Should either of these situations occur, it may be helpful to place the feet in a more parallel position.

does not exclude occasionally moving closer to the group during rehearsals or moving from one side of the room to the other to assist various sections.   But, for the most part, and certainly during a concert, the conductor should *stand still.*   On the podium the conductor should assert a necessary degree of forcefulness, based on a knowledge and surety of the music, and endeavor to communicate the composer's intentions to the singers.   Shyness, coyness, and the like are characteristics that must be masked and that should give way to clarity and definition.

One pitfall to which the beginning conductor often succumbs is the tendency to merely "draw" the patterns in the air in a somewhat mechanical way.   To minimize this tendency, the conductor should study the music carefully, identifying the various tensions created through rhythmic and harmonic movement and let them be reflected in his conducting.   Conducting thus becomes a real means of communicating musical ideas to a group of singers and not merely a mechanical exercise.

Facial expressions should reflect the mood or character of the music.   In short, the best advice that could be given is to endeavor to "look like the music."   Regular practice before a full-length mirror will reap dividends for the conductor desirous of improving this aspect of his conducting technique.

Self-Analysis

It is essential that undesirable traits be eliminated in the beginning stages, and not allowed to become reinforced and habitual. Following are some specific points of which young conductors should take careful note.

1 The wrist should be held firm, as any looseness or floppiness is distracting and the clarity of the point of each beat is lessened.
2 The elbows should be flexible and not held too closely to the body, as freedom of movement is inhibited.   They should at least be high enough to allow the palms of the hands to face the floor.   Conversely, the elbows should not be extended too far outwardly as this also is distracting.

3 The fingers should be held close together. With young conductors there may be a tendency to spread them somewhat apart, and this is not only distracting, but sometimes even humorous to the singers. Spread fingers have been referred to as "Dracula" hands, and a distended little finger has been referred to as the "teacup hand position."

4 One should conduct most of the time primarily in front of the body so that the singers can perceive the conductor's beat patterns or gestures as related to his facial expressions and thus integrate them into a whole. Extended movements to one side of the body may be utilized for a special purpose only, but they should be the exception rather than the rule.

5 The conductor should maintain eye contact with the singers to the greatest extent possible and should never "bury his nose" in the music. It is essential to maintain eye contact at the beginning and ending of phrases, at fermatas, and during any change of tempo. The conductor should be familiar enough with the music so that he needs to use it only as an occasional reference point.

If a conductor could view himself as others see him, many problems would be eliminated or at least minimized. This is possible, of course, on a videotape recording: the various points mentioned above become not only more meaningful, but sometimes shockingly real. It is essential for the young conductor striving for proficiency to practice on specific aspects of technique on a daily basis. Practicing in front of a mirror is helpful, but it is of even greater benefit for two persons to pair off, to practice conducting each other alternately, and then to provide immediate "feedback" or reaction to the other's conducting.

Use of a Baton

Whether or not to use a baton is largely a matter of personal taste; however, for the beginning conductor use of a baton has a distinct advantage in that it helps to delineate the point of each beat to a greater extent—thus providing a degree of necessary and desirable discipline. The baton serves as an extension of the hand and arm and is helpful in working with larger groups—particularly with a large chorus and/or orchestra.

The advantage of using the hands only—rather than a baton—is that the conductor is able to achieve a somewhat more fluid and flexible beat. This is particularly advantageous in legato sections of a piece. Some conductors, however, have been known to use both techniques with a particular choral work— a baton when conducting the larger chorus/orchestral forces and the hands only during a more subdued, legato choral section of a work. A choral conductor who anticipates working with combined choral and instrumental organizations would be well advised to develop an adequate baton technique.

Determining the Tempo

Performing a musical work in the proper tempo is an important aspect of artistic interpretation. In the process of determining a tempo, the conductor should consider a number of factors.

Style and Historical Period

Any consideration of tempo should begin with an analysis of the musical style and the characteristics of the historical period from which the music was an outgrowth. Artistic forms of expression are shaped by various social, economic, and political forces which influence a composer during his life. Tempo, therefore, as well as other interpretative considerations, should reflect the basic spirit of the times. (For a discussion of tempo during the various historical periods, see Chapter 3.)

Changes between historical periods were not abrupt, but evolved slowly. Within a given period, one may find unique differences among the styles of individual composers. With a concept of the general characteristics of particular periods as a starting point, the conductor should carefully analyze the style of the composer whose music he is preparing to perform. Although such a procedure may seem like a never-ending task, all efforts in this direction will contribute to a clearer understanding of the essential factors influencing interpretation.

Metronome Markings

Some music will contain metronome markings indicating the desired tempo of the composer and/or the arranger. The metronome marking indicates the number of beats occurring within the duration of a minute, and the type of note that receives this basic pulsation. For example, the abbreviation M.M. $\quad\!\!= 60$ indicates that 60 quarter notes may be'sounded in the duration of one minute, or one quarter note each second.[7] If the metronome marking were M.M. $\quad\!\!= 120$, the tempo would be double that of the previous tempo, and 120 quarter notes would be sounded in the duration of one minute, or two quarter notes each second. Prior to introducing a new selection to the group, it is desirable for the conductor to check his own tempo concept with that indicated by the metronome marking. Although such markings need not be slavishly followed, they can be helpful in providing the conductor with a basis for determining his ultimately desired tempo.

Tempo Markings

Although all composers do not include metronome markings on their music, many will indicate the approximate desired tempo through the use of appropriate words, sometimes in English, but usually in Italian. Following is a basic group of Italian terms that the conductor is most likely to encounter:

Very slow:	*Largo*—large, broad, stately
	Grave—heavy, slow, ponderous
Slow:	*Larghetto*—slow (the diminutive of *largo*)
	Lento—slow
	Adagio—slow, leisurely
Moderate:	*Andante*—moderately slow, at a walking pace
	Moderato—moderate (tempo)

---

[7] The metronome, a mechanical device used to indicate a particular desired tempo, was invented in 1816 by Mælzel, hence the name Mælzel Metronome, or the abbreviation M.M.

Moderately fast: *Allegretto*—quite lively, moderately fast
       Fast: *Allegro*—lively, brisk, fast
              Vivace—brisk, spirited
  Very fast: *Presto*—very fast, rapid
             Prestissimo—as fast as possible

Although these Italian terms are only relative indications of tempo, they do provide the conductor with a general basis for determining the approximate tempo suggested by the composer or the editor. Equally important, however, are those terms indicating a change in the basic tempo. Some of the more common terms are:

Accelerando—gradually increasing in tempo
Ritardando—gradually decreasing in tempo
Rallentando—gradually decreasing in tempo
Allargando—gradual broadening of tempo, with slight increase in volume
Calando—gradual decrease in tempo and volume
Stringendo—gradually increasing in tempo and excitement
A poco a poco—little by little, gradually
Poco meno mosso—a little slower
Poco più mosso—a little faster
A tempo—return to the original tempo

In addition to the preceding terms, the conductor will encounter many others, particularly those pertaining to musical expression. Until the conductor becomes thoroughly acquainted with all such markings, it is suggested that he maintain, for quick and easy reference, a standard dictionary of musical terms.

Mood of the Text

A thorough study of the mood of the text will provide additional insight in determining the most desirable tempo. An excerpt from the Christmas spiritual "Go Tell It on the Mountain" (Galaxy, No. 1532) is included for illustrative purposes (Figure 19).

Go tell it on the moun- tain, O - ver the hills and
ev - 'ry - where, Go tell it on the
moun - tain that Je - sus Christ is born!

FIGURE 19 *"Go Tell It on the Mountain" (Christmas spiritual).* Copyright © 1945, 1973 by Galaxy Music Corporation. *Used by permission.*

The author has heard this spiritual performed at various tempi, ranging from approximately M.M. ♩ = 60 to M.M. ♩ = 130. With such a wide variance in tempi, just what should be the conductor's guiding criterion? Although the mood of some spirituals is somber and serious, the text of this particular one describes the joyous, happy news that "Jesus Christ is born!" With this prevailing thought in mind, the author is inclined to select a beginning tempo of approximately M.M. ♩ = 100. The tempo of contrasting sections within the music, however, should be considered separately in light of the prevailing mood of the text.

Ability of the Singers

The complexity of various vocal lines and the harmonic aspects of the music are highly important factors in determining the correct tempo. Certainly the skill with which the singers can execute a difficult florid passage must be considered. For singers with limited technique, it is a far better practice to perform a selection at a slightly slower tempo than the metronome markings might indicate or one might wish, and to sing it *well,* rather than in a slovenly, unmusical manner. Folk-song arrangements that are straightforward in nature can often be sung at a more rapid tempo, without sacrificing tonal stability, than can music with an unusual harmonic treatment.

Acoustics of the Performance Room

The acoustical properties of the rehearsal room or auditorium have a telling influence upon the total musical effectiveness of a selection. In comparison with instruments, the human voice —especially that of an inexperienced singer—has less sustaining quality. In rooms with little reverberation, a lifeless tonal quality, with an insufficient connection between various tones within the musical phrase, will often result. In such instances music may sound best at a slightly faster tempo than one would normally use in an auditorium or a room with reasonably good acoustics. Conversely, the conductor will find it desirable to employ restraint when rehearsing or performing in rooms with exceptionally live acoustical properties.

Achieving Expressive Conducting

In developing one's conducting technique the fundamental patterns merely provide a necessary basis from which to begin. The conductor must also consider such matters as the conducting plane or height of the beat, the size of the beat in relationship to tempo and dynamics, clarifying the beat, the style of the beat in relationship to the manner of articulation, preparing for changes in tempo and dynamics, the length of the musical phrase, the use of the left hand, and the cueing of entrances.

The Conducting Plane

The level of the conducting beat is determined by the size of the musical organization and the eye level of the singers. If the size of the organization is reasonably small and if the group is seated on risers, the plane of the conductor's beat, for the most part, should be from the shoulder level down to the waist. If the musical organization is exceptionally large, the conductor will find it desirable to raise the conducting plane slightly so that all singers may clearly see his beat.

The conducting plane may be raised or lowered to effectively indicate the shape of a phrase or an increase and decrease of phrase-wise tension within the musical phrase. The choral selection "A Thought Like Music" by Brahms (Plymouth, No. A.S. 103) is an excellent example of music necessitating this treatment (Figure 20). The phrase should be begun with a

FIGURE 20 *Excerpt from "A Thought Like Music" by Johannes Brahms, in which the conducting plane may be raised and lowered to indicate the rise and fall or increase and decrease of tension within the phrase. Copyright © 1958 by Plymouth Music Company, Inc. Used by permission.*

beat about chest high and gradually raised to the peak of the phrase in the second measure. After the peak of the phrase is reached, the conducting plane is gradually lowered. Another example of this treatment occurs in "How Lovely Is Thy Dwelling Place" by Brahms (Carl Fischer, No. 632).

Size of the Beat

The size of the conductor's beat should be determined by the dynamic level, the tempo and rhythm of the music, and the style of articulation (discussed in a following section), as well as by the general mood or character of the music. The conductor should determine the appropriate dynamics of the music and adapt the size of his beat accordingly. Music of a high dynamic level generally necessitates a larger, broader beat, whereas music of a low dynamic level requires a relatively smaller movement. Particularly with music of a subdued nature, some conductors are inclined to utilize movements that are too large, and often, therefore, unprecise and unclear.[8] For example, in the choral selection "Since All Is Passing" by Paul Hindemith (Schott, No. AP37), the size of the conducting pattern that is appropriate to the first phrase—marked *piano* (*p*)—need not be more than 6 inches in height; for the second phrase—marked *pianissimo* (*pp*)—the pattern should necessarily be reduced slightly in height; the third phrase—marked *forte* (*f*)—should be prepared for vigorously and should be approximately 14 to 16 inches in height. The dynamic level of the final phrase is identical to the second and should be conducted accordingly.

In the motet "Create in Me, O God, a Pure Heart" by Brahms (G. Schirmer, No. 7504), an extremely quiet beginning is necessitated and the conductor must strive for an appropriate dynamic level (Figure 21). To help achieve the desired effect, the conductor's initial preparatory movement should be

---

[8] The conducting movements for music of a low dynamic level should, for the most part, be immediately in front of the body; thus a more coordinated effort between the hand and arm movements and the facial expressions may be achieved.

extremely small—only a precise movement of several inches is necessary, as a larger movement may elicit too loud a response.

Dynamic contrast is a problem of considerable concern to many directors, some of whom have often stated—somewhat in jest—that their choral groups seem to know only two dynamic levels—loud and louder. In view of this seeming dilemma, it behooves conductors to give careful consideration to the appropriate size of their conducting movements as they relate to the dynamic level of the music. This is essential if their groups are ever to sing in an expressive manner.

The tempo of the music is also an important factor influencing the size of the beat. Because of physical limitations, it is necessary for the conductor to limit the scope of his beat with music of a relatively fast tempo if any degree of precision is to be achieved. For example, in the well-known Ukrainian carol

FIGURE 21 *Excerpt from "Create in Me, O God, a Pure Heart" by Johannes Brahms, in which the conductor must use an exceptionally small beat in the beginning to achieve the desired dynamic level. Copyright, G. Schirmer, Inc., 1931. Used by permission.*

"Carol of the Bells" by Leontovich (Carl Fischer, No. CM 4604), the tempo necessitates a relatively small beat. Although some parts of the music may be conducted one beat to a measure, the introductory section in particular requires a small, crisp three-beat pattern. And, to reiterate, if the pattern is to be clear and precise, it must be relatively small.

In conducting certain figures or patterns containing notes of unequal duration, it is often desirable, particularly in *legato* music, to reduce the size or scope of the beat on unaccented pulses (Figure 22). For example, in conducting the Negro spiritual "My Lord, What a Mornin' " (Ricordi, No. 412), it is desirable to minimize the movements for the second and third beats in measures 1, 3, and 4 (Figure 22*a*), and to minimize the movements for all beats except the first in measure 2 (Figure 22*b*). This modification is more expressive of the music, it serves to lessen the singers' physical response on unaccented pulses, and it facilitates a more *legato* effect. Although this example is but one, the principle is basic and may be applied in numerous rhythmic patterns as a means of eliciting a more musical response.[9]

Clarifying the Beat

With fast tempi there may not be adequate time to conduct each beat in the pattern in a clear, distinct manner. Although decreasing the size of the beat pattern will help (so that the hand does not have to move through so much space), the only solution is sometimes to eliminate or leave out certain beats in a measure. This is often referred to as *negation*. For example, in the "Neighbor's Chorus" by Jacques Offenbach

---

[9] It will be found helpful to practice conducting various rhythm patterns with the objective of negating, or reducing the size of, beats where there are rests or little rhythmic movement. For example:

$$\frac{3}{4} \, \downarrow \downarrow \downarrow | \downarrow \downarrow \downarrow | \downarrow \downarrow | \downarrow \downarrow | \quad etc.$$

Devise various other rhythmic patterns to conduct.

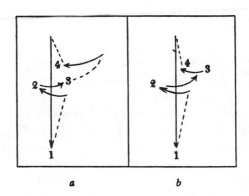

a   b

FIGURE 22 *Excerpt from "My Lord, What a Mornin'"* (Negro
*spiritual), arr. H. T. Burleigh (© 1924 by G. Ricordi & Co., New
York; used by permission of Franco Colombo Publications, a division of Belwin-Mills Publishing Corp.), in which the conducting
patterns are modified (a) for the rhythmic pattern* 4/4 ♩ ♩ ♫ |*, and
(b) for the rhythmic pattern* 4/4 ♩ ♩. |*. Note the rebound of the first
beat and the relatively short strokes of the following beats. Compare these patterns with Figure 3.*

(Broude Brothers, No. 130) the meter is 3/8 and the tempo marking is ♩. = 69 (Figure 23). Therefore, the most effective gesture is simply to conduct the music with one strong beat to a measure, thus either negating or at least minimizing the size of beats two and three in each measure. Occasionally,

FIGURE 23 *Excerpt from "Neighbor's Chorus" from* La Jolie parfumeuse *by Jacques Offenbach, in which beats two and three are either negated or reduced in size to clarify the conductor's gestures. Copyright, Broude Brothers, 1954. Used by permission.*

however, three small beats per measure may be conducted to indicate the restraint necessary at the end of a phrase, such as in measures 11 and 12. Measure 13, of course, returns to the original tempo.

The reverse of this situation occurs in "All Breathing Life, Sing and Praise Ye the Lord" by J. S. Bach (G. Schirmer, No. 7470) (Figure 24). In contrast, the conductor will want to utilize a small three-beat pattern to set the tempo and to indicate the rhythmic movement of the sixteenth-note figure. Then, two or three measures of this pattern may be followed by a "one-to-a-measure" pattern (with beats two and three being negated) for the remainder of the phrase. At the beginning of most phrases, however, the conductor will generally revert to the small three-beat pattern.

FIGURE 24 *Excerpt from "All Breathing Life, Sing and Praise Ye the Lord," from the motet* Sing Ye to the Lord *by J. S. Bach, in which a small, precise three-beat pattern is used to set the tempo and indicate the rhythmic movement of the sixteenth-note pattern.*

Style of the Beat

It is highly important that the conductor's beat reflect the manner or style of articulation of the music, that is, *legato, staccato,* or *marcato.*[10] In conducting music in a *legato* style, the director should maintain a continuous movement to his beat, for when it stops, the natural tendency is for the singers to stop also, or at least to lessen the flow of the breath. One of the difficulties involved, especially in slow, sustained passages, is maintaining control of the arm movement. When the arm moves too quickly and the end of the beat is reached too soon, the conducting will appear jerky and the smooth *legato* effect will be lost. To eliminate this fault, the conductor should imagine a definite resistance to his movements. Pretending to move one's hand through a pool of water will often produce the desired feeling.

Music in a *staccato* style must be conducted in a crisp, detached manner to indicate the desired articulation of the music. To do so effectively, however, the conductor should use a relatively small beat. As singing in a *marcato* style necessitates a sharp inward movement of the abdominal muscles on each note marked >, this action should be reflected in the conductor's motions. Thus music in a *marcato* style demands a vigorous movement, with a precise and definite point to each beat. Whereas many compositions may be found that are in either *legato* or *staccato* styles throughout, this is seldom if ever the case with *marcato* style.[11] Phrases indicating *marcato* are so marked for special effect and, to be effective, should be in contrast to other sections. Figure 25 includes an excerpt from the "Last Words of David" by Randall Thompson (E. C. Schirmer, No. 2294), which illustrates a considerable use of *marcato.* Note the relationship of the *marcato* markings to the text of the music. "Glory to God" by J. S. Bach (Ricordi, No. NY 1397) is an excellent example for analysis and performance that alternates between *marcato* and *legato* styles. An example com-

10 For a discussion of the relationship of diction to these basic styles of articulation, see section titled "Styles of Diction" in Chapter 2.
11 For examples of music in *legato, staccato,* and *marcato* styles, see section titled "Styles of Diction" in Chapter 2.

FIGURE 25 *Excerpt from "The Last Words of David" by Randall Thompson, illustrating a* marcato *style, which necessitates vigorous and marked conducting gestures. Copyright, E. C. Schirmer Music Co., 1950. Used by permission.*

bining all three styles—*legato, staccato,* and *marcato*—is "When Love Is Kind" (English Folk Song) —arr. Salli Terri (Lawson-Gould, No. 843).

Controlling Tempo and Dynamics

A conductor must retain absolute control of the tempo of a choral group. Under certain circumstances singers may be inclined either to rush or drag the tempo—neither of which helps to achieve a musical performance. At the very least they may not be as responsive to the conductor as is necessary. When a conductor is in control, he has the feeling that the singers will respond to his gestures for the most subtle of nuances (almost like one being in command of a "mighty" organ). First of all, the group must be trained to watch the conductor carefully, and the conductor should not always necessarily conduct a piece at the same exact tempo (sometimes due to the varying acoustics of the performance halls). Also, the treatment of phrase endings may be handled slightly differently. The conductor, in this respect, should not always be predictable; if he is and the group feels that they can "second guess" him, so to speak, they are not likely to be quite as attentive as necessary.

Additionally, for the conductor to control the tempo of an ensemble, two conditions are essential: the precision of the initial beat and the clarity of the afterstroke, or "rebound." There should be a definite point to each beat followed by a clear rebound to the next beat. It is the preciseness of the point of each beat that enables a choir to maintain a steadiness of the pulse, and it is the nature of the rebound that enables the conductor to change the tempo—either faster or slower. Effective changes in tempo are not achieved by merely slowing down or speeding up the conducting pattern. Rather, the pattern must be modified in a way that will both attract the attention of the singers and signal the intentions of the conductor.

For the conductor to express his desire for *accelerando,* the size of the overall conducting pattern should be lessened in size, but with particular attention being giving to a gradual quickening of the rebound of each beat. For a *ritardando,* the first half of each beat should be gradually lengthened, but the rebound in particular should consume slightly more time by moving through more space, i.e., the point of each subsequent beat is not reached quite as soon.

The problem of the choir determining their own *ritardandos* (which they are sometimes inclined to do) results in too many versions of tempi, inaccuracy, and overexaggeration of the *ritard.* To alleviate this problem, the conductor should insist that the group maintain a steady tempo—like a team of horses pulling a heavy load (or any other analogy), and he should "pull on the reins" ever so slightly when he feels it is necessary. Such an approach helps to maintain the intensity and drive of the pulse and places the conductor more in command of his choir.

As to dynamic changes, the size of the beat is paramount. An almost ludicrous situation seems to exist when the conductor asks for a *pianissimo* verbally and through his facial expressions but continues to flail away with a relatively large conducting pattern. Soft passages necessitate a small, precise conducting pattern which may be increased in size according to the relative level of dynamics. For one to become more sensitive to what is being asked of the choir, some periodical practice in front of a mirror can be most helpful. The key question to be asked by the conductor is: "Do I like what I see and how would I as a singer respond to the conducting gestures observed?"

Extending the Musical Phrase

Some singers are inclined to take unnecessary breaths between short phrases or in the middle of phrases. The conductor can eliminate some of this difficulty by making a circular movement toward the group—indicating that a breath is not to be taken and that the musical phrase is to be extended. This circular movement should commence at least one beat, and in faster tempi, two beats, prior to the end of the phrase that is to be carried over.

The Left Hand

Conductors, as a general rule, are inclined to overuse the left hand. Some fall into the habit of allowing the left hand to follow the pattern of the right. As overuse of the left hand renders it relatively ineffective for special situations, it should, for the most part, be held near the waistline. Conductors may then more effectively use the left hand for special emphasis, such as sudden accents, abrupt changes in tempo, cueing entrances of certain sections, *crescendo* and *decrescendo*, and to assist in effecting clear, precise attacks and releases.

In actual practice many conductors do use both hands simultaneously in conducting the basic patterns. There is nothing terribly wrong with this practice, particularly when it is used, for example, to convey a certain dramatic intensity in the music or to rhythmically solidify a chorus of considerable size. It does become unnecessary, however, when conducting music of a restrained nature and a low dynamic level. In this instance, too much arm movement is inimical to the best artistic performance of the music and simply might best be described as "overkill."

Cueing

Effective cueing should provide a sense of security to the singers and facilitate the precision of attacks and an improved musical interpretation. It also allows the singers to become more aware (if they watch) of important entering solo voices or sections that are generally of musical importance to the listeners. This concept should be communicated to the singers so that they understand the necessity for some voices to occasionally predominate and others to be subservient to the melodic line.

Cueing has been referred to as "effective phrasing with a timely look in the proper direction." Several methods of cueing are currently utilized. The conductor may employ any of the following approaches, depending upon the tempo of the music, the style of the music, and the frequency of the entering parts:

1 Use of the *hands*, providing there is adequate time to execute the movements.
2 Use of the *head*, when a multiplicity of entrances occur in the music.
3 Use of *facial expressions*, appropriate in dealing with more subtle and delicate entrances.
4 A *combination* of two or more of the preceding methods.

Some subtle cues may be indicated by a very slight hand movement combined with appropriate facial expressions, such as a nod of the head, or perhaps by mouthing the vowels in the first word or so. Other entrances may necessitate a more vigorous motion, sometimes with both hands being used. The appropriate gesture depends, of course, upon the dynamic level of the music, the tempo, and the multiplicity of entrances required.

A good many cues that involve the entrance of only one part may be best accomplished by simply pointing the beat or hand and arm in the direction of the group or section whose entrance needs to be assisted. When several sections or the entire choir is cued, it is generally best to reinforce the gesture by the use of both hands.

Cueing entrances of various parts is essential to rhythmic security and should be given the same careful treatment and preparation as the entire ensemble is given at the beginning of a choral selection.

Conducting Accent and Changing Meter

Basic conducting patterns often need to be modified in a variety of ways to reflect the character of the music and to elicit the proper musical response from the group. Rhythm, meter, and accent account for many of these modifications; therefore, the following procedures are suggested for conducting syncopated figures, off-beat accents, displaced rhythmic accents, and changing meter and shifting accents.

Syncopated Figures

The conducting of certain syncopated figures may be made more effective by utilizing a vigorous rebound to the beat preceding each accented or syncopated note in the figure, and shortening or reducing the size of the following beat. See, for example, the excerpt from "Ching-A-Ring Chaw" adapted by Aaron Copland (Figure 26), and the illustration of the modified conducting pattern for the figure $\frac{2}{4}$ ♩ ♪♩ ♩ |.

For a similar example involving the same conducting

FIGURE 26 *Excerpt from "Ching-A-Ring Chaw" (minstrel song), from* Old American Songs. *Adapted by Aaron Copland; arranged for SATB by Irving Fine. A modified conducting pattern is used for the syncopated figure* $\frac{2}{4}$ ♩ ♪ ♩ | —*(a) for faster tempi, as in the example, and (b) for music with slower tempi. A slight pause occurs at the top of the rebound, especially in conducting faster tempi.* © *1954, 1955 by Aaron Copland. Reprinted by permission of Aaron Copland, Copyright Owner, and Boosey & Hawkes, Inc., Sole Publisher and Licensees.*

FIGURE 27 *Excerpt from "Now Is the Hour of Darkness Past" by Daniel Pinkham, in which the conductor combines an accentuated rebound and negation to achieve clarity. Copyright 1975 by Ione Press, Inc. Sole selling agent: E. C. Schirmer Music Co., Boston. Used by permission.*

principle—yet somewhat more complex—see the final three measures of "Now Is the Hour of Darkness Past" by Daniel Pinkham (Figure 27). It will be noted that the accents fall on the second beat, the second half of the third beat, and the second beat of the following measure, and that the music is marked *senza rall.* While a conductor might initially be inclined to simply conduct the rhythm of the words, this creates difficulties in terms of rhythmic accuracy. One is advised to conduct a strict three beat pattern with an accentuated rebound on the second half of the third beat in measure 3. The size of the first beat in the following measure should be negated or minimized to allow for a clearer emphasis on the accented second beat.[12]

Off-beat Accents

A group of off-beat accents, *i.e.*, those occurring on the second half of each beat or pulse may be conducted effectively by utilizing a slight downward movement of the hands and arm on the first half of the beat, followed by a definite and precise upward movement on the second half of the beat. The pat-

---

[12] In addition to the conductor's gestures, it is helpful, in this instance, to ask the chorus to count aloud together—one, *two*, three *and*, one, *two*, three, one, etc. In counting, emphasize the accents and repeat as many times as necessary.

tern should be entirely up and down, with the rebound re-
tracing the path of the downbeat (see the excerpt from "Ezekiel
Saw the Wheel" and the illustration of the suggested conducting
pattern in Figure 28).

FIGURE 28 *Excerpt from "Ezekiel Saw the Wheel" (spiritual), arr.
Simeone, in which the modified pattern above is used for conducting
the off-beat accents* $\frac{2}{4}$, ♩ ♪ | ♪ ♩ ♪ |. *From the Fred Waring choral
arrangement.* © *Copyright MCML, Shawnee Press, Inc., Delaware
Water Gap, Pa. 18327. Used by permission.*

Displaced Rhythmic Accents

The use of accents on beats other than those expected, *i.e.*, the strong beats of a measure, is a rhythmic device used by various contemporary composers. One means is the use of traditional rhythmic patterns in nonsymmetrical forms. For example, in the composition "It Is Good To Be Merry" by Jean Berger (Kjos, No. 5293), the traditional 9/8 pattern of $3 + 3 + 3$ is altered to $2 + 2 + 2 + 3$ (see Figure 29). In Leonard Bernstein's "America" (from *West Side Story*), the 6/8 pattern of $3 + 3$ is altered to $3 + 3 + 2 + 2 + 2$ (see Figure 30). In "Ballad of Green Broom" by Benjamin Britten (Boosey & Hawkes, No. 1875), the 6/8 pattern of $3 + 3$ is altered to $3 + 1\frac{1}{2} + 1\frac{1}{2}$ and $1\frac{1}{2} + 1\frac{1}{2} + 3$ (see Figure 31).

In conducting such patterns, the director must first analyze the music for the shift of accents and then determine the most appropriate movements to convey clarity and evoke rhythmic precision from the group. The conducting pattern should not be too large if precision is to be achieved. Following the downbeat, it is suggested that the subsequent movements (beats) be made from right to left in a crisp, short, decisive manner (see Figures 29–31).

Changing Meter and Shifting Accents

In preparing to conduct selections with changing meter and shifting accents the conductor should carefully analyze the music, identify the significant aspects of the rhythm that need to be clarified or conveyed to the singers, and then determine the most appropriate gestures or patterns to convey musical meaning and the intentions of the composer.

In Randall Thompson's "Glory to God in the Highest" (E. C. Schirmer, No. 2470) (see Figure 32), for example, the first six measures change alternately from 2/4 to 3/8 to 2/4 (2 measures) to 5/8 to 2/4.[13] A suggested approach to conducting this

---

[13] Other suggested selections for study with changing meter are "It Is Good To Be Merry" by Jean Berger (Kjos, No. 5293) and "Festival Te Deum" by Benjamin Bitten (Boosey & Hawkes).

ance,   The mer - ry heart _ make - eth   a

ance,   The mer - ry heart _ make - eth a

The mer - ry heart   The mer - ry heart _ make - eth a

The mer - ry heart   The mer - ry heart _ make - eth a

FIGURE 29   *Excerpt from "It Is Good To Be Merry" by Jean Berger, together with a conducting pattern for the nonsymmetrical figure* ⅜ ♩ ♪♪ ♩ ♪♩ | (2+2+2+3). *Used by permission of Neil A. Kjos Music Co., San Diego, Calif. Copyright 1961.*

section of changing meter, as illustrated in Figure 32, is as follows.   In measure 1 (in 2/4), a two-beat pattern with a strong full downbeat and a short precise secondary beat should be used. In measure 2 (in 3/8), because the eighth note maintains the

FIGURE 30 *Excerpt from "America" from* West Side Story *by Leonard Bernstein, arr. William Stickles, and patterns for conducting the nonsymmetrical figure* 𝄴♪♪♪♪♪♪|♩♩♩| (3+3+2+2+2) *(a) for measures one and three, and (b) for measures two and four.* © 1957, 1959, by Leonard Bernstein and Stephen Sondheim. Used by permission.

FIGURE 31 *Excerpt from "Ballad of Green Broom" from* Five
Flower Songs, *Op. 47, No. 5. Words anonymous; music by Benja-
min Britten. Conducting pattern (a) for measure one:* § ↕ ↱ ♪ ♪ |,
pattern (b) for measure two: § ♪ ♪ ♪ ♪ ♪ |, *and pattern (c) for meas-
ure three:* § ♪ ♪ ♪ ♪ ♪ |. © *1951 by Boosey & Co., Ltd. Renewed
1979. Reprinted by permission of Boosey & Hawkes, Inc.*

same value as in the previous measure ($\downarrow = 120$) and since it
would be awkward, and not really necessary, to conduct three
distinct movements, beats two and three should be negated and
only one strong beat conducted in the measure. (Actually there

is a pause on the second beat and the rebound from the down-beat occurs on the third beat). Measures 3 and 4 should be conducted in two, as in measure 1. In measure 5 (in 5/8), the first eighth note is conducted with a downbeat, on the second eighth note the beat is negated, and the third eighth note is indicated by the rebound, which is restricted with the hand and arm returning only part way. The conductor will thus be in a position

FIGURE 32 (continued)

FIGURE 32 *Excerpt from "Glory to God in the Highest" by Randall Thompson. Suggested conducting patterns for (a) measures 1 and 4, (b) measures 2 and 11, (c) measure 5, and (d) measure 12. Copyright E. C. Schirmer Music Co., 1958. Used by permission.*

for the secondary beat of a two-beat pattern, with the last two eighth notes in the measure being conducted as in measure 1. The principal reason for using this pattern, and particularly for negating the second beat in the measure, is because of the moderately rapid tempo (♩ = 120) and the need for clarity in the conducting pattern. Each of the five eighth notes should be equal in duration, and if the conductor executes the pattern as described, no problem of unevenness should occur. Measure 6 (in 2/4) should be conducted with a strong downbeat, but with a short movement on the secondary beat to indicate the duration of an eighth note followed by the eighth-note rest.

In measures 11–13, the accents shift from the third beat, to the second, to the first. In conducting measure 11 (in 3/8), the first beat should be conducted with a vigorous downbeat— but short and precise; the second beat should be negated (with a slight pause); and the third-beat accent should be indicated by a precise, directly upward, movement or rebound. In measure 12 the downbeat on beat one should be followed by a precise upward rebound on beat two and the third beat should be negated. In measure 13, the first beat is accented with a precise downbeat.

Another interesting example involving changing meter (see Figure 33) may be found in "Walking on the Green Grass" by Michael Hennagin (Boosey & Hawkes, No. 5443). Measure 12 (in 2/4) and measure 13 (in 6/8) are both conducted with a two-beat pattern; however, the tempo of the eighth note remains constant ($\quarternote = \quarternote$), with the rebound to the downbeat occurring on the second eighth note in the 2/4 meter and on the third and sixth eighth notes in the 6/8 meter. Measure 14 (in 5/8 meter) may be considered a composite of the two previous measures: the conducting pattern for the first two eighth notes is the same as that used for measure 12, and the pattern for the remaining quarter and eighth note is the same as that used in the last half of measure 13. In other words, the rebound of the beat pattern used for 2/4 meter occurs on the second half of the beat, whereas the rebound for the 6/8 meter occurs on the third and sixth eighth notes in each measure.

It must be remembered that the conducting pattern used depends on the rhythm. For example, in measure 14 of "Walking on the Green Grass" the basic rhythm is 2 + 3, whereas in measure 5 of "Glory to God in the Highest" the basic rhythm is 3 + 2. Compare the suggested patterns for conducting each of these rhythms and practice each alternately as follows:

FIGURE 33 *Excerpt from "Walking on the Green Grass" by Michael Hennagin, with suggested conducting patterns for measures 12–15: (a) for measure 12, (b) for measures 13 and 15, and (c) for measure 14. Note that the conducting pattern for measure 14 (in 5/8) uses the first half of the pattern for measure 12 (in 2/4) and the last half of the pattern for measure 13 (in 6/8).* © 1962 by Boosey & Hawkes, Inc. *Reprinted by permission.*

Alternate the practice of 5/8 patterns with 2/4 and 6/8 patterns until you can move from one to another with *security*.

Conducting 7/8 meter at a moderate-to-fast tempo also necessitates the use of a pattern different from that used for slow tempi. Although the precise technique used will vary according to the rhythm within each measure, a practical approach is to conduct a basic 4/4 pattern with an accentuated rebound on each beat except the last, which is negated with the rebound returning, on the seventh pulse (if felt or conducted in 8/8) in the measure, to the next downbeat (Figure 34). Benjamin Britten's "Festival Te Deum," Opus 32 (Boosey & Hawkes) contains several examples of 7/8 meter that may be conducted in the manner just described.

Another alternative is to conduct the 7/8 measures with the first two movements or beats of a triple-meter pattern (with the rebounds accentuated) and the last half of a 6/8 pattern, as illustrated in Figure 35. (This pattern is preferable for conducting the first three measures of the excerpt.) excerpt.)

The principle in the selection of beat patterns, then, is to analyze and break down the rhythmic patterns into their basic components, usually units of two or three (duple- or triple-meter patterns), and identify patterns or movements that are the simplest to coordinate, particularly during moderate-to-fast tempi. Economy of movement is necessary if rhythmic clarity and precision are to be achieved. Gestures that are too large and too numerous can impede rhythmic drive and lessen the intensity and effectiveness of the interpretation. In measures with irregular meter, one should look not only to the rhythm but the text to determine the most appropriate conducting patterns.

Following is a list of other examples of choral music containing changing meters, in many but not all instances, from measure to measure. These are all excellent study, as well as performance, pieces for the conductor. Each should be thoroughly analyzed as regards the most appropriate and effective conducting patterns to be used, and practiced until one's technique becomes stable and secure. The sequence of meter changes is indicated following each selection.

Hindsight—Brent Pierce. Walton Music Corp. No. 2964. (6/8, 5/8, 6/8, 5/8, etc.)
A Fancy—Emma Lou Diemer. Carl Fischer No. CM8011. (2/2, 3/2, 2/2, 3/2, etc.)
Who Hath a Right to Sing?—Lloyd Pfautsch. Lawson-Gould No. 52048. (6/8, 5/8, 6/8, 5/8, etc.)
Shout the Glad Tidings—Larry Willcoxen. Harold Flammer No. A-5583. (3/8, 5/8, 9/8, 5/8, etc.)

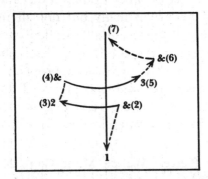

FIGURE 34   *Excerpt from "Festival Te Deum," Op. 32, words liturgical; music by Benjamin Britten, in which the measures in 7/8 may be conducted with the pattern indicated.* © *1945 by Boosey & Co., Ltd.; renewed, 1972. Reprinted by permission of Boosey & Hawkes, Inc.*

FIGURE 35 (a) First two movements of a triple-meter pattern (with accentuated rebounds), (b) last half of a 6/8 pattern, and (c) combination of (a) and (b) into a 7/8 pattern for conducting selected measures in Benjamin Britten's Festival Te Deum.

The Ninth of January—Dmitri Shostakovitch. G. Schirmer No. 12123. (6/8, 5/8, 3/8, 3/4, 4/4, 7/8, 5/8, 3/8, 2/4, etc.)

Praise Ye the Lord—John Rutter. Oxford University Press No. 42.357. (3/4, 4/4, 3/8, 5/8, 3/8, 4/4, 7/8, 4/4, 6/8, 4/4, etc.)

Mary Hynes (from Reincarnations)—Samuel Barber. G. Schirmer No. 8908. (4/4, 3/2, 3/8, 4/4, 3/8, 5/8, 3/4, etc.)

Festival Te Deum—Benjamin Britten. Boosey & Hawkes. (3/4, 5/8, 7/8, 4/4, 3/4, 3/8, 5/8, 2/4 . . . ; 2/4, 7/8, 3/4, 11/8, 7/8, 5/8, 2/4 . . . ; 6/8, 18/8, 4/8, 5/4, 4/4, 7/8, 3/4, 5/8, 3/4, etc.)

Symphony of Psalms—Igor Stravinsky. Boosey & Hawkes. (Part I: 2/4, 4/4, 1/4, 3/2, 4/4, 3/2, etc.; Part II: 4/8, 3/8, 2/8, 4/8, etc.; Part III: 4/4, 3/2, 4/4, 3/2, 2/2, 3/2, etc.)

Chichester Psalms—Leonard Bernstein. G. Schirmer, Inc. (Part I: 6/4, 3/4, 3/8, 5/4, 2/4, 5/8, 6/4, 2/4, 5/4, 7/4, etc.; Part II: 3/4, 2/4, 3/4, ¢ 3/2, 3/4, C, ¢; Part III: 9/4, 10/4, 5/2, 9/2, 12/2.)

Preparing the Score

In preparing for a rehearsal the conductor should first thoroughly study his score (singers generally resent the conductor who learns the music along with the choir). Before introducing a new choral selection, it is suggested that first he peruse and analyze the text to determine the overall mood and then play the music on the piano to acquaint himself with the musical means that the composer used to express his creative thoughts. Rhythm, tempo, dynamics, harmony, and the texture of the music—all have a bearing upon the conductor's choice of gestures, which should grow out of his understanding and desire to effectively interpret the music.

After careful study, it is suggested that the conductor mark his score by either underlining, encircling, or drawing over portions of the music. For example, tempo and dynamic indications might be underlined or encircled; accents, phrasing lines, and changing meter signs, and moving parts that need to be emphasized or brought out may be encircled. (Some conductors prefer to highlight their markings by using a red- or blue-colored pencil). These markings may effectively serve as a reminder for the use of appropriate conducting gestures during either subsequent study and/or actual rehearsals.

In studying the score, the conductor should read through the music and endeavor to conceptualize his interpretation. Specific consideration should be given to each measure and no matters left to guesswork. To illustrate this point, guidelines for preparing the first twelve measures of "Create in Me, O God, a Pure Heart" by Brahms (G. Schirmer, No. 7504) are given in Figure 36.

In summary, and perhaps to overstate the obvious, conducting should never be simply a matter of establishing the tempo, conducting a meter pattern, and then "watching the notes go by." Young conductors, in particular, should know their scores, develop some specific musical expectancies, and then express them to the choir both verbally and through their conducting. Try preparing a number of selections in detail, as indicated above, and then note the development of your conducting technique!

Topics for Discussion

1 Recall and identify the personality attributes of successful conductors you have known. With this information as a basis, dis-

Measure	Suggested Conducting Gestures
Incomplete	Use extremely small movement, as a large gesture will elicit too loud a response.
1	Use small beat pattern; negate beats two and three.
2	Raise plane of beat slightly; place slight stress on third beat.
3	Negate beats two and three; support tone with left hand.
4	Lower plane of beat; indicate decrescendo with left hand.
5	Negate beats two and four; make precise sideways movement (from left to right) to indicate the release of the second and the beginning of the third beat in measure.
6	Negate first beat; cue soprano line on second beat.
7	Conduct quarter-note movement in baritone line.
8	Restrain volume with left hand; raise plane of beat gradually.
9	Continue to restrain volume on first beat; gradual crescendo beginning with second beat may be indicated by raising slightly the conducting plane.
10	Lower conducting plane gradually; indicate decrescendo by lowering the left hand.
11	Negate second beat; cue and stress entrance of bass line on third beat.
12	Indicate descrescendo of tenor line by lowering left hand and conducting plane.

FIGURE 36 *Guidelines for conducting the first twelve measures of "Create in Me, O God, a Pure Heart" by Johannes Brahms.*

cuss the factors that you believe are important to conducting success.

2 Recall and identify the facets of effective conducting technique that you have observed in various conductors.

3 Describe in class some of the conducting problems not usually encountered. Discuss the most appropriate means of handling these problems.
4 Discuss the differences in interpretation of a choral composition as illustrated in two or more recordings. Which interpretation do you believe is most effective, and why?
5 What effect do tempo, dynamics, accent, rhythm, phrasing, style, and mood of the music have upon the basic conducting patterns?

Selected Readings

Cain, Noble, *Choral Music and Its Practice*. New York: M. Witmark & Sons, 1942. (Chapter 14.)

Christy, Van A., *Glee Club and Chorus*. New York: G. Schirmer, Inc., 1940. (Chapter 1.)

Davison, Archibald T., *Choral Conducting*. Cambridge, Mass.: Harvard University Press, 1945. (Chapters 1 and 2.)

Decker, Harold H., and Julius Herford, *Choral Conducting: A Symposium*. Englewood Cliffs, N.J.: Prentice-Hall, Inc., 1973. (Chapter 5.)

Finn, William J., *The Conductor Raises His Baton*. New York: Harper & Row, Publishers, 1944.

Jones, Archie N., *Techniques in Choral Conducting*. New York: Carl Fischer, Inc., 1948.

Kjelson, Lee, and James McCray, *The Conductor's Manual of Choral Music Literature*. Melville, N.Y.: Belwin Mills Publishing Corp., 1973.

Krone, Max T., *Expressive Conducting*. Chicago: Neil A. Kjos Music Co., 1949.

McElheran, Brock, *Conducting Techniques: For Beginners and Professionals*. New York: Oxford University Press, Inc., 1966.

Moe, Daniel, *Problems in Conducting*. Minneapolis: Augsburg Publishing House, 1968.

Pooler, Frank, and Brent Pierce, *New Choral Notation*. New York: Walton Music Corporation, 1971.

Roe, Paul, *Choral Music Education*. Englewood Cliffs, N.J.: Prentice-Hall, Inc., 1970. (Chapter 8.)

Rudolf, Max, *The Grammar of Conducting.* New York: G. Schirmer, Inc., 1950.

Sateren, Leland B., *Mixed Meter Music and Line in Choral Music.* Minneapolis: Augsburg Publishing House, 1968.

Stanton, Royal, *The Dynamic Choral Conductor.* Delaware Water Gap, Pa.: Shawnee Press, Inc., 1971. (Chapters 2 and 3.)

Tone and Diction

Tone quality is the very substance of choral singing. Without properly produced tones, coupled with correct diction, effective choral singing is impossible to attain. Dynamic contrasts, proper blend and balance, accurate pitch and intonation, and effective phrasing are all dependent upon correct vocal production. Furthermore, projection of the mood or spirit of the music is dependent upon correct diction, as well as on proper tone quality. Since good tone quality and correct diction are fundamental considerations in the training of choral groups, the conductor should develop a well-defined concept of all factors influencing tone and diction. Because choral groups react in varying ways, he should also develop a wide variety of techniques for achieving his objectives.

The Vocal Instrument

The human vocal instrument possesses the three components that are essential to the functioning of all musical instruments: an *actuator*, a *vibrator*, and a *resonator*. In addition, it has a component unique only to the human voice—an *articulator*. Generally, the components of the vocal instrument (see Figure 37) may be identified as follows:

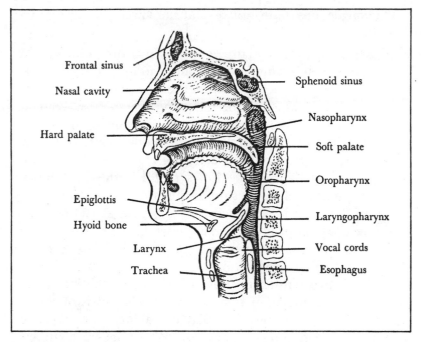

FIGURE 37 *Relative locations of the larynx, the resonating cavities (pharynx, mouth, and the nasal cavity), and the articulating organs (tongue, lips, teeth, palate, and the lower jaw). Note the divisions of the palate (hard palate and the velum, or soft palate), and the pharynx (laryngopharynx, oropharynx, and the nasopharynx).*

1 The respiratory or breathing muscles serve as the actuator.
2 The vocal cords (sometimes referred to as vocal folds) serve as the vibrator and are the source of the sound.
3 The pharynx, mouth, and nasal cavity serve as the resonator, which amplifies the sound.[1]

[1] Some authorities also consider the paranasal sinuses, the trachea, the bronchi, and the chest cavity to be part of the resonating system. The concept of the nasal and sinus cavities as resonating chambers appears to be rather widely accepted among voice teachers. There is a contrary opinion, however, that rejects the concept of both the nasal and sinus cavities as resonating chambers and scientific evidence is cited against the latter. For statements of these opinions, see Richard Luchsinger and Godfrey Arnold, *Voice-Speech Language* (Belmont, Calif.: Wadsworth Publishing Co., 1965), p. 458, and John Carroll Burgin, *Teaching Singing* (Metuchen, N.J.: The Scarecrow Press, Inc., 1973), pp. 84–87. Whatever the opinion held by various persons, perhaps greater agreement might exist on at least the "sensation" of head resonance. This is not to say that it occurs physiologically but that it is at the very least a pedagogical device for achieving voice placement.

4   The tongue, lips, teeth, palate, and the lower jaw serve as the articulator.

The principal muscles utilized in normal breathing are the diaphragm, the abdominal muscles, and the intercostal muscles. Although there is still some difference of opinion concerning the action of these muscles, the following is generally accepted. During inspiration, the diaphragm contracts and pushes downward, while the contraction of the intercostal muscles lifts or raises the ribs. The combined action of these muscles enlarges the thorax, which allows the lungs to fill with air. During normal expiration there is supposedly no muscle contraction necessary; the chest is decreased in size by the elastic recoil of the thoracic wall. In prolonged expiration, such as in singing a sustained note, the abdominal muscles gradually contract while the diaphragm slowly relaxes, and the intercostal muscles maintain enough tension to prevent bulging of the intercostal spaces. During the act of singing, breath control is of the essence; therefore, a delicate interplay or balance must exist between these opposing sets of muscles. When one set contracts, the other set should relax—but not completely—as their mutual activity provides for the best utilization of the air in the lungs.

The larynx functions somewhat like a valve—when open it allows the singer to inhale and exhale air to and from the lungs. The vocal cords or folds are the vibrating edge of the thyroarytenoid muscles, the posterior ends of which are attached to the arytenoid cartilages. The anterior or front ends of the vocal cords are attached to the thyroid cartilage, commonly known as the "Adam's Apple." The vocal cords are tensed by the contraction of the cricothyroid muscles. The tension of the vocal cords is decreased by the contraction of the thyroarytenoid muscles of which they are a part. The vocal cords are approximated or brought together by muscles controlling the position of the arytenoid cartilages, and are set into vibration by the flow or pressure of the breath during exhalation. The fissure or opening between the vocal cords is referred to as the glottis. During deep inspiration, the glottis assumes a somewhat round shape, but during quiet or normal breathing it assumes a V-shaped position. When one sings a high pitch, the vocal cords come very close together and the glottis become a thin, narrow slit or opening (see Figure 38).

The pitch of the tone is determined by the tension of the vocal cords and the pressure of the breath against the vocal cords. If this pressure or breath support is inadequate, the laryngeal muscles often function incorrectly in their effort to obtain the correct pitch. This induces fatigue and undue strain on the voice.

In general, the resonating cavities may be divided into two types—fixed and adjustable. The nasal cavity is fixed, whereas the pharynx and mouth are capable of special utilization. On each side and above the vocal cords are cavities that amplify the vibrations produced by the vocal cords and increase their intensity as they are projected from the larynx. These cavities are fully utilized as resonance chambers only when the throat is relaxed and kept open. Similarly, the mouth is best used as a resonance chamber when all the muscles, including the tongue, are relaxed and the cavity of the mouth is enlarged, thus allowing for an increased resonance chamber. The nasopharynx and the nasal cavity are most effectively utilized as resonance chambers when a slight opening between the oropharynx is maintained, thus allowing for an extension of the vibrating column of air emanating from the larynx.

Flexibility of the articulating organs—the tongue, lips, velum (soft palate), and the lower jaw—is highly important

a   b   c

FIGURE 38 *The larynx as observed through a laryngoscope, illustrating differences in the size of the glottis (a) while taking a deep breath, (b) during quiet or normal breathing, and (c) during phonation.*

if the vocal mechanism is to function at optimum efficiency. Procedures for coordinating the various components of the vocal instrument are discussed in the following sections.

Developing Choral Tone

In the process of developing the tonal quality of a choral group, the conductor should take into consideration a number of factors: correct singing posture, proper breath control, the function and value of particular vocalises, and the development of deep-set vowels and high-forward resonance. Development of the high range, particularly in male voices, and the achievement of vocal flexibility are also areas of special importance and concern.

Achieving Correct Posture

Correct posture is necessary to the development of good tone production. Since vocal tone is affected by all the muscles of the body, an alert bodily position must be maintained while singing, whether the individual is standing or sitting (Figure 39).

When in a standing position, one should place his feet approximately 6 inches apart and the left foot preferably should be several inches in front of the right. This stance affords the singer better balance and lays the foundation for the proper use of the breathing muscles. The weight of the body should rest to a great extent on the balls of the feet—not on the heels. The abdomen should be drawn in and the spine should be kept as straight as possible. The singer's upper back should feel as wide as possible and the chest should be held relatively high, but without strain or excess tension. Since the throat functions as an organ pipe, the head must be kept perpendicular to the shoulders in order that this "pipe" be kept clear and open. The music must be held in such a position that the di-

FIGURE 39   *Correct posture for standing and sitting.*

rector may be easily seen without the singers lowering or raising their heads, as any deviation in the position of the head is likely to affect the tone quality.

When the singer is seated, the correct posture from the waist up will be almost identical with the standing posture. The only basic difference is that the legs assume a bent position. While in a sitting position, the singer must keep both feet on the floor and lean slightly forward, away from the back of the chair, if they are to maintain adequate breath support. Some of the bodily weight must be distributed to the lower limbs and the feet. The proper coordination between the breathing muscles and the vocal apparatus will result only if this correct posture is maintained while singing.

Improving Breath Control

The next consideration in developing good choral tone is the establishment of correct breathing habits. This is necessary to ensure the steady flow of the breath to the vocal cords and is fundamental to both tone quality and tone control.

Clavicular or collarbone breathing does not fill the lungs to capacity and the resultant tension in the upper chest and shoulder muscles affects the muscles around the larynx and inhibits the proper action of the vocal cords.[2] Improper breathing habits that have developed over a period of years are not always easily corrected. First, the singer must throughly understand the effect of poor breathing habits upon his own tone production and upon the tone quality and blend of the choir. He must achieve a conception of the correct method of breathing.

In singing, it is necessary to use the muscles around the entire midsection of the body, not just the diaphragm. The muscles of the upper chest and shoulders should be relaxed, with the greater amount of work being done by the intercostal muscles, the diaphragm, and the abdominal muscles. These are the muscles used in correct breathing technique (see section titled "The Vocal Instrument" earlier in this chapter).

The director should continually emphasize the formula, *breathe deeply, expand around the entire midsection—in the back and around the sides, as well as in front.* Have the choir members bend over, from a standing position, until the upper part of the body is parallel to the floor. In this posture clavicular breathing is difficult and somewhat unnatural. By pressing the hands against the waist, with thumbs to the back, one can get the "feel" of correct breathing. Try it! Another procedure, which is more easily managed in a crowded rehearsal room, would have the group lean forward in their chairs, placing one elbow on the knee. Proper breath action may then be checked by pressing the other hand against the waist. After the singers learn how the muscles are utilized in correct breathing, they must strive toward the attainment of proper breath control until it becomes automatic. Proper breath support and control will improve only through continual emphasis.

---

[2] This type of incorrect breathing is exemplified in the inspiration movements utilized by a child in preparation for blowing out a candle.

Use of Vocalises

Choral conductors generally employ vocalises as a part of the vocal training of their choir members. They are used specifically for the improvement of choral tone and blend. Some conductors utilize vocal exercises only as a part of the warm-up period, as athletes use mild exercise to prepare themselves for the more strenuous rigors of competition. Other conductors feel that exercises employed for such purposes are largely a waste of time, since they are not directly connected with the immediate problem of improving the performance of the choral music. This latter group will often take a troublesome portion of the music out of context and utilize it as a vocal exercise.

Although some conductors may feel that only one of the previously mentioned procedures should be followed, it seems reasonable to assume that both practices have considerable merit and that each approach should be employed to some extent. To be effective, vocal exercises must be varied periodically. Continued concentration on particular devices or exercises will eventually lead to boredom, lack of concentration, and less than maximum physical effort. As a result, more harm than good may occur. Therefore, *variety* is the watchword—variety in vowel sounds, in the types of exercises, and in the time of the rehearsal period during which they are utilized.

Vocal exercises should be employed discriminately, since each exercise, if performed correctly, will produce a different type of color or tone quality. It is important to realize, then, that the overuse of one exercise to the neglect of another will not always produce the best or desired results. For example, if the choir sings with an overly dark tone, the conductor should avoid too much vocalization on the darker vowels, such as **aw** and **oh**. It might be well for the choir director or voice teacher to think of various vocal exercises as a physician might think of a prescription or a form of therapy—that is, as a remedy or treatment for a specific individual or group need. For choral blend, a uniformity of vowel production must be achieved. Although the conductor is definitely concerned with individual voices and needs, the problem in practice is, for the most part, one of dealing with the tone problems of a large group.

Let us first of all examine the type of tone quality desired for high school, college, and community choral groups. There are several schools of thought concerning the "ideal" quality, and in addition, certain choral selections require subtle changes in voice quality. Nevertheless, it is essential that the conductor develop his concept of tone through private voice study and by listening to numerous choruses and choral recordings, and then strive toward that goal. A word of caution, however! Sometimes the inexperienced high school conductor is overzealous in his attempts to achieve the mature quality found only in adult choirs, and in his eagerness develops a tenseness and rigidity in the youthful voices. High school choirs have characteristic qualities common to this age level. These qualities should be carefully nurtured and allowed to develop slowly. Only in this way will the ultimate in high school choral singing be achieved.

Individuals participating for the first time in a choir generally display an abundance of technical faults. Some may sing with a throaty tone, others with white, nasal, or colorless tones. Without uniformity in tone production, blend is practically unattainable.

Just what type of voices are we endeavoring to develop? There are two characteristics that the conductor should strive to develop in voices at the outset: (a) a deep-set vowel, and (b) a high-forward resonance. When these two characteristics are present, the tone quality is rich and beautiful, and capable of lending itself to the wide gamut of emotions found in choral literature. Various exercises contribute to the development of these qualities and will be presented on the following pages.

Achieving Deep-Set Vowels

The deep-set vowel is usually associated with maturity and roundness of tone and with naturalness of production. It is achieved through minimizing unnecessary tension in the vocal apparatus and by correctly utilizing the resonance cavities of the mouth and throat. As has been previously discussed, correct posture and breath control are essential conditions. Clavicular breathing should be avoided, since the resultant tension in the shoulder muscles and upper regions of the chest is oftentimes reflected in the muscles surrounding the larynx, thus inhibiting the proper functioning of the vocal mechanism.[3]

The writer has observed high school and adult choral groups in various sections of the country. One of the most objectionable faults is that many teen-age youths, as well as adults, sing with a tight, rigid jaw. Some individuals believe that this condition is a reflection of environmental tensions. More likely, the condition results from lack of proper vocal training and individual awareness of the problem. Whatever the exact cause, the effect is disastrous upon choral singing. Tenseness in the jaw and facial muscles results in strident, pinched, and colorless tones. Depth of tone and subsequent choral blend is impossible to attain until the condition is alleviated. Following are suggested devices, techniques, and exercises to help eliminate this problem.

1   Singers should be instructed to concentrate upon relaxing their facial muscles. Gently stroking the face with the fingertips is one means of eliminating excessive tension that may be utilized in rehearsals. To develop further the singers' understanding of the importance of this relaxation, choir members should be asked to observe the facial expressions of a recognized concert singer on television. In addition, they should compare their mental conception of this singer with their own facial expressions by checking in a mirror. (Enlargements of closeup group photographs taken during rehearsals provide a further objective means for the singers to analyze their difficulties.)

2   In addition to relaxing the lips and facial muscles, the jaw must be relaxed and the mouth opened wide if the deep-set vowel is to be achieved. The darker vowels, such as **oh, aw,** and **ah,** should have a great deal of depth and should be formed low in the

[3] This is a particularly troublesome problem with high school boys, since large chest expansion seems to be associated with manliness. The problem here can be lessened somewhat by means of a frank and open discussion concerning athletes who employ deep abdominal breathing in order to increase their own breath control.

throat. In order to make them round and full, one should think of singing the vowels up and down, rather than across. The jaw should be free from any rigidity. Exercise 1 is an excellent device for loosening the jaw and "rounding out" the tone.

EXERCISE 1

Yah, yah, yah, yah, yah,   Yah, yah, yah, yah, yah, *etc.*

1   Vocalize from low B♭ (below the staff) to E♭ (fourth space, treble clef). Much of the value of the exercise is lost if it is sung in the extreme high range of the voice.
2   In this exercise use lots of jaw action. A helpful physical device is for the singer to place the tips of each index finger on the approximate hinge position of the jaw. This procedure serves to increase one's awareness of the jaw movement.
3   In singing this exercise, there is an unconscious tendency for some singers to pull the upper lip downward over the upper front teeth. This practice should be discouraged since it is likely to darken the tone quality too much. Singers should be instructed to hold the upper lip stationary, with just a portion of the upper teeth remaining visible. A useful device is to have the singer check this position with a hand mirror. It should prove enlightening to him.
4   It has been found profitable for the singers to check one another's jaw movements on this exercise. This procedure seems to provide the proper motivation for those persons who have difficulty with the exercise.

When the vowel **ah** is used, Exercise 2 is also helpful in developing the deep-set vowel. It has an added ear-training value, in that it provides an opportunity for the singers to hear more clearly their parts in relationship to the other tones in the chord.

EXERCISE 2

1 Director should cue each entrance.
2 Singers should hold back the breath, explode the attack, and drop the jaw.
3 Crescendo, then decrescendo on final chord.
4 Proceed upward or downward by half steps.
5 For the purpose of developing uniformity of vowel production, the exercise should also be sung on the various other vowels. Each vowel should be preceded by the consonant **M**.

Developing High-Forward Resonance

The preceding exercises, if used consistently, develop depth in the voices and transform the thin, shallow voices of inexperienced singers into rounder and deeper voices. If used to the total exclusion of other exercises, however, they will make the voices dark and throaty, and as a result flatting sometimes occurs. To be most effective, these devices and exercises must be coupled with exercises designed to develop focus or high-forward resonance in the voices.

When sound is produced by vibration of the vocal cords, it moves in many directions and is resonated and amplified in the various cavities of the body—that is, the chest, the pharynx, the mouth, and the nasal cavity. A sound, unrestricted by muscular tension, will seek and utilize *all* these resonating areas. Muscular tension and interference, however, often limit the maximum use of these resonating chambers. Tension in the throat muscles prevents the most effective use of the pharynx as a resonator and, as previously mentioned, a tight, rigid jaw and an unruly tongue reduce the size of the oral cavity and lessen its effectiveness as a resonator.

Of particular concern to the choral conductor is the development of focus or high-forward resonance in the voice. By this is meant simply the maximum utilization of the resonating cavities or chambers above the oropharynx and the mouth, specifically the nasopharynx and the nasal cavity. The key to the most effective use of these resonating areas is to maintain a sensation of an opening between the oropharynx and the nasopharynx. The organ that regulates the size of the opening is the velum, or soft palate (see Figure 40). When food is swallowed the velum moves posterosuperiorly and maintains contact

Velum (soft palate)

FIGURE 40 *The velum, or soft palate—a controlling factor in the utilization of the nasopharyngeal cavity and the nasal cavity as resonance chambers. The dotted lines indicate the velum in its lowered or relaxed position.*

with the posterior wall of the pharynx. This muscular adjustment also occurs in the articulation of certain consonants. If
this adjustment did not occur, air would escape through the
nose and the precise articulation of these consonants could not
be achieved. As the nasal consonants **m, n,** and **ng** are produced, the velum is in its relaxed or lowered position, the nasal
port is widely open, and the nasopharynx and the nasal cavity
serve as a more predominant center of tonal resonance. The
velar opening or nasal port may be maintained, however, by a
means other than relaxing or lowering the soft palate. It also
may be opened by an upward and forward tension of the velum
—as experienced in a deep yawn.[4] This suggested movement
of the velum is contrary to the velopharyngeal contact utilized
in articulating certain consonants.[5]

According to a survey by Burgin there appears among voice
teachers to be a general acceptance of the concept of a raised
soft palate in singing. Yawning serves the purpose of raising
the soft palate, as well as opening the throat. Also, according
to Burgin, "this device [the yawn] appears to be among the
most popularly accepted in the broad scope of training the
singing voice."[6]

Singers should strive to develop a high-forward arch to the
velum or soft palate, so that the nasal port may remain slightly
open, thus allowing for an extension of the vibrating column
of air emanating from the larynx and a more effective use of
the upper resonating cavities.[7]

Thus singers should think of the nasopharynx as an extension of the oropharynx and concentrate on drawing the breath

[4] *Cf.* G. Oscar Russell, *Speech and Voice.* New York: Macmillan Publishing Co.,
Inc., 1931, p. 18.
[5] *Cf.* Robert F. Hagerty and others, "Soft Palate Movement in Normals," *Journal of Speech and Hearing Research,* Vol. 1, No. 4, December, 1958, pp. 325–330.
[6] John Carroll Burgin, *Teaching Singing.* Metuchen, N.J.: The Scarecrow
Press, Inc., 1973, p. 77.
[7] There is not complete agreement on the extent of the opening between the oropharynx and the nasopharynx. X-ray studies during phonation indicate a changing size, depending on the vowel produced, and variations on the same vowel
among different singers. However, regardless of the size of the opening, the
imagery of directing the tone through this space is helpful in achieving high-
forward resonance.

"inward and upward." Many choral conductors recommend yawning as a means of developing a sensation of the high-forward arch of the velum. Other directors simply suggest singing with a sensation of a high arch in the back of the mouth. Both devices, however, achieve the same desired purpose and can be utilized to facilitate this necessary physical adjustment.

Muscles work in pairs throughout the body. When one set is in tension to effect a specific movement or action, the opposing set of muscles should be relaxed. When the opposing set of muscles is not relaxed, unnecessary tension occurs, resulting in wasted energy. The singer, therefore, must endeavor to relax the opposing muscles, so that the others may function at optimum efficiency. This is the singer's goal. However, until the correct vocal adjustment becomes automatic in nature, the singer must apply a degree of conscious effort toward arching the velum and opening the passage between the oropharynx and the nasopharynx.

Sagging facial muscles are also detrimental to the development of high-forward resonance. The feeling of a short upper lip and a lifting of the facial muscles directly above the upper lip will aid in the development of this resonance. When the correct singing sensation is achieved and the process becomes automatic, then the singer will be able to produce fully resonated tones with a minimum of effort. Exercises 3–5, and the specific suggestions pertaining to their use, will be found helpful in developing high-forward resonance in the voice.

EXERCISE 3

Hah, hah, hah, hah, hah, hah, hah, hah.

1 Vocalize on the descending major scales, C, D♭ (C♯), D, and E♭. Sing each scale slowly, taking a "catch breath" between each scale step.
2 Sing with the tips of two fingers between the teeth. This ensures an open mouth and a freer emission of the tone.

3 The feeling of the high arched roof of the mouth, as in yawning, is necessary for the proper adjustment of the velum or soft palate and the correct focus of the tone or voice. Strive to develop this sensation.

4 When yawning, notice the position of the lips. In their most relaxed position, they are extended away from the teeth; the upper lip is raised slightly and a portion of the upper teeth is visible.

5 Concentrate on the sensation of drawing the breath inward in a relatively narrow stream and focusing the tone in the resonating cavities behind the bridge of the nose. (Using various physical devices will assist the singer in achieving the correct tonal focus. Drawing the hand inward toward the body facilitates the singer's concept of the correct direction of the flow of the breath.[8] Placing the fingertips on the bridge of the nose is also a reminder of the correct point of tonal focus.)

6 Vocalize all voices to their lowest tones. Avoid forcing the voices in the lower register.

7 Avoid distorting and altering the vowel sound. A common pitfall is to change the vowel **ah** to **uh** when vocalizing in the lower register of the voice.

After a sufficient degree of progress has been made toward achieving correct resonance, Exercises 4 and 5 may be alternated with Exercise 3.

EXERCISE 4

Hah, _____ hah, _____

hah, _____ hah. _____

1 Sing each scale (C, Db, D, Eb) slowly, taking a full breath between each descending scale.

---

[8] The flow of the breath is actually from the lungs, through the larynx, and into the resonating chambers or cavities. The sensation of drawing the breath inward simply assists in directing the tone into the cavities above the pharynx and the oral cavity.

2 Sing with the tips of two fingers between the teeth.
3 Vocalize all voices to their lowest tones. Avoid forcing the voices and distorting the vowel sounds in the lower register.
4 Concentrate on achieving correct tonal focus (see suggestions 3, 4, and 5 in Exercise 3).

EXERCISE 5

Hah, _____ hah, _____ *etc.*

1 Start on middle C and vocalize upward by half steps an octave or more.
2 Vocalize with the tips of two fingers between the teeth. A freer emission of the tone is thus assured.
3 Raise the upper lip and extend away from the teeth.
4 The feeling of the high arched roof of the mouth, as in yawning, is necessary for the proper adjustment of the velum. Strive to attain the sensation.

When practicing Exercise 5, male singers quite often become easily discouraged when their voices crack or break in the upper range. Considerable benefit can accrue to the singers if they are encouraged to continue the exercise upward in a light, head-voice or falsetto quality.

One of the obstacles to achieving the proper placement of voices relates to many singers' misconception that the darker vowels, such as *ah* and *oh*, are to be placed far back in the mouth or throat. In baritones and basses, in particular, this idea or concept often results in an overly dark sound that is difficult to blend and too heavy to be properly supported by the breath, thus resulting in pitch and intonation problems for the choir. Exercises 6 and 7, therefore, have the same basic objectives as Exercises 3, 4, and 5, but they may be used as alternatives and will be found particularly helpful for lightening and focusing the tone.

EXERCISE 6

1 Vocalize upward by half steps but stay primarily in the middle range of the voices.
2 Drop the relaxed jaw on the *ah* vowel, endeavoring to keep the placement forward. Strive for a bright *ah* vowel, and avoid the darker sound that occurs if it is placed farther back in the mouth.

EXERCISE 7

1 Vocalize upward by half steps but stay primarily in the middle range of the voices.
2 Maintain a frontal placement on all vowels, *i.e.*, strive for a bright sound.

To afford further variety, Exercises 8, 9, and 10 also may be utilized periodically as warm-up exercises.

EXERCISE 8

Exercise 8 may be notated on the chalkboard or introduced by means of syllables (all voices sing the interval of the octave—

do to *do;* sopranos sustain *do,* altos descend to *mi,* tenors descend to *sol,* and basses descend to *do.*)

1 Singers should endeavor to maintain the forward placement of the **ee** vowel throughout the exercise; however, as the sound changes to **ah** the jaw should drop and be kept relaxed.
2 Singers should maintain adequate breath support and *crescendo* toward the end of the exercise.
3 The exercise may be repeated upward by half steps (not to exceed four or five half steps, depending on the maturity of the voices).

To afford variety, Exercises 9 and 10 may be alternated on subsequent days with Exercise 8.

EXERCISE 9

1 Sing the exercise in unison.
2 Combine two parts together—SA, TB, ST, AB.
3 Sing in four parts.
4 Repeat upward or downward by half steps.

EXERCISE 10

The use of the nasal consonants (**m, n,** and **ng**) as a means of establishing a sensation for and a feeling of correct resonance is a somewhat controversial subject. One position states that "humming is not singing" and that the two acts require a different adjustment of the velum. In the broadest sense, this statement is true; that is, in humming, the velum is in its relaxed or lowered position, whereas in singing this is seldom, if ever, the case.

The use of humming, prior to singing, the use of the consonants **m, n,** and **ng,** as a prefix to the vocalization of various vowels, and the vocalization of such words as **sing** and **hung** (immediately moving to and sustaining the **ng** sound) have become rather prevalent practices. Proponents of the value of humming maintain that it provides the best muscular setting for the attainment of resonance. In this respect, the use of the nasal consonants has value, because during this act the vocal mechanism is well coordinated. Excessive tension in any aspect of the vocal mechanism will prevent the attainment of a fully resonated tone. Therefore, humming and the use of the other nasal consonants have value in that they facilitate the beginning of phonation without excessive muscular tension. Because of this "relaxing effect," choir members should endeavor to retain the humming sensation while singing.

The humming exercise shown in Exercise 11 may be used for the purpose just described. In addition, it has a certain ear-training value, if the group is instructed to listen carefully and to hold the chord until it is perfectly in tune. Instruct

EXERCISE 11

Hm

the singers to avoid gasping for breath; when a breath is needed they should drop out of the ensemble, take a full breath, and then reenter as unobtrusively as possible. Some persons may hum incorrectly. To check, ask the group while humming to open their mouths at a given signal. If the tone changes into the vowel **ah**, the group is humming incorrectly. When the mouth is opened, the correctly produced tone should change from **hm** to **ng**. It is wise to use this checking device frequently. The **ng** sound has greater intensity than the **hm** sound, and may be found preferable for use with certain selections calling for a humming background. Some high school directors have even found this exercise to be a profitable time-saver—when the students in the chorus enter the rehearsal room, they immediately take their seats and commence humming their respective tones. After all the choir members have arrived, the director may immediately begin the rehearsal, since the group is in a more receptive frame of mind and less inclined toward verbal outbursts.

In striving for the development of deep-set vowels and a high-forward resonance, one could mistakenly get the idea that one vocal characteristic should purposely be developed prior to the other. In practice, both should be developed simultaneously.

If the utmost is to be gained from the previously mentioned exercises they should be sung with a free open throat. Excess tension in the muscles around the larynx should be eliminated insofar as possible. Vocalization on the vowel **oo** has been found to be helpful in opening the throat. When vocalizing on this vowel, it is suggested that the tips of two fingers be placed between the front teeth. This procedure assists in opening the throat and aids in a freer emission of the tone, substantially assisting in the development of the higher range of the voice.

Developing the Vocal Range

Voices with a limited vocal range make the performance of a considerable amount of choral literature prohibitive. If music with an extreme tessitura is used, the voices are likely to sound harsh, strained, and unmusical. Under such circumstances, blend, balance, and good intonation are impossible to attain. Therefore, developing the singers' vocal range is an important and essential task of the choral conductor.

The singing of correctly produced high tones is dependent upon an open throat (achieved through vocalization of the **oo** vowel) and a high-forward resonance (see Exercises 3 and 4). The heavy chest quality of the middle range is not easily produced in the upper limits of the voice and any attempt to do so will often result in unmusical sounds and breaks in the flow of the tone; therefore, the singers should try to lighten their voice quality in vocalizing Exercise 12, which is suggested for helping to develop the upper range.

EXERCISE 12

1 Vocalize, in the beginning, on the vowel **oo**. This vowel opens the throat and facilitates a freer production of tone. As progress is made, however, it is desirable periodically to alternate the **oo** with the **ah** vowel. The latter vowel will give greater brilliance and "ring" to the voice.
2 Vocalize with the tips of two fingers between the teeth. This device facilitates the dropping of the jaw, which is an absolutely essential condition in singing the high tones.
3 When singing *high,* think *low,* and vice versa. This thought facilitates the necessary muscular adjustment.

4　Vocalize all voices up to the extreme limits of their range. Sopranos and tenors should vocalize up to high C, and altos and basses at least up to high A♭.

Female voices will find Exercise 12 comparatively easy— that is, much easier than will the male voices. Treble voices are able to sing the higher pitches without the unique muscular adjustment problem that occurs with male voices. With treble voices, the range simply needs strengthening and developing. The problem is not quite the same with the male voice. In vocalizing Exercise 11, male voices will quite naturally and normally change into a "falsetto" quality at a certain point. At first there may be some embarrassment on the part of the younger singers, but this should be expected. They should be told of the many fine singers who have extended their ranges by first learning how to use correctly their falsetto voice. Indeed, there may even be places in the literature where such a quality will be desired by the tenor voices.

There will exist, however, many other instances where it will be necessary and desirable for the male singers to sing with a full resonant quality in their high range. In order to do so, it will be necessary to develop the so-called *covered tone*, in which the vowel sound is slightly altered or modified toward one which is more easily produced in the upper register. It is full and resonant and is devoid of any falsetto characteristics. In singing the covered tone, a certain firming of the vocal mechanism occurs and the vowels are slightly modified—generally toward the **uh** sound.[9] Exercise 13 is suggested as a means of obtaining the desired tone quality and placement.

Exercise 13

Beginning on first line E (treble clef), slur up an octave, keeping the resonance high and forward. The sounds **ing** and **ay** are generally the best to begin with; however, eventually the

[9] The covered tone versus the open tone has been a controversial subject for many years. For an historical background, as well as an experimental analysis, see Richard Luchsinger and Godfrey E. Arnold, *Voice-Speech Language*. Belmont, Calif.: Wadworth Publishing Co., 1965, pp. 103–106.

other vowels should be used as well. Remember that the jaw must be dropped on all high tones. On the open vowels, sing with the tips of two fingers between the teeth. In singing the closed vowels ee and ĭ, the back sides of the tongue should be held against the upper back teeth. This device facilitates an easier and freer production of tone. Basses should eventually vocalize up to high Ab and the tenors to high C.

In developing the lower range of the voice, it is suggested that the singers vocalize, using the vowel ah, on the descending five-tone scale (see Exercise 18 in Chapter 7). The exercise should be begun on about first space F (treble clef) and should be sung slowly downward. The voices should not be forced, but should be produced with a naturally resonant quality. The greatest deterrent to developing the lower range in both male and female voices is that the singers often fail to drop the jaw. As a result, a considerable portion of the lower range of the voice frequently remains undeveloped. In addition, when the jaw is not dropped the vowel sound will often change from ah to uh. Singing the exercise with the tips of two fingers between the teeth will help to alleviate this problem.

Developing Flexibility

A flexible voice is usually a freely produced voice—one that is devoid of excessive strain and tension. A marked degree of flexibility is essential if desired interpretative effects are to be achieved in choral music. Exercises 14a and 14b, shown here, should prove profitable in developing flexibility in voices.

EXERCISE 14

Ah, _____ etc.

Ah, _____ etc.

1   Vocalize only in the middle range of the voice. Proceed upward by half steps.
2   Insert the tips of two fingers between the teeth. This assists in a free emission of the tone.
3   Avoid singing too loudly. Excessive tension is sometimes created in this way, thus making the exercise more difficult and thereby decreasing the benefit from it.
4   At first, sing the exercise quite slowly—until the student becomes acquainted with it; then gradually increase the tempo.
5   Practice exercises in both a *legato* style and in a *half-staccato* style.

Achieving Correct Diction

Correct diction, necessary to the effective communication of the central thought of the text, is the overall manner of vocal utterance as it pertains to the conveying of meanings and ideas. Pronunciation, enunciation, and articulation are all integral aspects of diction; these terms are often used rather loosely, and frequently their precise meanings are misunderstood.

Pronunciation is the manner of uttering the words, as regards the use of appropriate vowel and consonant sounds and the proper accent of words and phrases. "Sing as you speak" is a statement often heard. This advice would be worthwhile, providing everyone spoke correctly and there was a reasonable degree of uniformity in the speech mannerisms and habits of individuals. Careful analysis of words spoken or sung by individuals will reveal a wide variety of similar, yet distinctly different, pronunciations of each vocal sound.

Vocal mannerisms characteristic of particular regional areas should be avoided and a standardized "general American" approach to pronunciation, as utilized by most radio and television announcers, should be adopted. In an attempt to become "educated," singers should avoid extreme alterations in pronunciation, lest they sound unnatural, affected, and ridiculous to local audiences. An exception to the use of a standardized general American approach to pronunciation in choral singing is readily evident in the performance of certain folks songs requiring a dialectal treatment. Pronunciation problems inherent in these choral selections should be carefully analyzed in regard to vowel and consonant sounds and accent or stress, and then diligently rehearsed. Careful attention must be given to all pronunciation problems if effective communication of the text is to be achieved.

Enunciation pertains to the manner of vocal utterance as regards distinctness and clarity of the various vowel and consonant sounds. Individuals who mumble their words, and who slur or omit consonants, have fallen into slovenly habits that are not conducive to good communication. The conductor should use every possible means to develop the singers' awareness of this problem. Demonstrating the singers' faults through imitation, and playing back tape recordings of rehearsals and performances, are suggested procedures for improving enunciation.[10] Only when effective enunciation is achieved will the central thought of the music be communicated to the listening audience.

Articulation pertains to the physical action of the articulating organs (tongue, lips, teeth, palate, and lower jaw) in forming and altering the channels and in projecting the various vocal sounds necessary to achieve intelligible communication. A further differentiation may be made between articulation and enunciation. When an individual is unable to speak distinctly because of lack of physical control, such as occurs with young children, he may be said to have poor articulation. When an individual's vocal utterance is indistinct because of slovenly diction and lack of concentrated effort, it may be said that his speech or singing is poorly enunciated.

Difference Between Vowels and Consonants

The vowels are utilized for sustaining the singing tone, and the breath flow is continuous. In sounding or articulating the con-

---

[10] Imitation of singers' faults always should be done in a spirit of joviality—never in a ridiculing manner. Imitation should be followed immediately by the conductor's demonstration of correct procedures, and the chorus's renewed efforts toward improvement.

sonants, the flow of the breath is momentarily interrupted. This is the basic difference between the vowels and consonants.

Vowels are the chief vehicle for sustaining the vocal tone, whereas the consonants have shorter sustaining qualities and in some instances may detract from the *legato* flow of the music. The vowels are all voiced sounds—that is, the vocal cords are set into vibration. However, approximately one third of the consonants are voiceless. Intelligibility of the consonants is dependent upon the precise movements of the articulating organs, while the vowels are dependent more upon duration and resonance for their identity.[11] Singing a choral selection on the vowels only is a useful device for achieving uniformity of vowel production and improving tonal blend. Moreover, it demonstrates the fact that vowels have little meaning by themselves, and that intelligibility of the text is dependent primarily on the precise articulation of the consonants.

Vowels

If uniform tone production and tonal blend are to be achieved, the choral conductor must be cognizant of the precise differences of vowel sounds utilized in speaking and singing, and he must develop a similar awareness on the part of his choristers. Singers as a group are usually familiar with the primary vowels (**ee, ay, ah, oh, oo**), since these are used rather extensively as a beginning point in vocalization. However, they are less familiar with the precise differences among the other vowel sounds. The vowel chart in Figure 41 illustrates the variety of vowel sounds that occur in the texts of choral literature. The International Phonetic Alphabet, with a specific symbol for each sound, was devised by phoneticians for the purpose of

---

[11] The formation of intelligible vowel sounds is, of course, dependent upon the adjustment of the articulating organs; however, the vowels are not so dependent upon such a rapid and precise adjustment as are the consonants.

Phonetic Symbols	Dia-critical Mark-ings	Illustra-tive Symbols	Examples
i (long e)	ē	ee	see, each, tree, Easter, free, glee, feet, sleep, deep, sheep, wheel
ɪ (short i)	ĭ	ĭ	sing, is, will, him, thing, ship, wish, April, similar, crib, been, king
e (long a)	ā	ay	say, faith, age, angel, rain, same, maiden, away, day, way, great
ε (short e)	ĕ	ch	yet, end, enter, help, never, every, let, men, said, then
æ (short a)	ă	ă	at, rang, mantle, ashes, agony, began, can, cat, that, than
a	ȧ	ȧ	ask, grass, laugh, bath, calf, craft, raft, chance, chaff
ɑ	ä	ah	father, Amen, alms, army, far, heart, calm, palm, psalm
ɒ (short o)	ŏ	ŏ	stop, hot, sorry, olive, God, watch, wander, John, yon
ɔ	ô	aw	law, all, awe, autumn, always, walk, warm, dawn
o (long o)	ō	oh	flow, old, road, hope, low, soul, snow, open, so, boat, home, cold
ʊ	o͝o	o͝o	look, bosom, took, foot, stood, should, would, book, full, brook
u	o͞o	oo	who, too, moon, whose, blue, true, through, flew, soon, tomb
ɝ	ûr	ur	birth, early, earth, world, worth, perfect, burden, were
ɚ	ẽr	er	ever, never, another, pleasure, mother, weather, measure
ə	ə,ȧ	uh	about, around, firmament, America, awhile, away, above
ʌ (short u)	ŭ	uh	but, sun, done, creation, other, until, wonder, thunder

FIGURE 41 *The single vowels frequently occurring in choral literature, with symbols and examples by which the conductor may illustrate and correct pronunciation difficulties.*

providing an accurate means of identifying and differentiating among the various vowel and consonant sounds. In the first column of this chart, the phonetic symbols for the different vowel sounds are listed. The diacritical markings for these vowels, as used in English dictionaries, are listed in the second column. Both the phonetic symbols and the diacritical markings are presented primarily as a reference for the choral conductor. Because their precise meanings would not always be readily evident to a group of amateur singers, various illustrative symbols for each vowel are included in the third column, and are suggested for use with the choir members. When pronunciation difficulties occur in rehearsals, the conductor should identify and isolate particularly troublesome vowel sounds. These illustrative symbols may be written on the chalkboard, discussed, pronounced, and sung as a means of clarifying in the singers' minds the desired vowel sounds. Numerous examples of specific vowels as they occur in various words are also listed and may be used for illustrative or comparative purposes.

The formation of each vowel in Figure 42 requires distinctly different adjustments of the articulating organs, with the exception of the following. The vowel ɝ (ûr) is the counterpart of ɚ (ẽr) and the adjustment of the articulating organs is quite similar. The vowel ɝ (ûr) occurs only on stressed syllables and the sound ɚ (ẽr) occurs on unstressed syllables. Also, the vowel ʌ (ŭ) is the counterpart of ə and the position of the articulating organs is almost identical. The vowel ʌ (ŭ) occurs only on stressed syllables, whereas the vowel ə occurs only on unstressed syllables.

The various vowels are determined by the relative size and shape of the mouth and throat cavities. Specific determinants are the position of the tongue, the jaw, and the lips. As indicated in Figure 42, the vowels ee and ĭ are formed high and forward, while the vowel oo is formed lower in the throat. In singing the ee and ĭ vowels, the tongue is relatively high, whereas in the oo vowel the tongue is back. In both cases the position of the jaw is high and the mouth is somewhat closed. Because of this condition, these sounds are often referred to as *closed vowels*. All other vowels are referred to as *open vowels*,

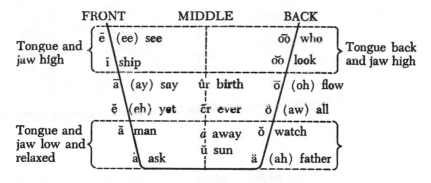

FIGURE 42   *Front-to-back vowel formation.*

even though the position of the tongue, lips, and jaw will vary to some extent. The tongue is most relaxed and the jaw at its lowest position while singing the vowel **ah,** as in the word **father.** Because of the lesser degree of tension, this vowel is the most freely produced and is therefore frequently used as a beginning point in vocalization.   (See also Figure 43.)

In his exuberance, the novice chorister may tense the tongue too much and restrict the proper functioning of the vocal mechanism; a thin, shallow tone quality is likely to result. A helpful device is for the conductor to suggest to the singers that, when singing the open vowels, the position of the tongue remain in the relaxed position of the **ah** vowel.   There is a limit, of course, to the practicality of this suggestion as it affects pronunciation; however, the device does facilitate the reduction of excessive tension in the tongue muscle.

When singing the closed vowels **ee** and **ĭ,** it is suggested that the singers place the back sides of the tongue against the upper back teeth.   When the position of the tongue is too high, this device serves to enlarge the oral cavity somewhat and allow for a freer emission of tone. It also prevents one from forming these vowels too low in the throat, which may cause throatiness and flatting, especially in the upper range of the voice.

If a choral group sings with a nasal, white, or colorless tone, then vowels with extreme forward placement such as **ee** and **ĭ** should be utilized sparingly in vocalization, and the vowels formed lower in the throat, such as **aw, oh,** and **oo,** should be

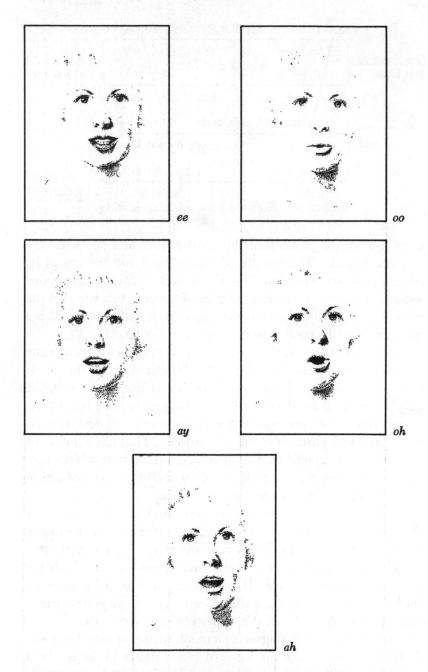

FIGURE 43 *Relative positions of the lips and jaw in forming the primary vowels* (**ee, ay, ah, oh, oo**). *Compare with Figure 42.*

utilized.   Conversely, if the group sings with an overly dark tone quality, then greater attention should be given the vowels formed high and forward.   All the primary vowels (**ee, ay, ah, oh, oo**), however, should be utilized to some extent in vocalization, and concentration on any one group of vowels to the total exclusion of the others should be avoided.

Diphthongs

The dipthong may be defined as a compound vowel, or a syllable in which the sound changes from one vowel to another.   In a simple or single vowel the articulating organs are held in a somewhat fixed position, whereas in a diphthong the articulating organs change position, thus altering the vowel sound.   Figure 44 shows the diphthongs as they occur in English.

Except for **ju** or **Iu**, the durational stress should be given the primary vowel, and the secondary vowel should be sounded just prior to the release of the diphthong.   It is often helpful if the secondary vowels are thought of in terms of the same durational stress as are the consonants.   This procedure should be followed whenever the musical notation and the tempo permit the *initial* vowel in the diphthong to be sustained for any reasonable length of time.   Thus the word **night** if sustained would be sung as **nah——ĭt,** not **nah–eet,** and the word **round** would be sung **rah——ŏŏnd,** not **rah–ōŏnd.**

The diphthong **ju** is actually a consonant-vowel combination. An example of this sound occurs in the word **beauty.**   In

Phonetic Symbols	Diacritical Markings	Illustrative Symbols	Examples
aɪ or ɑɪ	ī (long i)	ah—ĭ	night, high, light
aʊ or ɑʊ	ou	ah—ŏŏ	our, now, round
ɔɪ	oi	aw—ĭ	oil, rejoice, joy
eɪ	ā	ay—ĭ	day, faith, they
oʊ	ō	oh—ŏŏ	old, hope, low
ju or ɪu	ū	i-ŏŏ—	beauty, few, view

FIGURE 44   *The diphthongs as they occur in English.*

this instance it is the secondary rather than the primary vowel that should receive the durational stress. The word should always be pronounced bĭ-ōō——ty, rather than bēē-ōō-ty.

In the treatment of all diphthongs, a smoother transition from the primary to the secondary vowel will be achieved if the diphthong is thought of as a single, composite sound, rather than as two separate and distinct vowel sounds.

Classification of Consonants

Generally the consonants may be classified into two types—the voiced and voiceless (nonvoiced). The voiceless consonants include **k, p, t, f, h, s,** and **sh,** whereas the voiced consonants include **b, d, v, z, zh, l, g, j, w, r, y, m, n,** and **ng.** The consonant **th** is voiced in some words and voiceless in others. In producing the voiced consonants the vocal cords are drawn together, set into vibration, and the consonant is voiced as a result, whereas in the voiceless consonants there is no perceptible movement of the vocal cords. The voiced consonants are softer in character and less explosive than the voiceless (nonvoiced) consonants. As the voiced consonants have a slight sustaining quality, they may be used effectively to bridge the gap between various vowel sounds, especially in *legato* singing. Developing the singers' awareness of the essential differences between these consonant sounds will result in improved enunciation.

For a number of consonants, the adjustment of the articulating organs is similar. Only one adjustment is necessary for the following paired consonants: **t-d, p-b, f-v, k-g, s-z,** and **sh-zh.** The first consonant in the pair is voiceless, whereas the second consonant is voiced.[12] The words in Figure 45 serve to illustrate further the similarities between the adjustment of the articulators and the differences in sound duration. Words are listed that include the use of an initial, a medial, and a final consonant.

---

[12] Exceptions to the pairing of voiced and voiceless consonants are **h, r, y, w, l, m, n,** and **ng.** All of these consonants are voiced except the **h,** which is voiceless.

Voiceless	Voiced
t—time, turtle, part	d—day, garden, afraid
p—pretty, happy, harp	b—bright, above, crib
f—faith, before, life	v—voices, ever, above
k—kind, because, music	g—garden, finger, flag
s—sing, asleep, peace	z—zenith, music, eyes
sh—sheep, ocean, wish	zh—Jacques, pleasure, rouge

FIGURE 45   *Paired consonants, with similar articulator adjustments.*

Another means of classifying the consonants is by the manner in which the flow of the breath is released. The *explosive* consonants are **p, b, t, d, ch, j (dzh), k,** and **g.** The *continuants* are **w, wh, f, v, th, s, z, sh, zh, r, j (y), h, l, m, n,** and **ng.** In articulating the *explosive* consonants, the flow of the breath is momentarily interrupted by the contact between the articulating organs. An explosive sound is emitted as the articulating organs are separated precisely and the pressure of the breath is released. In producing the *continuants*, the articulating organs assume a relatively fixed position as the sound is emitted.

Still another means of classifying the consonants is by the position or placement of the articulating organs involved in producing the sounds. They are as follows:

Bilabial (**p, b, m, w**). Bilabial consonants are formed by the lower and upper lips. In forming the consonants **p** and **b,** the flow of the breath is interrupted momentarily as the lips are drawn together, and the breath is released in an explosive manner as the lips are suddenly opened; **p** is voiceless and **b** is a voiced consonant. The consonant **m** is voiced and is formed by closing the lips, thus causing the flow of the breath to be emitted through the nasal passages. The consonant **w** is voiced and is referred to as a *bilabial glide.* It is produced by the lips forming a position similar to the **u** vowel and then moving or gliding quickly to the subsequent vowel sound.

Labio-dental (**f, v**).   Labio-dental consonants are formed by the lower lips and the upper teeth.   The lower lip and the upper teeth are brought together and the breath is forced audibly between the two articulating organs; **f** is a voiceless consonant and **v** is voiced.

Lingua-dental (**th**).   Lingua-dental consonants are formed by the tip of the tongue touching the back side of the upper front teeth.   The breath is forced between these two articulators; **th,** as in the word **thousand,** is voiceless and the sound **th,** as in the word **there,** is voiced.

Lingua-alveolar (**t, d, n, l, s, z**).   Lingua-alveolar consonants are formed by the tip of the tongue and the upper teeth or gum ridge.   In forming the consonants **t** and **d,** the flow of the breath is interrupted momentarily by the contact between these two articulating organs.   The consonants are sounded and the breath is released in a slightly explosive manner as the contact between these organs is released; **t** is voiceless and **d** is voiced. The **n** is voiced and is formed by placing the tip of the tongue against the gum ridge and directing the sound through the nasal passages.   In the consonant **l,** which is also voiced, the tongue is placed against the gum ridge and the sound is emitted over the sides of the tongue.   In forming the consonants **s** and **z,** the sides of the tongue are kept in contact with the upper back teeth, and the tip of the tongue rests just behind the upper front teeth, although not touching directly.   The flow of the breath is directed over the tongue where it strikes the back edge of the upper front teeth, thus causing the hissing sound descriptive of these two consonants.   The **s** is voiceless and the **z** is voiced.

Lingua-palatal (**sh, zh, ch, dzh, j, r**).   Lingua-palatal consonants are formed by the contact between the tongue and the hard palate.   In producing the consonants **sh** and **zh,** the sides of the tongue are placed against the upper back teeth, as in the position for the consonant s, except that the tongue is drawn slightly back; sh is voiceless and zh is voiced.

In sounding the consonant combinations ch and dzh, the tongue contacts the hard palate at a point slightly farther back than for the consonant t. The tongue comes in contact with the upper back teeth and the flow of the breath is interrupted momentarily. As the tongue is released, the breath is emitted in an explosive manner. The consonant ch is voiceless, but the dzh is voiced.

The consonant j as it occurs in certain words, is pronounced dzh, as in judge and joy. In other words, such as hallelujah, it assumes a softer, nonexplosive quality as in the consonant y in such words as yet, year, and beyond. The y is considered by many authorities to be a voiced consonant; however, some writers classify it as a semivowel.

In pronouncing the consonant r, the sides of the tongue contact the upper back teeth. The tip of the tongue is curled or drawn back toward the hard palate and, as the sound is emitted, it glides smoothly to the adjustment necessary for the following vowel sound. This adjustment is common in such words as run, around, and read. In some words, however, the tongue assumes a much lower position in the mouth, and the glide occurs in reverse order. This action occurs in such words as heard, her, and creator, where the preceding vowel sound is stressed. In this case, the consonant is articulated as the syllable is released. The consonant r is a voiced consonant.

Velar (k, g, ng). Velar consonants are formed by arching the back part of the tongue and pressing it lightly against the soft palate. In the k and g sounds, the flow of the breath is interrupted momentarily. As the contact is released and the tongue is lowered, the breath is exploded. The consonant k is voiceless, but the g is voiced. In forming the consonant ng, the position of the tongue is similar to that of the k and g sounds, except that the soft palate or velum is lowered slightly and the tongue is more relaxed, thus allowing the sound to be emitted through the nasal passages. The consonant ng is voiced.

Glottal (h). Glottal sounds are formed in the glottis or the opening between the vocal cords. The vocal cords come together in a position that restricts the flow of the breath slightly, but not enough to set the cords into vibration. The consonant **h** is voiceless and is produced by forcing the breath between the nonvibrating vocal cords. This sound is often referred to as the *aspirate h.*

Styles of Diction

There are three basic styles of choral diction; namely, *legato, staccato,* and *marcato.* Each of these styles is distinctly different and each must be treated in a specific manner if effective interpretation is to be achieved.

Legato diction is smooth and connected. A minimum of emphasis should be given to the rhythmic stress or pulsation of the music in *legato* style. *Legato* phrases should be thought of in terms of long, soaring and descending musical lines. In addition, the explosive qualities of the consonants should be minimized if they are to be smoothly blended with the vowel sounds.[13] In achieving this effect, the singers should carry over the final consonants of one syllable or word to the following syllable or word. The following examples serve to illustrate this concept: **My Lord, what a mornin'** is sung **mah-ee law—rd hwah-tuh maw—rn–nĭn. Lost in the night** is sung **law—stĭ–n–thuh nah—ĭt. My love dwelt in a northern land** is sung **mah-ee luhv dweh–l–tĭn nuh naw–r–thern lă—nd.**

Any exception to this rule occurs as a result of the diction being unintelligible or creating a somewhat ludicrous effect. In the following examples, it is desirable to separate the sounds, as indicated by the diagonal lines, with a slight break in the flow of the breath.

---

[13] To achieve a smooth blending between the consonants and the vowels in *legato* diction, it will be helpful to request the singers to sustain the consonants as well as the vowels. This device, although seemingly quite unorthodox, lessens the explosive qualties of the consonants and contributes substantially to the desired *legato* effect.

"She's / like the Swallow" (from "She's Like the Swallow," New-foundland folk song, Oxford, No. X64).
"Slumbers / not nor sleeps" (from "He Watching Over Israel"—Felix Mendelssohn, G. Schirmer, No. 2498).
"We Three Kings of Orient / Are" (John H. Hopkins).

When the second syllable occurs on a stressed beat, one may further clarify the sound through careful articulation. That is, in the first example, articulate the word *like* with a "capital L."

Examples of octavo choral selections requiring a *legato* treatment of diction are included in the following list.[14]

Ave Verum Corpus—Wolfgang A. Mozart. G. Schirmer, No. 5471.
Alleluia—Randall Thompson. E. C. Schirmer, No. 1786.
God So Loved the World (from *The Crucifixion*)—John Stainer. G. Schirmer, No. 3798.
How Lovely Is Thy Dwelling Place—Johannes Brahms, ed. H. R. Wilson. Ricordi, No. 1515.
I Wonder As I Wander (Appalachian carol)—arr. John Jacob Niles and Lewis Henry Horton. G. Schirmer, No. 8708.
Lost in the Night (Finnish folk song)—arr. F. Melius Christiansen. Augsburg, No. 119.
Mary Had a Baby—William L. Dawson. Tuskegee, No. 118.
My Love Dwelt in a Northern Land—Edward Elgar. G. Schirmer, No. 2366.
O Divine Redeemer—Charles Gounod. Schmitt, Hall & McCreary, No. 1602.

In *staccato* diction, the words should be sung in a detached style as if there were a slight rest between each note. Good *staccato* diction depends upon distinct and precise articulation of the consonants. The lips should be flexible and devoid of excessive tension, and the lip movements should be exaggerated. The singers should refrain from singing too loudly, since excessive volume is likely to inhibit the precise articulation of the words. (Excessive volume tends to shift the focus from careful articulation to weighty tonal effects.) The vowels should be modified slightly and formed closer to the front of the mouth; words should be thought of as being formed on the

[14] For complete names and addresses of the publishers referred to in this and subsequent lists, see Appendix.

lips, since sounds formed too far in the back of the mouth tend to become weighty, cumbersome, and difficult to articulate in a short, detached style. Exercise 15 will be found helpful in developing precise lip movements and in improving *staccato* diction.

EXERCISE 15

Bah, bah, bah, bah, etc.   *(repeat one-half step higher, etc.).*

1   Use various consonants on this exercise (b, p, t, f, d, etc.).
2   Vocalize only in the middle register.
3   Work for clearness and precision of consonants and for flexibility. Flexibility will aid in developing freedom of voice production.

Examples of choral octavo publications requiring a *staccato* treatment of diction are included in the following list.

Cicirinella (Italian folk song)—arr. Max Krone. Witmark No. 5—W2952.
Hasten Swiftly, Hasten Softly—Richard Kountz. Galaxy No. 1750.
I Saw Three Ships (traditional English)—arr. Alice Parker and Robert Shaw. G. Schirmer No. 10188.
Rock-a My Soul (spiritual)—arr. Joseph De Vaux. Bourne No. 667.
Sleigh, The—Richard Kountz. G. Schirmer No. 7459.
We Wish You a Merry Christmas (English folk song)—arr. the Krones. Kjos No. 4006.
Younger Generation—Aaron Copland. Boosey & Hawkes No. 1723.

In *marcato* diction each note is sung with an accent and the rhythm is quite pronounced. Effective *marcato* diction necessitates correct muscular action, which is precisely a sharp inward movement of the abdominal muscles.[15] Perhaps the most effective means of teaching this concept is to ask the singers to "grunt" each note in the correct musical rhythm. By placing the hand on the abdomen, singers are more likely

---

[15] For a discussion of the function of the abdominal muscles in the respiratory process, see section titled "The Vocal Instrument" in Chapter 2.

to "feel" the movement, thus facilitating the achievement of this concept. With attention focused upon this muscular movement, it is helpful to have the group recite the text in correct musical rhythm before attempting further to apply the concept to actual singing. A *marcato* treatment of diction is required in sections of the following choral octavo publications, which are included for study and analysis.

Hallelujah (from *Mount of Olives*)—Ludwig van Beethoven. G. Schirmer No. 2215.

Hallelujah, Amen (from *Judas Maccabaeus*)—George F. Handel. Witmark No. 5–W3026.

Let Their Celestial Concerts All Unite (from *Samson*)—George F. Handel. E. C. Schirmer No. 312.

Psalm 150—Louis Lewandowski, ed. H. R. Wilson. Schmitt, Hall & McCreary No. 1640.

While by My Sheep (17th-century hymn)—arr. Hugo Jungst. G. Schirmer No. 2532.

Although many choral compositions require only one specific type of treatment as regards the style of diction, others will contain contrasting sections and phases, each requiring a different treatment. Prior to introducing a selection to the chorus, the conductor should analyze carefully the text and the music, giving particular attention to the diction requirements. If in doubt about the style of diction, one should always look to the text of the music. The mood and emotional content of the text will reveal many things to the conductor, including various shadings and nuances necessary for the most effective interpretation of the music.

The Sibilant S

Of the sibilants or hissing sounds in English (s, z, sh, zh, ch, and j), the most troublesome, especially in *legato* singing, is the consonant s. Unless handled correctly, the singing of this consonant may remind one of sounds emanating from a snake pit. An example of this may be found in the words "God so loved the world" from the chorus in John Stainer's *The Crucifixion*. Unless careful attention is given to the sibilant s in the word **so,** considerable difficulty may occur with amateur choral groups. Amateurs are often likely to sing the phrase as **Gaw——dssssssoh—luh—vd thuh wuh—rld.** The difficulty here lies primarily in the lack of the singers' accurate response to the rhythmic duration of the first measure. The **s** is anticipated with a resultant hissing sound. Tight, rigid jaws also contribute to the problem. If the jaw is not relaxed and the mouth kept open, the consonants **d** and **s** will inevitably follow too quickly the preceding vowel sound.

A solution to this specific problem, which also will apply to other problems of a similar nature, is first to concentrate upon the development of rhythmic accuracy in the chorus. The fact that the first measure has three beats must be understood and felt by all the singers. Having the group clap or tap the basic pulsation, or even conducting the traditional pattern for triple meter, will be found helpful. Next, have the group sing the phrase on a neutral syllable, such as **loo.** After rhythmic accuracy has been achieved, the group should endeavor to prefix the vowel sound **oh** in the second measure with the consonants **ds.** The final result should sound as shown in Figure 46.

Some directors have found it particularly helpful, in dealing with the hissing **s**'s, to assign the singing of them to only a particular portion of the chorus, with the remainder of the group singing only the vowel sound. The use of this approach certainly depends upon the requirements of the musical situation, and its success depends upon a clear understanding on the part of the singers as to their particular assignments.

In certain choral selections it will be helpful to minimize the **s** sound by changing it to the shorter **z** sound. Certainly

Gaw ____ dsoh - luh - vd thuh wuh ____ rld.

FIGURE 46 *Excerpt from "God So Loved the World" (from John Stainer's* The Crucifixion).

the obvious advantage of this procedure becomes apparent in singing the words "slumbers not" from Mendelssohn's *He Watching over Israel.*

The Troublesome R

The consonant **r** is often the source of unmusical sounds in amateur choral groups. The difficulty usually encountered is the overanticipation of the consonant, often caused through the singer's inaccurate response to the rhythmic duration of the music. Words such as **ever** and **world** are particular examples. How often has one heard the sound **eh–vuhrr** or the equally obnoxious sound of **wuhrrrr–ld?** To alleviate the problem, singers must not only be made more conscious of rhythmic duration, but must also be instructed to sustain the vowel preceding the consonant **r** sound, and to add the **r** only briefly upon the release of the syllable. Thus **ever** should be sung as **eh–vuh——r,** and **world** as **wuh——rld.**

The Consonants M, N, and L

Although most of the consonants have a comparatively short duration, the consonants **m, n,** and **l** are particular exceptions and have a certain degree of sustaining power. As such they may be effectively used, especially in *legato* singing, to bridge more smoothly the gap between the various vowel sounds. For example, in singing the word **amen** the pronunciation **ah—mehn** contributes little to the smoothness of the *legato* phrase. A more effective procedure is to sing the word as **ah—m—mehn.** In this manner the consonant **m** serves to bridge the gap between the vowels **ah** and **eh,** thus creating an improved *legato* effect (Figure 47). To accomplish this successfully, the mouth must be closed momentarily upon the release of the first vowel and opened upon the attack of the second vowel sound. (Obviously, this treatment is appropriate only when dealing with *legato* diction. Utilizing this approach with a vigorous, Handelian chorus would be out of character and

FIGURE 47 *An example of bridging the gap between two vowel sounds. Note (a) how the word is written, and (b) how it is effectively sung.*

highly inappropriate. In most cases the approach used will be dictated by the demands of the musical situation.)

A similar treatment is suggested in dealing with the consonant **n.** In the words **mine eyes** the tongue should touch the back side of the upper front teeth as the **n** is sounded. The tongue should drop immediately before the first syllable of the word **eyes.** The phrase should be sung as **mah–een–nah–eez.**

In most cases, when dealing with the double consonants, the first of the two should be eliminated. Usually this procedure is dictated by common sense. For example, the word **better** is pronounced **beh—tuhr** and not **beht—tuhr;** the word **torrents** is pronounced **tŏ-rĕnts** and not **tŏr-rĕnts.** An exception to the rule, however, is the treatment of the double consonant **ll.** In the word **allelujah,** for example, both **l**'s should be sounded if *legato* diction is to be clear and connected. The word **allelujah** should be sung **ahl—lay—loo—jah,** rather than **ah—lay—loo—jah.** The initial **l** should be added upon the release of the first vowel and the second **l** should prefix the second vowel. Examples of this suggested treatment may be found in the following compositions:

Alleluia—Wolfgang A. Mozart. Carl Fischer, No. 541.
Alleluia—Randall Thompson. E. C. Schirmer, No. 1786.

The Aspirate H

The aspirate **h** is effected by means of a rapid flow of the breath, and when this condition does not prevail the sound is often strident and ineffective. For example, in the word **hallelujah** in the chorus "Hallelujah, Amen" from the oratorio *Judas Maccabaeus* by Handel, the initial consonant is often slighted, thus resulting in a poor attack and a tightening of the vocal mechanism. To avoid this pitfall, singers should be instructed to anticipate the attack and precede the initial vowel with a rapid push or flow of the breath. When singing in *marcato* style, a sharp inward movement of the abdominal muscles will help to activate the flow of the breath. Adequate preparation on the part of both the conductor and the chorus is essential. Singers should be poised, alert, and ready for the attack, and the conductor should provide a clear, precise preparatory beat.

The aspirate **h** will often cause difficulty when combined with another consonant. For example, the word **when** often is pronounced as **wehn** rather than **hwehn**. In addition to activating the flow of the breath, singers must strive for careful, precise lip action to ensure the correct articulation of this consonant combination.

Vowel—Consonant Balance

The concept of "singing on the vowel," important as it is, should not be stressed at the expense of the consonants. Overemphasis upon the vowel sounds to the neglect of the consonants may result in beautiful choral tone, but the singing will generally lack luster and the desirable expressive characteristics.

To achieve correct, understandable diction, a balance must be maintained between the vowels and the consonants. When given only equal stress, the vowel sounds usually predominate over the consonants because of their sustaining characteristics. Therefore, to achieve a desirable balance the consonants should be overexaggerated—not in duration, but in the degree of intensity.[16] Emphasis should be placed upon careful and precise

---

[16] A word of caution! An exception to this treatment occurs in dealing with music in a *legato* style, as discussed earlier in this chapter under "Styles of Diction." Too much emphasis upon the intensity of the consonants is likely to disturb the *legato* flow of the music. In this style, emphasis should be placed upon the smooth connection of vowels and consonants.

articulation, rather than upon excessive duration of the consonants. It should be understood, however, that clear diction will not guarantee good voice production and that any attempt toward precise articulation should not cause unnecessary tension in the vocal mechanism. Articulation should occur away from the throat!

More effective results will be achieved by graphically illustrating on the chalkboard the relative degree of emphasis required in balancing the vowels and consonants, as in Figure 48.

Final Consonants

Amateur singing groups often do not finish their words, especially at the ends of phrases. The poetical qualities of the

A word sung as follows

| C | V | C | V | C |

will sound to the audience as

| C | V | C | V | C |

Therefore, to achieve a proper balance

| C | V | C | V | C |

the singers should stress the consonants as follows

| C | V | C | V | C |

FIGURE 48

text are thereby lost and projection of the mood or spirit of the song becomes relatively ineffective. The conductor should be careful to provide a clear, precise release to the phrase so that the group may utilize this movement as a signal to add the final consonants. In addition, the conductor should endeavor to develop in his singers an increased consciousness of the problem. One effective approach is for the director to sing a series of words from which the final consonants are omitted; then ask the singers to identify the words. The variety of guesses will serve to illustrate the importance of including the final consonants of all words.

Tone and diction are the chief means of transmitting the poetic qualities of the music to the audience. Without properly produced and appropriate tone quality the effectiveness of the music is lessened considerably, and without correct diction choral tone becomes meaningless and little more than instrumental in character. Good tone quality and correct diction are essential to effective interpretation and, to be achieved, must receive the detailed, exacting attention of the choral conductor.

Commonly Mispronounced Words

A brief list of some common errors in pronunciation is shown in Figure 49.[17] This list, though incomplete, may serve as a starting point for the conductor who wishes to develop his own list of mispronounced words—or words that are troublesome in his particular locality.

---

[17] This list, of course, does not pertain to songs necessitating a dialectal treatment.

Word	Pronunciation
angel	ayn-j*eh*l, not ayn-juhl
beautiful	bĭ-*ōō*-tĭ-f*ōo*l (bū-tĭ-fŏŏl), not be-ōō-tee-fuhl
Bethlehem	Bĕth-lē-h*ĕ*m, not Bĕth-lē-ham
can	k*ă*n, not kĭn
Christmas	Chrĭs-m*ă*s, not Chrĭs-muhs
creation	kree-ay-sh*uh*n (kre-ā-shŭn), not kree-ay-shĭn
dew	dĭ-*oo* (dū), not d*ōō*. (Other words necessitating a similar pronunciation of the diphthong ĭ-ōō are: new, beauty, few, view, pure, and human.)
for	f*ô*r, not fûr
forget	fŏr-g*eh*t, not fŏr-gĭt
forgiveness	fŏr-gĭv-n*eh*s, not fŏr-gĭv-nuhs
Galilee	gă-lĭ-lē, not gă-luh-lē
get	g*eh*t, not gĭt
glory	gl*oh*-ree, not glaw-ree
government	guh-*vern*-mehnt (gŭ-vĕrn-mĕnt), not guh-ver-mehnt
heaven	heh-v*eh*n, not heh-vuhn
judgment	jŭj-m*ĕ*nt, not jŭj-muhnt
kindness	kah-ĭnd-n*eh*s (kĭnd-nĕs), not kah-ĭnd-nuhs
listen	lĭs-*eh*n, not lĭs-uhn
Lord	L*aw*rd (Lôrd), not Lahrd, or Lowrd
love	l*uh*v (lŭv), not lahv
manger	mayn-j*er* (mān-jĕr), not mayn-jĭr
Mary	M*eh*-ree (Mâ-rē), not May-ree
mountain	moun-t*eh*n, not moun-uhn
night	nah-ĭt (nīt), not naht, or nah-eet. (Other words containing the long ī [a diphthong] include high, sigh, fly, etc.)
open	oh-p*eh*n, not oh-puhn
poor	p*ōō*r, not pohr
pretty	prĭ-t*ē*, not prĭ-dē
roof	r*ōō*f, not ruhf
silent	sah-ĭ-l*eh*nt (sī-lĕnt), not sah-ee-luhnt
spirit	spĭ-rĭt, not spĭ-ruht
the	th*ee* before words beginning with a vowel, or the silent *h* (th*ee* everlasting, th*ee* hour). th*uh* before words beginning with a consonant (th*uh* night, th*uh* heavens).
triumphant	trī-ŭm-f*ă*nt, not trī-ŭm-funt
virgin	vûr-jĭn, not vûr-juhn
wheel	*h*weel, not weel
when	*h*wĕn, not wĕn (wehn)
worship	wûr-shĭp, not wûr-shup
your	y*ōō*r, not yuhr

FIGURE 49 *Common errors in pronunciation.*

Terms Pertaining to Choral Tone and Diction

Actuator—the part of the vocal mechanism that actuates or begins the flow of the breath, i.e., the lungs, the diaphragm, the intercostal muscles and the abdominal muscles.

Articulation—the action of physical adjustment of the articulating organs in the formation of intelligible sounds.

Articulators—the part of the vocal mechanism that forms or shapes the various language sounds and that determines their particular distinguishable characteristics. Specific determiners are the tongue, lips, teeth, lower jaw, the hard palate, and the velum, or soft palate.

Aspirate h—a vocal sound characterized by a slight constriction of the vocal cords; the cords are approximated, but not close enough to be set into vibration.

Bilabial—the consonants formed by the upper and lower lips (**p, b, m, w**).

Breath support—the flow or pressure of the breath against the vocal cords in an amount sufficient to effect the vibration necessary for a given pitch; considered to be adequate when phonation occurs without unnecessary constriction or tension in the laryngeal muscles.

Closed vowels—the vowels ee, ĭ, and oo, classified as such because of the relatively small oral cavity caused by the high position of the tongue in the mouth.

Consonants—the vocal sounds formed by precise, articulate movements of the lips, tongue, and jaw and characterized by an interruption or restriction of the flow of the breath. Consonants give intelligibility to vocal expression.

Covered tone—a slightly modified or altered vowel sound utilized by male singers in the production of tones in the upper register. The covered tone is full and resonant and lacking in any falsetto characteristics. A firming of the vocal mechanism occurs and the vowel being sung is modified toward the **uh** vowel.

Deep-set vowels—vowels characterized by a roundness and fullness of tone quality, and a naturalness of tone production, creating a sensation of being formed low in the throat. Essential physical conditions are a relaxed tongue and an open throat.

Diaphragm—a broad muscular partition located between the chest cavity and the abdomen. The diaphragm is one of the principal muscles used in inhalation. It is arched and dome-shaped in its relaxed state. As the diaphragm is tensed, it contracts and flattens out, thus pushing downward against the organs in the abdominal region. Coupled with the action of the rib muscles, the diaphragm contributes to the enlargement of the chest cavity, and as a result the air pressure is lowered. The lower air pressure is equalized by air entering the lungs. When the diaphragm relaxes, it returns to its normal state and pressure is made upon the small air sacs in the lungs, thus effecting or causing exhalation, and completing the cycle of breathing.

Diphthong—a compound or double vowel, in which the vowel sounds change smoothly from one to the other. For example, the word **round** contains the diphthong **ou (ah and oo)** and is pronounced **rah-oond.**

Enunciation—the manner of vocal utterance as regards distinctness and clarity of vowels and consonants.

Falsetto—a light, head voice, lying above the natural or normal range of the male voice. In singing a falsetto tone, only the inner edges of the vocal cords vibrate.

Final consonant—the last consonant in a word.

Glottal—relating to, or produced in, the glottis; the aspirate consonant **h,** formed in the glottis.

Glottis—the fissure or opening between the vocal cords or bands.

Hard Palate—the portion of the roof of the mouth between the alveoli and the velum or soft palate. The hard palate is a structure of bone with a layer or cover of tissue.

High-forward resonance—a focusing of the tone in the "mask," or more specifically in the frontal cavities of the head. Essential physical conditions are an open throat and an arched velum.

Hooty tones—a muffled tone quality lacking in correct tonal focus.

Initial consonant—a consonant situated at the beginning of a word.

Intercostal muscles—the muscles that lie between the ribs and that partially control the process of respiration.

Labio-dental—the consonants formed by the lower lip and the upper front teeth **(f, v).**

Laryngeal muscles—the muscles that regulate the size of the glottis, control the degree of tension of the vocal cords, and close off the larynx during swallowing.

Larynx—sometimes referred to as the voice box; a cartilage that houses the vocal cords, situated at the upper part of the trachea or windpipe.

Legato diction—a style of diction in which the vowels and consonants are smoothly connected. The explosive qualities of the consonants are minimized, and the final consonants of most syllables or words are carried over the prefix the following syllable. For example, the words night time are sung nah–ĭ taheem.

Lingua-alveolar—the consonants t, d, n, l, s, and z, formed by the tip of the tongue touching the alveoli (teeth or gum ridge; portion of the jaw where the sockets for the upper teeth are situated; area between the teeth and the hard palate).

Lingua-dental—the consonants formed by the tip of the tongue touching the upper front teeth (th as in thousand, and th as in there).

Lingua-palatal—the consonants formed by the contact between the tongue and the hard palate (sh, zh, ch, dzh, j, and r).

Marcato diction—a style of diction in which each note in the music receives an accent and the explosive qualities of the consonants are exaggerated.

Medial consonant—a consonant situated within a word.

Nasality—an undesirable, exaggerated nasal quality often arising from some obstruction in the nasal cavity. When the nasal cavity becomes infected and swollen, as with a head cold, this quality usually occurs.

Open throat—an expression used to describe the feeling of a relaxed throat; an essential condition to correct voice production.

Open vowels—all the vowels with the exception of ee, ĭ, and oo. They are classified as open vowels because of the relaxed tongue position and the relatively low position of the jaw. The basic open vowel is ah, as in the word father. This vowel is the most naturally produced and is widely used as a beginning point in vocalization.

Palate—the roof of the mouth (*see also* Hard palate; Velum).

Pharynx—cavity extending from the base of the skull to the esophagus.

Phonation—the act of uttering or producing vocal sounds in singing or speaking.

Pronunciation—the manner of pronouncing words as regards the selection of appropriate vowels and consonants, and the proper accent of words.

Registers—the compass or range of the voice in which the singer is able to sing without readjustment of the vocal cords. Principal classifications are the chest and head registers; however, some authorities consider the middle range of the voice as a third register. Certain other authorities emphatically deny the existence of vocal registers.

Resonance—the amplification and enrichment of a fundamental tone emanating from the larynx—by means of supplementary vibrations in the bodily resonance cavities.

Resonator—the part of the vocal mechanism that amplifies or resonates the tone and provides its characteristic timbre—specifically, the pharynx, the mouth, the nasal cavity, and the sinuses. (Some authorities believe that the trachea, the bronchi, and the chest cavity also contribute to vocal resonance.)

Respiration—the process of breathing, involving the alternate inhaling and expelling of the breath; inspiration followed by expiration.

Sibilants—the hissing sounds caused by the raised tongue position and the flow of the breath being directed at the back side of the upper teeth. The sibilants in English are **s, z, sh, zh, ch,** and **j.**

Soft palate—(*see* Velum.)

Sonorous—a full, richly resonant tone quality.

Staccato diction—a style of diction in which the notes and the words are distinctly separated or detached.

Strident quality—a harsh, grating, unpleasant tonal quality.

Sustained consonants—consonants with a longer degree of sustaining power, such as **l, m,** and **n.**

Syllable—a single sound or a part of a word, which may be pronounced separately without interruption.

Tessitura—the average range of the melodic line or a voice part.

Throaty quality—an excessively dark tone quality sounded or resonated deep in the throat.

Tonal focus—direction of the vocal tone to a particular localized area of the frontal resonators.

Tremolo—an excessively wide and slow *vibrato* that detracts from the expressive qualities of the voice.

Velar—the consonants formed by arching the back part of the tongue and pressing it against the velum or soft palate (**k, g, ng**).

Velum, or **Soft palate**—a muscular membrane, continuous with and attached to the bone of the hard palate. It serves an important function in phonation in that it may be raised to prevent the breath from entering the nasal passages during the articulation of certain consonants.

Vibrato—a rapid fluctuation of vocal tone alternately above and below a given pitch level—for the purpose of adding beauty and warmth to the tone.

Vibrator—the part of the vocal mechanism in which the sound originates; the vocal cords or membranes that are attached to the inner portion of the larynx and that are set into motion or vibration by the flow of the breath.

Voiced consonant—a consonant phonated with a distinguishable movement of the vocal cords.

Voiceless consonant—a consonant phonated without movement of the vocal cords.

Vowels—the vocal sounds utilized for sustaining the tone and in which the flow of the breath is continuous. The primary vowels are **ee, ay, ah, oh,** and **oo.**

Topics for Discussion

1 What environmental factors cause a singer to utilize clavicular or high-chest breathing, when, as a child, one quite naturally employs abdominal breathing?

2 Discuss the tone quality of various choirs and choruses you have heard either in concert or in recordings. What tonal characteristics do you feel are desirable? What characteristics are undesirable?

3 What is the relationship between flexibility and good tonal quality?

4 Differentiate between the terms *pronunciation, enunciation,* and *articulation.*

5 What truths and what fallacies exist in the statement "sing as you speak"?

6 How may the choral conductor employ the concept of *front-to-back vowel placement* as a device for the improvement of tone quality?

7 Which consonants are likely to cause a choral group the most difficulties? Why? What procedures may be utilized to overcome these difficulties?

8   Why does each varying musical style require a distinct type of treatment in terms of diction?   In terms of tone quality?

9   Why is it desirable for the choral conductor to have a *variety* of techniques for achieving good tonal quality and correct diction?

Selected Readings

Adler, Kurt, *Phonetics and Diction in Singing: Italian, French, German, Spanish.* Minneapolis: University of Minnesota Press, 1967.

Brodnitz, Friedrich S., *Keep Your Voice Healthy.* Springfield, Ill.: Charles C Thomas, Publisher, 1973.

Burgin, John Carroll, *Teaching Singing.* Metuchen, N.J.: The Scarecrow Press, 1973.

Cain, Noble, *Choral Music and Its Practice.* New York: M. Witmark & Sons, 1942. (Chapter 10.)

Christy, Van A., *Glee Club and Chorus.* New York: G. Schirmer, Inc., 1940. (Chapter 4.)

Darrow, Gerald F., *Four Decades of Choral Training.* Metuchen, N.J.: The Scarecrow Press, 1975.

Dewey, Philip, *Bel Canto in Its Golden Age.* New York: King's Crown Press, Columbia University, 1950.

Dykema, Peter W., and Karl W. Gehrkens, *The Teaching and Administration of High School Music.* Boston: C. C. Birchard & Co., 1941, pp. 90–94. (Chapter 8.)

Fields, Victor A., *Training the Singing Voice.* New York: King's Crown Press, Columbia University, 1947.

Finn, William J., *The Art of the Choral Conductor.* Boston: C. C. Birchard & Co., 1939. (Chapters 2, 3, 4, 13, and 14.)

Frisell, Anthony, *The Tenor Voice.* Boston: Bruce Humphries, 1964.

Hammer, Russell, *Singing—An Extension of Speech.* Metuchen, N.J.: The Scarecrow Press, 1978.

Howerton, George, *Technique and Style in Choral Singing.* New York: Carl Fischer, Inc., 1958. (Chapters 1–4.)

Huls, Helen Steen, *The Adolescent Voice: A Study.* New York: Vantage Press, 1957.

Jones, Archie N., *Techniques in Choral Conducting*. New York: Carl Fischer, Inc., 1948. (Chapters 2 and 3.)

Kagen, Sergius, *On Studying Singing*. New York: Holt, Rinehart and Winston, Inc., 1950. (Also Dover edition.)

Krone, Max T., *The Chorus and Its Conductor*. Chicago: Neil A. Kjos Music Co., 1945. (Chapters 4 and 5.)

Marshall, Madeline, *The Singer's Manual of English Diction*. New York: G. Schirmer, Inc., 1953.

Moriarty, John, *Diction*. Boston: E. C. Schirmer Music Co., 1975.

Reid, Cornelius L., *The Free Voice*. New York: Colman-Ross Co., Inc., 1965.

Roe, Paul F., *Choral Music Education*. Englewood Cliffs, N.J.: Prentice-Hall, Inc., 1970. (Chapters 4 and 5.)

Shewan, Robert, *Voice Training for the High School Chorus*. West Nyack, N.Y.: Parker Publishing Company, 1973.

Stanley, Douglas, *Your Voice*. New York: Pitman Publishing Corporation, 1945.

Stanton, Royal, *The Dynamic Choral Conductor*. Delaware Water Gap, Pa.: Shawnee Press, Inc., 1971. (Chapters 4 and 5.)

Sunderman, Lloyd F., *Some Techniques for Choral Success*. Rockville Centre, N.Y.: Belwin, Inc., 1952. (Chapters 2 and 3.)

Vennard, William, *Developing Voices*. New York: Carl Fischer, Inc., 1973.

Westerman, Kenneth N., *Emergent Voice*. Second Edition. Ann Arbor, Mich.: privately published, 1955.

Wilson, Harry R., *Artistic Choral Singing*. New York: G. Schirmer, Inc., 1959. (Chapters 6 and 7.)

The following references pertain primarily to the anatomy and physiology of the human vocal mechanism.

Appelman, D. Ralph, *The Science of Vocal Pedagogy*. Bloomington, Ind.: Indiana University Press, 1967.

Berg, Janwillem van den, "Calculations on a Model of the Vocal Tract for Vowel /i/ and on the Larynx," *Journal Acoustical Society of America*, Vol. 27, 1955, pp. 332–338.

———, "Myoelastic Aerodynamic Theory of Voice Production," *Journal of Speech and Hearing Research*, Vol. 1, No. 3, September, 1958, pp. 224–227.

————, "Transmission of the Vocal Cavities," *Journal Acoustical Society of America*, Vol. 27, 1955, pp. 161–168.

————, and A. Sporr, "Microphonic Effect of the Larynx," *Nature*, Vol. 179, 1957, pp. 525–626.

————, J. T. Zantema, and P. Doornenbal, Jr., "On the Air Resistance and the Bernoulli Effect of the Human Larynx," *Journal Acoustical Society of America*, Vol. 27, 1957, pp. 626–631.

Boone, Daniel R., *The Voice and Voice Therapy*. Englewood Cliffs, N.J.: Prentice-Hall, Inc., 1971.

Borchers, Orville J., "Practical Implications of Scientific Research for the Teaching of Voice," *Music Teachers National Association, Volume of Proceedings*, 1947, pp. 209–215.

————, "Vocal Timbre in Its Immediate and Successive Aspects," *Music Teachers National Association, Volume of Proceedings*, 1941, pp. 346–358.

Brody, Viola, *An Experimental Study of the Emergence of the Process Involved in the Production of Song*. Unpublished Ph.D. thesis, University of Michigan, 1947.

Denes, Peter B., and Elliot N. Pinson, *The Speech Chain, the Physics and Biology of Spoken Language*. Baltimore: Bell Telephone Laboratories, 1963.

Farnsworth, D. W., "High Speed Motion Pictures of the Human Vocal Cords," *Music Teachers National Association, Volume of Proceedings*, 1939, pp. 305–309.

Hagerty, Robert F., and others, "Soft Palate Movement in Normals," *Journal of Speech and Hearing Research*, Vol. 1, No. 4, December, 1958, pp. 325–330.

Hixon, E., *An X-ray Study Comparing Oral and Pharyngeal Structures of Individuals with Nasal Voices and Individuals with Superior Voices*. Unpublished M.S. thesis, State University of Iowa, 1949.

Husler, Frederick, and Yvonne Rodd-Marling, *Singing: The Physical Nature of the Vocal Organ; A Guide to the Unlocking of the Singing Voice*. London: Faber & Faber Ltd., 1965.

Jones, David S., Richard J. Beargie, and John E. Pauly, "An Electromyographic Study of Some Muscles of Costal Respiration in Man," *The Anatomical Record*, Vol. 117, No. 1, December, 1953, pp. 17–24.

Lewis, Don, "Vocal Resonance," *Journal Acoustical Society of America*, Vol. 8, 1936, pp. 91–99.

Luchsinger, Richard, and Godfrey Arnold. *Voice–Speech Language*. Belmont, Calif.: Wadsworth Publishing Co., 1965.

Negus, V. E., *The Mechanism of the Larynx*. London: William Heinemann Ltd., 1929.

Norris, M. A., *X-ray Studies of Vowel Production as It Is Related to Voice*. Unpublished M.A. thesis, State University of Iowa, 1934.

Russell, G. Oscar, "First Preliminary X-ray Consonant Study," *Journal Acoustical Society of America*, Vol. 5, 1934, pp. 247–251.

————, *Speech and Voice*. New York: Macmillan Publishing Co., Inc., 1931.

————, *The Vowel*. Columbus: Ohio State University Press, 1928.

————, "X-ray Photographs of the Tongue and Vocal Organ Positions of Madame Bori," *Music Teachers National Association, Volume of Proceedings*, Vol. 27, 1932, p. 137.

Secord, Arthur E., *An X-ray Study of the Hyoid Bone, Thyroid Cartilage and Cricoid Cartilage in Relation to Pitch Change in the Human Larynx*. Unpublished Ph.D. thesis, University of Michigan, 1941.

Strong, Leon H., "The Mechanism of Laryngeal Pitch," *Anatomical Record*, Vol. 63, No. 1, August, 1935, pp. 13–28.

Vennard, William, *Singing: The Mechanism and the Technic*. Revised Edition. New York: Carl Fischer, Inc., 1967.

Westerman, Kenneth N., "Resonation," *Music Teachers National Association, Volume of Proceedings*, 1949, pp. 295–300.

Westlake, Harold, *The Mechanics of Phonation, An X-ray Study of the Larynx*. Unpublished Ph.D. thesis, University of Michigan, 1938.

Williams, R. L., "A Serial Radiographic Study of Velopharyngeal Closure and Tongue Positions in Certain Vowel Sounds," *Northwestern University Bulletin*, Vol. 52, No. 17, pp. 9–12.

Wolfe, W. G., *X-ray Study of Certain Structures and Movements Involved in Naso-Pharyngeal Closure*. Unpublished M.A. thesis, State University of Iowa, 1942.

Style and Interpretation

The primary function of the conductor is to interpret the music. He must interpret it in such a way that the intentions of the composer are "brought to life" and projected to the audience. To do this properly, the conductor must have, among other qualities, a clear concept of the music's basic style. *Musical style* may be simply defined as the distinctive manner or mode in which musical thought is expressed. It includes those characteristics that make a particular musical work uniquely different from others.

An understanding of the main historical periods, as well as the different styles within each period, is a requisite to the proper interpretation of any composer's music. Basic styles of art expression change periodically as a result of various social, political, and economic forces. Although the characteristics of the music of any one period begin to develop in the previous period and carry over to the next, various points of demarcation may be determined. The main currents of musical expression since the year 1400 may be divided into five periods as follows: *the Renaissance period* (c. 1400–1600), *the Baroque period* (1600–1750), *the Classic period* (1750–1820), *the Romantic period* (1800–1900), and *the Modern period* (1890 to the present).

Although the characteristics of the music of each period could be presented in a variety of ways, we have chosen the following five factors for discussion: meter and stress, tempo, dynamics, texture, and expressive aspects of the music. These factors have undergone change, were often distinctly different during the various periods, and can be controlled somewhat by the conductor in striving toward his interpretative goals.

The Renaissance Period

Although we should not forget that cultural change is a slowly moving process and that ascribing particular dates to certain periods is an arbitrary matter, the approximate 200-year period that we call the *Renaissance* (c. 1400–1600) does have certain salient characteristics. In some circles of European society, the religious orientation declined before rising secular interests. Ultimately this shift of interest was to culminate in the development of the modern scientific inquiry of the seventeenth century. The Renaissance intellectual began to emphasize his destiny here on earth, rather than considering life only as a prelude to the hereafter. He developed new confidence in his ability to solve his own problems and to determine his own fate. The wisdom of the church usually was not denied, but, in addition, the claims of other sources of truth were staked out.

Considerable discussion has taken place as to the exact beginnings of the Renaissance period in music. There appears to be some uncertainty as to the beginning of the period; however, the year 1400 seems to be the most suitable date. Jeppesen concurs with this point and offers the following well-founded reasons:

As far as can be discerned at present, there is a marked and very significant boundary line, especially in a musico-technical respect, at about the transition from the 14th to the 15th century. What happened at that time may be characterized as a change in the conception of consonance—the definite, practical recognition of the 3rd and 6th as not only having privileges in musical art equal to the 4th, 5th and 8th, but moreover as main consonants—tonal combinations decidedly preferred above all others, and regarded as fundamental factors in musical composition.[1]

Meter and Stress

Most of the music of the Renaissance period was unmetered, with stress occurring only through the emphasis of particular syllables in important words. The barline, with the resultant stress on the first beat of the measure, generally was not used during this period. Although the barline did come into being during the latter part of the period, it was utilized only as a "measure" of elapsed time and as a means of keeping the singers together.[2] When metrical stress is used for music of this period, the inherent beauties and flow of the vocal lines are destroyed.

In Figure 50a, an excerpt from Palestrina's *Missa Papae Marcelli* is shown illustrating the use of the traditional barlines. The normal syllabic accents occurring on the words "*Ple*-ni sunt *coe*-li et *ter*-ra" are obscured and the rhythmic counterpoint so necessary to the music does not occur with this manner of barring. Figure 50b, however, is barred according to the natural accent of the text, thus revealing the beauties of the rhythmic complexity of the music.

The conductor should be always alert to the tendency for singers to stress certain figures or rhythmic groupings in a manner that is inimical to the proper interpretation. For example, in the motet *Cantantibus Organis* by Marenzio (Pustet, No. B32), there often exists a tendency for some singers to stress, in a somewhat mechanical manner, the first and third of each group of four eighth notes (Figure 51). This practice should be avoided, as stress should occur only through the natural ac-

[1] Knud Jeppesen, *The Style of Palestrina and the Dissonance.* Second Edition. Copenhagen: Ejnar Munksgaard, Publisher, and New York: Oxford University Press, Inc., 1946, p. 222. Used with permission.
[2] As a convenience to the singers, modern-day publishers employ several means to facilitate the reading of Renaissance music. Some employ the use of regular barlines; others utilize dotted barlines as a means of minimizing the natural stress following the barline. Still other publishers use a short vertical line before certain words at regularly spaced intervals to serve as a guide to the singers.

FIGURE 50 *Excerpt from* Missa Papae Marcelli *by Palestrina: (a) illustrates the use of traditional barlines; (b) is barred according to the natural accent of the text. From* A History of Music and Musical Style *by Homer Ulrich and Paul A. Pisk, © 1963 by Harcourt Brace Jovanovich, Inc.*

FIGURE 51   *An excerpt from the serie* Cantantibus Organis. *Madrigal by Luca Marenzio, in which mechanical stress should be avoided in the eighth-note groupings in measures 2, 3, and 4, and the music performed in a smooth, flowing manner. Used by permission of Otto Heinrich Noetzel Verlag, Wilhelmshaven BRD.*

cent of particular syllables in important words. The sacred music of this period, in particular, should be performed in a smooth, flowing manner, and phrases should be thought of in terms of long ascending and descending lines.

The conductor should remind the singers to think always melodically and never chordally, except when tuning various intervals, and to avoid the regular recurring accents common to barred music. To help achieve the correct syllabic stress, ask the singers to read the text aloud with accents in the correct place and in accordance with the rise and fall of the various vocal lines. The conductor should utilize the tactus, or downward and upward movement of the hand and arm, to minimize any tendency toward metrical stress and to allow for the interplay of rhythmic polyphony.[3]

Tempo

The tempo of Renaissance music is determined largely by the syllabic setting of the text and the mood of the music. When one syllable is set to a melodic figure (melisma), the tempo should be restrained so that the inherent beauty of the vocal line may be revealed. On the other hand, when each syllable is set to a different note, of a comparatively longer duration, the tempo may be pushed slightly forward.

The tempo should remain relatively steady throughout the entire composition, or at least throughout a particular section. Any change in tempo should result only through a contrasting change in the mood of the text and a resultant change in the musical texture. Any changes in tempo within a given section should be extremely gradual and subtle, lest the symmetry of the music be destroyed.

Rallentando, as we know it today, did not exist in the music of the Renaissance period. Composers of the period were, however, aware of this effect, and when it was felt desirable they made it a part of the music itself. That is, they

[3] Each tactus has two beats in opposite directions—up-down or down-up (usually the latter is employed)—each one at a tempo ranging between M.M. = 50–60. This tempo was related to man's normal heartbeat (during quiet respiration) or his leisurely walking stride; thus the tempo of Renaissance music remained relatively steady. Both movements of the tactus were made with equal force whether it was conceived as down-up or up-down. For a further discussion of tactus, see Curt Sachs, *Rhythm and Tempo* (New York: W. W. Norton & Co., Inc., 1953), pp. 202–233.

achieved the effect by simply broadening or lengthening the musical notation. Therefore, conductors should avoid the deliberate use of *rallentando*, as this would only distort the musical interpretation.[4]

A somewhat greater freedom, however, may be said to exist in the performance of madrigals and related genre than with the masses and motets of the Renaissance period. Madrigal composers were captivated by the expressive qualities of the words. The mood of the text, therefore, is an essential determining factor in the selection of the correct tempo (and the proper dynamics). Restraint and avoidance of extremes, however, should always be paramount in the conductor's mind.

Dynamics

The dynamics of the music of this period is related to and is dependent upon any changes of mood in the text. Changes in dynamics would occur only as with changes in tempo—that is, with a contrasting mood between sections of the music. Within the overall framework of the music, however, dynamic levels should be moderate; extremes should seldom occur. Owing to the high degree of consonance, the pervading imitation, the lack of harmonic complexity, and the restraints inherent in the style, a climax seldom occurred and was not even sought by composers of the period.[5]

Through the use of the "seamless" technique there existed an overlapping or dovetailing of cadences; that is, one phrase ended in two or more of the parts, while another began in the other parts. Through this technique many cadences were minimized, thus lessening the necessity for dynamic changes. It should be added, however, that dynamics, especially in the madrigal, frottola, and canto carnascialesco, may be realized simply through the natural tessitura of the voices, as well as in the intensity of the word symbolism.

[4] *Cf.* Curt Sachs, *Rhythm and Tempo: A Study in Music History.* New York: W. W. Norton & Company, Inc., 1953, pp. 218–219.
[5] *Cf.* Robert Stevenson, *Music Before the Classic Era.* London: Macmillan & Co. Ltd., 1955. p. 42.

Texture

The music of the period was primarily contrapuntal in texture, that is, the various vocal lines were conceived as horizontal in nature. Composers wrote using anywhere from three to six or more parts. Upon first examining music of the period, one might feel some compositions or portions of others were conceived harmonically rather than contrapuntally. Upon careful examination, however, one will often discover, for example, that the third in a particular part may be omitted in an effort to achieve the best movement in the various vocal lines.[6]

Imitation as a contrapuntal device was used by composers from Dufay throughout the remainder of the period. The term, "point of imitation," pertains to the introduction of a figure or motive in one part, which is taken up successively in the other parts. These points of imitation should be emphasized slightly. The entrances need to be definite and precise, but vigorous accents are out of place and should be avoided. These entering parts should be brought out slightly, but should never overshadow the other contrapuntal lines. As other parts enter, they should then recede into the background.

Expressive Aspects

The sacred music of the Renaissance period sounds remote and restrained, primarily because of the large degree of consonance. There was a wide use of unisons, thirds, fifths, sixths, octaves, and triad sounds. Dissonance of the unprepared variety was used sparingly and was considered something "vehement and violent." Therefore, the objective was to conceal or muffle it insofar as was possible.[7]

Renaissance music possesses very subtle points of harmonic arrival. As previously mentioned, with the "seamless" technique there existed an overlapping or dovetailing of phrases; that is, one phrase ended in two or more parts, while another began in the other parts. Through this technique many ca-

---

[6] See, for example, Jeppesen, *op. cit.*, p. 92.
[7] *Ibid.*, p. 108.

dences were somewat obscured and the tension of the cadence was minimized. The conductor should search out all the suspensions in Renaissance music, mark them in his score, and have the chorus "lean" on them ever so slightly during performance.

The masses and motets of the Renaissance are impersonal in nature and should be performed with an atmosphere of quiet reflection and sincerity of feeling—in other words, as a prayer unto God, and not as a concert. The tone quality, therefore, should be kept light. Heavy dramatic quality and excessive vibrato in the voices are inimical to the expressive character of the music; both should be eliminated.

As previously mentioned, Renaissance music, when performed correctly, sounds remote and restrained. The resonance in the church or hall in which it was originally performed contributed substantially to this effect. The impersonal quality of Renaissance sacred music is comparable to the detachment that may be observed in certain paintings of the period in which the Madonna is not caressing her child, but is maintaining a distance between Him and herself.[8]

A somewhat greater freedom existed with the madrigals and related secular styles of the period. Composers were well aware of the expressive qualities of the text and often employed word painting in their music. That is, they used the music to portray, in a variety of ways, the character of certain words. For example, leaps in the melody were often used to depict joy, while the voices might ascend on such words as "heaven" and descend on words such as "earth." To depict grief and sadness, a diminished or augmented triad was often used, and dissonance was employed to represent such words as "sadness" and "pain."

The conductor should study his score and identify the various word-painting devices employed by the composer and, for an effective performance, the singers must be led to an understanding of them. The music must be sung with an emotional expressiveness that can result only through proper under-

---

[8] See, for example, the painting *The Cowper Maiden* by Raphael (1483–1520).

standing of it. Secular music of the period, although light in texture, should never be sung in an insipid manner. The rhythmic interplay among the voices should be emphasized somewhat, and the text articulated in a crisp manner, especially in English secular music. While a firmness of approach is necessary to performance, the inherent emotion in the music should not be allowed to run rampant; rather, the music should be performed with a certain degree of restraint.[9]

The Baroque Period

The Baroque period began toward the end of the sixteenth century, and is generally considered to have ended by 1750— the year of the death of Johann Sebastian Bach. The word *baroque* is said to have originated from *barrôco*, a Portuguese word meaning "a pearl of irregular form." In the nineteenth century, the term *baroque* was used in a pejorative manner, implying that the exceptionally ornate style of the arts of this period was in poor taste and a debasement of the Renaissance style. Today, however, such a connotation of the word has largely disappeared and the Baroque is considered to be one of the greatest periods of dramatic expression.

The art forms of the Baroque period were characterized by expansiveness, grandeur, and impressiveness. Baroque architecture was expansive and monumental; paintings were dynamic, alive with color, and filled with the tension of opposing masses; and the interior decoration of churches was highly ornate and dramatic.

Through the Counter-Reformation, beginning about the middle of the sixteenth century, the papacy, utilizing all its resources, set out to regain the faith of the people previously lost to Protestantism. The Counter-Reformation sought converts by trying to reach the spiritual through the senses. A vigorous program, incorporating the impressive aspects of all the arts,

[9] For a further discussion on the interpretation of madrigals, see Charles Kennedy Scott, *Madrigal Singing*. London: Oxford University Press, 1931.

was put into action.   As a result, cultural forms were developed that were both grandiose and sublime.

The period of the early Baroque began to take form during the pontificate of Sixtus V (1585–1590), and the new Catholicism was reflected in all the arts.

> The early baroque was, at first, a period of Catholic churchly art, and it was again the Society of Jesus which gave this art its peculiar traits of character. From the sphere of quiet devotion, the faithful were lifted into the world of the triumphant Church whose cult was celebrated by richly decked clergy under the vaults of a mighty architecture, surrounded by statues and pictures, before scintillating altars ornamented with gold and silver, to the accompaniment of the impressive and resonant music of multiple choirs, orchestras, and organs. In elaborate processions with flags, candles, and torches, triumphal carriages, floats, and arches, with the marchers singing, accompanying soldiers' bands blaring forth with their trumpets, the bells tolling and cannon booming, priests and students, guilds and corporations with their emblems, princes and the populace all united to demonstrate their adherence to the regenerated triumphal Church.[10]

Whereas the Counter-Reformation prompted the creation of a vast amount of sacred art, Protestantism, on the other hand, showed little interest in pictorial and decorative art, presumably because such churchly ornamentation would be contrary to the evangelical precepts of the church.[11] Protestant piety held that the proper reverence to God's word would be weakened if the congregation's attention were diverted by ornaments and decorations.   In the main, therefore, the Protestant churches remained relatively simple, their architecture merely imitating that of pre-Reformation times. Although music also suffered as a result of this artistic hostility, it was the one art form that eventually became an integral part of the reformed

---

[10] From *Music in Western Civilization* by Paul Henry Lang. By permission of W. W. Norton & Company, Inc. Copyright 1941 by W. W. Norton & Company, Inc. Copyright renewed 1968 by Paul Henry Lang. Page 319.

[11] Extreme Calvinists sometimes went so far as to destroy stained glass windows and smash religious statues in their rejection of traditional symbolism.

faiths. After a while music came to epitomize the highest degree of artistic expression in Protestantism.[12]

Meter and Stress

The barline and metered music came into being during the Baroque period; accentuations, therefore, generally occur at regularly spaced intervals. To evoke these accentuations in the performance of Baroque music, the conductor should utilize a definite and precise beat. This approach is particularly appropriate for music such as, for example, Schütz's "Cantate Domino Canticum Novum" (Bourne No. ES 33). The conductor, however, should avoid a mechanical, machine-like stress following each barline. For example, in Carissimi's "Plorate Filii Israel" (Bourne, No. ES 34; E. C. Schirmer, No. 1172), a broad legato style is necessitated with a minimum degree of stress. The conductor should analyze each selection under consideration, and particularly each phrase, to determine those places requiring greater stress—sometimes those notes at the peak of the phrase.[13]

The frames of Baroque paintings usually did not encompass the entirety of a particular scene, but often cut through various objects, thus giving the illusion of boundless space.[14] Composers achieved a similar effect by often beginning their music on a beat following a rest, thus providing the feeling to the listener that the music was a continuation of something that had already been underway. This delayed entrance effected a tension and rhythmic drive leading to the nearest downbeat.[15]

[12] Lang, *op. cit.*, pp. 320–321.
[13] It should be mentioned that, in the Baroque period, two basic stylistic practices existed—the *stilo antico* and the *stilo moderno*. In the *stilo antico*, or old style, which was suitable for the church, the music dominated the text. In the *stilo moderno*, or new style, the text dominated the music. These styles are sometimes referred to as *strict style* and *free style*. Some composers (Eberlin, for example) mixed these styles, rather than keeping them separate.
[14] See, for example, the painting *Landscape with the Chateau of Steen* (1636) by Peter Paul Rubens (1577–1640).
[15] Sachs, *op. cit.*, p. 266.

The practice of lengthening the dotted note and shortening the complementary note is an important consideration in the proper interpretation of Baroque music.   For example, the rhythm

¢ ♪. 𝅘𝅥𝅮 𝅘𝅥 | should often be performed as ¢ ♪ ♪ 𝅘𝅥𝅮. 𝅘𝅥 |

and

𝄞 𝄽 𝅘𝅥𝅮. 𝅘𝅥𝅮𝅘𝅥𝅮 𝅘𝅥𝅮. 𝅘𝅥𝅮𝅘𝅥𝅮 | as 𝄞 𝅘𝅥𝅮.. 𝅘𝅥𝅮 𝅘𝅥𝅮.. 𝅘𝅥𝅮 |

Why is it that the composers did not indicate what they desired?   Simply because it was easier to tell the performers how the music should be performed than to write out the notation. This treatment of the dotted note began during the early part of the seventeenth century and carried through to the beginning of the nineteenth century.   The music of Monteverdi, Purcell, Bach, and Handel (as well as the later music of Haydn, Mozart, and Beethoven) all necessitate this treatment.[16]   During the latter part of the eighteenth century, however, composers began to indicate more carefully their desired intentions in the music.

The purpose of this practice is the achievement of a crisp, clear manner of articulation, as opposed to a lazy and sluggish treatment.   This manner of articulation also minimizes the tendency for performers to rush their parts.   Of course, the conductors should utilize discretion in applying this convention. One criterion for consideration is the general character of the music; that is, the lengthening of the dotted notes would be more appropriate to brilliant and majestic music and somewhat less appropriate to music of a lilting, graceful character.

A different treatment of dotted rhythms, however, should occur with trochaic rhythms in compound triple meter, which are sometimes written as dotted rhythms.   For example, the rhythm notated as ¾ 𝅘𝅥. 𝅘𝅥𝅮 𝅘𝅥. 𝅘𝅥𝅮 𝅘𝅥𝅮𝅘𝅥𝅮𝅘𝅥𝅮 | should be performed as

𝄞 𝅘𝅥 ♪ 𝅘𝅥 ♪ 𝅘𝅥𝅮𝅘𝅥𝅮𝅘𝅥𝅮 | .   To determine the proper handling of these rhythms the conductor should analyze the music; when the dominant rhythm is compound triple meter (often determined

---

[16] Thurston Dart, *The Interpretation of Music*. Revised Edition.   London: Hutchinson Publishing Group Ltd., 1960, pp. 81–82.

by the triplet groupings), then the passage should be performed as indicated in the latter example above.[17]

A somewhat more controversial problem is encountered in the handling of dotted eighth notes against triplets. An example of this occurs in the Bach sacred cantata No. 4, *Christ lag in Todesbandon* ("Christ Lay in Death's Dark Prison"), *Versus VI*.[18] The dotted rhythm ♩♪ ♩♪ in the bass line of the orchestral accompaniment (continuo) occurs against the triplet figure ♫♩ ♫♩ in the parts for soprano and tenor. As a general rule, duplets should yield to triplets.[19] In this case the dotted eighth note should coincide with the first two triplets and the sixteenth note with the last triplet (Figure 52).[20]

FIGURE 52

Tempo

The tempo of Baroque music should generally be somewhat moderate and deliberate and extremes should be avoided. Even fast tempi should be performed with some restraint. During the Baroque period Italian terms, such as *allegro* and *largo*, were used to indicate the character of the music, rather than as specific directions as to tempo. As a result some conductors, misunderstanding the meaning of these terms, are inclined to rush

[17] *Ibid.*, p. 89.
[18] Another example of this problem occurs in Bach's *Jesu, Joy of Man's Desiring* (E. C. Schirmer, No. 317).
[19] For an example of the suggested interpretation, listen to the recording by the Robert Shaw Chorale, RCA Victor LSC-2273.
[20] For a further discussion of dotted rhythms, see Sachs, *op. cit.*, pp. 303–306, and Dart, *op. cit.*, pp. 81–83, 88–89, 111, 125–126, and 171.

the music marked *allegro* and *vivace*, and to conduct too slowly music marked *adagio* and *largo*. Italian markings should be considered as an indication of mood rather than tempo. *Allegro* should be interpreted literally, as merry, lively, brisk, rather than as fast, while *largo* should be considered as simply broad, rather than as very slow.[21]

Handel often wrote the Italian marking *largo* at the end of many of his sacred choruses. The composer's intent in adding this marking at the end of a chorus implies simply that the quarter note for the *allegro* becomes exactly twice as long for the *largo*; for example, if the *allegro* has been conducted at $\downarrow = 120$, then the *largo* will be conducted at $\downarrow = 60$. He also, however, sometimes wrote notes of a larger or greater value as a means of achieving the desired intention of *largo*, that is, simply broad. For the conductor to further slow down the pulse of the music would make the ending too slow and thus distort the desired effect.[22]

In the early Baroque monody, a considerable flexibility existed in the tempo so that the emotions in the text and the music might be fully expressed. In the late 1630s, however, a reversal of this trend occurred and the tempi of music became more strict and restrained.[23] The relative freedom of emotional expression gave way to rhythmical shifts within a stricter tempo.

According to Machlis, one of the most notable characteristics of Baroque music is its steady pulsation or unflagging rhythm.[24]

The Baroque, with its fondness for energetic movement, demanded a dynamic rhythm based on the regular recurrence of

---

[21] Richard T. Gore, "The Performance of Baroque Church Music," *Music Teachers National Association, Volume of Proceedings*, 1950. Pittsburgh: The Association, 1953, pp. 156–157.

[22] *Ibid.*, p. 157.

[23] Sachs, *op. cit.*, pp. 265–266.

[24] Exceptions to this general characteristic of Baroque music are the *recitative*, which is sung in a declamatory style with stress or accent occurring as a result of important words or particular syllables, and the *arioso*, which in style lies somewhere between the recitative and the aria and possesess some of the characteristics of each.

accent. The bass part became the carrier of the new rhythm. Its relentless beat is an arresting trait in many compositions of the Baroque. This steady pulsation, once under way, never slackens or deviates until the goal is reached. It imparts to baroque music its unflagging drive, producing the same effect of turbulent yet controlled motion as animates baroque painting, sculpture, and architecture.[25]

Although a steady pulsating drive is important to proper interpretation, this does not mean that the tempo should be completely unyielding. For instance, at cadences immediately prior to subsequent sections, a slight holding back of the tempo is often desirable. The exact treatment of each cadence, however, will vary according to the music itself.[26] In reference to the handling of cadences *Grove's* states:

Each needs its own natural flexibility, though this may vary according to circumstances from the merest easing scarcely consciously perceptible, at the one extreme, to a majestic broadening at the other. It is for the performer to judge on the merits of each case between sentimental excess and self-conscious rigidity.[27]

Accelerando and *ritardando* (or *rallentando*) are inappropriate and out of place in Baroque music, principally because these concepts of gradually increasing or gradually decreasing the tempo did not exist in this period. These concepts grew out of the Mannheim school in the latter part of the eighteenth century. Another concept, often misunderstood, is the treatment of the *fermata*. A *fermata* in Baroque music simply indicates the end of a phrase and a point at which the singers may take a breath. The concept of the *fermata* as an untimed hold developed during the latter part of the eighteenth century, as did also the modern concept of *accelerando* and *ritardando*.

[25]Joseph Machlis, *The Enjoyment of Music*. Third Regular Edition. New York: W. W. Norton & Company, Inc., 1970, p. 356. Used with permission.
[26]For a discussion of conflicting viewpoints in regard to tempo changes, see Sachs, *op. cit.*, pp. 277–280.
[27]*Grove's Dictionary of Music and Musicians* (edited by Eric Blom), Volume II. New York: St. Martin's Press, Inc., Macmillan & Co. Ltd., 1954, p. 986. Used by permission of Macmillan, London and Basingstoke.

Dynamics

The concept of *crescendo* and *decrescendo* did not widely exist during the Baroque period, principally because the instruments of the period did not have the necessary flexibility to achieve these ends. The organ, for example, did not possess swell shutters, and the piano was not invented until the latter part of the period. Therefore, contrast was sought by other means.[28] Contrast in dynamics was achieved by adding or dropping out various instruments or voice parts. This was referred to as *terraced dynamics,* meaning various levels or plateaus of dynamics. Extremes in dynamics, therefore, should be avoided, as the concept of terraced dynamics would render them undesirable.[29] Usually the music itself will take care of the often slight dynamic changes in terraced dynamics and one should question editorial markings that seem to place undue emphasis upon these changes. Terraced dynamics is only part of the change, however, the other being in the density due to the increase or decrease of the number of voices participating. Composers up through J. S. Bach generally did not include dynamic markings, but in those instances where they did, it was to make clear a change that might not have been recognized in the performance practice of the time or where an absolute insistence of change seemed necessary by the composer. The conductor should utilize a dynamic range only from *piano* to *forte*. Extending the dynamics above or below these levels is inappropriate and should generally be avoided except upon rare occasions.

Texture

The beginning of the Baroque period ushered in a change from a texture of independent, but interrelated parts to a single melody or voice part supported by chords or chordal combinations. This change from modal polyphony to a homophonic style ne-

---

[28] According to *Grove's Dictionary of Music and Musicians*, crescendo and *decrescendo* were not entirely unknown to Baroque composers, as written indications of it are found in the mid-seventeenth-century music of the Italian composer Mazzochi (*Grove's*, Vol. II, p. 988).

[29] Gore, *op. cit.*, pp. 157–158.

cessitated a change in the harmonic system—from the medieval church modes to a system of major and minor tonality. Whereas the polyphony of the Renaissance symbolized the submissiveness of the individual, the new style fulfilled the need for greater individual expression. Secular music gained vastly in importance and the new style allowed for a greater emotional expression of the text. When polyphony returned, after a brief lapse, it did so within a different harmonic framework, that is, the system of major–minor tonality.[30]   Even when the new harmonic counterpoint became in vogue, some composers continued to write in the old style polyphony (*stile antico*), sometimes called the Palestrina style. Conductors, therefore. need to recognize and treat each style accordingly.

As Baroque polyphony functions within a harmonic framework of tonality and generally well-defined chord progressions, cadences are important aspects of arrival but may be different according to the overall texture of the music, *i.e.*, some may be lighter and others heavier (see previous section on tempo for a discussion on the treatment of cadences). Also, the complexity of the texture as well as the complexity of the chords, especially when some have been chromatically altered, may have an influence on the tempo of the music. In lighter textures the tempo may be pushed slightly forward, while in denser textures the tempo may be held back somewhat. As to imitations, answering voices should be replicas of the announcing voice's treatment of the subject, including specific rhythmic patterns, trills, and so on.

Expressive Aspects

In contrast to the Renaissance composer, who expressed emotion with considerable restraint, the Baroque composer gave freer vent to his emotions. Nevertheless, his music was still somewhat impersonal, with the emotion stemming not from an

---

[30] While polyphony was rejected by most composers during the early Baroque period, it was never abandoned by the famous three S's: Johann Herman Schein (1586–1630), Samuel Scheidt (1587–1654), and Heinrich Schütz (1585–1672).

individual struggle, as in the Romantic period, but from the tumultuous and dramatic forces affecting all mankind.[31]

Within the new system of major–minor tonality each chord assumed a definite relationship to the others. Harmonic tension and repose were well understood by composers of the period and were used as devices in composition. There were fewer but stronger cadences, and the drive to the keynote was apparent. There was a considerable increase in the intensity of the music and in the amount of dissonance that was used for the purpose of achieving emotional intensity. Whereas in the Renaissance period dissonance was permissible only when prepared—that is, when first heard with a consonant interval and introduced through a suspension, the use of unprepared dissonance became accepted and widely used as an expressive device.[32]

Tone painting, or the way in which the music portrayed the words, was increasingly given attention by composers of the period. Bach, for example, advised his students to "play the chorale [prelude] according to the meaning of the words." It must be understood, however, that although the text gave birth to the musical idea, it was the music itself that ultimately reigned supreme.[33]

The Baroque period marked the first time in history that instrumental music assumed an equal position with vocal music. The spirit of the times prompted the development of new instruments and the improvements of the old. The new status of instrumental music has caused certain persons to say that some music was conceived instrumentally rather than vocally. The performance of Baroque music, therefore, necessitates a most exacting rhythmic precision. Singers should thus be as exacting as instrumentalists. They should also maintain a steadiness and purity of vocal line, devoid of excessive vibrato, as this may adversely affect the intonation and thus blur the

[31] George Howerton, *Technique and Style in Choral Singing.* New York: Carl Fischer, Inc., 1957, p. 133.
[32] Claudio Monteverdi (1567–1643) is often credited with the first wide use of unprepared dissonance.
[33] Machlis, *op. cit.,* p. 355.

polyphonic structure.   These qualities are especially important in singing contrapuntal music.

The matter of the proper pitch level at which to perform Baroque music should be given due consideration.   Between approximately 1600 and 1820, the standard accepted pitch level —although there were many deviations—was about a semitone lower than the present A-440.   The implications of this fact are that, to perform Baroque music in as authentic a manner as possible, one ought to lower the pitch a half step to return it to its original key.   Of course, practical considerations such as the difficulty of transposing the orchestral parts, or even the piano or organ accompaniment, often make this practice unfeasible.   Another argument, however, against this practice is the additional brilliance which is often achieved through performance in the higher key.   On the other hand, when the tessitura of the various parts appears to be too high and thus negatively influences the tone quality, the conductor may consider lowering the pitch.   If he elects to do so, he then will have at least two justifications for his decision.   By and large, however, the conductor will find his problems minimized if he performs the music in the key in which it is presently written.

The Classic Period

While Bach and Handel were carrying the Baroque style to its culmination in the first half of the eighteenth century, forces were already at work leading toward the formulation of a new style.   The Classic era, generally considered to cover the period from 1750 to 1820, includes such diverse aesthetic trends as the Rococo (*Stile galant*), *empfindsamer Stil* (literally, "sensitive" style), Enlightenment, and *Sturm und Drang* (storm and stress). The Classic period thus lacked any unifying social and aesthetic philosophy, such as shaped artistic expression in the Baroque period.   While each of these aesthetic trends had its proponents, it was the master composers of the period—Haydn, Mozart, and Beethoven—who were able to synthesize the elements of each into their music.

The Rococo style (c. 1720–c. 1770) repudiated the massive forms of the Baroque. The endless vistas gave way to intimate glimpses; the grandeur of Baroque decoration changed to delicate, often unnecessary, ornamentation; monumental sculpture decreased in size to figurines for the mantle; the center of life moved from the ballroom to the boudoir; and the grandiloquent language of the Baroque changed in manner and tone to witty, tête-à-tête conversations.[34] The expansiveness, grandeur, and impressiveness of Baroque music gave way to an expression of elegance in delicate proportions The polyphony of the later Baroque was abandoned in favor of a homophonic style, with interest focused on the soprano line that often was adorned with a proliferation of ornamentation.

Whereas the music of Rococo was elegant and ornate, and written to please the aristocracy, the *empfindsamer Stil* (or expressive style) was more the music of the middle class. This bourgeois style reflected the attitudes of honesty and goodness and often approached the borders of sentimentality. It is reflected, for example, in the title of a collection of songs by the German composer J. F. Reichardt, "Lullabies for Good German Mothers."[35]

The eighteenth-century Enlightenment, or Age of Reason, began as a reaction against supernatural religions, formalism, and authority. The underlying philosophical belief was that man should be "natural" in all these respects—that is, natural behavior as opposed to formality, and individual freedom as opposed to submission to authority.[36] Denis Diderot's *Encyclopédie,* or *Classified Dictionary of Sciences, Arts, and Trades,* was published serially beginning in 1751 and symbolizes rationalism and the spirit of scientific inquiry. Thomas Paine's book, *The Age of Reason,* also reflects such rationalism. The Marquis de Condorcet's book, *The Progress of the Human Spirit* (1774), set forth ten stages through which man had progressed from

[34] William Fleming and Abraham Veinus, *Understanding Music: Style, Structure, and History.* New York: Holt, Rinehart and Winston, Inc., 1958, pp. 309–310.
[35] *Ibid.,* p. 312.
[36] Donald Jay Grout, *A History of Western Music.* New York: W. W. Norton & Company, Inc., 1960, p. 411.

primitive life to nearly ultimate perfection. This philosophy expressed the belief that man, through the use of his rational and moral powers, could ultimately control his environment. Jean Rameau was an outstanding exponent of rationalism and sought to restore reason to musical thought. There is evidence of this philosophy in the optimism expressed in some of the music of Beethoven, who was the movement's most articulate spokesman.[37]

The *Sturm und Drang* (storm and stress) movement in Germany ran counter to the elegance of the Rococo, the optimism of the Enlightenment, and the restricted emotionalism of the *empfindsamer Stil.*[38] These aesthetic trends were rejected in favor of a search for emotional truth and a more flexible use of the imagination. This philosophy may be seen in the literary works of both Goethe and Schiller. The best-known literary example is Goethe's *Faust.* Faust rejects the tenets of the Age of Reason, ceases to search for nature's secrets in books, and seeks the ultimate truth in experiences and emotion. It is felt by some authorities that Haydn, Mozart, and Beethoven were all influenced by this philosophy, as indicated by the pathos and sometimes violent outbursts in some of their music.[39]

The center of cultural life in the Classic period was the palace. The ruling aristocracy surrounded itself with the arts, which it considered its privileged right. Beauty of expression and elegance of manner became formalized and permeated its existence. The artist of the period created for his patron, who was far above him in social rank. Composers were employed for what they could contribute to the aristocracy's "cultural" surroundings. In general, the patron was interested in the artist's creative products, rather than in him as an individual. In other words, a certain degree of reserve existed between employer and employee. In this social setting, where the emphasis was upon courtly manners, the artist avoided becoming too personal in his art, as this would have been considered in poor

[37] Fleming and Veinus, *op. cit.*, p. 313.
[38] Some authorities feel that the *empfindsamer Stil* and the *Strum und Drang* are only different manifestations of an overall Classic-Romantic style.
[39] *Ibid.*, p. 314.

taste.   Objectivity and reserve, therefore, became a necessary part of the artist's creative expression.

Meter and Stress

The art of the Classic era, the Rococo style in particular, strove for elegance and more delicate proportions.   These general characteristics were also reflected in the music of the period. Therefore, the pulsation of the music was more delicately marked than in the Baroque period.   In order to convey clearly this style to his performers, the conductor should, therefore, utilize a lighter beat, yet with a definite or marked precision to delinate the crisp rhythmic patterns of the music.[40]

Tempo

Tempi in the Classic period were generally moderate and extremes avoided.   Beginning with the Classic period composers indicated to a much greater extent what they desired in their scores.   Markings indicating the desired tempo, correct phrasing, and tonal quality were often included.   Tempo was often indicated through the use of Italian words (*i.e.*, *allegro, adagio,* etc.), and signs indicating dynamic changes were written in.[41] In the waning years of the Classic period, composers, Beethoven in particular, were able to prescribe the desired tempo of their compositions through the use of metronome markings (as noted previously, the metronome was invented by Maelzel in 1816) .

Tempo rubato originated from the vocal art and eventually was utilized as a device in the interpretation of instrumental music.   It was first discussed in a book on singing by Pier Francesco Tosi, published in 1723.   The letters of Mozart reveal that he was well aware of the device and used it in his piano

---

[40] Howerton, *op. cit.,* p. 142.
[41] Frederick Dorian, *The History of Music in Performance.*   New York: W. W. Norton & Company, Inc., 1942, p. 155.

performances. In addition, Philipp Emanuel Bach (1714–1788) discussed *tempo rubato* in Volume Two of his *Versuch*.[42] It is reasonable to assume that other composers of the period were also aware of this interpretative device. It is suggested, however, in performing music of this period, that *tempo rubato* be used with discretion and restraint, and that its more exaggerated use, as in the subsequent Romantic period, be avoided. In general, the principle of strict time should be followed. The exceptions where *tempo rubato* seems desirable will usually be dictated by the poetical aspects of the text.[43] The use of *ritardando* and *accelerando* became more frequent, especially during the latter part of the period. In accordance with the general characteristics of the music of the period, such alterations in tempi should be slight and performed with restraint.

Dynamics

Although dynamic contrast was an important part of the music of the period, composers did not seek the extremes that occurred during the later periods. One of the most significant developments growing out of the latter part of the eighteenth century was that of *crescendo–decrescendo*. Such a concept was in marked contrast to the terraced dynamics of the earlier Baroque period. While the concept of *crescendo–decrescendo* was not entirely unknown and had been utilized to some degree in Italy from the beginning of the century, it had not been widely used elsewhere. Through the efforts of Stamitz, the precision of the orchestra at Mannheim was developed to such a high degree that this carefully controlled *crescendo* became known as the *Mannheim crescendo*. In choral performances the *crescendo–decrescendo* should be performed with some restraint, considering the general dynamic level of the passage. The *crescendo* should not begin from as low a dynamic level, nor reach as high a level, as it would during the Romantic period. Generally, in *crescendo* and *decrescendo*, the dynamic level

---

[42] *Ibid.*, pp. 186–193.
[43] For a further discussion of *tempo rubato*, see Sachs, *op. cit.*, pp. 306–310.

should change gradually just one degree higher or lower—for example, from *p* ——————— *mp;* and rarely from *p* ——————— *f.*

The *forte–piano* contrast was an unwritten law of dynamic execution; that is, repeated phrases and/or periods should be performed *piano,* as in an echo. Periods performed *piano* the first time should be performed *forte* on the repetition.[44] The harmony itself will provide the conductor with further clues for the treatment of dynamics.

> Philipp Emanuel Bach points out that every tone foreign to the key can very well stand a *forte,* regardless of whether it occurs in dissonance or consonance. . . . Quantz distinguishes clearly three classes of dissonances, to be played *mezzo forte, forte,* and *fortissimo,* respectively. He also explains that the theme of the composition calls for dynamic emphasis. Likewise, all other notes of importance (in a theme, in a contrapuntal passage, or in a harmonic structure) must be stressed by means of dynamics. The notes introducing the theme must be marked; the dissonance must be made stronger than its resolution.[45]

It is also often necessary and desirable to adjust the dynamics to the acoustical conditions of the performance hall. The conductor needs to consider the character of the music, the number and maturity of the performers, and the size and the acoustical conditions of the performance hall or auditorium. To maintain the classic proportions of the music, it should never become overbearing from the dynamic standpoint. An overly large musical organization, coupled with an auditorium with exceptionally live acoustical properties, can create a dynamic level that is much too high; to be effective, the dynamic level must be reduced in size and/or scope.

Texture

Composers sought for lightness and simplicity in their music. In place of the heavy Baroque texture, there was a combination

---

[44] Dorian, *op. cit.,* p. 166.
[45] From *The History of Music in Performance* by Frederick Dorian. New York: W. W. Norton & Company, Inc., 1942, p. 168. Copyright renewed 1970 by Frederick Dorian.

of textures in which chordal patterns, running figures, unsupported melodies, and other devices were used alternately, depending upon the expressive intentions of the composer. Contrapuntal devices were also sometimes used, particularly in the masses; however, polyphony was generally not sought by composers of the period. During the Baroque period a polarity existed between the melody and the bass parts. The bass supported the melody, while the inner voices sometimes only completed the harmonies. During the Classic period, the inner voices assumed greater importance, and the previous supporting function of the bass part gave way to one of greater flexibility and interplay with the inner voices.[46]

Expressive Aspects

In contrast to the late Baroque period, where the cadences were relatively infrequent and somewhat inconspicuous, and the phrases were "spun-out," the composers of the Classic period utilized phrases of a regular two- or four-bar length that were shorter and more distinct. There were generally rather strong points of harmonic arrival and the period structure was well defined. Although the harmonic vocabulary did not differ substantially from the late Baroque period, the harmonic progressions were certainly less weighty.[47] Melody reigned supreme; the other parts served to support and enhance it, and were often subordinate to it. Ornamentation developed to its fullest bloom. This embellishment of the melodic line, however, was only reflective of the spirit of the times, where elegance and grace were considered so highly important, particularly to the patrons of the arts.

The music of the Classic period was generally abstract in nature and "discreet" in taste and was an integral part of a sophisticated mode of living. It was moderate in style, avoiding the extremes of the later Romantic period. Emotional content was less important and unity of design became the composer's

[46] Homer Ulrich and Paul A. Pisk, *A History of Music and Musical Style*. New York: Harcourt Brace Jovanovich, Inc., 1963, pp. 322–323.
[47] Grout, *op. cit.*, p. 417.

goal. Form served to eliminate the personal qualities and universalized the style. Symmetry, balance, clarity, and restraint summarized the composer's artistic creations.

The Romantic Period

The French Revolution, beginning in 1789, resulted in the breakdown of the aristocratic way of life and led to the development of nineteenth-century liberalism. In the world of the arts, it was paralleled by the rise of the Romantic movement, in essence a revolt against formality and authority. Previously, composers had for many centuries worked under the patronage of either the church or princely courts. Under this system, composers generally wrote music to please their patrons. They were careful not to let their music become too personal in nature. With the breakdown of the patronage system composers were free to express themselves individually. They were no longer inhibited or restricted by a patron's demands, and were able to please their equals—the general public. With their greater freedom, composers sought out new and unique means of expression. This led to a greater display of emotion, heretofore largely restrained.

Although the composer, no longer bound to his patron, was able to express himself more freely, his financial insecurity, on the other hand, often caused him to withdraw from the world about him. He sometimes became preoccupied with his own inner problems and became even pessimistic about the future. Nevertheless, these situations or conditions involving withdrawal, escape, mysticism, religion, as well as the need for self-expression, all were often expressed in the composers' music, and they enriched the repertoire as a result.

The term "Romanticism," as it pertains to the nineteenth century, is inexact and somewhat misleading. The Romantic period contained many diametrical differences, which seemingly run counter to its name. According to Machlis:

> The nineteenth century included many opposites: liberalism
> and reaction, idealism and the crassest materialism, bourgeois

sentimentality and stark realism, mysticism and scientific inquiry, democratic revolution and royalist restoration, romantic optimism and no less romantic despair.[48]

Meter and Stress

Composers in the Romantic period, in their search for freedom from rules, often sought to break the strictness of the rhythm, yet remain within the time-honored rules. A widely used device to achieve this objective was through the use of meter changes without changing the meter signature.[49] An example of this device may be found in the Brahms *Requiem*. Such metric alteration results in displaced accents—that is, accents where they are not normally expected—in a relatively short space of time. Whereas Romantic composers achieved these unique rhythmic effects within the boundaries of the accepted rules, the modern-day composer would normally utilize alternately different meter signatures (see later section "The Modern Period" in this chapter and discussion on meter and stress, for examples). Other varied means of syncopation also became widely used during this period as an expressive device and as a means of evoking interest. Intricate rhythmic patterns and rhythmic surprise were characteristic of the music of the period. Composers sometimes used a phrase structure that was irregular, that is, of varying lengths. Brahms in particular was noted for his elongated or extended phrases; in some cases they were absorbed into contrapuntal textures so that it is difficult to determine where they actually do end.[50]

Tempo

The restraint typical of the Classic period was abandoned during the Romantic era. It was a period of extremes—fast tempi were often performed exceptionally fast and slow tempi excep-

[48] Joseph Machlis, *The Enjoyment of Music.* Regular Revised Edition. New York: W. W. Norton & Company, Inc., 1963, p. 85. Used with permission.
[49] Sachs, *op. cit.,* p. 344.
[50] Ulrich and Pisk, *op. cit.,* p. 485.

tionally slow. Tempo was closely aligned with mood, and as the composer was often expressing varying moods within a composition, extreme, abrupt changes in tempo often occurred. *Accelerando* and *ritardando* became more frequently used than in the previous period. As an element of expressiveness *tempo rubato* was developed to its ultimate.

During the Romantic period two diametrically opposed schools of interpretative thought existed. One, represented by Mendelssohn, was based on classical principles; the other was the highly romantic, sometimes called the "Neo-German" type of interpretation, which was initiated by Liszt and exemplified by Wagner. The Mendelssohn school sought to preserve the Classical tradition and to eliminate some of the practices which they felt were extreme. Mendelssohn was an exponent of regularity of rhythm and fluency of tempo. Wagner, on the other hand, favored broad, singing melody, and considerable liberty in tempi.[51] He felt that the correct tempo could be determined only through "a proper understanding of the melos."[52]

Although composers may be said to have had tendencies toward one or the other of the above positions, and certainly were influenced in one way or another, it would be unwise, as well as impossible, to categorize them all in either group. The music of each composer must be considered individually. Only through a thorough analysis and study of the music will a proper tempo be determined. For example, music with a light texture may be performed in a faster tempo than should music with a heavy, sonorous texture. The latter should be performed somewhat slower if it is to be effective. Relating to this point, the following statement by Robert Schumann is both interesting and revealing:

> You know how I dislike quarreling about tempo, and how for me only the inner measure of the movement is conclusive. Thus, an allegro of one who is cold by nature always sounds lazier than a slow tempo by one of sanguine temperament. With the orchestra, however, the proportions are decisive.

[51] Dorian, *op. cit.,* pp. 230–231.
[52] *Ibid.,* p. 281.

Stronger and denser masses are capable of bringing out the detail as well as the whole with more emphasis and importance; whereas, with smaller and finer units, one must compensate for the lack of resonance by pushing forward in the tempo.[53]

Dynamics

In contrast to the restraint of the Classic period, composers of the Romantic period often used extremes in dynamics ranging from *fff* to *ppp*, but with a slight leaning toward the use of the lower dynamic levels. Some editions of the Verdi *Requiem*, it may be noted, even contain dynamic markings of *ppppp*.

Crescendo and *decrescendo,* or the gradual swelling and diminishing of tone, became a widely used expressive device by nineteenth-century composers. In certain compositions it was used to create the illusion of distance—that is, of a group or object gradually coming closer and then receding into the distance.

Some composers employed a slight *accelerando* with a *crescendo* and a slight *ritardando* with a decrescendo. Rossini, in particular, was noted for his combining "a gradual dynamic increase with a great rhythmic momentum."[54]

Composers in the nineteenth century endeavored to indicate more clearly on their scores their intentions through the use of a variety of tempo and dynamic markings. Some of these terms encompassed both tempo and dynamics. For example, *morendo* (dying away) indicates that the music should be both slower and softer, and *andante maestoso* (moderately slow and majestic) implies a moderate tempo yet with a full sonority.

In addition to *crescendo* and *decrescendo,* the use of more sudden climaxes also became a common practice. Grieg, for example, employs this device to a considerable extent in his *Psalms* (C. F. Peters). The use of dynamic accents, such as *sforzando* (*sfz*) and *sforzato*(*sf*), occurred with much greater

---

[53] From *The History of Music in Performance* by Frederick Dorian. New York: W. W. Norton & Company, Inc., page 227. *Cf.* Sachs, *op. cit.,* p. 379.
[54] Ulrich and Pisk, *op. cit.,* p. 455.

frequency. See, for example, the Choral Finale to the *Ninth Symphony* by Beethoven (H. W. Gray; G. Schirmer), *Elijah* by Mendelssohn (G. Schirmer), the *Requiem Mass* and the *Stabat Mater* by Dvořák (G. Schirmer), and the *29th Psalm* by Elgar (Novello). In contrast to the moderately sized ensembles utilized in the various princely courts of the Classic era, the combined forces of large orchestras and choirs became the ideal medium for the expression of the dynamic extremes of the Romantic period.

Texture

New harmonic relationships were explored by composers of the Romantic period. Dissonance became more widely used and an increasing use of melodic and harmonic chromaticism gave the composer a wider range of expressive devices.[55] There was a lessening of harmonic drive, with an increased tendency toward the use of deceptive resolutions and obscured cadences. That is, cadences were sometimes avoided, or resolved deceptively. In contrast to "wandering" chromaticism, composers sometimes utilized sudden harmonic and enharmonic changes, or shifts of tonal center.

Although a balance between harmony and counterpoint is said to have existed during the late Baroque period, the nineteenth-century Romanticist altered the balance in favor of harmony. The Romantic composer, however, often alternated the texture within a short time span. Counterpoint, when used, focused upon the opposition of masses, rather than upon vocal lines. In contrast to the light and clear texture of the Classic period, the texture of music in the Romantic period was often somewhat dense and heavy.

[55] The effectiveness of dissonance is certainly related to tempo, as the listener's aural comprehension of a complex and dissonant passage may be blurred by a tempo that is too rapid.

Expressive Aspects

During the Romantic period some composers expressed their opposition to formality, convention, authority and tradition, while some others expressed a longing for the past—the "golden age"—and made efforts to recapture it in some way. Whereas the Classic composer was highly concerned with expression within a particular form, the Romanticist was not to be restricted by it. He was not to be bound by the previous forms and strove to develop a freer form through which he might better express himself.

Individual expression became the composer's principal goal. To express emotion freely, the composer drew on all the multitude of musical resources at his command. As a means of creating tension and expressing emotion, composers of this period experimented considerably in the field of harmony. Unusual harmonic effects, as well as unusual rhythmic effects, wide contrasts in dynamics, changing moods, and varying textures were all used as expressive devices.

While tone color has always existed as an integral aspect of music, it took on a new importance during the Romantic period. Through tone color composers sought to express sensuous beauty and tonal enchantment. Musical terms, such as *con amore* (with love), *con fuoco* (with fire), *con passione* (with passion), *dolce* (sweetly), *gioioso* (joyous), and *mesto* (sad) were increasingly used by composers as an indication of their intention to the performers. These terms, in addition, indicate the frame of mind of the composers of the period. Music of this period, both vocal and instrumental, was influenced by the lyricism of the human voice. It is notable that many of the themes of instrumental music of the period have been adapted into popular songs. Their popularity is, in part, affected by their singability.[56]

---

[56] Machlis, *op. cit.*, pp. 86–88.

The center of musical life in the nineteenth century was in the concert hall, rather than in the palace or the church. Because of the lack of restrictions in regard to size of performance organizations, composers during the latter part of the period increasingly wrote for larger groups and in a more colorful and grandiose style than was characteristic of the earlier part of the period.[57]

The Modern Period

Toward the end of the nineteenth century the subjective expression of Romanticism had run its course. Some composers, however, continued to write in a modified Romantic style. Among the more notable of this group of late Romanticists were: Sergei Taneyev (1856–1915), Edward Elgar (1857–1934), Gustav Mahler (1860–1911), Richard Strauss (1864–1949), Alexander Gretchaninov (1864–1956), Enrique Granados (1867–1916), Max Reger (1873–1916), and Sergei Rachmaninoff (1873–1943). Most composers, however, began to seek new means of expression. The main currents of musical expression in the Modern period are now described.

Impressionism

Impressionism developed as a reaction against the emotionalism and subjective aspects of Romanticism. It emerged during the last quarter of the nineteenth century and was exemplified in the music of Claude Debussy (1862–1918) and Maurice Ravel (1885–1937). Debussy was highly influenced by the Impressionist painters and the Symbolist poets, who avoided the exact and clear-cut representation of things, but rather sought to create a momentary impression of them. The painters often did not mix their paints, but juxtaposed daubs of pure color on the canvas, with the "mixing" left to the eye of the viewer.

[57] *Ibid.*, p. 88.

Also seeking new paths, the Symbolist poets rejected emotionalism and turned to nebulous suggestion and dreamlike evocation of mood.[58]

Expressionism

Appearing about 1910 as a reaction against the "vagueness" of Impressionism, Expressionism is sometimes referred to as the German answer to French Impressionism. Expressionism also received its impetus from painting and poetry. Artists, perhaps influenced by Sigmund Freud's work in psychology, endeavored to capture on canvas the myriad thoughts from the unconscious. Distorted images, expressing the artist's inner self, took the place of the traditional concepts of beauty. Composers also rejected older aesthetic concepts and sought new means of expression.[59] Expressionistic music is characterized by its continuous intensity, high level of dissonance, angular melodic fragments, complex rhythms, and fluctuating tempi. The expressionist composer utilized all the devices at his command to express the conflicts, fears, and anxieties of man's inner self. The outstanding exponents of Expressionism are Arnold Schoenberg (1874–1951), Alban Berg (1885–1935), Anton von Webern (1883–1945), and Ernst Krenek (1900–).

Neo-Classicism

In the phase of musical expression called Neo-Classicism, which appeared after World War I, composers sought to recapture the ideals of the eighteenth century, where the emphasis was upon craftsmanship rather than on emotional expression. They sought to restore the proper balance between form and emotion and rejected the excesses of the Romantic period. The return to form was a primary consideration in composition, with emotional expression being a secondary factor. The Neo-

[58] Joseph Machlis, *Introduction to Contemporary Music.* New York: W. W. Norton & Company, Inc., 1961, pp. 111–112.
[59] *Ibid.*, p. 335.

Classicists decried the idea of program music and gave more stress to the intellectual aspects of music. Composers who have written in this style include Igor Stravinsky (1882–1971), Paul Hindemith (1885–1963), Darius Milhaud (1892–1974), Francis Poulenc (1899–1963), William Schumann (1910–   ), Benjamin Britten (1913–1976), Irving Fine (1914–1962), Vincent Perischetti (1915–   ), and Lukas Foss (1922–   ).

Some musicologists have applied the labels of Neo-Classicism and Neo-Romanticism to specific composers, most of whom have written in various styles. It is impossible to categorize the works of all composers in this manner. Each student will need to analyze each work under consideration to determine the "tag" that most appropriately applies.

Neo-Romanticism

Twentieth-century composers have not all found the styles of Impressionism, Expressionism, or Neo-Classicism to their liking. Some, therefore, have utilized means of expression more closely aligned with the ideas of the Romanticists. This group has been referred to as the Neo-Romanticists. Music in the Neo-Romantic style is usually rich in sonorities, contains frequent climaxes, and is comparatively easy for the nonmusician to listen to. The Neo-Romantic composers utilize many of the tonal and rhythmic devices of the Neo-Classicist, but they convey it in a subjective manner—in such a way as to instill emotion and warmth in their music.

While, during the first part of the twentieth century, the majority of composers had rejected the ideals of the nineteenth century in favor of other modes of expression, the political and economic situation of the second quarter of the century led the way to a more emotional means of expression. World War II, in particular, created an atmosphere more receptive to romantic ideals and a need in some composers for a more personal means of expression, in which greater emphasis is placed upon the poetical and dramatic aspects of music.[60] Some rep-

---

[60] *Ibid.*, p. 314.

resentative composers of this style are Ernst Toch (1887–1964),
Carl Orff (1895–   ), Howard Hanson (1896–   ), William Walton (1902–   ), Paul Creston (1906–   ), Samuel
Barber (1910–   ), Gian Carlo Menotti (1911–   ), Norman Dello Joio (1913–   ), and William Bergsma (1921–
).

In addition to the styles of musical expression just discussed, separate consideration must be given to those composers
who utilize folk material in their music. This group has often
been referred to as the Nationalists. Among the more prominent are Ernest Bloch (1880–1959), Zoltán Kodály (1882–
1967), Ralph Vaughan Williams (1872–1958), Charles Ives
(1874–1954), Randall Thompson (1899–   ), Aaron Copland (1900–   ), Heitor Villa-Lobos (1887–1959), Carlos
Chávez (1899–1978), and Alan Hovhaness (1911–   ).

Whereas the nineteenth-century composer utilized folk
material more for color effects and altered it when it did not
fit his compositional scheme, the twentieth-century Nationalist
incorporated more of the flavor of the original folk idiom in his
music. Modal music and material with asymmetrical rhythms
are often used to create fresh, new effects.[61]

Meter and Stress

Impressionistic music possesses less tension and rhythmic drive
than does music in the Romantic period. Impressionist music,
particularly that of Debussy, gives the impression of being
"suspended in space." While Impressionistic music may give
the feeling of vagueness, it is, however, quite precise. The
conductor should avoid any exaggeration of tempo fluctuations,
and the beat should be clear and precise but flexible and responsive to all the subtle nuances in the music.

In contrast to Impressionism, Expressionistic music possesses considerable rhythmic incisiveness; that is, the rhythm
is even more clear-cut. The rhythm of the music is generally

[61] *Ibid.,* p. 257.

aligned with the durational values of the text; however, as a means of achieving tension, the Expressionists often distorted the normal accentuations of words. This alteration usually necessitated the use of changing meter to accommodate the resultant rhythm.

A particular characteristic of Neo-Classic music is its rhythm. As a means of avoiding the monotony of the regular stress following the barline, composers employ various devices. One procedure is to alter the meter with each measure.[62] The same effect, however, may be achieved by simply shifting the stresses or accents from point to point within the measure, but without changing the meter signature. In conducting rhythmic patterns with shifting accents, the conductor should limit the scope of his patterns and utilize a precise rebound to each beat. On accented notes—whether on a downbeat or an upbeat—the stress should be reflected in the tension of the arms and shoulders, whereas limited, yet precise, movements should occur on the unaccented notes.

Additive rhythm, in which each measure includes one more or one less pulsation than the preceding measure—for example, 4/4, 3/4, 2/4, or 2/4, 3/4, 4/4—is also frequently employed. Still another rhythmic device is the use of traditional rhythmic patterns in nonsymmetrical forms. For example, in 4/4 meter the eighth notes might be divided as 3 + 3 + 2, or 3 + 2 + 3, rather than 4 + 4. (Another way of stating these rhythmic groupings is 1 2 3 1 2 3 1 2, or 1 2 3 1 2 1 2 3.) In 6/8 meter, a two-measure pattern might be alternately written as 3 + 3 + 2 + 2 + 2. In conducting rhythms in nonsymmetrical forms, the conductor must alter his patterns to conform to the basic rhythm of the music.[63]

Although the Neo-Romantic composer will use many of the rhythmic devices of the Neo-Classicist, he will do so in moderation. He places a greater emphasis on the poetical aspects of music and a means of personal expression that is more

---

[62] See, for example, various works by Jean Berger: "It Is Good to Be Merry" (Kjos), "The Good of Contentment" (Presser), "Lift Up Your Heads" (Summy-Birchard), and "Seek Ye the Lord" (Augsburg).
[63] For a discussion of this technique see section titled "Syncopated Figures" in Chapter 2.

universally understood.   When modern-day rhythmic devices contribute to this end they are used, and when they do not they are avoided.

Tempo

With Impressionistic music most tempi tend toward the moderate and the slow, with exceptionally fast tempi usually being avoided.   A considerable degree of modern music following this period, however, exhibits a strong rhythmic drive.   As movement and speed are an integral part of our modern-day life, so too are these characteristics reflected in much of our modern-day music.   The rhythm of Expressionistic music is generally somewhat irregular and rather complex.   As a result of the normal accent of words being sometimes deliberately distorted, the tempo, therefore, often fluctuates with the use of pauses, *ritardandos,* and *accelerandos.*

Tempo, of course, is related to both rhythm and mood, and, in determining the proper tempo, the conductor should consider carefully both of these factors.   As clarity of line is essential to the performance of Neo-Classic music, a tempo that is too fast will impede the articulation, whereas a tempo that is too slow will sometimes lessen the intensity and rhythmic drive.   Mood is an important consideration in determining the tempi of Neo-Romantic music.   With emotional expression being relatively important, the projection of textual meanings often necessitates a greater flexibility in tempi.

Dynamics

In contrast to music of the Romantic period, Impressionistic music possesses a relatively low level of dynamic intensity. *Fortissimo* occurs rather infrequently, with the medium and the lower dynamic levels, *mezzo forte, piano,* and *pianissimo,* being used primarily.   *Crescendo* and *decrescendo,* when employed, should be used with considerable care and restraint. In performing music from this period, the conductor should take care to adapt the scope of his beat to the dynamic levels of the music. In conducting a *pianissimo* passage, for example, the movements should be very slight.

Following the Impressionistic period there has gradually developed an increasing use of dynamic extremes. Contrast is often achieved through a rapid change from an extremely low dynamic level to one of great intensity and volume. Modern-day composers are inclined toward using a multiplicity of dynamic effects in their music, including extreme contrast in dynamic levels, rapid *crescendos* and *decrescendos,* dynamic accents, and uniform levels of intensity.[64]

Texture

Composers of the Romantic period were highly interested in harmonic experimentation. This interest was intensified by composers of the Modern period. The Impressionists sought to escape the restrictions of the major–minor system of tonality. In the process, Debussy used a variety of devices, including the medieval modes, the whole-tone scale, and the pentatonic scale. Parallel fourths, fifths, and octaves were often used above a pedal point, which resulted in unusual effects from the clash between the sustained and the moving harmonies.

Although previous harmonic systems focused upon the relationship of chords and their progression from one to another, the Impressionists utilized individual chords for the sonorous and coloristic effects they created. Thus the tendency for chord resolution was certainly lessened. While triads were sometimes used, seventh, ninth, and eleventh chords were frequently employed either separately or in succession. Composers, furthermore, often utilized these chords on various scale degrees by shifting them up and down without alteration. This "gliding" use of chordal movement, utilizing blocklike chords in parallel motion, was an integral stylistic feature of Impressionism. Escaped chords—that is, those that are not resolved, but seem to "escape" to another key—were also an important char-

[64] Howerton, *op. cit.,* pp. 179–180.

acteristic of Impressionistic music. Impressionist composers often achieved a feeling of rest, or point of harmonic arrival, by simply using a less dissonant chord than those preceding it. Tonal color became equated with melody, harmony, and rhythm during this era.

Debussy often deliberately created a vagueness within his music, coupled with an indefiniteness of phrase structures. Ravel, on the other hand, utilized traditional forms and phrases to a much greater extent. The whole-tone scale was not utilized by Ravel, as it was by Debussy, as he desired a more definite triad outline, clearer phrase structures, and more functional harmony.

Expressionism is generally considered to have begun with Schoenberg, and, as twelve-tone music is associated with him, the two terms have become somewhat synonymous. It should be understood, however, that all Expressionist music is not twelve-tone music, as the Expressionistic movement began before this development. In Schoenberg's earlier works (his oratorio *Gurre-Lieder* [Universal], for example) he developed his use of chromaticism to its maximum potential. He then began to seek new means of expression.

Schoenberg's experimentation led to the development of the *twelve-tone method* or *serial technique* about 1923. With this method, all compositions are based upon an arbitrary arrangement or *set* of the twelve chromatic tones. Each tone row or set is handled in such a manner that no particular tone becomes any more important than the others. No tone is allowed to be repeated until every other tone has been used at least once. This is in marked contrast to the conventional major–minor tonal system. The row or set serves as a unifying factor in the music. After the basic set has been introduced, it may be repeated through a variety of means. It may be inverted— that is, turned upside down—it may be performed backwards (retrograde), or inverted and performed backwards (a retrograde of the inversion). The tone row is a type of variation technique in which great variety is achieved with only a minimum of material.[65] The guiding thought is that no idea

[65] Machlis, *Introduction to Contemporary Music, op. cit.*, pp. 340–342.

should be repeated except in a new form. The older style of repetition and sequence, and balanced phrases and cadences was rejected by the Expressionists.

In the nineteenth century, rhythm, harmony, and tone color were often considered as entities unto themselves, whereas Neo-Classicism considered each of these separate elements as subservient to the whole. The use of counterpoint by the Neo-Classic composers became increasingly important. To differentiate it, however, from the "harmonic" counterpoint of the Romantic era, this new polyphony is often referred to as "linear counterpoint." It is often marked by its transparency of texture and its dissonance and driving rhythm. While striking dissonance often occurs as a result of clashes between vocal lines, each line must maintain its forward drive or thrust.

In the music of the Neo-Romanticists, extreme harmonic complexity is usually avoided. Their music is generally characterized by its sensuous lyricism and its richness of harmony. It is often simply and directly stated, although some music possesses considerable rhythmic drive and intensity. Neo-Romantic music is primarily tonal in nature. Dissonance is used, but generally for comparatively brief periods to highlight the emotional and poetical aspects of the text. Although a considerable portion of Neo-Romantic music is harmonically conceived, some composers utilize contrapuntal devices as well. While their compositional techniques vary considerably, their one common characteristic is a more personal means of expression.

Expressive Aspects

The Impressionistic composer's aim was simply to suggest rather than boldly to state. Music of this period, therefore, should be approached in an objective manner and performed with considerable restraint. The excesses and extremes of the Romantic period should be avoided.

Expressionistic and Neo-Classical music should be approached with an even more objective point of view. Perhaps the most outstanding characteristic of Expressionistic music is its continuous dissonance (and lack of consonance that would allow for a lessening of the tension).   Dissonance, along with such other devices as angular melodic fragments, irregular rhythm, and abrupt changes in tempi, are used as a means of expressing the conflicts of man's inner self.   The composer's concern is the use of these varied devices to portray these inner feelings, rather than the expression of pure emotion in itself.

The Neo-Classicist is concerned largely with craftsmanship and with the statement of his material in an impersonal, objective manner.   Emotional expression is minimized.   Although it will vary from composer to composer, it is always carefully controlled.   The Neo-Classicist endeavors to recapture the classic spirit by striving for symmetry and balance in his music, by utilizing more transparent textures, and by limiting the size of his musical forces.

The Neo-Romanticist, however, seeks a more universalized type of expression.   His goal is different from the Neo-Classicist, as he desires his means of communication to be more personal in nature.   Although he uses many musical devices similar to those of the Neo-Classical composer, since his purpose is different he uses them in a different way.   The conductor should analyze his music and determine the *raison d'être* for each device if he is to employ it for its intended purpose.

In performing music of the Modern period, particular attention should be given to the tone quality and the manner of articulation.   With Impressionistic music, the singers need to use a *legato* style of diction so as not to disturb the smooth flow of the carefully voiced chords often moving in parallel motion. [66]

The melody of Expressionistic music often moves in wide angular leaps, thus creating some serious intonation problems for the performers.   Singers, obviously, need to listen carefully. And, as any rigidity in the jaw will inhibit proper articulation, they need to maintain a rather relaxed jaw to facilitate a cleaner articulation of the various interval leaps.

[66] For a discussion of *legato* diction, see section titled "Styles of Diction" in Chapter 2.

In Neo-Classic music it is usually desirable to lessen the dramatic qualities of the voice so that the clarity of the structure may be brought out. Voices with excessive vibrato or tremolo are particularly detrimental to the interpretation of this style of music. In performing music in a Neo-Romantic style, the voice quality should be warm and expressive so as to convey best the subjective aspects of the music.

Music with Electronic Tape and/or Nonconventional Notation

The continued search for new means of musical expression has brought forth, particularly during the decade of the 1970s, a variety of types of new choral music, including voices combined with electronic tape sounds, choric speech with singing, aleatoric (chance) music, and multimedia presentations. (We are presently in the midst of many new developments and therefore lack the perspective that we have of earlier music. It thus seems appropriate to include this material in a section separate from other twentieth-century music.)

Conventional notation for the vocal parts is usually employed in choral music with electronic tape. In some music, the time for specific cues is indicated in the score, and a stopwatch is necessary to coordinate the two separate sound sources. In other instances, a graphic illustration of the electronic sound is indicated in the score, thus assisting both the conductor and the singers to coordinate their efforts and making the use of a stopwatch unnecessary. Examples of both types are illustrated in Figures 53 and 54.

As composers continue to explore new means of music expression, they find that the conventional means of music notation do not allow them sufficient flexibility, nor do symbols always exist for the expression of their musical ideas. This has resulted in the creation of an entirely new means of notation. Specific notation now has been devised for spoken pitches, raising and lowering the pitch of the voice, shouts, screams,

FIGURE 55 *Excerpt from* Hymn of the Universe *by Richard Felciano. Score indicates the elapsed time in seconds for coordination of the tape with the choral parts. The vertical lines with the arrows indicate the conductor's cue to the singers. The small notes indicated on the tape line part provide the pitches for the entering voice parts. Copyright, 1974, by E. C. Schirmer Company, Boston. Used by permission.*

laughter, varying dynamic levels, tone clusters, staccato pronunciations, whispers, various lip sounds, tongue clicks, coughs, hissing sounds, giggles, hand claps, glissandos, vibrato, tempo, duration, *accelerando, ritardando,* and various other tonal effects.[67] Excerpts from a number of compositions representing this type of notation are illustrated in Figures 55–66.

FIGURE 56 *Excerpt from* Psalm 27 (Part III) *by Robert Karlen. Notation indicates, as closely as possible, the pitch of the spoken sounds. Copyright, 1968, A.M.S.I. Used by permission.*

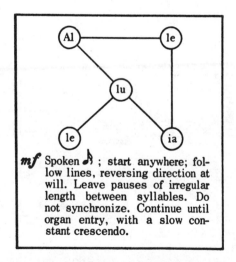

FIGURE 57 *Excerpt from* Pentecost Sunday *by Richard Felciano. Chart designed to elicit irregular, nonsynchronized speech sounds. Copyright, 1967, World Library Publications, Inc., 2145 Central Parkway, Cincinnati, Ohio 45214. All rights reserved. Used by permission.*

[67] For a helpful and useful compilation of all these symbols, along with explanations, see Frank Pooler and Brent Pierce, *New Choral Notation.* New York: Walton Music Corporation, 1971.

FIGURE 58   *Excerpt from* All the Ways of a Man *by Knut Nystedt. Rhythm and text given, but (A) pitch changes indicated by ascending and descending lines and (B) dynamic accents or "shouts" indicated by* /fz\ . *Copyright, 1971, Augsburg Publishing House. Used by permission.*

FIGURE 59   *Excerpt from* Suoni (Part II) (Op. 62) *by Knut Nystedt.* ▲ ▼ *indicates the pitch level, which should be as high (▲) or as low (▼) as possible. Copyright © 1972 by Associated Music Publishers, Inc. Used by permission.*

FIGURE 60 Excerpt from Pshelley's Psalm by Richard Felciano. Note combination of designated pitches with other sounds, including hisses, shouts, and hand claps. Copyright, 1974, E. C. Schirmer Company, Boston. Used by permission.

FIGURE 61 *Excerpt from* Aleatory Psalm *by Gordon H. Lamb.* *The box* �_ *represents a tone cluster within the confines of the symbol (in this instance—a minor seventh in each part). Singers should endeavor to avoid a pitch sung by another person. Copyright, 1973, World Library Publications, Inc., 2145 Central Parkway, Cincinnati, Ohio 45214. All rights reserved. Used by permission.*

FIGURE 62 *Excerpt from* "The Creation" *from* The Family of Man *by Michael Hennagin. (a) Approximate pitch level of vowel sound indicated by lines, and (b) special effects, such as tongue clicks. Copyright, 1971, Walton Music Corp. Used by permission.*

FIGURE 63   *Excerpt from* Praise to God *by Knut Nystedt.   In the rhythm indicated, each singer ascends differently and arrives at a distribution of pitches within the diagram.   Copyright © 1968 by Associated Music Publishers, Inc.   Used by permission.*

FIGURE 64 *Excerpt from* Two Moves and the Slow Scat *by Dennis Kam. Dotted lines divide measures into two parts, with the solid line indicating the cue for the downbeat and the dotted line the cue for the upward beat. The size of each notehead indicates the relative dynamic level (p, mf, f) and their location within the box for each part indicates the pitch range (high, middle, low). The thickening of a line indicates a crescendo. Copyright, 1973, Belwin-Mills Publishing Corp., 1973. Used by permission.*

(Sus. Pedal)

FIGURE 65 *Excerpt from "Winter" from* The Rising Sun *by Frank Pooler and Brent Pierce. Score indicates a) a tone cluster in soprano and alto parts produced by individual voices consecutively sustaining a notated pitch, b) tongue clicks by five voices, c) flutter tongue between lips by three voices, and d) random finger pick on piano strings. Copyright, 1973, Somerset Press, a division of Hope Publishing. Used by permission.*

FIGURE 66 *Excerpt from* Rondes *by Folke Rabe. Boxed staccato.
Dots inside each box indicate approximate pitch level and melodic
contour. Width of box indicates relative duration. Copyright ©
1967 by Edition Wilhelm Hansen, Stockholm, AB. Used by permission. The complete music also published by G. Schirmer, Inc.,
New York, for the U.S.A. and Canada.*

As part of the total musical diet, avant-garde music has value in that it adds a new dimension to sound as an expressive art, and it can "open singers' ears," so to speak, to new as well as older sounds. Young singers are generally receptive to music of this type, as it is not necessarily that far removed from their own popular musical culture. For the conductor who is especially attuned to music of other types and styles, a selective list of choral music with electronic tape and with non-conventional notation will be found in the Appendix. Most of this music will include explanatory information concerning the notational symbols and how to interpret them. Examination and study of these compositions by the conductor, and performance of certain selected works will balance out the musical diet of the choir or chorus.

Some Concluding Thoughts

Certainly one characteristic of twentieth-century music is the wide diversity of musical styles. It is often difficult to place composers neatly in the previously mentioned categories, as some change their styles during their composing years. Other composers might be said to possess an "eclectic" style; that is, they draw from the techniques and devices of various schools, depending upon the musical thought to be expressed. The conductor, therefore, if he is to interpret properly the works of any particular modern-day composer, should study and analyze the music, as well as the writings of the composer under consideration. What a composer says about his own music has obvious implications for the conductor seeking the proper interpretation. Whenever such writings do not exist, or are unavailable, the conductor may well turn to the vast number of books on twentieth-century composers (as well as those of other periods). What others have written about the lives and music of particular individuals will often provide the inquiring, analytical reader with fresh insights into the interpretation of music.

The study of style and interpretation is not a subject to be dealt with on a one-time basis—it should be studied throughout one's musical career. The intent of this chapter has been to provide a summary of the most salient points for consideration. To be most meaningful, however, they must be studied in connection with actual music. With this background information, the conductor should carefully study and analyze his scores. Only through reflective thought on the composer's intentions will the proper interpretation be achieved. The choral conductor should also listen critically to the interpretations of various choral organizations—on recordings and in the concert hall. The listener will most likely find that the interpretation of a particular composition will vary somewhat from one conductor to another. "What is stylistically correct and what is incorrect about these performances?" and "What do I like and dislike about the performances?" These questions must be always present on the listener's mind if he is to make the proper evaluation essential to further musical growth. The young conductor must give these questions careful consideration if he he is ultimately to achieve the correct interpretation for his own choral groups.

Finally, the effective conductor must also be a scholar. He should devote considerable time to further reading in various sources of the main points discussed in this chapter. He should also develop a broad historical understanding of the various periods of artistic achievement. For these purposes, a selected list of publications recommended for further study is included at the end of this chapter.

Topics for Discussion

1 What are some problems one might encounter when trying to perform Baroque music as it was originally intended?
2 Discuss the benefits and drawbacks of the old system of princely patronage of composers. What ideas have been advanced for the support of composers in our present-day society?

3 What specific techniques might a choral conductor use in teaching an appropriate style for any given period and/or composer? Discuss each historical period and cite particular composers and works.

4 How should the conductor's beat vary in conducting music of various periods?

5 In striving toward an authentic performance, to what extent should authenticity give way to the conductor's personal idiosyncrasies?

6 Discuss the effect of geographical influences upon the style and mode of expression of particular composers.

7 The Romantic era has been referred to as a "period of opposites." What is meant by this expression, and what are the implications for understanding the music of particular composers?

8 What is meant by the term "an eclectic style"? Give some examples.

Selected Readings

Aldrich, Putman C., "The 'Authentic' Performance of Baroque Music," *Essays on Music in Honor of Archibald T. Davison.* Cambridge, Mass.: Harvard University Press, 1957.

Apel, Willi, *Harvard Dictionary of Music.* Second Edition, revised and enlarged. Cambridge, Mass.: Harvard University Press, 1969.

————, *The Notation of Polyphonic Music,* 900–1600. Cambridge, Mass.: Mediaeval Academy of America, 1942.

Artz, Frederick, *From the Renaissance to Romanticism.* Chicago: University of Chicago Press, 1962.

Blume, Friedrich, *Renaissance and Baroque Music.* New York: W. W. Norton & Company, Inc., 1967.

————, *Classic and Romantic Music.* New York: W. W. Norton & Company, Inc., 1970.

Borroff, Edith, *The Music of the Baroque.* Dubuque, Iowa: Wm. C. Brown Company, 1970.

Bukofzer, Manfred F., *Music in the Baroque Era: From Monteverdi to Bach.* New York: W. W. Norton & Company, Inc., 1947.

————, "On the Performance of Renaissance Music," *Music Teach-ers National Association, Volume of Proceedings*, 1941. Pittsburgh: The Association, 1942, pp. 225–235.

Calvocoressi, M. D., *A Survey of Russian Music*. Baltimore: Penguin Books, Inc., 1944.

Dart, Thurston, *The Interpretation of Music*. Revised Edition. London: Hutchinson Publishing Group Ltd., 1960.

Decker, Harold H., and Julius Herford. *Choral Conducting: A Symposium*. Englewood Cliffs, N.J.: Prentice-Hall, Inc., 1973. (Chapters 3 and 4.)

Dolmetsch, Arnold, *The Interpretation of the Music of the XVIIth & XVIIIth Centuries*. London: Oxford University Press, 1946.

Donington, Robert, *The Interpretation of Music*. London: Faber & Faber Ltd., 1963.

Dorian, Frederick, *The History of Music in Performance*. New York: W. W. Norton & Company, Inc., 1942.

Einstein, Alfred, *The Italian Madrigal* (3 vols.). Princeton, N.J.: Princeton University Press, 1949.

————, *Music in the Romantic Era*. New York: W. W. Norton & Company, Inc., 1947.

Etherington, Charles L., *Protestant Worship Music: Its History and Practice*. New York: Holt, Rinehart and Winston, Inc., 1962.

Fellowes, Edmund H., *The English Madrigal Composers*. Second Edition. London: Oxford University Press, 1948.

Fleming, William, and Abraham Veinus, *Understanding Music: Style, Structure, and History*. New York: Holt, Rinehart and Winston, Inc., 1958, pp. 309–310.

Gore, Richard T., "The Performance of Baroque Church Music," *Music Teachers National Association, Volume of Proceedings*. 1950. Pittsburgh: The Association, 1953, pp. 155–163.

Grout, Donald Jay, *A History of Western Music*. New York: W. W. Norton & Company, Inc., 1960.

Grove's Dictionary of Music and Musicians. Fifth Edition (9 vols.). New York: St. Martin's Press, Inc., Macmillan & Co. Ltd., 1954.

Hansen, Peter S., *An Introduction to Twentieth Century Music*. Second Edition. Boston: Allyn and Bacon, Inc., 1967.

Harman, R. Alec, and Anthony Milner, *Late Renaissance and Baroque Music*. London: Barrie & Rockliff, 1959.

Heger, Theodore E., *Music of the Classic Period.* Dubuque, Iowa: Wm. C. Brown Publishers, 1969.

Howerton, George, *Technique and Style in Choral Singing.* New York: Carl Fischer, Inc., 1957.

Jeppesen, Knud, *The Style of Palestrina and the Dissonance.* Copenhagen: Ejnar Munksgaard, Publisher, 1946.

Jorgensen, Owen, *Tuning the Historical Temperaments by Ear.* Marquette: Northern Michigan University Press, 1977.

Kjelson, Lee, and James McCray, *The Conductor's Manual of Choral Music Literature.* Melville, N.Y.: Belwin-Mills Publishing Corp., 1973.

Lang, Paul Henry, *Music in Western Civilization.* New York: W. W. Norton & Company, Inc., 1941.

Leonard, Richard, *A History of Russian Music.* New York: Macmillan Publishing Co., Inc., 1957.

May, James D., *Avant-Garde Choral Music: An Annotated Selected Bibliography.* Metuchen, N.J.: The Scarecrow Press, Inc., 1977.

Machlis, Joseph, *The Enjoyment of Music.* Fourth Edition. New York: W. W. Norton & Company, Inc., 1977.

———, *Introduction to Contemporary Music.* Second Edition. New York: W. W. Norton & Company, Inc., 1979.

Morley, Thomas, *A Plain and Easy Introduction to Practical Music.* London, 1957. Modern edition by R. Alec Harman, London, 1952.

Palisca, Claude, *Baroque Music.* Englewood Cliffs, N.J.: Prentice-Hall, Inc., 1968.

Pattison, Bruce, *Music and Poetry of the English Renaissance.* London: Methuen & Company Ltd., 1948.

Pooler, Frank, and Brent Pierce, *New Choral Notation.* New York: Walton Music Corporation, 1971.

Quantz, Johann Joachim, *Versuch einer Anweisung die Flöte traversiere zu spielen.* Berlin, 1752. Translation and study by E. R. Reilly. Unpublished Ph.D. dissertation. University of Michigan, 1958.

Reese, Gustave, *Music in the Renaissance.* New York: W. W. Norton & Company, Inc., 1954.

Rosen, Charles, *Classic Style.* New York: The Viking Press, 1971.

Rothschild, Fritz, *The Lost Tradition in Music: Rhythm and Tempo in J. S. Bach's Time.* New York: Oxford University Press, Inc., 1953.

———, *Musical Performance in the Times of Mozart and Beethoven: The Lost Tradition in Music,* Part II. New York: Oxford University Press, Inc., 1961.

Sachs, Curt, *Rhythm and Tempo: A Study in Music History.* New York: W. W. Norton & Company, Inc., 1953.

Scott, Charles Kennedy, *Madrigal Singing.* London: Oxford University Press, 1931.

Sparks, Edgar, *Cantus Firmus in Mass and Motet, 1420–1520.* Berkeley, Calif.: University of California Press, 1963.

Stevenson, Robert, *Music Before the Classic Era.* London: Macmillan & Co. Ltd., 1955.

Strunk, Oliver, Ed., *Source Readings in Music History.* New York: W. W. Norton & Company, Inc., 1950.

Tartini, Giuseppe, "Treatise on Ornamentation" (translated and edited by Sol Babitz), *Journal of Research in Music Education,* Vol. 4, No. 2, Fall, 1956, pp. 75–102.

Ulrich, Homer, *A Survey of Choral Music.* New York: Harcourt Brace Jovanovich, Inc., 1973.

———, and Paul A. Pisk, *A History of Music and Musical Style.* New York: Harcourt Brace Jovanovich, Inc., 1963.

Vinquist, Mary, and Neal Zaslaw, *Performance Practice: A Bibliography.* New York: W. W. Norton & Company, Inc., 1971.

Young, Percy M., *The Choral Tradition.* New York: W. W. Norton & Company, Inc., 1962.

Rehearsal Techniques

The success of the choral concert is determined in the rehearsal room. Effective musical results are dependent upon a conductor's well-defined concept of his musical objectives, and his ability to transmit them to the members of the choral group. Although careful planning assists in the clarification of objectives, the conductor must possess various techniques for implementing his ideas. Through judicious employment of these devices, he will strive toward a consistently improved performance. Efforts in this direction will result in higher musical standards and increased satisfaction for both the performers and the audience.

Prerehearsal Planning

Choral directors are constantly asked to perform, and many, especially school music directors, feel that allocated rehearsal time is inadequate to develop their groups to the proper performance level. In view of this situation, rehearsals must necessarily be well planned if the director is to make the most effective use of his time. Careful prerehearsal planning is also likely to result in more meaningful learning experiences, which in turn provide the climate necessary for subsequent learning experiences. Following are some general suggestions concerning overall rehearsal planning.

A director should include in the choral rehearsal a variety of music from all historical periods. If choir members are to develop an understanding of, and appreciation for, various types of music, they should have some experience with choral music of the Renaissance, Baroque, Classic, Romantic, and Modern periods, as well as with folk music.[1] Furthermore, when variety is provided by alternating selections with contrasting styles, moods, and tempi, student interest is more readily maintained.

A conductor should never attempt to learn the music concurrently with his singers, but should study it carefully prior to each rehearsal. To familiarize himself with the music, he should read through the choral parts on the piano. Specific difficulties or pitfalls that the singers are likely to encounter, such as intricate rhythmic patterns, difficult intervals in the various parts, unusual harmonic progressions, and particular diction problems, all should be noted. It is helpful for the conductor to mark his score with a colored pencil, indicating the anticipated difficulties.

Consideration should be given, of course, to teaching procedures for clarifying and solving rhythmic and tonal problems, and specific conducting techniques should be analyzed and practiced. It is advisable to sing through any portions of the vocal parts that are likely to cause the singers difficulty, so that they may be demonstrated adequately to the choir. The conductor should also examine the text for words with an unusual pronunciation, and when in doubt, a dictionary should be consulted. Any textual subtleties reflected in the score should also be noted as a basis for achieving the proper interpretation.

In addition, the conductor will want to draw upon all his resources and musical background in achieving an effective musical interpretation. The practical application of knowledge gained in music theory and history classes will at this point be of inestimable value. The conductor should apply his knowl-

---

[1] For a chronological listing of choral composers, see Appendix.

edge of musical styles in various historical periods, and more specifically his understanding of the unique styles of individual composers.

In determining the procedures for accomplishing one's objectives, the director ought to prepare and write out a set of sample sentences on how to state what he desires to say or do. Such a procedure will enable the director to be more objective and precise about his procedures. Not too much should be said! Be succinct and consider the *impact* of what you plan to say or do! If you later find that your procedure is not really effective, then try another way. Your written plan will provide you with some basis for evaluating your actions.

There are three basic ways or procedures for achieving one's objectives: 1) through a verbal expression of what one desires, 2) by demonstrating through singing to illustrate tone quality, pronunciation, enunciation, phrasing, and so on, through clapping or chanting to correct rhythmic difficulties, and 3) through some psychological device or motivation such as "let the tone float—just as light as a feather." The director must decide which of these three procedures will be most effective in solving the problem at hand.

It is important that the director utilize reinforcement through words of approval or positive actions. Students, if they are to improve, need to know what they have achieved and what problems still remain to be solved. In short, they need careful guidance. Some teachers feel they shouldn't comment upon progress until the rendition of a specific choral selection is almost perfect. This approach is not advisable—conductors should endeavor to give *some* approval whenever possible. Teachers, however, should make an honest assessment. Actually, progress occurs in degrees, and directors may likewise respond with varying degrees of approval ranging from minimal approval to great satisfaction. The following succinct statements are provided as examples.

Minimal approval—"That's better! You have the idea!"
Moderate approval—"That's good! Much improved!"
Maximum approval—"I like it! That's great!"

The young conductor may sometimes have a concept in his mind as to how the music should sound and then conduct blithely away, seemingly oblivious to the reality of the situation. At times during a rehearsal he may wish to make corrections but is receiving so many *stimuli* that he is unable to find the words to express what he desires. By identifying potential problems—and this skill improves through experience—and writing out appropriate statements or ways of seeking solutions, the director is thus better able to respond to the situation. By writing out succinct statements the director will, it is hoped, avoid the opposite pitfall of saying too much—to the extent that the impact is lost and valuable rehearsal time is lost.

Prior to the rehearsal, the conductor should determine the order of the selections to be rehearsed and place them on the chalkboard. Singers, after they enter the rehearsal room, can then place their music in order, thus saving time and eliminating or at least minimizing any confusion prior to working on each selection.

Make certain that the accompanist is provided any new music in ample time prior to the rehearsal, with instructions as to tempo, dynamics, mood, and the like. The most carefully laid rehearsal plans can be of little avail, unless the accompanist is adequately prepared.

After each rehearsal, it is desirable to take a few moments to evaluate the group's progress and to notate, either on the music or in a notebook, those points in the score that need further attention, and any approaches that might be effectively used in subsequent rehearsals.

The First Rehearsal

The success of a choral group depends to a great extent upon the success of the initial rehearsal. In recruiting members, one of the best advertisements is a group of inspired singers. The word soon "gets around" that choral singing is an exciting adventure, and the question "Why don't you join too?" may be frequently asked.

Young singers entering the rehearsal room for the first time may possess mixed feelings about choral singing—they may eagerly anticipate an activity that they feel will be exciting and enjoyable, and yet be somewhat dubious of the outcome or the wisdom of their choice. It is the responsibility of the director to plan the rehearsal so that it will move smoothly toward its objective.

After the group has been seated, the conductor should endeavor to set the group at ease with a few words of welcome. Next, it will be necessary to explain the general rehearsal procedures, and tell the singers what they must do in order to retain their membership. Initial remarks, however, should be kept to a minimum, and the business of the actual rehearsal should be undertaken without unnecessary and needless delay. Also it should be kept in mind that overemphasis upon technique in the beginning can have a deadly effect upon a young choral group. These details are generally best introduced as the requirements of the music dictate—and only a few at a time.

In selecting the music for the first rehearsal, the conductor should consider the musical background of the group. Perhaps the singers have not been exposed to the standard choral literature and are generally unaware and unappreciative of its inherent beauties. In the beginning, it is helpful to concentrate upon a variety of folk-song arrangements of a rhythmical nature. In situations where the singers' backgrounds are extremely limited, it will be found desirable to intersperse a few easy rounds and canons with the rest of the repertoire. By providing the singers with music commensurate with their abilities and backgrounds, the conductor can minimize individual feelings of frustration and a more successful and enjoyable rehearsal will result. In the beginning, the singers should be provided with music they like, as long as it is within the limits of good musical taste. There will be ample time for raising musical standards and improving individual tastes.

The importance of having the first concert as soon as possible cannot be underestimated. Individuals constantly need a goal before them to guide their work if they are to make strides toward a consistently improved performance. This is especially important in the early stages of the development of a newly organized group. Soon the singers will anticipate the rehearsals for the sheer beauty of the music itself and the enjoyment and satisfaction that they receive. At this point the conductor should implement his plans, on a gradual basis, for broadening the singers' musical interests and raising their tastes and musical standards.

Introducing Music

In teaching new music, the best procedures are those which facilitate learning and achieve artistic singing in the shortest period of time. Some choral directors employ what is called the "note approach"—that is, after an attempt is made to read the music, each part is worked out separately with the aid of the piano, and finally all the parts are sung together. Such a procedure is extremely tedious, discipline is often difficult to maintain, and artistic singing is not readily achieved. One of the greatest objections to this procedure is that few of the emotional qualities of the music survive this mechanical approach. The following suggestions are given in an attempt to remedy this dilemma.

If the singers have a fair amount of reading power, they should endeavor to sing the entire number through from beginning to end (with or without the aid of the piano—depending upon the development of their musicianship). In this way, not only will the reading ability of the group improve, but also an overall concept of the music will be attained.

In presenting difficult compositions, the accompanist may play the music on the piano while each singer follows his part. If a good recording is available, it can be an invaluable aid in presenting new music. Although one would certainly not recommend that choral recordings be slavishly imitated by any group or conductor, they can serve as an extremely useful guide and rehearsal aid. After the choir members have been introduced to the music and have an overall conception of it, then various sections may be rehearsed in detail.

Many choral conductors have found through years of experience that once the rhythmic problems have been overcome, the notes and parts come faster. In studying sections of the music, a very helpful device is to have the singers recite together the text of the composition in correct musical rhythm. Such an approach helps to solve simultaneously problems of rhythm, diction, phrasing, and the proper dynamics.

This procedure does not preclude the necessity for occasionally devoting special attention to a particular voice part. At a specific point in the rehearsal, this may be the only means of achieving the desired musical results. Difficulties do sometimes arise, however, when directors devote too much to this procedure. Discipline problems may be lessened considerably if the director strives to maintain the group's interest at all times and if he stresses the importance of using all of the rehearsal time to the group's best advantage. In achieving this objective, the following procedures may be used alternately. First, while one part is being rehearsed, each of the other singers should be asked to study his part and listen to it in relation to the other parts. Second, all singers might be asked to sing a troublesome part in unison. This procedure also has value in developing an awareness of the relationships between parts. Third, request the choir members to *hum* their own parts softly while the troublesome part is being rehearsed.

Successful directors have found that effective rehearsals must be stimulating and must move quickly. When the director maintains a fast pace and the singers are kept busy, not only is much more accomplished, but confusion is reduced to a minimum.

Improving Music Reading

In most areas of learning, conceptual understandings are likely to be most meaningful when learning is through a discovery process, and not through simply being told the answer. Similarly, in music, sight-reading skills will improve most when a singer has to struggle a bit to interpret the score. Once he hears the music through a recording or on the piano, he no longer needs to rely on his musical memory in an attempt to recall the correct rhythm and pitches, for he already *has* the answer. To improve music-reading skills, singers need to be provided with challenges involving a wide variety of rhythmic and tonal experience.

If individuals are to improve, they must recognize and feel a need for improvement. Some persons are strongly motivated toward achieving success in all areas and have a strong desire for self-improvement. Such minds are highly receptive to improving music-reading skills. However, everyone does not possess this degree of motivation and the director can assist these other persons best by helping them to feel the satisfaction of achievement. He should be positive in all his remarks and plan all music-reading experiences so that they are as challenging and interesting as possible. Any devices used should generally grow out of a problem in actually reading music. At least, they should relate to a specific problem of music reading. Abstract drills, unrelated in any way to actual music, can become most dull and serve little purpose.

If the sight-reading abilities of a choir are to be developed, attention must be given to their development during each rehearsal period. Sight-reading can be improved only by practice, based upon musical understanding. Perhaps just past the midway point of each rehearsal, it desirable to include at least one selection for sight-reading purposes. Procedures followed at music competition-festivals are suggested. The music should be carefully examined by the choir members while the director points out and discusses various pitfalls inherent in it. Upon first examination, singers should accustom themselves to looking first at the meter and key signatures and at the beginning chord, and then scanning their respective parts for intricate rhythmic patterns or figures, unfamiliar intervals (particularly wide ones), any chromatic alterations, and expression markings. Next, pitches should be given and the group should attempt to sing the music completely through from beginning to end without a break. General suggestions which the group should keep in mind are (*a*) keep the eyes moving ahead to grasp patterns or groups of notes; (b) respond to the pulse of the music in some way—perhaps by wiggling the toes inside the shoes;[2] (c) keep going and do not stop or fret about mistakes; (d) look for familiar patterns in the music both before and during the reading process. Following the initial reading, difficult aspects of the music should again be discussed and, if time allows, the selection should be repeated in an effort to eliminate previous errors.

In many instances, problems of rhythm and pitch arising from reading sessions will be dealt with simultaneously. In other cases, the learning process may be facilitated when each is dealt with separately. Suggestions for achieving rhythmic responsiveness and tonal awareness follow.

Rhythmic Responsiveness

A singer's perception of rhythmic patterns and and the accuracy of his response constitute an important part of music-reading skills. The following approaches are suggested as a means of increasing a choir's responsiveness to rhythm.

1 Reciting the text of the music in correct musical rhythm, as discussed in the preceding section, is an excellent means of facilitating the learning of difficult rhythm patterns. To develop individual rhythmic responsiveness, however, the singers should be asked to peruse the rhythmic patterns silently by themselves before the group endeavors to chant them together.
2 Clapping the troublesome rhythm patterns is a good way to elicit a bodily response to rhythm. Opportunity should be provided for everyone to respond in various ways—individually, in quartets, or in sections, rather than just in the entire group.
3 The director may accumulate a number of rhythmic problems confronted by the singers. To encourage more careful listening coupled with bodily response, he should chant a one- (or two-) measure pattern, with the group responding immediately afterwards. The response is more effective if the group taps the heel or toe prior to the chanting, and maintains this steady response to the pulse throughout the activity. Rhythmic patterns may

---

[2] For other means of encouraging a response to the pulse of the music, see later in chapter under section titled "Attacks and Releases."

vary from the simple to the complex and encompass all musical styles. (For an illustration of this idea, see the discussion on rhythmic precision as it relates to attacks and releases, and Figure 68, later in the chapter.

4   Isolate particular rhythm problems in the music and write them on the chalkboard. Analyze them and then respond in some way by chanting or clapping, or by some counting system.

5   Some students have difficulty reading music in meters other than 3/4 and 4/4 because, as a result of their limited experience, they usually expect each beat to be a quarter note. To correct this misconception, and to broaden their experience, it is helpful to write on the chalkboard a familar tune in a meter other than the original. A tune originally in 4/4 meter might be written, for example, in 4/8, 4/2, or 12/8 meter. The familiar tune serves as a common element and through singing and comparing different ways of notating a tune, students gain insight into the relatedness of rhythms.

6   Write a phrase of a familiar song on the chalkboard and, after the group has sung it through once, alter the rhythm in some way. Use simple rhythmic alterations, but soon include the more difficult until a considerable number of rhythm patterns have been experienced. The familiar song provides a base from which to begin, so that attention may be focused on the rhythm and not the tonal problems.

Tonal Awareness

The ability to perceive differences and relationships in pitch and to reproduce them accurately is essential to achieving any degree of skill in music reading. The following procedures are suggested as a means of developing greater tonal awareness.

1   A keen awareness of the tonal relationships between various intervals is essential to the achievement of good intonation, as well as to skill in sight-reading. One suggested device is the singing in unison of various intervals without aid from the piano. The director may request the group to sing "up a major third" and back to the initial pitch, then "up a perfect fifth" and back, then "down a perfect fourth" and back, and so on, until various intervals have been sung. Extended over a period of time, this device may encompass a wide gamut of interval experience, which will contribute substantially to the singers' musicianship. The introduction of this procedure presupposes, of course, some

preliminary instruction in the theoretical aspects of intervals, and some initial practice in singing them with the aid of the piano and observing them on the chalkboard as they are sung. The practicality of this device, in terms of improving sight-reading skills, lies in the singers' ability to establish the connection between this aural experience and the visual recognition of the intervals. Therefore, to establish the connection more firmly, the director should, during the rehearsal of certain selections, ask the singers to identify specific intervals, recall their relationships and then sing them with a reasonable degree of accuracy.[3]

Another device closely related to the above is to train the group to sing the pitch A = 440 without aid from the piano. In the initial stages, periodical checking of the pitch with the piano will be necessary and will illustrate to the group their relative degree of success. After a while the singers will develop this skill and a degree of confidence will result from the accomplishment. Once the pitch has become firmly established in the singers' minds, a basic starting point is also provided for the singing of various intervals.

2 When intonation difficulties occur within the group, the pitch variation is usually less than a half tone, since otherwise the group would be singing a wrong note, and most individuals would recognize such a discrepancy. A helpful device is therefore to train the choir to sing *quarter tones*. First, select a note in the middle range and have the group sing downward a whole tone and back, then down two half steps and back, then down two *quarter tones* and back. Immediately check the pitch with the piano. In the beginning, the choir will find this procedure difficult, but after repeated daily attempts they will soon be able to sing quarter tones with comparative ease. One might ask: "Just what is the value of such an exercise?" After singers have developed an acute consciousness of pitch, the director often will be able to signal various sections of the choir to make the slight adjustments sometimes necessary for maintaining accurate pitch.

3 Singing the resolutions of dominant seventh chords develops a feeling for tonality and for modulation to new keys and, as a result, has a direct relationship to music-reading skills. A seventh chord creates tension and each pitch possesses a "pull"

---

[3] Some teachers prefer to cement these tonal relationships by relating the intervals to those found in familar songs. For a listing of intervals and suggested songs, see Robert L. Garretson, *Music in Childhood Education*, Second Edition. Englewood Cliffs, N.J.: Prentice-Hall, Inc., 1976, pp. 83–84.

toward another. Initially, it is desirable for the choir to experience all the resolutions in the different inversions of the chord. Then, they may sing the key circle progression given in Figure 67. The use of notation, however, is not necessary. Each section is asked, upon signal, to move to the closest possible note that will create a feeling of rest. The soprano, alto, and tenor parts will move upward or downward either a half or whole step, or they will remain on the same tone. The bass part moves downward a fifth and upward a fourth, except in third inversion chords (V₂) when the seventh is in the bass part. Begin on a major triad, then direct one of the upper voice parts doubling the root of the chord to move downward a whole step, thus creating the dominant seventh chord. Give the choir lots of time to feel the "pull" of their notes before resolving each seventh chord.

4 An excellent device for developing tonal awareness is for the director to teach the choir members to recognize the chord progressions that they sing. A good starting place is to identify the cadences. Too many individuals sing the simple V-I cadence without knowing what it is. A few minutes of each rehearsal can be well spent in explaining to the group the function and purpose of the cadence, and the part each note plays in the chord. The director may want to take the chord progression

FIGURE 67 *Resolving the dominant seventh.*

out of context and drill each chord until it is perfectly in tune —each time making sure that the singers are able to identify the progression.

As the group improves in their identification of chord sounds, the director will be able to extend the process to more complicated chord progressions and eventually even to modulation. Such a practice, if carried on over a long period of time, will most certainly show results not only in improved reading ability, but also in better intonation and all-around musicianship.

5 Encourage the choir to maintain the pitches in their minds when they are stopped for corrections and/or suggestions. Do not always provide the pitch on the piano, but ask them to remember it and sing upon direction. At first they may flounder and begin to sing in a variety of keys. Soon, however, they will retain and recall the correct pitches. The general alertness necessary to remember the pitches will often have a beneficial effect on the rehearsal.

6 As a further means of developing tonal awareness, and as a check to determine how well the singers know their notes and if they are hearing them in tune, the device of "silent singing" is suggested.

First, give the pitch of a selection the group knows reasonably well. Then ask the choir to sing the music "silently" together at the tempo indicated by the conductor. At the appropriate time, the conductor should prepare the group to sing aloud with the verbal command, "Sing!" spoken on the previous beat. Initially, the group may sing silently for only four to eight measures, but as they become more proficient, the activity may be extended in length. The choir may also be directed to sing aloud at the beginning of a new phrase or, again, as they develop proficiency, at any point within the phrase. Silent singing will be found to be an excellent means to stimulate concentration and alertness and to "rejuvenate" a sluggish choir.

Attacks and Releases

Precision of attacks and releases is essential to artistic choral singing and is dependent upon several factors—namely, the general attentiveness of the group, the rhythmic response of the group, and the basic technique of the conductor.

A choral group with high morale, in which each individual possesses a feeling of "belonging" and exhibits a singleness of effort toward the group's objectives, is relatively easy to motivate toward a consistently improved performance. The attentiveness of the choral group depends to a very great extent upon this group morale and upon a high degree of motivation. Difficulties usually arise not in the early stages of rehearsing a selection, but in the latter stages, just prior to the perfection of the number. The conductor should therefore be constantly in search of means to stimulate interest and capture the singers' imagination. Individuals who are highly motivated and desirous of improving their group's musical standards will not succumb to the pitfalls of slovenly bodily attitudes and the resultant lack of precision.

Rhythmic security in the music not only aids in the precision and the vitality of the performance, but also reduces to some extent excessive muscular tension and improves the tone quality of the group. Rhythmic security can be increased by encouraging a stronger rhythmic response to the music.

Here is an approach to rhythmic responsiveness which usually creates enthusiasm on the part of the singers. After setting the tempo, instruct the choir members to tap their feet (not too loudly) in response to this basic pulsation. Continue for several measures until the group is responding together precisely. While the group continues the tapping, the director sings a rhythmic or melodic pattern one or two measures long. In the following measure or measures, the group responds and imitates the pattern previously sung by the director (Figure 68). When figures extend to the last beat of a measure, it is best for the group to wait out a full measure and enter on the subsequent measure, often on the cue of the director. Patterns should be varied and may be sung on a single pitch or a melodic or "scat" pattern (see the section on scat singing in Chapter 5).

School age youth especially enjoy responding to different rhythmic patterns. Try it—the possibilities are unlimited! In

FIGURE 68 *Patterns for developing singers' rhythmic responsiveness.*

addition to evoking rhythmic response, this procedure is also beneficial as an ear-training device.[4]

Singers should develop a strong feeling for the pulsation of the music they are singing, especially if it is in a *staccato* or *marcato* style. They are more likely to feel the pulsation if they make some large bodily movements while singing. Having the group either beat out the basic pulsation of the music on the knee or conduct the traditional conducting patterns can be exceedingly helpful.

The conductor should thoroughly prepare for all attacks and releases if they are to be clear to the performers. Many choral directors take too much for granted in this respect. Most singers soon learn to adjust to the indecisive movements of the conductor, yet as a group they are never quite sure of his intentions. The choral conductor's movements should be clear, precise, rhythmical, and should reflect the mood of the music. Daily practice in front of a mirror can be very helpful. *See if you can follow yourself!*

[4] This device is intended to be used in conjunction with music of a rhythmic syncopated nature, such as the vigorous spiritual "Rock-a My Soul." It would provide an excellent means of evoking the necessary excitement and rhythmic awareness required for effective singing of this selection. Conversely, using the procedure immediately prior to a Bach chorale would by comparison make the chorale seem rather dull and would serve no purpose.

Balance and Blend

In achieving correct balance, one must consider the voice quality of the individual singers, the range in which the voices are singing, the number of persons singing the various parts, and the harmonic aspects of the chords and the relative importance of the various vocal lines.

Voices of unusual and distinct tone quality oftentimes protrude from their sections, thus destroying the choral balance and blend. These voices must be subdued and blended with the group if artistic choral singing is to be achieved. The director must be continually on the alert for such occurrences and should strive to develop the singers' awareness of the problem. Often the difficulty results from poor voice production and improper breath control. In such instances, especially in the case of a wide tremolo, individual assistance is often necessary to correct the problem.

The problem of the tremolo, or excessively wide vibrato, usually occurs when a person endeavors to sing with an overly large, dramatic quality and does so without the proper breath support. To eliminate this condition, the director should emphasize adequate breath support, a somewhat lighter tone quality, and practicing with a fairly straight tone. Through constant attention, the situation can be remedied.

When individuals are singing in the extreme high range of the voice, distortion is likely to occur. Voices with greater power and brilliance (resonance) in the upper registers must be subdued to the level of the entire group. If the proper balance and blend is to be maintained throughout the vocal range, choral groups should avoid using all their bodily energy in an effort to sing "as loud as possible." Distortion cannot help but result. The best advice is always to save some energy in reserve by singing only up to approximately 75 percent of the maximum vocal effort, and by concentrating on resonance and improved tone quality. Maximum dynamic levels will, of course, vary from group to group, and the most effective dynamic ranges must necessarily be determined by the director for each specific group.

In music with divided parts, it may be necessary to redistribute some of the voices and assign them to the weaker parts in order to achieve the proper balance. It is suggested that a few selected voices in the chorus be designated as "roving" singers. This would mean, for example, that a few of the second sopranos need not be given a definite voice assignment, but may sing either the soprano or alto part as the musical situation demands.

Moving parts, especially when they occur in the lower voices, should be emphasized and brought out. When some of the parts are sustained, these moving parts often indicate a change of harmony and are of special interest to the listener. A much more musical effect often can be created by emphasizing the rhythmical movement of the vocal line, rather than by just singing the part a little louder. The problem of bringing out the melody usually occurs when it is in the lower parts. In such instances it might be well to mark the melody on all the music. Close attention to dynamics is most essential in securing balance between the melodic line and the supporting harmonic parts.

Other factors influencing choral blend, aside from those previously mentioned, pertain specifically to uniform vowel production and tonal and harmonic awareness. In singing, the tone is sustained upon the various vowel sounds. Each vowel produced must be clear and distinct and uniform in production throughout the choir if any degree of blend is to be achieved. The choral director should stress the importance of *singing on the vowel*. As a basis for achieving good blend, it is suggested that the following two concepts be presented to the group and continually emphasized.

1 Following the initial consonant, move to the vowel sound as quickly as possible—and *sing on the vowel*.
2 Listen carefully and endeavor to blend your vowel sounds with the group.

Many directors have found it profitable to utilize all of the primary vowel sounds in an exercise in which careful attention can be given to uniform production within the group. (See Exercise 16, for blending the vowels.)

EXERCISE 16

Mah may mee moh   moo,   mah may mee moh   moo,

1 Vocalize within the middle range of the voice only.
2 Move smoothly from one vowel to another.
3 Listen carefully—strive for uniform production within the group.

Some singers appear to be completely unaware of the other voices in the group. Good blend, balance, and intonation will not be achieved unless all the singers are trained to listen to the entire ensemble as well as to themselves.[5] Singers should be advised never to sing so loudly that they can't hear the individuals and the parts next to them. Humming the music sometimes will allow the singers to hear the other parts better. This device can be used to improve the blend of all the parts, especially in *legato* singing. On easy and familiar choral selections, it has been found profitable for the singers occasionally to switch parts. This helps to develop an awareness of the other parts and subsequently may improve the blend of the group.

A procedure that has been found to give the most immediate (and sometimes startling) results is to place the the entire choral group in quartets (SATB), or in the arrangement known as the *scrambled setup*.[6] Achieving results from these arrangements presupposes that the students know their parts. These seating arrangements separate the students who lean upon each other and lessen the stridency in voices of students accustomed to sitting together. They generally result in a tone quality and blend extremely satisfying to the group. In addition, they reveal the extent to which students have learned their parts.

A tape recorder can be put to very effective use in the choral rehearsal. Recordings of the group serve to reemphasize the suggestions made by the director. They are also valu-

---

[5] For a further discussion of the importance of singing without accompaniment, see "Rehearsing A Cappela" later in the chapter.
see "Avoiding Fatigue and Vocal Strain" later in the chapter.
[6] For diagrams of both these seating arrangements, see Plans 6 and 7 in Chapter 7.

able as a means of evaluating progress and determining future lines of endeavor.

Pitch and Intonation

Faulty pitch and intonation in choral groups are one of the most troublesome problems confronting choral directors today. Some have learned to live with the problem, so to speak, and have accepted it as being common to untrained voices. The majority, however, continue to strive for perfection, and many have achieved a reasonable consistency of performance in their groups.

Accurate pitch and intonation are basically dependent on (a) correctly produced tones, properly supported by the breath, and (b) the degree of tonal awareness that each individual singer possesses. In addition to these two basic factors, both previously discussed, there are other varied causes of poor intonation, which the director should be cognizant of if he is to deal effectively with the problem.

The Slurring Attack

Attacking the notes from below and sliding or slurring to the proper pitch is a particularly obnoxious fault common to singers. The problem can be somewhat alleviated if the choir members are instructed to think of approaching the notes from above, rather than from below the pitch. Another helpful device is to think of singing the consonants on the same pitch as the vowels.

Repeated Tones and Scale Passages

Intonation difficulties frequently occur on repeated tones. Since there is sometimes a tendency to sing each repeated tone a bit lower, it is helpful if the singers are instructed to think of each repeated tone as being a bit higher.

Intonation difficulties also often occur on ascending and descending scale passages. Many individuals are likely to sing the ascending scale steps too small and the descending scale steps too large. Both practices, of course, result in flatting. It is therefore suggested that choir members be asked to think purposely of singing the ascending scale steps larger and of singing the descending scale steps smaller.

Diction

Lack of attention to careful enunciation of the words can create intonation difficulties. The best advice that can be given the singers in such instances is: "Vitalize your words," or "Be more precise in your tongue, lip, and jaw movements and work for clarity of diction."

Breath Control

The problem of breath control usually occurs on long, extended phrases. Singers should be advised to refrain from using all their available breath supply, since this would result in an irregular flow of the breath and resultant gradations in volume and slight variations in the pitch. The group should be instructed in the "staggered" method of breathing. On long, extended phrases, each individual should drop out when in need of breath, take a full breath, and unobtrusively reenter. For best results, certain sections or groups probably should be told when to breathe in order that the best possible effect may be achieved.

Classification of Voices

Adolescent voices are unsettled and generally in a state of change. For this reason, and for the protection of the voices against unnecessary strain, it is advisable to retest each singer's voice frequently. Baritones singing tenor parts and altos singing soprano parts can lead to many difficulties.

Bodily Attitudes and Fatigue

Incorrect bodily attitudes, which generally reflect a lack of genuine interest, can have a decided effect upon performance. It behooves the director to be ever alert to this problem and to convince the choir members as best he can that they should maintain correct posture while singing. Correct posture and alert bodily attitudes are essential to properly supported tones, and when singers fully realize this fact they are usually more eager to cooperate. One idea found profitable in action is to insist that the group maintain correct posture only when singing; between numbers they should relax in a position most comfortable to themselves. Good posture can become a habit. Strive for it!

The best time of day for the choral rehearsal is believed to be the middle or late morning hours. Individuals generally do not sing as well immediately following lunch or late in the afternoon when bodily fatigue begins to occur. It is recognized that some school schedules prohibit the utilization of the most desirable hours for rehearsal, and that many directors have little voice in determining the scheduling of classes. It is felt, however, that the director should at least discuss the problem with his school administrator. Administrators are eager to provide the best possible education for their students and, if presented with a reasonable argument for making changes in the schedule, are usually most anxious to cooperate if they can.

When rehearsals become dull and uninteresting, bodily fatigue is bound to occur regardless of the time of day or the length of the rehearsal. Directors should, therefore, carefully plan and endeavor to make all rehearsals exciting events for the choir members.

Tempo

The tempo of the music can have a decided effect upon intonation. The tempo selected for a previous choral group—or the tempo originally chosen by the conductor—may not always be the best one. The conductor should become most sensitive to the problem and should endeavor to determine through experimentation the tempo that is most suitable for his present group and, of course, for the most effective rendition of the music.

Seating Arrangements

In choral groups where a strict tryout is not mandatory for membership there will usually exist a few voices that might be classified as "chronic flatters." If these individuals are allowed to sit together, their tone qualities are seemingly reinforced and can cause havoc within the group as regards intonation. The problem, however, can be somewhat alleviated by judiciously placing each of those offenders between two or more stronger singers. In this way they are more likely to produce the tone qualities desired.

Acoustics

Many factors, including the size and shape of the room and the finishing materials utilized, affect the acoustics of the rehearsal room or the auditorium stage. Again, the tempo in which the music is performed should be determined to some extent by the acoustical properties of the performance room. As a general rule, it will be found that in rooms with little reverberation one should avoid singing the music too slowly if accurate pitch is to be maintained, whereas in rooms that are "exceedingly alive," one should avoid singing the music at too fast a tempo, lest the sounds emitted meet each other coming and going and produce a discordant and distasteful result.

Atmospheric Conditions

Atmospheric conditions also have their effect upon intonation. On dark, dismal days most individuals do not respond physically in the same way that they do on bright, clear days. At such times, spirits are sometimes low and the group does not always display an abundance of vitality. It has been said that a person's vitality is to some extent dependent upon the relative degree of humidity present in the atmosphere. During highly humid days, bodily fatigue occurs sooner, the tone is generally not supported correctly, and many intonation problems result. What can be done to alleviate the situation? The director can only point out to the group the pitfalls that may occur, and through increased group effort hope to avoid some of the difficulties. If this procedure does not produce the desired results, then all concerned would be wise to charge the difficulty to "just one of those days."

Ventilation

Poor ventilation in the rehearsal room creates a stuffy, stale atmosphere that can have a decidedly detrimental effect upon intonation. The director should recheck this condition periodically during the rehearsal. It is often advisable to assign the task to one or more interested and helpful persons.

Growing Stale

Most directors have experienced the problem of having choral selections grow stale. There is only one solution to this problem. Set the number aside and return to it at a later date. The problem can be avoided somewhat if the season's repertoire is planned early in the year. This provides ample time for singers to learn a new selection which can then be set aside until rehearsals are renewed just prior to its presentation. This procedure can have a definite beneficial effect upon raising standards of musical performance.

Other Rehearsal Considerations

The effectiveness of a given rehearsal begins from the moment the choir members enter the rehearsal room. The conductor should encourage the singers to secure their music folders and immediately take their seats so that the rehearsal may begin promptly with a minimum of confusion. This process is facilitated if each singer's music is kept in an assigned folder and stored in music cabinets near the entrance door. Following are suggestions that will contribute to more effective and satisfying rehearsals.

Rehearsal Pace

Rehearsals should move quite rapidly—when they lag, disciplinary problems may arise. Confusion between selections can be lessened if the rehearsal order is carefully planned and written on the chalkboard prior to the rehearsal. Choir members should not be given the opportunity to waste time. In most cases, they will appreciate the director's efforts to make efficient use of rehearsal time.

Warm-up Exercises and Ear-Training Devices

Many conductors prefer to begin their rehearsals with a warm-up exercise or an ear-training device. To avoid monotony, it is desirable to alternate these exercises and devices, and above all to keep them *short*. Get to the music as soon as possible.

Establishing and Maintaining Rapport

It is advisable to begin rehearsals with *familiar* music of a reasonably vigorous nature that is straightforward, uncomplicated, and not too demanding vocally. Selections that are demanding vocally and/or include various subtle nuances and shadings may be better dealt with later in the rehearsal when the singers are more adequately warmed up.

The conductor should study the technical aspects of the music before each rehearsal, and know what he wants to accomplish. He should use the music as a reminder, glancing at it only when necessary. Thus he is free to concentrate upon maintaining "eye" contact with the group. Whenever possible, the conductor should inject a bit of humor into the rehearsals. A good laugh can lessen group tension and contribute substantially to the rehearsal's outcome. Through bodily attitudes, the conductor should project his enthusiasm for the music to the group and endeavor to spur the singers toward greater musical accomplishments.

Maintaining Correct Posture

If tones are to be adequately supported, correct posture must be maintained while singing. Unless the singers are continually encouraged, they are likely to fall into poor posture habits. Since the length of many choral selections will average about three minutes, choir members should be expected to maintain 100 percent effort for this minimum length of time. Between selections they should be instructed to stretch and relax. This same philosophy applies to those individuals who feel they must communicate with each other during the singing of a specific selection. The following rule should apply: *No talking during actual rehearsal! Time between selections will be allotted for questions and communication regarding musical problems of concern to the group.*

Avoiding Fatigue and Vocal Strain

There is a limit to what can be accomplished with a given selection during a single rehearsal. When the singers show signs of fatigue and boredom, set the music aside and return to it at the following rehearsal.

It also is highly desirable for the director to provide a short break at the midway point in the rehearsal period. This time may be effectively utilized for special announcements, such as forthcoming concerts and musical events.

Rehearsing A Cappella

Too often singers become overly dependent upon the piano as a means of tonal and rhythmic support. As a result, they listen primarily to this instrument and not to the other vocal parts. Therefore, it is absolutely essential to rehearse some of the choral selections without accompaniment. Only in this way will the maximum degree of vocal independence, rhythmic security, and effective blend and balance be achieved.

Making Corrections

Errors in rhythm, pitch, and phrasing, should be corrected immediately, before they become habitual. The conductor, however, should not be overcritical in his remarks or belittle the singers, as this may have a discouraging and detrimental effect upon the group. The director should be positive in his remarks —commenting about progress already made, as well as about the portions of the music that still require improvement.

When the conductor resorts to excessive talking, however, the singers' enthusiasm is lessened and valuable rehearsal time is lost. Therefore, he should be succinct in his comments and proceed with the rehearsal as quickly as possible.

The conductor should concentrate on rehearsing the troublesome parts of a choral selection. Much time can be wasted by simply repeating the sections that the singers already know. It is also advisable to rehearse periodically the treble and male sections of the choir separately. This practice is essential if minor discrepancies in rhythm and pitch are to be corrected and if sectional tone quality and blend are to be improved.

Prior to the repetition of selections, the conductor should avoid merely saying "Let's sing it again." If singers are to improve, they must know what they are striving for. Therefore, he should tell clearly what he wants in every repetition.

Consideration should be given to possible starting points after the choir is stopped for corrections. A general procedure is to identify the point by referring to first the *page*, then the *score*, the *measure*, and finally the *beat* within the measure.

After the choir is reasonably familiar with the music, a particular word or phrase may be identified as the starting point. After the singers have gained even further knowledge of the musical score, starting points may be identified as, for example: (a) after the double bar, (b) at the key change, (c) at the tenor entrance (thus forcing the other singers to identify this portion of the music to orient themselves).

Although demonstrating desired musical improvements and occasionally singing certain entrances is justifiable, the director should avoid continually singing with the group. Instead, he should devote his attention to critical listening and assisting the group to a more effective interpretation of the music through his conducting technique.

Stimulating Concentration

It is important that singers give their undivided attention to the conductor and that they concentrate upon achieving artistic singing. Following are suggestions that will contribute toward this objective.

Rehearsing from a Standing Position. Singers become weary and fatigued when rehearsing all the music from a sitting position. In addition, the maximum group effort cannot always be achieved unless the singers stand, assume the correct singing posture, and concentrate upon artistic singing. Therefore, alternate selections should be sung from a standing position.

As a further means of developing more careful attention, it is advisable for the conductor to time each selection with a stopwatch. While the resulting information is essential in planning the length of the final concert program, it has the added advantage of stimulating an extra group effort, particularly if the singers understand the purpose of the timing and the importance of being alert and responsive to the director's conducting movements.

"Erratic" Conducting. When singers seemingly have their eyes glued to the music, and are unresponsive to the subtleties of

the conductor's movements, then it is helpful for him to purposely alter the tempo—faster and slower and employing the
fermata at will.   Singers enjoy this activity, and the challenge
of "following" the conductor is an excellent means of developing attentiveness and responsiveness in a choir.

"Silent Singing."   Mentally thinking together the pitch,
rhythm, and tempo of a selection under a conductor's direction,
before being asked to sing aloud at a designed point, is an excellent means of stimulating concentration and alertness.   (For
a more detailed discussion of this procedure, see end of section,
"Tonal Awareness," earlier in this chapter.

Encouraging Individual Responsibility

The conductor should encourage the choir members to analyze
their difficulties and to request assistance with particularly troublesome parts or sections of the music.   Although the conductor
necessarily must use discretion and be the final judge as to which
problems should be undertaken first, he should encourage individual responsibility in regard to the various problems encountered in the music.   Encouraging individual effort produces
greater group solidarity, improved musicianship, and eventually
a more effective interpretation of the music.

Ending the Rehearsal

The conductor should schedule a selection relatively familiar
to the group during the final portion of the rehearsal—one that
the singers particularly enjoy, so they will leave the rehearsal
room with a feeling of genuine aesthetic accomplishment.   The
director should be prompt in ending the rehearsal, as most individuals have a demanding time schedule.   Nevertheless, the
dismissal time must be considered the director's prerogative—
the singers should not be mere "clock watchers," but should
wait to be dismissed.

Interpretation

In achieving the artistic interpretation of choral music, a conductor must take into consideration a number of factors. The following suggestions will assist the conductor in achieving his goals.

Style of the Music

Prior to the initial rehearsal of a choral selection, the conductor should give ample thought to the style of the music. These considerations will provide a guide to the achievement of a more artistic interpretation. Essential points are the characteristics of music in various historical periods, and the specific treatment of meter and stress, tempo, dynamics, texture, and expression. The unique characteristics of the music of each individual composer should also be understood.

Consideration should also be given to the stylistic features or characteristics of particular types of compositions, such as the chorale, the motet, the madrigal, the cantata, the oratorio, the mass, liturgical music, the folk song, the ballad or love song, and music in a popular idiom.

Another fact of style is the manner in which it is articulated—that is, *legato*, *staccato*, and *marcato*. The mood of the text as well as the musical markings will generally reveal these basic styles. Each musical selection requires a specific treatment in terms of diction, as well as in the projection of the mood or spirit of the song to the audience. The singers, therefore, must become aware of the differences in style if artistic interpretation is to be achieved.

Dynamic Range and Contrast

The dynamic range of a particular choral group depends upon the age level, physical maturity, and vocal development of the singers in the group. The relatively immature voices of a junior high school chorus, for example, are obviously unable to achieve the same full *fortissimo* effects as an adult choral group.   Conductors should avoid being overambitious and striving for effects that may prove harmful and injurious to younger students' voices.   Contrast of dynamics is, of course, one of the objectives of the conductor.   One should remember, however, that dynamics are relative, and that to achieve this goal the dynamic extremes of one group need not necessarily equal those of another choral group.   Through experimentation, a conductor should determine the maximum dynamic level that voices of his particular group may sing without distortion of sound and undue vocal strain—and then compensate at the other extreme of the dynamic range by reducing the level of the *pianissimo* effects. Although immature vocal groups will be unable to achieve the same *pianissimo* effects as an adult group, some adjustment toward the goal of achieving dynamic contrasts must necessarily occur at this end of the continuum.   Only in this way will the voices be protected from undue vocal strain.

A director must devote considerable attention to the achievement of effective dynamic contrasts.   *Crescendo* and *decrescendo* markings should be adhered to.   In the absence of such markings a slight *crescendo* on ascending vocal lines and a slight *decrescendo* on descending vocal lines will generally enhance the effectiveness of the interpretation.   When in doubt about the general dynamic level, a thorough study of the text will reveal certain subtle implications—each suggesting, sometimes from phrase to phrase, a change in dynamic effects; to achieve effective interpretation the director must assist the singers in developing an awareness of the importance of dynamic contrasts.   Through the use of teacher demonstrations, the tape recorder, choral recordings, and other means, the ineffective portions of a selection must be brought to the singers' attention and the importance of dynamic contrasts should be continually stressed.

Tempo

Although choral conductors will often differ in their opinions concerning the "correct" tempo of a selection, the majority will agree that they must determine the most effective tempo for their own groups. Factors determining the proper tempo are the basic style of the music, the mood of the text, the given musical markings, the physical maturity of the group, and the acoustical properties of the rehearsal room and the auditorium. One may best advise the conductor to experiment in an effort to determine the most effective tempo for his particular group.

Nuances

Nuances may be defined as delicate changes in musical expression, either in tone, color, tempo, or volume. The various nuances and shadings necessary for the most effective performance of the music quite naturally develop as the singers gain increased understanding of the text. The singers should recite and study the words of the music individually and as a group. Only through this approach will certain subtle, hidden meanings—essential to the best interpretation of the music—be revealed.

One type of nuance, perhaps obvious only to the director, is the slight degree of tension and relaxation within each phrase essential to the most effective interpretation of choral music. The tension or emotional surge is usually characterized by a slight quickening of one phrase, whereas the relaxation aspect of the cycle is reflected through a slight slowing down of the tempo. The tension is not only balanced but also complemented by the relaxation. Improvement of a problem moves through three stages: an awareness of the problem, an evaluation or appraisal of present progress, and a renewed effort toward improvement. Therefore, to implement these effects in the music, the conductor must demonstrate his desired objective by singing various vocal lines, and by playing back tape-recorded portions of the music so that the group may evaluate their performance.

Projecting the Mood

Projection of the mood or spirit of a song is essential to an effective choral performance. Capturing the proper mood of a selection may occur only through diligent study of the text. The director should discuss the implications of the text with the singers, the proper mood should be established for each selection, and an effort should be made to improve the projection with each subsequent researsal.

In achieving this goal, it has been found helpful to give special attention to the consonants. For example, in certain words, such as *thunder* and *glory*, the prevailing thought is quite dynamic. Therefore, the initial consonants should be stressed—almost "exploded." Often the advice "Sing these as *Capital Consonants*" assists in creating in the singers' minds the desired mental picture. Conversely, other initial consonants, in such words as *dreams, softly*, and *lullaby*, demand the opposite treatment and must be handled more subtly and sung in a smooth *legato* style.

Finishing the Musical Phrase

Perhaps one of the most obvious differences between a professional and an amateur choral group is the seeming inability of the latter to complete their musical phrases. Often, because of lack of proper breath control, choral groups anticipate the release of the phrase ending. A choral director may eliminate this difficulty, to some extent, by employing what is called "staggered breathing," thus enabling the singers to sustain the phrase until it is released by the conductor. Singers often are inclined to anticipate the release of the phrase. It is often helpful if, during rehearsals, the director employs a slightly modified type of interpretation by holding certain phrases a bit longer than others. In this way, choir members are trained to watch the conductor more carefully, especially at the beginning and the end of phrases.

One of the most troublesome faults in choral singing is that groups do not finish their words. Such singing is slovenly and detrimental to an effective projection of the mood or spirit of the music. Singers should be trained to include the final consonants on all words, and should be especially careful to in-

FIGURE 69   *Excerpt from "April Is in My Mistress' Face" by Thomas Morley.*

clude the final consonant upon the release of the phrase by the conductor.   For example, a problem often arises when one or more sections of the choir release the phrase at the end of the second beat, while another section begins a phrase on the third beat of the music.   This is essentially a conducting problem, and the difficulty can be avoided if the singers are instructed that the attack for one section will serve as the release for the other section (Figure 69).

Eliminating Excessive Slurring

Exaggerated slurring or scooping is the scourge of effective choral singing.   According to studies by the music psychologist Carl Seashore, some degree of "gliding attack" is characteristic of the human voice and is even desirable.[7]   However, definite

---

[7] C. E. Seashore, *Psychology of Music.*   New York: McGraw-Hill Book Company, 1938, p. 271.

steps should be taken to avoid excessive slurring. Most objectionable slurring occurs because the jaw is tight and rigid and the mouth is kept too tightly closed. Slurring can be eliminated, to a considerable extent, if the singers are requested to drop their jaws prior to the initial attack or prior to wide pitch changes. When choir members learn to anticipate wide pitch or interval changes, and properly adjust the vocal mechanism, choral singing can be much more effective.

Facial Expressions and Bodily Attitudes

Many choral concerts are rendered less effective as a result of the stoic, expressionless faces of the singers. Especially since the advent of television, choral directors are becoming more cognizant of the importance of facial expressions and bodily attitudes to the ultimate success of the concert program. A correct bodily attitude may be defined as "that entire bodily posture or stance which reflects the mood of the music." Appropriate facial expressions are equally important to the effective performance of a selection, and considerable attention must be devoted to each individual singer if the desired results are to be achieved.

Memorizing the Music

If the mood of the music is to be projected effectively to the audience, music performed for programs and concerts must be thoroughly memorized. When music is memorized the singers are able to watch the director more closely and concentrate on the interpretative aspects. The director is able to establish better rapport with the group and to transmit, through his conducting technique, his bodily attitudes, and his facial expressions, the desired musical interpretation.

Some choral groups are able to memorize music more quickly than others. Memorization can be facilitated through increased musical understanding and through the principle of association. Students with a greater understanding of the musical score—that is, knowledge of form, harmonic structure, styles of music, and the like—will memorize their parts more quickly. Memorization of the text may be facilitated by identifying particular key words in the text and associating them with various facets of personal experience. When one connection fails, often one can rely upon others to assist in the "recall" process.[8] Memorization is dependent upon a well-defined concept of the entire musical composition, and the relationship of the various parts to the whole. In short, a systematic, well-planned program of instruction, designed toward the goal of improving the musicianship and understanding of the singers, will reap many benefits—only one of which is improved memorization.

Topics for Discussion

1 What are some of the personal characteristics of successful choral directors you have known?

2 In your experience as a participant in various choral groups, have you ever sensed or felt that the director was unprepared for the rehearsal? What were your feelings? What was the reaction of the group?

3 Discuss the effects upon a chorus of a mechanistic approach to the teaching of new music.

4 Identify, if possible, the causes of poor pitch and intonation in some of the choral groups in which you have participated.

5 Recall the techniques utilized by the conductor for achieving effective interpretation in groups in which you have participated. Which techniques were most effective? Which were relatively ineffective?

[8] An approach to the identification of key words is as follows. Write the complete text of the choral selection on the chalkboard, and ask the group to follow it when singing, rather than the text in the octavo publication. Prior to the next repetition, erase certain nonessential words, such as *and, or, to,* etc. Then, gradually, on each subsequent repetition erase other words, until only a small group of key words remains. Then suggest to the group that they give vent to their imaginations and associate these key words with as many related ideas as possible. Finally, erase all the words from the chalkboard and test the singers' recall ability.

6   Select a specific publication and try to analyze the difficulties that a particular group might encounter in rehearsals.

7   Why should accompanied selections be rehearsed, at least part of the time, without accompaniment?

8   Discuss the factors that prevent the attainment of effective balance and blend in a choral group. How would you remedy them?

9   Analyze the difficulties, if any, that hamper your memorization of music.

10   Should music be memorized for all performances? For what reasons would you justify memorizing the music? For what reasons would you justify using the music at programs and concerts?

Selected Readings

Boyd, Jack, *Rehearsal Guide for the Choral Director.* Champaign, Ill.: Mark Foster Music Company, 1977.

———, *Teaching Choral Sight Reading.* West Nyack, N.Y.: Parker Publishing Company, Inc., 1975.

Cain, Noble, *Choral Music and Its Practice.* New York: M. Witmark & Sons, 1942. (Chapters 9, 11, and 12.)

Christy, Van A., *Glee Club and Chorus.* New York: G. Schirmer, Inc., 1940. (Chapters 4 and 5.)

Davison, Archibald T., *Choral Conducting.* Cambridge, Mass.: Harvard University Press, 1945. (Chapters 4 and 5.)

Ehret, Walter, *The Choral Conductor's Handbook.* New York: Edward B. Marks Music Corporation, 1959. (Chapters 1–7.)

Finn, William J., *The Art of the Choral Conductor.* Boston: C. C. Birchard & Co., 1939. (Chapters 5–12.)

Garretson, Robert L., *Helpful Hints for the Choir Director.* Champaign, Ill.: Collegiate Cap & Gown Co., 1956. (Chapter 2.)

———, *Music in Childhood Education.* Second Edition. Englewood Cliffs, N.J.: Prentice-Hall, Inc., 1976, pp. 81–84.

Hoggard, Lara G., *Improving Music Reading in the Choral Rehearsal.* Delaware Water Gap, Pa.: Shawnee Press, Inc., 1947.

Jones, Archie N., Ed., *Music Education in Action: Basic Principles and Practical Methods.* Boston: Allyn and Bacon, Inc., 1960, pp. 172–184 and 186–199.

Krone, Max T., *The Chorus and Its Conductor.* Chicago: Neil A. Kjos Music Co., 1945. (Chapters 3, 6, and 7.)

Murray, Lyn, *Choral Technique Handbook.* Great Neck, N.Y.: The Staff Music Publishing Co., 1956.

Pfautsch, Lloyd, "The Choral Conductor and the Rehearsal," *Choral Conducting: A Symposium.* (Edited by Harold Decker and Julius Herford.) Englewood Cliffs, N.J.: Prentice-Hall, Inc., 1973.

Sunderman, Lloyd F., *Some Techniques for Choral Success.* Rockville Center, N.Y.: Belwin, Inc., 1952. (Chapters 6 and 7.)

Van Bodegraven, Paul, and Harry R. Wilson, *The School Music Conductor.* Chicago: Hall & McCreary Co., 1942. (Chapters 2, 4, 5, and 6.)

Wilson, Harry R., *Artistic Choral Singing.* New York: G. Schirmer, Inc., 1959. (Chapters 3, 4, 9, and 11.)

5

The Jazz/Show Choir

Following World War II, some choral directors began to add popular music to the repertoire of their small ensembles. Throughout the 1950s many professional groups appeared on television and gradually began to have an influence on the attitudes of school music directors. They came to recognize the range of possibilities as well as the educational benefits that might accrue to their singers. In the last two decades, popular vocal music ensembles steadily increased both in quantity and quality and are presently widely considered to be an integral part of the choral music curriculum. Music publishers in turn have responded to the movement and currently offer high quality arrangements of music in various styles.

Some choral directors place their emphasis on vocal jazz exclusively, while others focus upon the show choir and the performance of popular music with choreography and staged productions. While some directors emphasize one or another type of music exclusively, there appears to be a growing tendency for some directors to present a broader range of musical styles to their students so that their musical experiences may be as diverse as possible.

The vocal jazz ensemble movement, which is particularly strong in the Pacific Northwest, emphasizes the jazz idiom as exemplified by the stage band movement and stresses the importance of vocal improvization—and thus creativity—necessitating an understanding of harmonic progressions and the development of an aural sensitivity to the essence of jazz. The show choir, on the other hand, may perform a variety of styles of music, including pop, rock, and broadway show tunes as well as some vocal jazz, but with an emphasis on bodily movement that appropriately reflects and usually enhances the presentation of the music. Singing-dancing groups can be seen on television and provide ample illustration of effective choreography.

Both the vocal jazz ensemble and the show choir movement have valid educational concepts, and to allow students to experience all these varying styles and to gain proficiency and understanding is a tall order indeed. Whatever choices the director makes, however, the purpose of this chapter is to provide some practical insights into the various problems and procedures involving jazz and show choirs.[1]

Jazz and show choirs may range in size from sixteen to thirty-two singers, depending on the available talent in the school and the director's philosophy about the ideal size to fulfill or meet the group's objectives. Whereas vocal jazz ensembles generally perform on three-step risers, show choirs utilizing active bodily movement need space in which to maneuver effectively. Therefore, twenty-four singers is generally considered the maximum number that can be accommodated.

Auditions

Auditions should be held at a designated time of the year. Some conductors prefer to hold their auditions in the fall, whereas many others prefer the late spring. The advantage of spring, particularly for secondary schools, is that the student body knows about the group and upper-class students are given first chance to audition. After the results are announced, discussions can be held to determine the outfits of the group, students can be sized, and the outfits ordered. Also, during the summer

---

[1] Readers may wish to write to music publishers listed in the Appendix and request a catalog of their current offerings in order to facilitate the choosing of music for jazz and show choirs.

the conductor and singers can peruse music, and the conductor can make certain decisions as to selections based on the ability of the group and can order the music. In addition, since participation in such a group is quite time consuming, those students who are not selected are free to make decisions relative to other activities, jobs, and the like. Furthermore, students who are selected may be motivated enough to begin the study of private voice. If others are already studying, they may even desire to increase their efforts.

In selecting members of the group, several criteria are important and should be kept in mind: (a) the singer's vocal ability and musicianship; (b) each singer's experience, flexibility, and ability to learn and remember various bodily movements or dance routines[2]—students with "two left feet," so to speak, would be detrimental to the purposes and objectives of the group; and (c) proficiency with some musical instrument —for example, drums (trap set), guitar, electric or acoustical bass, flute, etc. If students within the group have these capabilities, they can occasionally be drawn from the ensemble for certain selections to add variety and another dimension to the performance. (If the singers who audition do not have these capabilities, then they should be sought out from the instrumental music department of the school.) Finally, although spring auditions are desirable, if the "right" singers do not audition, the conductor may opt not to choose the entire ensemble, but to leave some openings for supplementary auditions in the fall or to modify somewhat the size of the group.

While conductors of jazz and show choirs in secondary schools generally prefer to hold their auditions in the spring, conductors of college groups will often prefer to hold their auditions in the fall of the year immediately before the beginning of school, for the simple reason that in comparison to secondary schools, there is probably a larger percentage of stu-

---

[2] If the group is going to be concerned with choreography, then personal appearance is also an important factor to be considered. Appearance involves grooming, height to weight ratios, and how they use the qualities they have. Appearance in this sense does *not* mean looks or innate beauty. Well in advance of the auditions, some directors even make available to students a "height-weight" table so they can make an assessment of themselves.

dents who either don't return to school for financial reasons or scholastic difficulties or transfer to another institution. Additionally, of those students remaining in school, some may develop class-schedule conflicts with established rehearsal times or decide to pursue other activities.

Selecting Music and Programming

Finding just the right music for a jazz/show choir can be a time-consuming task but that is essential to the success of the group. Following are some suggestions for the director's consideration:

1 Contact music publishers (see Appendix for list) and ask to be placed on their mailing list for announcements of all their new publications. Some publishers provide samplers of their latest publications (often photo-reduced), promotional records, or brochures on new releases, and some will provide sample examination copies. In writing publishers it is desirable to do so on school letterhead stationery.[3]

2 Many music stores maintain a single-copy file of music of various types and styles, generally in alphabetical order. Look through these files whenever possible and ask to be notified when new releases are obtained.

3 Keep in touch with the media (radio, newspapers, magazines, TV) on what is current—also check with the students, as they are well aware of the current favorites. Before purchasing the latest pop tune, ask yourself, "Will it last or will its popularity be only momentary?" While this is often difficult to ascertain, the director should, nevertheless, consider the matter. Take a chance on some of the latest pop music, but consider also the many tastefully done arrangements of the old standards; they are certainly much safer. However, the arrangements of some old standards done years ago are rather bland in comparison to the fresh and innovative ideas used today. Compare and decide!

4 Reading sessions and workshops are often sponsored by university and/or commercial establishments (sometimes in coopera-

---

[3] Some publishers offer a library plan where for a yearly fee one receives all their latest publications.

tion). Take advantage of these sessions whenever you hear about them.

5   Select quartets comprised of students who can read fairly well, and review single copies of music that you have on approval. Solicit their opinions! Sometimes a second reading on another day will even provide further insights. A director may, for example, feel that a particular tune or arrangement is "great," but if the students reject it, especially after it has been purchased, then both money and effort have been wasted.

6   In making your final decisions (always in consideration of the budget available), it is desirable to select a variety of types and styles of popular music including current pop tunes, old standards, and vocal jazz. Medleys are good and a number are available, some including the music of particular composers and others featuring the favorites of previous decades.[4] The rationale for selecting a variety of types and styles is the same as that for the conductor of the concert chorale. Would you approve of performing on a program only music from a particular historical period? What would be the audience reaction? Variety helps the conductor to fulfill his educational mission better.

As to the length of programs, thirty to forty-five minutes is a range within which the director should operate. When working within a given time frame such as a school assembly, programs may be lengthened if necessary by including solos by members of the group. Don't use too many, however, and give consideration to their judicious placement between sets of selections by the group. Obviously, selections should not be included on a program if they are not adequately prepared.

As to the sequence of selections, begin with a rousing opener to establish rapport with the audience. Consider the intensity of the various selections and the impact each will have on the audience at a particular point in the program. It may be helpful to diagram the intensity of the music and rearrange the order whenever necessary and desirable.

Some directors prefer to write a narration for their programs and others do not. There are reasons to support either position. Persons opposed to narrated programs feel that this only interrupts the continuity or flow from one number to the next.

---

[4] See the Shawnee Press catalog.

Those directors who advocate narration feel it may be used to link the separate musical numbers together into a meaningful whole, sometimes with the use of a theme. If narration is used, comments should be relatively short and carefully conceived with a special effect in mind. Narration need not occur between every number but between identifiable sets—with a definite purpose in mind. Thus, it should contribute to the continuity of the performance and never detract from it.

Interpretation

In the interpretation of popular music, the conductor who has had no prior experience performing in an ensemble of this type, or in playing in a jazz ensemble, is somewhat at a disadvantage. His interpretation may be tabbed as somewhat "square," in other words too stiff and unyielding or too loose and "sloppy" —the effect in either case of which is unmusical. The same criticism has been leveled at instrumentalists during their initial experiences in playing in a jazz ensemble. The choral conductor who has had no prior experience with a jazz or show choir, however, can, with diligent study, develop proficiency in this area.

Rhythm

A basic aspect of interpretation pertains to the treatment of eighth notes. In most pop/rock tunes they are usually performed with equal duration and are generally notated that way. For example:

The underlying even eighth-note pattern in the percussion part of the combo accompaniment is an integral part of the style and helps to perpetuate the rhythmic drive. (Certain

5 From "Sausalito Strut" by Carl Strommen (Alfred Publishing Co.).

performers even say that they feel the music in 8, or at least a strong "and," or second half of the beat.)   Some publications provide directions in various ways.   For example, in "Crazy Rhythm" by Meyer and Kahn, arr. Ellis Bretton (Warner Bros.), the initial directions are "Funky Rock (equal eighth notes)."   In "Sausalito Strut" by Carl Strommen (Alfred Publishing Co.), the music is marked "Bright Rock ($\downarrow$ = 120)" and the drum part is notated | ♪ ♪ ♪ ♪ ♪ ♪ ♪ ♪ |. In "Just the Way You
Light Rock beat
Are" by Billy Joel, arr. Ed Lojeski (Hal Leonard), under "Performance Notes" is the comment, "Rehearse slowly, counting each eighth note," and at measure 21 the percussion part includes the directions "Bossa Nova–rock feeling."[6]   Eighth notes are also generally of equal length in music of a particularly slow tempo.   Textual cues and notation within the total configuration of the music will usually enable the director to determine the proper desired effect.   Directions and clues for performance in a pop/rock style may be found at various places in the music and, if none are there, then the director must make his own assessment of the musical style and/or perhaps listen to a current recording of the music.

Singers should always endeavor to feel and respond to the pulse or forward drive of the music.   Particularly after a rest, ♩ ♪ . |, the entrance of the group must be together, which is not likely to occur unless the singers feel the pulse of the third beat and respond precisely on the rebound or second half of the beat (pop/rock style).

In performing off-beat rhythms, ♩ ♪♪ ♪♪ ♪♪ ♪♪, for example, such as occur in "Just the Way You Are" by Billy Joel, arr. Ed Lojeski (Hal Leonard)[6], "Can't Stop Dancin' " by Ray Stevens and John Pritchard, arr. Harry Simeone (Charles Hansen), and "You've Got Your Troubles" by Roger Greenaway and Roger Cook, arr. Paris Rutherford (Belwin-Mills), singers should avoid simply trying to read individual notes, but should endeavor to develop a feel for the entire phrase.   In pop/rock music the off-beat accents occur on the second half of the beat, while in vocal jazz they usually are held back and

[6] For an interpretation of this song by the singer/composer, see the album, *The Stranger*, Columbia 34987.

performed on the last third of the beat (see the following section on swing style). Directors should, therefore, determine the basic style and then assist their singers in its interpretation accordingly.

In the tune, "You've Got Your Troubles" (Figure 70), there is a tendency for some singers to rush the figure ♪♩ ♪♩, particularly the eighth followed by the quarter note, thus creating a stiff or square effect. Singers should be advised to stretch out or "lay back" on these two notes to create a more relaxed (and less corny) style.

In swing style, both equal eighth notes and dotted eighth and sixteenth notes are performed with a two-to-one rather than a three-to-one ratio. For example, the dotted eighth and sixteenth-note pattern in the old standard "Louise" notated as $\frac{4}{4}$ ♫. ♫. ♩ ♫. | ♫. ♫. ♩ |, is not sung as indicated, but as $\frac{12}{8}$ ♩♪ ♩♪ ♩. ♩♪ | ♩♪ ♩ ♩♪ |. The three-to-one durational pattern would create a stiff or "square" effect, whereas the two-to-one relationship (as indicated in the example) makes the choir "swing." Another way of notating the two-to-one relationship is as follows: $\frac{4}{4}$ ♩ ♪♩ ♪♩ ♩ ♪| ♩ ♪♩ ♪♩ |. However, in certain instances this notation can be somewhat difficult to read. An increasing number of arrangers are indicating on the score the style they desire. For example, in "I Hear Music" by Loesser and Lane, arranged by Larry Lapin (Warner Bros.), the directions "Moderate Swing" (♫ = ♩♪) are indicated (Figure 71). While all the eighth notes in this arrangement are written equally, the directions clearly indicate to the director that a two-to-one relationship is necessary in performance. If the music is not marked "swing style," then one may be inclined to assume that equal eighth notes should be performed as written. However, there can be exceptions to this and the director must use his own musical judgment. In swing style, the dotted quarter note is similarly performed as: ♩. ♪ = ♩ ♩♪ . Also in swing style, one may periodically encounter the rhythmic figure $\frac{4}{4}$ ♩ ♩ ♫. ♫ |. As to the last two equal eighth notes, they have been performed in three different ways:

FIGURE 70 *Excerpt from "You've Got Your Troubles" by Roger Greenaway and Roger Cook, arranged by Paris Rutherford. Copyright © 1976 by Mills Music Ltd. Used by permission.*

FIGURE 71 *Excerpt from the introduction to "I Hear Music" by Frank Loesser and Burton Lane, arranged by Larry Lapin. Copyright © 1978 by Famous Music Corporation. Copyright © 1967 renewed by Famous Music Corporation. Used by permission.*

♫, ♩♪, and ♪♪. In such situations, try the pattern several ways, *i.e.*, experiment, think about what you feel is the most effective or sensitive way, and then do it!

In the first measure of the introduction to the arrangement of "I Hear Music," each chord (syllable) is notated on the second half of the first, second, and fourth beats respectively; however, they are performed on the last one-third of each of the beats indicated. (Note the directions by the arranger— "Moderate Swing ♫ = ♩♪ .") For the singers to respond to the rhythm accurately they must feel the beginning of each beat and "bounce off" so to speak, so the accents are as precise as possible.

The question is often asked why arrangers don't notate the music the way they would like it to sound. Figure 72 shows the notated rhythm of the excerpt from "I Hear Music" followed by notation indicating the correct performance style. The latter two ways are obviously more difficult than the first to read. It is for this reason that the traditional means of musical notation is generally used with an indication of "swing style" given. Once a person comprehends the basic swing style, the reading of the notation is usually facilitated quite readily.

In interpreting jazz rhythms, there are innumerable patterns that the director will encounter. For further study and

FIGURE 72 *Rhythmic patterns from the introduction to* "I Hear Music" *as notated and as performed.*

reference, the reader is referred to Clark Terry and Phil Rizzo, *The Interpretation of the Jazz Language*, M.A.S. Publishing Co., Bedford, Ohio, 1977. In this publication, various rhythmic patterns are notated, with a suggested appropriate jazz interpretation included on a line underneath.

Tempo

In the rendition of any vocal jazz or pop tune the finding of the "right groove" is essential for the most effective articulation and overall effect of music. Directors will find the metronome markings helpful, but they should experiment a bit as, for example, the personnel of a group and the acoustics of the performance hall may have a subtle effect on the tempo that will seem right for the group. Once this is determined and marked on the conductor's score, many conductors like to refer to a pocket metronome to make certain of the tempo before it is given to the group. Performance conditions can have subtle effects on the groups and they should be advised to hold rigidly to the given tempo, *i.e.*, don't rush and don't drag—keep on the beat!

On up-tempo tunes, there is often a tendency for the group to drag, or sing behind the beat. Conversely, on medium to slow tempos there is sometimes a tendency for a group to rush the tempo. As previously mentioned, an inward response to the pulse of the music is essential to maintaining a steady beat. On up-tempo tunes the singers should keep on top of the beat, so to speak, and have a feeling of leaning forward, *i.e.*, they should anticipate and respond to the "front" side of the beat. (However, they should avoid rushing up-tempo tunes to the extent that articulation becomes blurred.) On slow tempos, singers should be advised to "lay back," relax, and respond to the back side of the beat.

There is also sometimes a tendency for singers to rush staccato notes that fall on the beat. They should be advised to "lay back" and allow for the separation that should occur between the quarter notes. An example of this problem occurs in measures 58 and 59 of "Let There Be Love" by Lionel Rand

and Ian Grant, arranged by Kirby Shaw (Hal Leonard Publishing Corp.), shown in Figure 73.

Tone Quality

In vocal jazz, as well as in most pop tunes, singers should be advised to sing with a straight tone during all unison passages and in those with close or tight harmony; otherwise the intonation and blend will be adversely affected. Note, for example, the voicing in measure 2 of the excerpt from "When I Fall in Love" (Hal Leonard), shown in Figure 74. With the bass, tenor, and alto parts an interval of a major second apart, the clarity of the chord structure would most certainly be "muddled" were any vibrato to be used. Some vibrato, however, may be used occasionally for coloring purposes but primarily on solo passages.

The same basic principles of correct tone production as related in Chapter 2 generally apply to pop singing (see section titled "Developing Choral Tone" in particular). As to diction, initial consonants should be clearly and precisely articulated, though the intensity of *middle* and *final* consonants should be minimized. The consonant *t* in particular, needs to be softened. For example, on the final consonant in doot, minimize the *t* and keep the tongue in contact with the palate. Also, the function of the *t* in doot is to stop the sound.

As to the treatment of diphthongs, the second vowel will usually be omitted or at least softened. One of the most troublesome problems of choral singers, regardless of the music style, seems to be their dogged determination to anticipate the second vowel in diphthongs and, of course, not all at the same time, thus resulting in problems with choral blend. With pop singers, however, they have numerous models to whom they listen regularly, so the director can perhaps more readily make his point. In summary, tone and diction in pop style should not be forced, but should be somewhat relaxed and easygoing.

FIGURE 73 Excerpt from "Let There Be Love" by Lionel Rand and Ian Grant, arranged by Kirby Shaw. © Copyright 1940, Renewed by Shapiro, Bernstein & Co., Inc. Used by permission.

229

FIGURE 74   Excerpt from "When I Fall in Love" by Adward Heyman and Victor Young, arranged by Phil Azelton. © Copyright 1952, 1973 by Northern Music Corp., a divission of MCA Entertainment, Inc., and Victor Young Publications.   Used by permission.

Vocal Jazz Articulations and Inflections

The following symbols are generally accepted as standard articulations and inflections for arrangements of vocal jazz ensemble music.

Accent markings—there are several different types.

$\tilde{\mathbf{r}}$ = heavy accent held to fullest value. May occur on or off the beat.

$\hat{\mathbf{r}}$ = heavy accent, usually on the beat and held less than full value.

$\hat{\mathbf{r}}$ = heavy accent, but short as possible.

Tenuto and staccato

$\bar{\mathbf{r}}$ = note held to fullest value.

$\dot{\mathbf{r}}$ = short and detached.

Shake

$\widetilde{\mathbf{r}}$ = a rather fast alternation between the written pitch and minimally a major second above. Some directors prefer a minor third or even a major third. Shakes need not be synchronized within the group.

Flip

$\mathbf{r}\searrow$ = sound first note written and just before its release raise the pitch and drop quickly to the next note.

Smear

$\mathbf{J}$ = a slide into a note from below, reaching the pitch just before the next note. The length of the smear then depends on the length of the note.

Falloff

$\mathbf{\mathbf{\mathbf{\mathcal{A}}}}$ = a descending slide which may be either short or lond depending on the style and the tempo of the music. (The sigh is the essence of the falloff).

Doit

$\int$ = an ascending slide of from one to five steps.

Plop

$\int$ = a descending slide to the indicated note. Sing the
               main note at the last instant and "land" with force.

Indefinite sound (ghost notes)

$\uparrow$ = an indefinite pitch for notes needing a soft but
               vital sound.

Glissando (Gliss)

$\int$ = a slide from one pitch to another which may be
or   up, down, short, or long. Some arrangers simply
$\int$ mark the music as $\int$.

Downward turn or dip

$\check{\rho}$ = an inflection, generally occurring on the first beat
                of a measure in which the singers bend a note
                downward, usually a half step, and resume the
                original pitch.[7]

In rehearsing the jazz/show choir there are many subtleties of interpretation of which the choral director should become aware. The following additional suggestions, therefore, are offered to enable the conductor to develop greater sensitivity: (*a*) listening to and analyzing recordings of outstanding popular groups, (*b*) discussing with his colleagues various matters of interpretation (most school systems have at least one person who has had experience with instrumental or vocal jazz ensembles), (*c*) by attending concerts of other jazz/show choirs in the area, and (*d*) by openly discussing interpretative matters with the students in the ensemble. Their "young ears"

---

[7] For further performance suggestions, as well as musical examples for study purposes, see Kirby Shaw's *Vocal Jazz Style*. Milwaukee, Wisc.: Hal Leonard Publishing Corp., 1976.

generally are tuned to the current popular music on radio and TV and, as a result, they often quite naturally interpret popular music in an acceptable manner, which, although perhaps not perfect, is stylistically preferable to the approach of the uninitiated conductor. Following are several performing groups whose recordings are suggested for listening and study: "The Four Freshmen," "Manhattan Transfer," "Singers Unlimited," "The Hi Lo's," and "The Anita Kerr Singers."

Scat Singing

Scat singing, or a free improvised solo, is an integral part of the vocal jazz movement and can be of benefit to those students who desire the opportunity for free creative vocal expression. It will be of special appeal to those students who have innovative ideas they would like to express but would find it difficult to notate.

There is little question that the steps involved in learning to scat sing can develop increased musical understanding and musicianship. Doug Anderson delineates six basic ingredients of scat singing.[8] They are:

1 Chord patterns—singers must know and hear the progressions underlying the music.
2 Chord structure—singers must understand and hear the notes or pitches involved in the basic chords in the progression.
3 Phrase form—singers should understand that phrases are like sentences, that they are statements of varying length (usually four measures), and singers must fit their musical ideas into these phrases or time frames.
4 Melodic form—singers should construct their solos around the basic melody, and as skills develop (and not until) they may stray further from this basic melody.
5 Rhythm—singers should experiment with various rhythmic patterns ranging from sustained notes to intricate patterns. Listening to various recordings will increase students' understanding of the range of possibilities.

[8] For further suggestions upon these basic ideas, see Doug Anderson, *Jazz and Show Choir Handbook*. Chapel Hill, N.C.: Hinshaw Music, Inc., 1978, pp. 58–67.

6 Inventive human sounds—the human voice is very flexible and the mind is very inventive. Experimentation with both the range and variety of sounds can lead to the development of unique styles.

As a beginning point in teaching improvization, try the twelve-bar blues (in 4/4 meter) with the following chord progression in successive measures:

B♭, B♭, B♭, B♭, E♭, E♭, B♭, B♭, F, E♭, B♭, B♭

1 As an instrumental group (or a recording) plays the basic chord progression above, ask the group to listen for chord roots and then to sing them. Next, repeat the process on the third and then the fifth of the chord.
2 Devise some interesting rhythms for the group to sing using the root and third of the chord.
3 Remember that music is a combination of sounds and silences, so see how effective the use of rests can be.
4 All chord roots have upper and lower neighbors. Experiment with them, but always return to the root of the chord.
5 Strive for variety in the use of different vowel and consonant sounds. Eventually use various words and phrases.

The preceding outline is only an introduction on getting started. For further information, as well as a basic instructional book along with a cassette tape, see Dominic Spera, *Blues and the Basics* (Winona, Minn.: Hal Leonard Publishing Corp., available for C treble clef and C bass clef, as well as for instruments in B♭ and E♭).[9] Another recommended book, available with a record, is Jamie Aebersolds *Nothin' But the Blues* (JA-1211) Lebanon, Ind.: Studio P/R, Inc.

Choreography

For show choirs the director will want to involve the group in some type of movement that will enhance the effectiveness of

---

[9] As a part of the Jazz Improvizational Series, *Blues and the Basics* may be followed with the book and casette tape, *Making the Changes*. Milwaukee, Wisc.: Hal Leonard Publishing Corp., 1977.

the music. Choreography adds a new dimension to the total performance. If one has had relatively little experience with choreography there are several avenues open to the director.[10] In some instances the director may find it helpful to enlist the help of a dance specialist in the women's physical education department. Or perhaps one is acquainted with a professional dance teacher in the community or with a dance major in a local or nearby college or university. Any of these persons may be willing to work with your group on ideas in basic movement, as well as choreographing special choral selections. Also, they may be willing to work with certain students in your group who are both interested in, and capable of, planning choreography.

After the program has been initiated, it may be found that some of the most unique and effective ideas will come from the students in the ensemble, and if their pride is exceptional, they may even request that they be allowed the opportunity to choreograph the music rather than a person from "outside" the group. Students interested in developing the choreography for a particular song should be encouraged to do so and to bring their ideas to the director for evaluation before presenting them to the group. Through the development and utilization of individual talent within the group, the director is often able to identify and then appoint a "chief" choreographer who will coordinate other students' ideas in a way that contributes to the cohesiveness of the entire group. Some directors prefer to have both a male and female choreographer to provide leadership and assistance whenever necessary to the members of their sections.

In evaluating choreography, several matters should be considered. Does the movement enhance or add to the effectiveness of a piece? If not, then how may it be modified? Certainly avoid the mistake of using too much bodily movement that not only detracts from the music itself but leaves the singers in a somewhat "breathless" state unable to do justice vocally to the music. Remember that both singing and bodily

[10] Choreography involves artistic bodily movement, but as music is a combination of sounds and silences, choreography also has its moments of rest.

movement take energy, and to do both well is difficult indeed! Some compromise, therefore, is needed.   For up-tempo tunes also make certain that the choral arrangement is not overly complex.   Up-tempo tunes, including some unison and two-part harmony, may be all the group can handle musically, especially if involved with active choreography.   Does the choreography relate to the tempo, rhythm, various textual cues, and the overall mood of the selection?   Up-tempo tunes, especially show-stoppers used for opening and closing programs, should have energetic movement.   For moderate tempo tunes the movements should be more flowing, while slow ballads often are most effective with no movement at all.   The contrast is thus appreciated by the audience, and the preceding and following numbers become even more effective by contrast.

Finally, when students are creating the choreography, the role of the director should be to guide them in every way possible.   For example, a particular movement—although interesting and effective the first time you see it—can become terribly dull after excessive repetition.   Therefore, the director should identify a basic step and ask the choreographer(s) the question: "How many ways can this movement be modified or expressed?"   In other words, take the same idea and modify or build upon it to add interest and variety to your routines.

When the choreographer presents the movements to a group, they need to be not only attentive but open-minded as well.   This is not the time for critical analysis; it may only result in a chaotic situation.   Give the choreographer's ideas a chance, and then after the rehearsal they may be reevaluated.   If necessary, modifications may be suggested by the director or by certain students, but always in a positive manner.

During the introduction of the choreography, the singers should be advised not to ask questions but to *watch* and *listen!* This procedure helps to focus their powers of concentration. Students are often inclined to ask questions as a "stall," *i.e.,* because they couldn't accomplish a particular move.   Also, when student choreographers are used, have them write their schedules of free periods on the chalkboard so that the singers can get together with them for extra help if necessary.

Show choirs may differ considerably in the extent and
nature of their choreography. Some groups will utilize more
active bodily movement than others; yet basic to the consideration of any choreography are the formations or positions out of
which movement may most naturally evolve. Different formations are, of course, more appropriate for use with specific
selections, where arrangements may range from somewhat stationary positions to those adaptable for active movement. As
a point of departure consider the following:

1 The ensemble is arranged in pairs (boy–girl, boy–girl, etc.)
   in a semicircle formation (partners should be matched in consideration of their relative heights). Tall pairs of partners are
   generally placed together and can be situated either on the
   outside or the inside of the group; it is generally preferable,
   however, to place them on the inside so that the visual configuration of the ensemble from the view of the audience would
   appear to be reasonably uniform.
2 The boys stand behind the girls, but just a bit to one side, so
   that the boys' faces and a partial view of their bodies can be
   seen.
3 On slow ballads, or music with complex harmony, the choir
   may be placed in a tableau or grouping to "make a picture."
   Another term to describe this is a "sculpture"—a shaping of
   artistic forms through a carefully considered placement of
   persons in the group. As a beginning point, try seating part
   of the singers on stools (thirty inches in height) with the remainder standing behind. Then experiment by moving persons around until the right visual effect is achieved. For example, some persons on the stools may sit at a slight angle, and
   two singers may even share a stool back-to-back. Anything to
   avoid a stilted look!
4 The use of elevated platforms of differing levels, with portions
   of the group placed on each level, can create an interesting
   visual effect. At one point in the piece the singers can either
   change levels (higher, lower), or move to the stage level. The
   gradual movement of the entire ensemble to the front of the
   stage can help create a dramatic effect.
5 The girls sit sideways on stools (thirty inches in height) with
   heels placed on the bottom rung; the boys stand behind.
6 Props such as the stools just mentioned are most useful in enabling a group to create a variety of formations. Shorter stools
   (about twelve inches in height) are also desirable—for example,

when a portion of the ensemble, either boys, girls or a combination of each, needs to be only slightly elevated for a special
effect.

In determining bodily movements, remember to keep them
simple, especially in the initial stages of a group's development,
and vary them periodically throughout a selection.   Among the
simpler movements are the following:

Swaying (only slightly)
Holding and swinging hands (with minimal movement)
Boys' hands on girls' waists (particularly when assisting them on
   or off stools)
Boys and girls in a back-to-back position (sometimes with arms
   folded, perhaps to indicate disdain or poutiness) and then turn-
   ing to face each other, indicating a complete change of mood
Girls walking slowly around the boys, with boys turning their
   heads to one side to watch their departure and then to the other
   side to anticipate their return
Boys hiding behind girls and "peeking" to one side or the other
Upraised arms to indicate joy and exultation
A "chorus line" kick of the right leg crossing in front of the left
   and then the left leg in front of the right
Short side steps on each beat of 4/4—left, right, left, right toe
   touch (in front of left), then reverse direction—right, left, right,
   left toe touch (in front of right)
Slight shoulder movements—front to side on each beat (or every
   other beat), reversing sides on every other measure
Boys hold girls' hands straight above their heads while girls slowly
   turn about
Diagonal thrust of arms to left and right sides (alternate between
   measures)
Precise upward movement of arms one section at a time—left front,
   right back, right front, left back

For certain disco-type tunes, many other diverse movements may be used.   Watch the students dance and help them
to identify appropriate disco steps for choreography; then find
music they can choreograph.   Two suggested arrangements of
this type are "Rubber Band Man" by Linda Creed and Thom
Ball, arr. Lojeski (Hal Leonard) and "Copacabana" by Barry
Manilow, arr. Metis (Big 3 Music Corp.).

Singers should endeavor to see television variety shows, movie musicals, and musical theater productions whenever possible and make notes on movements that might be adapted to particular selections that the group is currently rehearsing. Ideas for choreographing choral selections seem to grow and to invoke still further ideas. The process becomes easier as the group gains experience.

Whether one brings in a dance specialist to do the choreography or whether students within the group are assigned this task, the director still has the ultimate responsibility for the final result. Therefore, he or she will want to become as knowledgeable as possible about dance and bodily movement. This may be accomplished by studying books and articles on the topic, observing TV variety shows involving choreography, movie musicals, musical theater productions, attending programs of show choirs from other high schools and colleges, participating in special workshops offered by colleges and universities, or by enrolling in dance courses during the academic year or a summer session.

Directors should give consideration to the following teaching sequence:

1   The group must first learn and memorize the music. To introduce choreography before that is accomplished would be an exercise in futility! Besides, in teaching a new routine, the choreographer may periodically give word cues to clarify and facilitate the learning of the movement.
2   Teach the choreography in sections. Explain and demonstrate the movements, then have the group "walk through" the sequence. Make certain the group can execute the movements reasonably well before introducing a new section; in other words, don't endeavor to teach too much at one time.
3   After the choreography has been introduced and reasonably well learned, return to a rehearsal of the music to focus entirely upon such matters as tone, blend, enunciation, pitch and intonation, balance, and so on. (Rehearsing by SATB quartets seated in a circle facilitates more careful listening.) If the music is not periodically focused upon, it can deteriorate in sound, thus negating the entire purpose of the choreography, which is to enhance the musical presentation.

4   Alternate rehearsals, with the emphasis on the choreography or the music alone, whenever necessary and appropriate.
5   In the final rehearsal, especially on the day of a performance, don't sing at full voice, but save it! Work toward the achievement of both precision of movement and vocal articulation.

Stage Presence

Anything that affects the impact of the performance upon an audience, whether it be visual or aural, is importantly involved and must be considered no matter how minute it may seem. Some of the nonmusical considerations are as follows:

1. *Facial expressions.* The facial expressions of the singers must reflect the mood of the music. This is important for all choirs but absolutely essential to the effectiveness of jazz and show choirs. Singers must "turn on" to up-tempo tunes and should avoid a solemn expression on ballads. The essence of the music's sensitively conceived text should be projected to the audience.

Most directors will face the problem of helping certain students with a stoical expression on their faces. Sometimes this occurs because they are trying too hard, which may be alleviated through the development of individual confidence. The director may periodically need to encourage them to relax, loosen up, and "smile a bit." Another way to assist the singers with a stoical expression is to encourage them to select someone in a friendly audience (perhaps a parent or student friend) and endeavor to transfer to this person the feeling or mood of the song—for example, happiness, sadness, or love.

2. *Eye contact.* The singers should never forget their mission and role as performers—to project the essence of the poetic and musical ideas to the audience and to do so in an entertaining manner. Even when the body is turning sideways in choreographic movements, singers should endeavor to keep their heads facing the audience. The sound will thus project better too!

3. *Body language.* All bodily attitudes—posture, positions, and movements—project a message to the audience, *i.e.,*

how the singers feel about the music as well as about themselves. When they feel secure in their performance, a more positive image will be projected. Normally, students who enjoy and "get into" the music as well as the choreography, have less difficulty in this respect; however, most singers need a continual reminder about its importance. The director may advise the singers to "go home and sing to yourself in the mirror, and if you don't like what you see no one else will"!

Building confidence in the group's abilities is an important task of the director and will occur as a part of the growth process necessitating periodical reassessment and the establishment of immediate as well as long-term goals. It seems that progress occurs by degrees. The group may function on one plateau for a while then move to a higher performance level. When this occurs it's time for a celebration!

While all the movements of a show tune may be precisely and effectively executed, what happens between selections? Consideration, therefore must be given to the movements to the new position so that they are accomplished to effect a smooth transition.

4. *Acknowledgment of audience applause.* When and how often will the singers recognize the applause of the audience? Certainly not after each selection as this might interrupt the continuity of the performance. (However, at the end of each selection the director may wish to recognize the applause if he or she feels it is necessary. Certainly one should not confuse the audience or do anything to keep them from applauding). Some directors plan group bows at the end of sets of music and others at the end of the program. Two suggested ways are group bows from the waist (given on cue) and the other a ripple bow. Some groups like to use both types. On the waist bow, the movements must be together. It is helpful to designate a centrally located leader from which the group will take its initial cue. Two waist bows may be executed with the group counting silently to themselves: down, two, three, four; up, two, three, four; and down, two, three, four; up, two, three, four. After a brief pause the waist bow may be repeated or a ripple bow may be executed: beginning from stage left with

each singer bowing successively in turn until the entire group has bowed. The "ripple" then reverses itself and each individual successively assumes an erect position beginning on stage right. To make the movements effective, each singer must be keenly aware of the movements of the singer next to him or her. An effective ripple bow should be as smooth as a gentle ocean wave.

An alternative is for the director to give the bowing cues, provided he is in an appropriate position to do so. Following the singers' bows, the instrumentalists should be recognized by the director. (If carefully planned and coordinated they may also be recognized upon cue by the singers as well.) In summary, all of the above aspects of stage presence must be discussed with the singers and then thoughtfully considered and rehearsed. This will not happen through wishful thinking but only by diligent practice.

To assist in the development of stage presence, videotaping the group is an excellent teaching aid. When students are able to see themselves as others see them, the conductor's comments become far more meaningful. Videotaping should be scheduled periodically; however, it is helpful if, for at least one complete session, the camera focuses on the hands of the singers. (Singers often betray their nervousness through an awkward use of their hands. Once they surmount this obstacle, however, they will perform more confidently.) The director must be equally cognizant of the person who overacts. Videotaping often helps this type of person to identify his problem and to be better able to blend into the group.

Social functions held periodically can also contribute to the development of group cohesiveness and help to dispel the self-consciousness that a particular member or singer might have.

Importance of Solo Performance

The jazz/show choir director should do all he can to encourage solo performances by each individual singer in his group. Such experience contributes to the individual, as well as the ensemble, in the following ways:

1 It helps each singer to learn the strengths and limitations of his or her voice.
2 It encourages listening to other singers and the development of one's unique style.
3 It develops vocal independence and provides valuable ear training that enables each singer to function more effectively in the larger group.
4 It develops self-confidence and the necessary ability to "sell" a song to an audience. The ability of a jazz/show choir to project enthusiasm as a total group may be strengthened considerably through the singers' solo experiences.

In preparing their solos, singers may be helped by practicing their songs in front of a mirror. Also videotaping the singers in the performance of their songs may help each person to gain a realistic perspective of their performance and can lead to a critical analysis that will foster improvement.

Achieving Special Effects

An important aspect of a choreographic venture is the costuming, which can be most creative if left to the imagination of the members of the group. Changes of costume between sets are often effective. When dresses are worn by the girls, they should be of a type that allows for freedom of bodily movement. Many show tunes may be enhanced through the use of special props such as top hats and canes, small pastel-colored umbrellas for the girls and straw hats for the boys, and various other paraphernalia depending on the character of the music. In addition, an imaginative stage crew, knowledgeable about special lighting effects, can also contribute substantially to the overall effectiveness of a performance. Each selection has a specific mood, and color changes in the lighting can serve to highlight these moods.

Obviously, it is unnecessary for the director of such an ensemble to endeavor to conduct a group during public performances, as this would only detract from the performance of the singers. The conductor is best advised to remain backstage and contribute what he can to assistance with the lighting effects and the overall timing or pacing of the show. Exceptions to the general rule will occur when the establishment of a precise and definite tempo is essential to an effective performance. In such instances, the conductor may establish the tempo from the center or the side of the stage and then exit. The only other justification for the conductor being "on stage" is when the music being performed has varying tempo changes and the singers are unable to effectively execute them. The singers, however, should be given the opportunity to perform without the conductor in front of them. In this situation they will necessarily have to listen to each other more carefully, and thus an opportunity is provided for the further development of their own musical sensitivities.

Most groups enhance their performances by utilizing a small instrumental combination, including piano, guitar, acoustical or electric bass, and drums to accompany the group.[11] Not only is the rhythm of the singers solidified as a result, but the added "tonal color" of the instruments contributes substantially to the overall effectiveness of the presentation.

Groups, such as a jazz/show choir, are often used to provide variety on a school choral program and often appear on programs with the school chorus or choir. In other instances, however, when the repertoire of the group is sufficient, they are able to present complete programs by themselves. Again to provide variety, as well as a needed rest between sets, vocal and/or instrumental solos are often utilized. The performance demands on school choral programs are often excessive, and the organization and utilization of a group such as a show choir not only relieves certain performance pressures for the other choral organizations, but more often than not is the ideal group,

---

[11] It is suggested that two piano accompanists be a part of the total group, not just to cover illness, but because on some selections it may be desirable to use a four-hand piano accompaniment.

both in terms of size and repertoire, to present performances before luncheon or dinner groups, such as, for example, local service clubs.

One final word! Before any public performance is scheduled, the conductor must make certain that the choreography is just as well rehearsed as is the music. Although slight slips of memory as regards the music can sometimes be "covered up" (to the uninitiated ear, at least), miscues or mistakes in the choreography are not only obvious to everyone, but are embarrassing to the singers, as well as to the conductor. The dedication in terms of both time and effort to perfecting all movements must match, if not exceed, that put forth during the music rehearsals if performances are to be even reasonably adequate and if the ensemble is to achieve its aesthetic goals. With a jazz/show choir, the mental preparation of the group for a performance is highly important. The mental warm-up, or getting ready to perform, is even more important than the vocal warm-up.

Topics for Discussion

1 List several of the specific criteria for the selection of new members in a jazz/show choir and describe how auditions might be held.

2 When introducing choreography to singers, what means can be used to help ensure that they comprehend the movements and can learn to execute them with a minimum of confusion?

3 Describe various means by which singers can be assisted in overcoming certain inhibitions that are detrimental to the overall effectiveness of a group's performance.

4 Describe the tone quality appropriate for jazz/show choirs. Discuss means by which the "ideal" quality may be achieved.

5 Discuss various special effects that a jazz/show choir might achieve through unique costuming ideas.

Selected Readings

Aebersold, Jamie, *Nothin' but the Blues* (JA-1211). Lebanon, Ind.: Studio P/R, Inc. (Book and record.)

Anderson, Doug, "Improvisation for Vocal Jazz Ensembles," *Music Educators Journal*, Vol. 66, No. 5, January 1980, pp. 89–94.

————, *Jazz and Show Choir Handbook*. Chapel Hill, N.C.: Hinshaw Music, Inc., 1978.

Bower, Jordan Hamm, "Ideas from a Choreographer," *The Choral Journal*, December, 1978, pp. 25–26.

Davidson, John, and Cort Casady, *The Singing Entertainer*. Sherman Oaks, Calif.: Alfred Publishing Co., Inc., 1980.

Glenn, Stanley L., *The Complete Actor*. Boston: Allyn and Bacon, Inc., Chapters 1–7.

Grier, Gene, Editor, "Get Down!" Jazz and Show Choir Corner, *The Choral Journal*. (Issued 9 times yearly: September–May.)

Kysar, Michael, David Cross, Ken Kraintz, and Frank DeMiero, *Vocal Jazz Concepts*. Chapel Hill, N.C.: Hinshaw Music, Inc., 1976.

Leatherman, Gary, *Jazz Show Choirs*. Cherokee, Iowa: Rapid American Press, 1978.

Lockhart, Aileene, and Esther E. Pease, *Modern Dance: Building and Teaching Lessons*. Dubuque, Iowa: Wm. C. Brown Company Publishers, 1977.

Murray, Arthur, *How to Become a Good Dancer*. New York: Pocket Books, 1976.

Peck, Abe, *Dancing Madness*. Garden City, N.Y.: Anchor Press/Doubleday, 1976.

Shaw, Kirby, *Vocal Jazz Style*. Milwaukee, Wisc.: Hal Leonard Publishing Corp., 1976. (Vocal Jazz Style Pak includes 1 teacher's manual, 20 student books, and 1 cassette tape.)

————, *Warm-ups for the Jazz and Show Choir*. Milwaukee, Wisc.: Hal Leonard Publishing Corp., 1978. (Pak includes 30 SATB student scores.)

Smallwood, Richard, "Gospel and Blues Improvisation," *Music Education Journal*, Vol. 66, No. 5, January 1980, pp. 89–94.

Spera, Dominic, *Blues and the Basics*. Milwaukee, Wisc.: Hal Leonard Publishing Corp., 1975. (Pak includes book and cassette tape. Books available separately. C treble clef instrumental/vocal, C bass clef instrumental/vocal.)

————, *Making the Changes.* Milwaukee, Wisc.: Hal Leonard Publishing Corp., 1977. (Pak includes book and cassette tape. Books available separately. C treble clef instrumental/vocal, C bass clef instrumental/vocal.)

Strommen, Carl, *The Contemporary Choir: Jazz, Pop, and Rock.* Sherman Oaks, Calif.: Alfred Publishing Co., 1980.

Terry, Clark, and Phil Rizzo, *The Interpretation of the Jazz Language.* Bedford, Ohio: M.A.S. Publishing Co., 1977.

6

Programs and Concerts

Practically all choral conductors have at one time or another encountered difficult problems in the preparation and presentation of choral programs. Problems of special concern include: locating a variety of worthwhile choral materials, planning and staging programs of an artistic nature, and planning and implementing effective publicity. The individual conductor solves these problems as best he can, and, in so doing, is constantly obtaining new ideas. Following are suggestions that may be helpful.

Selecting the Music

The basic consideration in planning a choral program is selection of the music, since the success of the program depends to a great extent upon the quality and appropriateness of the music performed. Following are criteria that will serve as a guide and help the conductor select good, usable choral materials.

1 Is the text worthwhile? Does it contain a message of sufficient value?
2 Is the music artistically conceived, and does it reflect the mood of the text?
3 Does the selection fit the needs and interests of the particular age group for which it is being selected? Does the music have emotional appeal for the singers?

4 Does the music fit the physical limitations of the singers? Is the *tessitura* of the parts too extreme? Are there extreme, awkward jumps in the voice parts which might prove difficult to execute?
5 Are the voice parts handled in such a manner as to make each part sufficiently interesting?
6 If the selection is an arrangement, is it done in an authentic musical style? Is the authenticity of the music sacrificed for clever musical effects? (This criterion applies to arrangements of the masters, as well as to folk-song arrangements.)
7 Does the music justify the rehearsal time necessary to prepare it?
8 Are all the various types and styles of choral music being represented in your selections, so that the singers may have the broadest educational experience possible?

Considering the Audience

The choral conductor should consider the audience in his selection of music for particular programs. Music has a variety of moods and must be appropriate to the occasion. Aside from individual musical tastes, the nature of the event quite often determines the receptivity of the group to various types of music. Performances provided for certain festive banquets, for example, quite often preclude the exclusive use of sacred music. If the occasion warrants the use of popular and novelty tunes, they should be used. This need not imply a lowering of musical standards, for to include in the program a variety of styles and types of music is often the most effective way of evoking enthusiastic audience reaction.

It is important to the success of the program that rapport be established as soon as possible between the audience and the performers. Prior to the beginning of the choral concert, the audience is usually unsettled, as evidenced by considerable shuffling around, coughing, and general confusion. The conductor, therefore, should begin the program with music of a reasonably straightforward and vigorous nature in order to gain the complete attention of the audience. Placing selections of a quiet and subdued nature at the beginning of the program should be avoided, for here their effect would be lost. Such numbers would be more effective if placed later in the program when the audience is in a more receptive mood.

The conductor also should consider the audience in planning the length of the program. Fatigue decreases not only the efficiency of the singers, but also the receptivity of the audience. Choral programs generally should not exceed an hour and a quarter, including intermission. It is desirable to end the program with the audience wanting to hear more, since such attitudes will promote more enthusiastic support of the choral organization.

Achieving Unity and Variety

For an effective choral program, it is important that both unity and variety be maintained. Musical *variety* may be achieved by selecting numbers that contrast in style, mood, length, mode, and key. Variety in the program also may be obtained by:

1 Featuring vocal and/or instrumental soloists, either within or in addition to the choral selections.
2 Featuring either or both the treble and male sections of the choir in selected SSA and/or TTBB literature.
3 Presenting several of the school's music groups, both vocal and instrumental, in a combined program.

Unity, as well as variety, is often achieved in the choral program by selecting publications that fall into three or more groups and that have some definite literary or stylistic relationship to each other; for example, sacred songs, folk songs, and contemporary music. A prevalent practice is to begin the program with a group of sacred selections, representing various historical periods, and end the program with music of a lighter mood—either folk songs or contemporary music, depending upon the nature of the music. Program I illustrates this idea.

Program I

I
SACRED MUSIC

Jubilate Deo .... Orlandus Lassus
Day by Day We Magnify Thee .... George F. Handel
Contentment .... W. A. Mozart
Nunc Dimittis .... B. S. Kalinnikov
The Last Words of David .... Randall Thompson

II
CONTEMPORARY MUSIC

It Is Good to Be Merry .... Jean Berger
The Lobster Quadrille .... Irving Fine
Old Abram Brown .... Benjamin Britten
Sure on This Shining Night .... Samuel Barber
Whether Men Do Laugh or Weep .. Ralph Vaughan Williams

III
FOLK SONGS

My Pretty Little Pink .... American Folk Song
arr. Joyce Barthelson
Dance to Your Daddie .... Scottish Nursery Song
arr. Edmund Rubbra
I Know My Love .... Irish Folk Song
arr. Parker-Shaw
May Day Carol .... English Folk Song
arr. Deems Taylor
Didn't My Lord Deliver Daniel? .... Spiritual
arr. Ralph Hunter

The program sequence from serious to lighter moods and from early periods to contemporary compositions is, of course, heavily enmeshed in tradition and has many merits. However, some directors feel that the group of sacred songs is likely to be better received if it is placed later in the program. Furthermore, they believe that audience rapport may be more firmly established if the program is begun with music of a lighter mood. Program II is presented as an alternative approach. The use of a choral prelude and a choral postlude may contribute further to the overall effectiveness of the program.

Program II[1]

CHORAL PRELUDE

O Sing Your Songs .... Noble Cain

FOLK SONGS

Chiapanecas .... Mexican Dance Tune
arr. Harry R. Wilson

Shenandoah* .... Early American Barge Song
arr. Tom Scott

Soon-Ah Will Be Done† .... Spiritual
arr. William L. Dawson

Charlottown .... American Folk Song
arr. Charles F. Bryan

SACRED MUSIC

O Filii et Filiae .... Volckmar Leisring

Ave Verum Corpus .... W. A. Mozart

Salvation Is Created .... Paul Tschesnokov

Glory to God in the Highest .... Randall Thompson

---

[1] In this and subsequent programs, symbols indicate that selections are to be sung by: (*) girls' glee club, (†) boys' glee club, and (‡) choir and audience. Undesignated selections are to be sung by the mixed chorus.

CONTEMPORARY MUSIC

Younger Generation .... Aaron Copland

Old Abram Brown .... Benjamin Britten

Monotone .... Normand Lockwood

Stomp Your Foot (from *The Tender Land*) .. Aaron Copland

CHORAL POSTLUDE

Onward, Ye Peoples .... Jean Sibelius

As any given audience will usually contain persons with varied musical tastes, the conductor may wish to evoke maximum audience response and enthusiasm by including on the program a variety of musical styles and ensembles. In Program III, for example, Part I includes sacred choral literature from various periods. In Part II, while the singers are given a brief rest, the accompanist may be featured in two or three piano selections. Including an extended choral work of some type in Part III serves to highlight the first portion of the program, as well as providing a valuable musical experience for the participants. Following an intermission, it is often desirable to include music of a less serious nature. A group of folk songs from various countries, therefore, is appropriate at this point (Part IV). Further variety may be achieved by featuring one or more smaller vocal ensembles. Part V includes music particularly suitable for a men's octet, while in Part VI is included music most appropriate for a small mixed ensemble of twelve to sixteen voices. As the culminating part of the program, the entire chorus may be featured in music of a light character. Selections from light opera and Broadway musicals are particularly appealing to most audiences and generally are enthusiastically received. Program III illustrates these ideas.

Program III

I

Cantantibus Organis .... Luca Marenzio
Cantate Domino Canticum Novum .... Heinrich Schütz
Plorate Filii Israel .... Giacomo Carissimi
Ave Maria .... Sergei Rachmaninoff
Alleluia .... Alan Hovhaness

II

Reflets dans l'eau .... Claude Debussy
Alborada del gracioso .... Maurice Ravel
Mary Jones, Pianist

III

Polovetzian Dance and Chorus
    (from Prince Igor) .... Alexander Borodin

INTERMISSION

IV

Marching to Pretoria .... South African Veld Song
                          arr. Joseph Marais & Ruth Abbott
Ho-La-Hi .... German Folk Song
                                    arr. Roger Fiske
Ching-A-Ring Chaw .... Minstrel Song
                           arr. Aaron Copland & Irving Fine
When Love Is Kind .... English Folk Song
                                    arr. Salli Terri
Ezekiel Saw the Wheel .... Spiritual
                                    arr. Harry Simeone

V

Josh'a Fit de Battle .... Spiritual
                                    arr. Harvey Enders
All Through the Night .... Old Welch Song
                                    arr. Roy Ringwald
Men's Octet

VI

A Wonderful Day Like Today .... Leslie Bricusse
& Anthony Newley
arr. Norman Leyden

Touch Me in the Morning .... Michael Masser
arr. Bernard Harding

I Can't Give You Anything but Love .... Dorothy Fields
& Jimmy McHugh
arr. Paris Rutherford

The Modernaires

VII

Neighbor's Chorus
(from *La Jolie Parfumeuse*) .... Jacques Offenbach

Man of La Mancha (Choral Selections) .... Mitch Leigh

Utilizing a Theme

Another means of achieving unity is to build the choral program around some central theme. In choosing a theme, the
conductor should consider the various alternative subtopics
around which the music may be grouped. Provided the text
of the music under consideration is related to the central theme
or topic, a careful analysis of it will often reveal many possibilities for natural groupings. Christmas, Easter, and other
important holidays or seasons provide a most natural opportunity for this type of thematic treatment. For the imaginative choral director the possibilities are unlimited. Consider
the following suggestions.

Christmas Programs. A most effective Christmas choral program may be achieved by selecting numbers that fall into one
of the following three categories or groups: "The Advent,"

"The Nativity," and "The Rejoicing." By utilizing this theme, directors will find their problems somewhat minimized, since most of the choral publications of Christmas music may be placed into one of these three important periods of the Christmas season. Program IV illustrates this idea.

Program IV

CHORAL PRELUDE

Fanfare for Christmas Day .... Martin Shaw

THE ADVENT

While Shepherds Watch'd .... Old Yorkshire Carol
arr. Gustav Klemm

As Joseph Was A-Walking .... Don Malin

Lost in the Night .... Finnish Folk Melody
arr. F. M. Christiansen

The Three Kings .... Healey Willan

THE NATIVITY

Jesus, Jesus, Rest Your Head .... Appalachian Carol
arr. Niles-Warrell

Gentle Mary and Her Child .... Finnish Folk Melody
arr. Lundquist

Slumber Song of the Infant Jesus ... François Auguste Gevaert

Silent Night* .... Franz Gruber

THE REJOICING

Hodie Christus Natus Est .... Jan Pieters Sweelinck

Go Tell It on the Mountain .... Spiritual
arr. John W. Work

Glory to God in the Highest .... G. B. Pergolesi

CHORAL POSTLUDE

Joy to the World‡ .... George F. Handel

Other categories that may be utilized in a similar manner for a Christmas program are: "The Star of Bethlehem," "The Nativity of the Christ Child," and "Joy to the World."

"Christmas Around the World" is a flexible theme for a school assembly program. The program may be built around carols from all countries. The use of a narrator may further enhance the effectiveness of the program.

Whereas some directors prefer to use all-sacred music at Christmas, others may wish to include some secular, as well as sacred, music on their programs. When this is done the selections must be given careful consideration and judiciously placed on the program according to some particular plan. To help achieve this purpose, the theme "Music at Christmastide" is suggested. Appropriate categories for developing this theme are "Christmas Hymns and Carols," "Christmas Symbols and Greetings," and "Songs of Youth and Childhood." The program may be made even more effective through the use of an organ prelude, a brief choral prelude or "fanfare" prior to the processional, and the inclusion of selected masterworks for combined choirs immediately after the processional and just before the recessional. Further variety may be achieved by featuring different choral groups on all or part of each of the three major sections of the program. Program V illustrates this idea.

Program V

Music at Christmastide

ORGAN PRELUDE

Pastorale .... Arcangelo Corelli
Carol Rhapsody .... Richard Purvis
                Organist: Mary Jones

CHORAL PRELUDE

Fanfare for Christmas Day .... Martin Shaw

PROCESSIONAL AND GLORIA

Adeste Fideles .... Old Latin Hymn
Gloria in Excelsis Deo .... Joseph Haydn
Combined Choirs

CHRISTMAS HYMNS AND CAROLS

Christmas Hymn .... 17th Century German
God Rest Ye Merry, Gentlemen .... Old English Carol
Still, Still, Still .... Austrian Carol
Carol of the Drum .... Czech Carol
Concert Choir

CHRISTMAS SYMBOLS AND GREETINGS

Now Is the Caroling Season .... Dorothy Priesing
O Tannenbaum .... Traditional German
Silver Bells .... Jay Livingston
Mistletoe .... Fred Waring and Jerry Toti
Mixed Chorus

SONGS OF YOUTH AND CHILDHOOD

Sleigh Ride .... Leroy Anderson
Winter Wonderland .... Felix Bernard
Chestnuts Roasting on an Open Fire .... Torme and Wells
Toyland .... Victor Herbert
The Modernaires

CHORAL POSTLUDE AND RECESSIONAL

Hallelujah Chorus (from *Messiah*) .... George F. Handel
Combined Choirs
Joy to the World‡ .... George F. Handel
Audience and Combined Choirs

Other categories or titles for grouping choral selections are: "Music of the Masters," "Now We Go A-Caroling!," "The Many Moods of Christmas," "Christmas Favorites," "Yuletide Carols," "Loud Their Praises Sing!," and "Carols from Faraway Lands."

Interfaith Programs. In schools and colleges where the student body or the membership of a choral group is representative of several faiths, a particularly appropriate program may include music from various religions. Program VI illustrates this idea.

Program VI

I

O Magnum Mysterium	Tomas Luis da Vittoria
Verbum Caro	Gaspar von Weerbeke
Angelus ad Pastores	Hans Leo Hassler
Weihnachts Motette	Luca Marenzio

II

Mi Y'Mallel (Hanukkah Song)	Julius Chajes
Shuvu Adonay (Psalm 126)	Joseph Topel
Harken to My Pray'r (based on a Hebrew motif)	Julius Chajes
El Yivneh Hagalil ("The Lord Will Build Galilee")	Julius Chajes

III

Break Forth, O Beauteous Heavenly Light	J. S. Bach
Joseph Tender, Joseph Mine	Seth Calvisius
Lo, How a Rose E'er Blooming	Michael Praetorius
Hallelujah Chorus (from *Messiah*)	George F. Handel

Easter Program. An effective grouping of music for a sacred Easter program may be achieved by selecting music that falls in one of the following three categories: "The Holy Week," "The Crucifixion," and "The Resurrection."

General Sacred Programs. Groupings that may be used for general sacred choral music programs are: "The Spirit of Glorification," "The Spirit of Trust," and "The Spirit of Peace."

Secular Programs. Appropriate groupings for a secular program are: "Songs of Work," "Songs of Love," and "Songs of Play," or "Songs of Nature," "Songs of Love," and "Songs of Travel." "I Hear America Singing" may be used as an appropriate title for a spring concert in which both sacred and secular music is included (Program VII).

Program VII

I HEAR AMERICA SINGING

CHORAL PRELUDE

A patriotic selection

OF HER FAITH

Sacred music of various faiths

OF HER PEOPLE

Secular or sacred music about particular societal organizations or famous individuals

PRAISE TO THE LAND OF THE FREE

Appropriate patriotic music

CHORAL POSTLUDE

America the Beautiful‡

Memorial Day Program. An effective Memorial Day program may be achieved by grouping the music into the categories "The Ideals," "The Men," and "The Land." Program VIII illustrates the use of this theme.

Program VIII

LEST WE FORGET

CHORAL PRELUDE

The Star-Spangled Banner‡ .... John S. Smith

THE IDEALS

Born to Be Free .... Ralph E. Williams
What Makes a Good American? .... Singer-Gearhart
Give Me Your Tired, Your Poor .... Irving Berlin

THE MEN

Anchors Aweigh .... Miles & Zimmerman
The Caissons Go Rolling Along .... E. L. Gruber
The Marines' Hymn .... L. Z. Phillips
The U.S. Air Force Song .... Robert Crawford
Reading: *O Captain! My Captain!* .... Walt Whitman

THE LAND

This Is My Country .... Al Jacobs
Homeland .... Noble Cain
God Bless America .... Irving Berlin
America the Beautiful .... Samuel A. Ward

POSTLUDE

Taps‡ .... U.S. Army Bugle Call

Publicizing the Concert

Adequate publicity is essential to the overall success of concerts and programs. Singers perform best before an interested and enthusiastic audience; therefore, the director should continually search for means to increase the size and quality of the audience and to develop community support for the choral music program. Following are some suggested publicity techniques.

Newspaper Articles

Newspaper articles should be well written, giving all the vital information, such as date, time, place, soloists, and other special features of the program. This information, along with a copy of the program, should be forwarded to local newspapers well in advance of the program date. Most newspaper editors welcome such information and are usually willing to allot a limited amount of space in their publications as a public or community service. The younger set may be best reached by placing articles and announcements in the school newspaper. To provide a desirable learning experience for secondary school students, the director should designate individuals in the choral organization to handle this latter aspect of public relations.

Radio Announcements

In communities displaying a high degree of interest in school, church, and community affairs, certain local radio stations have cooperated by broadcasting spot announcements of programs, sometimes during local news broadcasts, a few days before the event is to occur. Some radio stations provide this assistance as a public service, without charge. In certain instances, stations have been known to interview choir members on radio broadcasts concerning aspects of a coming musical event or program.

Complimentary Tickets

Perhaps one of the most effective means of publicity is the distribution of a specified number of complimentary tickets to concerts for which there normally would be no admission charge. Tickets may be mailed to selected persons or a certain number may be provided each choir member for distribution. Individuals do not, as a rule, destroy so quickly items to which they attach some value; tickets may lie around a person's home in various conspicuous places, or be shuffled daily from one coat pocket to another. In this way, the tickets are a constant reminder of the coming event.

Mailing of Programs

In many instances, a certain clientele may be lured by mimeographed copies of the actual program. In contrast to the more formal appearance of a printed announcement, the actual program creates greater interest for the reader. Recognition of a familiar or favorite choral selection sometimes provides the necessary extra motivation for one to leave the confines of a comfortable home on a cold winter night.

Posters

Attractive, eye-catching posters can also be an effective means of attracting attention and stimulating interest in choral programs. Posters may be printed by local printing shops for a nominal fee, or in the school printing shop, where facilities exist. In most organizations there are a number of persons with artistic ability who are willing to prepare some atttractive posters. These same individuals will usually assume the task of distribution. Posters should be placed where traffic is heavy —in locations where they will be seen by the largest number of persons—in schools, churches, stores, and various other locations in the community.   Adequate study given to determining the best locations will reap later dividends.

Handbills and Public-Carrier Advertisements

Although handbills and public-carrier advertisements are used infrequently because of their prohibitive cost, the distribution of the former throughout a specified section of the community and the use of the latter posted in or outside buses or other types of public transportation are additional means of publicity. Their use would probably be justified only for certain types of programs which are financially self-supporting and presented on several consecutive evenings.

A less expensive means that may be profitably utilized is the distribution of automobile bumper stickers that advertise a specific event.

"Word-of-Mouth"

For many performances, a large segment of the audience will always consist of parents, relatives, and friends.   This group is motivated to attend programs and concerts largely because of their individual interests in particular members of the performing organization.   The "personal touch" is exceedingly important in all areas of human relations.   Effective results may be achieved, therefore, if each participant in the organization is requested to extend a cordial, verbal invitation to at least 25 persons outside his immediate family.   Each singer may be provided with a printed reminder, perhaps in the form of an invitation, to make certain that he remembers to pass the word.

The Final Rehearsal

When programs are to be presented in a school or church auditorium, it is of paramount importance that the final rehearsal be held there so that the choir members may become accustomed to the acoustics and to the routine of the performance. (Indeed, the final rehearsal for any concert should always be held at the place where the concert is to be given.) The group should even practice marching on and off the risers so that this may be accomplished with a minimum of confusion.

Not everyone in an audience is capable of judging the musical accomplishments of a choral group, but most will surely be impressed one way or another by the singers' general appearance. The importance of uniform dress is discussed in Chapter 7. In addition, the director should emphasize the importance of bodily attitudes and facial expressions that reflect the mood of the music. Concentration upon the emotional qualities of the music not only will result in an improved performance and greater audience appreciation, but also will serve to reduce excessive nervousness in the singers.

The choir should be advised always to keep their eyes on the conductor and not on the audience, never to turn their heads to look at the person next to them, never to call attention to any mistakes, and to maintain absolute silence between selections and when offstage. In short, the group should endeavor to be as "professional" as possible.

It is suggested that the director turn part of the rehearsal over to a student conductor or a qualified assistant and listen from the back of the auditorium for choral balance, blend, precision, intonation, and general effect. Most persons generally wish to do their best, and last-minute suggestions are sometimes taken more seriously than advice given during previous rehearsals.

When the music has been memorized, the singers are able to pay closer attention to the conductor and to his interpretative wishes. Most individuals will have memorized the music by the time it is perfected and ready for performance. There may be occasions, however, when it is necessary to use the music. In such instances the singers should be reminded to hold their music so that they can easily see the director—they should keep their noses out of the music and watch him as closely as possible, especially at the beginnings and ends of phrases.

Final instructions concerning the dress for the performance and the meeting time and place prior to the concert, should be reiterated at the last rehearsal. To avoid any misunderstanding, it is advisable to place these final instructions on both the bulletin board and the chalkboard. When the performance involves a number of different school, church, or community groups, it has been found profitable to mimeograph the instructions and distribute a copy to each individual involved.

The placement of the piano in relationship to the chorus must be considered if it is to enhance the effectiveness of the music and if the correct balance and maximum security of the singers is to be achieved. Generally, the best location for a grand piano is immediately in front of the chorus, rather than at either side. If it is in this position, generally all singers can hear equally well. If only an upright piano is available, then the risers may be divided in the middle and the piano placed between the two sections in such a position that the director can be easily seen. This arrangement has the obvious disadvantage of dividing the singers, but it is outweighed by the increased tonal and rhythmic security they receive.

When a band or orchestral accompaniment is used, the chorus is usually placed on risers, or on the stage, immediately behind the band or orchestra (Plan 1). From the visual standpoint this arrangement is highly desirable. In addition, it usually enables all the performers to see the conductor more easily. The major problem that usually occurs with this arrangement lies in achieving a proper balance between the two groups. Unless an especially large choral group is performing, it is necessary to lessen considerably the volume of the instrumental group. This is sometimes best accomplished by assigning only one player to a part.

When a satisfactory balance still cannot be achieved, the problem can be lessened to some extent by placing the chorus on one side of the stage, as illustrated in Plan 2. This arrangement allows for a somewhat better projection of the voices.

Still another possibility is to divide the chorus and place them on both sides of the instrumental group and to the front of the stage (Plan 3). This arrangement allows for the highest

PLAN 1

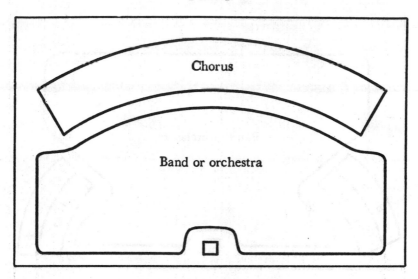

degree of voice projection, but has the obvious disadvantage of lessening, to some extent, the tonal and rhythmic security of the singers.

Musical productions presented on a stage with adequate facilities can be made much more effective by utilizing appropriate lighting. Through the use of various colors, such as

PLAN 2

PLAN 3

amber, red, blue, green, and pink, during the various choral selections, the emotional effects of the music can be heightened considerably. Colored gelatin for covering spot and stage lights may be obtained in a wide assortment of colors and hues (approximately 95). The imaginative director will be able to identify the predominant color mood or moods of each selection by careful analysis of the music. A cue sheet or marked copy of the program should be prepared for the electrician, and all lighting effects should be carefully set during the final rehearsal.

The director should stress the importance of an adequate warm-up before the performance. Choir members should be in the rehearsal room at least 45 minutes prior to the concert. It is important that the temperature of the rehearsal room be approximately that of the auditorium stage. Extreme differences in temperature can have a detrimental effect upon the singers' voices.

A little time devoted to vocalization, reviewing general procedures, and renewing in the singers' minds the tempi and general moods of the choral selections can prove a profitable aid in achieving an improved performance. It is especially important to review the order of the selections. It has been found helpful to start each number and sing at least the first phrase or so. This procedure helps the group accustom themselves to the routine of the program. Singers are often likely to be somewhat nervous and "on edge" immediately prior to the concert. The director, therefore, should endeavor to exert a calming influence on the group by talking and chatting informally with them in the warm-up room, prior to entering the auditorium stage.

Careful planning and attention to all the preceding details will contribute substantially to the overall effectiveness of the choral concert.

Topics for Discussion

1 Maintain a file of programs of various types. Discuss the aspects of particular programs you like or dislike, in terms of musical value, unity and variety, and general format.

2 Discuss the importance of achieving audience rapport. By what means may this be achieved?

3 As a class project, prepare individual programs utilizing a unique thematic idea. Discuss the strengths and weaknesses of these programs in terms of the purposes for which they were designed.

4 Discuss the lighting effects that you feel would enhance the effectiveness of a particular choral program.

5 Discuss the effects of a good program of public relations upon concert attendance and school–community relationships.

6 Recall from your past experience as a singer, situations in which the director's careful attention to details during the final rehearsal contributed substantially to the effectiveness of the choral concert.

Selected Readings

Cain, Noble, *Choral Music and Its Practice*.   New York: M. Witmark & Sons, 1942.   (Chapter 13.)

Christy, Van A., *Glee Club and Chorus*.   New York: G. Schirmer, Inc., 1940.   (Chapter 8.)

Davis, Ennis, *More Than a Pitchpipe*.   Boston: C. C. Birchard & Co., 1941.   (Chapter 8.)

Graham, Floyd F., *Public Relations in Music Education*.   New York: Exposition Press, 1954.   (Chapter 7.)

Krone, Max T., *The Chorus and Its Conductor*.   Chicago: Neil A. Kjos Music Co., 1945. (Chapters 9 and 10.)

Wilson, Harry R., *A Guide for Choral Conductors*.   Morristown, N.J.: Silver Burdett Company, 1950.   (Chapter 4.)

7

Planning and Organization

A practical knowledge of planning and management procedures is as important to the choral director as the techniques of teaching. It is in this area that the ultimate success of the music program many times depends. The choral conductor is first an organizer, secondly a teacher, and finally a conductor. A conductor without an understanding of organizational procedures may be seriously impaired in his efforts to develop outstanding musical groups. Certain administrators often judge the effectiveness of the music director by his ability to plan and organize, rather than by his musicianship. They generally assume that the music teacher has had an adequate training in music; they cannot, however, always assume that the person is an effective organizer.

Recruiting Members

The organization and development of new choral groups in various educational institutions, or the improvement of established programs, may in some instances pose a considerable problem to the inexperienced director. A successful choral group demands at least a specific minimum membership, without which it is difficult to achieve any measurable degree of success; naturally the long-range development of a program depends to some extent upon this initial success. Following are suggestions that should prove profitable in the development of the choral music program.

Endeavor to show all individuals that singing can be an enjoyable and rewarding experience—not an uninteresting mechanical ritual! In schools this may be approached, in the beginning, through well-planned school assembly and community sings.[1] In churches, informal sings may be promoted as an integral part of the program provided or sponsored for various age groups—that is, boy and girl scouts, youth groups, young married couples' groups, men's organizations, and women's societies.

At the outset of this program, one should utilize many familiar songs, sung in unison. Unison songs, sung with good tone quality and clear diction, can be a satisfying musical experience. This activity, plus the singing of many rounds and canons, provides the background for and serves as a means of stimulating interest in the later group harmonization of favorite songs. Although the emphasis should always be upon the recreational and not the technical aspects of the music, it is possible for the leader to stress the importance of good tone quality and clear diction as it relates to expressive singing. Remarks such as "When you open your mouths wide, you sound so much better," and "Enunciating your words make this song more enjoyable to sing" contribute toward this end. Several highly successful choral programs were begun in this manner. From the musical seeds sown in these informal sings and assemblies grew a strong desire on the part of many individuals to explore further the vast wealth of choral literature.

With particular reference to school situations the following suggestions are offered. Inviting outstanding choral groups from neighboring schools and from the community at large to present assembly programs may serve to stimulate interest in singing and provide further impetus to the choral music pro-

[1] For a variety of songs for recreational singing, see the listing at the end of this chapter.

gram. One of the local barbershop quartets might prove of special interest to the male students. If individuals are to improve, they must know what they are striving for. Hearing other choral groups provides a means through which students may evaluate their own attitudes and progress.

In certain schools, the problem of recruiting students for choral groups centers not in enrolling girls, but in obtaining an adequate number of boys to sing four-part music. The reasons for this problem are many, including schedule conflicts with other school activities and athletics. The problem usually resolves itself to ferreting out the remaining number of boys and/or making the choral program so attractive that an adequate number of singers are drawn from other conflicting activities. The organization of a male quartet or octet that may be called upon to sing in the school assembly or elsewhere in the community can have a most desirable effect upon boys who consider choral singing to be a nonmasculine activity. To combat this attitude, many successful directors have devoted special attention toward establishing rapport with, and subsequently recruiting in the organizations, the "leaders" of the school athletic teams. Once this group has been won over, the problem of recruiting additional boys is, for obvious reasons, lessened considerably.

Enlisting the cooperation of other teachers in the school to be on the lookout for students who display an interest in music, and who from all indications will be able to meet the established membership qualifications, has in many cases proven most profitable. Some are, to a greater or lesser extent, desirous of participating in choral groups, but are either unaware of their capabilities or lack courage enough to express their desires to the choral director.

It is advisable to heed the old adage, "Nothing succeeds like success." The director should assume an attitude of believing in the success of his choral groups. In other words, he should avoid pessimistic attitudes and should always be optimistic; he should think in positive terms and avoid negative thoughts. Such a positive attitude is contagious and can have a decidedly beneficial effect on one's singers.

Stimulating Interest

Individuals are normally motivated in a variety of ways toward music participation. There are relatively few persons whose initial interest is entirely *intrinsic;* that is, whose desire to study music emerges primarily from a love of the music itself. Nevertheless, such interest not only is admirable, but also might well be considered one of the ultimate goals of music education. The skilled director who displays a great enthusiasm for music will normally make great strides in developing in individuals a love for music and the desire to explore and experience the vast wealth of music literature. It is not suggested, however, that the choir director depend entirely upon this intrinsic interest in the development of the choral music program. In a normal situation one will find that everyone is interested in music to a greater or lesser extent. The problem usually occurs with the half-interested person who either is "exploring" the activity or is merely anxious to remain in the company of his friends. The experienced director, however, takes a realistic attitude and utilizes many means to help accomplish his goal or purpose. Sometimes these techniques or methods are described as *extrinsic* means of motivation; that is, the director motivates such a person by taking advantage of interests that lie outside the music itself.

Following are suggestions that might be placed in either of the previously mentioned categories and, if utilized, will not only stimulate interest in music participation, but will also result in other values that contribute toward the development of the choral music program.

Exchange Concerts

Exchange concerts with neighboring communities are valuable in that they provide the singers a "yardstick" for the evaluation of the progress of their own music groups, as well as serving as an introduction to varied types of music literature. In addition, valuable and lasting friendships are sometimes made with individuals from other schools or communities.

Guest Conductors

Utilizing guest conductors for rehearsals and/or concerts can be a valuable musical experience for chorus members. As a result of this experience, singers necessarily become more alert to the conducting movements of the director and develop an awareness of varying types of musical interpretation. Such an arrangement can usually be made on an exchange basis with directors from neighboring institutions. Whenever financial arrangements can be made, however, it would seem highly desirable to invite a nationally known choral conductor to work with the choir or chorus for a day or two. These rehearsals may be culminated with a public concert. A practice that is quite prevalent, and certainly more economical, is for a number of neighboring schools or churches to join together and direct their efforts toward one large musical festival. Between schools, lines of communication usually are set up by the principals; therefore, it is quite natural for those in the same activities conference to join together for this event.

Attending Concerts

Group solidarity and a feeling of belonging—so important to the ultimate success of an organization—is often facilitated when members of a choral organization attend as a group various musical events presented in the community or in nearby towns or cities. In addition, a broader understanding and appreciation of music is often developed by the group.

Choral Recordings

Recordings of professional, collegiate, church, and community choral groups often are utilized for the introduction of new musical selections to the group, and as a means of studying various types of interpretation. A variety of listening experiences is helpful in broadening the singers' musical horizons, and in improving their musical tastes.

Tape Recordings as a Rehearsal Aid

The use of a tape recorder during rehearsals can be a most effective means of facilitating the singers' musical development. As an aid in improving the interpretation of a musical selection it is in many ways unsurpassable. Often the well-chosen words of the director, expressing a specific desired effect, are comparatively ineffective, whereas the playback of a tape recording usually has a profound effect on the listeners.

Production and Sale of Recordings

Provided the musical development of the organization warrants it, it may be found profitable to produce and sell recordings of the group. Such a project not only serves to stimulate the singers' interest, but also focuses the community's interest on the choral music program—certainly a most desirable objective.

Group Photographs

The experienced director is well aware of the enthusiasm created when organization pictures are taken. They have for a long time been utilized as a means of developing an *esprit de corps* in groups. Persons of all ages enjoy pictures; however, school-age youth are especially interested in photographs that include themselves and their peers.

The Rehearsal-Room Bulletin Board

The bulletin board may be used advantageously in many ways. It may be utilized for posting general announcements, magazine or newspaper articles of general interest, organization photographs, and various other types of pictures and cartoons dealing with music topics. All of these are effective means for stimulating interest in music.

Radio and Television Broadcasts

The choral group that is fortunate enough to participate in radio or television broadcasts will usually be highly motivated to prepare for the program.[2] As a result, most directors would agree that such opportunities are a profitable educational experience for the persons involved. Many local stations, it will be found, are desirous of scheduling programs of general public interest. Because the nature or content of choral music programs is especially appropriate for programming during the Christmas and Lenten seasons, many community music groups may be heard at these times. Unfortunately, in some localities, opportunities such as these are not frequently available for all choral groups. In such instances, however, many directors endeavor to utilize these educational media in other ways—by announcing at rehearsals various noteworthy programs, or posting notices of them on the bulletin board. In this way the choir members may benefit considerably from the programs themselves, as well as from discussions of them later.

Publication of Yearbooks or Newsletters

Many school music groups have found it extremely profitable, in terms of developing individual interest, to publish a yearly booklet in which photographs, comments on noteworthy performances, and various anecdotes of the organization's members are included. Other groups have published periodically a newsletter with equal success. In most groups there will be found persons who have a keen interest in writing, and who will benefit especially from this experience.

Awards

The presentation of letters, pins, or keys to outstanding students, or to students who have participated for a specified length

[2] Choral conductors should acquaint themselves with the hand signals utilized in television studios. See last section in the Appendix.

of time, has long been found to be an effective means of stimulating interest in school music groups.   Some directors have
found the establishment of a point system to be quite effective
in implementing such a plan.   That is, to receive an award a
student must be accredited with a specified number of points.
For example, points may be given for attendance at regular and
special rehearsals, participation in concerts and music festivals,
or participation as a soloist or a member of an ensemble at competition-festivals or at various functions in the community.   It
is usually advisable for a committee, selected by the students,
to work with the director in setting up the system of awards.

Social Events

Dances, mixers, and parties provide a splendid opportunity for
the development of *esprit de corps* and the feeling of belonging
which can contribute so much to the eventual success of an
organization.   In addition to serving as a means of strengthening personal relationships within the group, they can be utilized
as money-making activities.

Newspaper Publicity

Adequate newspaper coverage of concerts can be of considerable assistance in the development of the choral music program.
Newspaper editors are eager to receive information concerning
news events that they believe will be of special community
interest.   Many newspapers have a prescribed format to be followed in preparing news items.   Learning and following these
procedures will often facilitate communication and the release
of the news item.   Also, early submission of an item that has
no particular release time enables a paper to use it whenever
it will fit their makeup.   The importance of maintaining
friendly relationships with the local newspaper staff, and sub-
mitting articles that are carefully written, cannot be overem-
phasized.

Competition-Festivals

Music competition-festivals may contribute substantially to the development of the music program. Adjudicators' remarks may prove helpful to singers and director alike. Opportunity is also provided for hearing other school music groups and for making many lasting acquaintances with individuals from other communities. Perhaps the major criticism levied against contests—not the only one, however—is that too much emphasis is placed upon the competitive aspects, and that singers often become emotionally disturbed and upset over the preparation, performance, and the final ratings. In certain instances this criticism may be true; however, it should not be interpreted as a final condemnation of contests. Prior to participation in such events, the director must prepare his groups emotionally for any eventual outcome. He will encourage concentrated effort during rehearsals and performances. Nevertheless, he will strive to develop in his singers a realistic life attitude. In our present-day society, too much emphasis is placed upon winning "first prize" in various fields of endeavor, or being named the star of the show or hero of the game. Individuals failing to reach their goals often assume a defeatist attitude. The director can render a genuine service to his singers by helping them to develop a proper perspective.

The Evaluation of Chorus Members

The evaluation of choir members should be a continuous process from the first rehearsal to the end of each formal grading period. Without specific established criteria, directors may easily succumb to the pitfall of giving all the students the same grade. This is certainly an undesirable practice, for if a group is to progress at a desired level, then the students must be evaluated on the basis of their accomplishments.

For a group to be properly evaluated, students must know the course objectives and the teacher's expectations. In this respect, it is suggested that teachers prepare a course syllabus that would include the following: objectives of the course; content of the course, i.e., music to be rehearsed and performed (this information is helpful to parents as well); expectations as regards attendance; performance dates, time, and place, and an indication of the total number that will occur during the school year; the importance of attitude toward the achievement of the group's performance objectives; the care of choir robes or other attire; and specific criteria that will be utilized in the grading procedure and the percentage allocated to each.   For example:

Written examinations	40%
Performance (singing exams)	40%
Attendance, effort, and attitude	20%
Total	100%

Examinations are, of course, time consuming in both their preparation and in the grading, but it is felt that there should be some balance between the written and performance types, as both contribute to improved musicianship.   Various types of written tests may be given. One might simply cover the text of the music. A particular phrase could be given with directions for the student to write, in the blank space provided, the words of the succeeding phrase. This type of quiz may be given periodically and is helpful in that it stimulates singers to make a special effort to memorize the words of a piece. Some students learn words more readily than others; however, some could sing a piece an entire semester or even longer and not memorize the text by simple repetition. These students, in particular, need the stimulation of forthcoming quizzes to force them to make a special effort. In the memorization of poetry, students are advised to identify and memorize the key words in each phrase to help trigger their recall.[3]

Written exams or quizzes may also be given on such musical content as musical markings, texture, harmonic structure of

[3] For further suggestions or procedures on memorization, see the section titled "Memorizing the Music" near the end of Chapter 4.

a particular piece, rhythmic patterns, and melodic patterns (for example, "circle the wrong pitch or note in the following phrase").

In evaluating performance capabilities, the director will want to consider each singer's tone quality, ability to carry his or her own part, and blend and balance with the other singers. To help set a procedure for determining this, the director may divide the entire choir into quartets (SATB) and during the evaluation period identify the quartet and the specific beginning point in a particular selected piece. The length of time each quartet sings will depend upon the director having adequate time to focus upon each individual singer in the quartet and make a judgment on tone, blend, balance, phrasing, and the ability to carry their part. It is advisable to rotate the selections used for various quartets, and when exams are given periodically the director will wish to notate both the grade in his gradebook as well a code number for the selection so that a different one may be used on the next exam. Some directors may prefer to set aside a particular time and have each quartet sing in his office; however, this is more difficult to arrange and certainly more time consuming. One advantage of the quartet assignment is that students may be encouraged to practice together during out-of-school hours in preparation for the next exam. When this occurs, many benefits may accrue to the singers as a result of this small ensemble experience where they all more readily hear their own parts, which will facilitate the development of improved tone quality, balance, blend, and general musicianship.[4]

Testing and Classifying Voices

Among choral directors, it is accepted procedure to audition individuals before admitting them to membership in an or-

---

[4] As an alternative to the assignment of students in quartets, the director may wish to play three parts on the piano, with the singer filling in the fourth part to make up the quartet.

ganization. In some cases, the audition is utilized as a means of limiting membership and obtaining the best voices for the choir or chorus. Directors using the procedure primarily for this purpose justify it as a necessary means of providing the selected singers with the best possible musical experience. It is most desirable ·to develop and maintain highly selective choral groups, provided that the remaining individuals are not prevented from participating in some group as a result. Opportunity for participation in a wide variety of choral groups and ensembles should be provided, so that the musical and social needs of *all* interested persons are met. Auditions also provide a means of determining the singer's vocal range and voice quality so that he may be assigned the voice part to which he is best suited, and by which he can make the best contribution to the group. Since most adolescent voices are quite unstable and are still in the process of change, it is advisable to retest voices periodically in order to avoid unnecessary strain from singing in the improper vocal range.

In classifying voices, two criteria must be taken into consideration—*range* and *quality*. The following procedure is suggested as a means of determining these factors.

EXERCISE 17

Ah, —————————————— Ah, ———————————————— *etc.*

EXERCISE 18

Yah, yah, yah, yah,   yah,   Yah, yah, *etc.*   *etc.*

1 Determine the approximate middle range of the student's voice and start there.

2   Utilizing Exercise 17, vocalize upward, noting the point at which execessive strain occurs and/or when the quality of the voice changes to any noticeable degree.
3   Utilizing Exercise 18, vocalize from the middle range downward, noting the point at which the quality of the voice changes. The low range is as important as the higher limits of the voice. Little benefit can come to a voice that is forced downward in an attempt to sing too low a part.

The voice ranges in Figure 75 are only approximate classifications, and the ranges of many singers do not always fall easily into these categories. The vocal range of some individuals may be considerably smaller than, and some may conceivably cover the ranges of two or more of, the classifications presented. In any case, one must listen carefully to the quality of the voice and determine the range in which it sounds most natural—that is, where the person sings with the best voice quality and with the least amount of strain or effort. This is most readily accomplished by utilizing some easy song material. The well-known English folk song "Drink To Me Only with Thine Eyes" is excellent for this purpose, and may be found in many song books compiled for community singing.

As a further guide in determining the proper voice classification of singers, the following voice qualities are considered characteristic:

First Soprano—light, flutelike, lyric quality.
Second Soprano—similar in range to the first soprano, but has a fuller, more dramatic type of voice quality.

FIGURE 75 *A general classification of voice ranges of untrained singers.*

First Alto—similar in quality to the second soprano, but has a more fully developed lower range.

Second Alto—a heavier, deeper voice quality, especially in the lower range, which is more fully developed than the first alto voice.

First Tenor—light, lyric quality, especially in the upper range limits.

Second Tenor—similar in range to the first tenor, but has a fuller, more dramatic, voice quality.

Baritone—often similar in quality to the second tenor, yet has a more fully developed middle and lower range. (Initial voice characteristics may be deceiving—it is in this category that many true tenor voices may be identified and developed. Periodical retesting is recommended.)

Bass—a heavier, darker, deeper quality, especially in the middle and lower ranges of the voice.

In addition to determining voice quality and range, many directors like to test the singer's ability to read music and to carry a harmony part independently. The above-mentioned song is also excellent for this purpose. A suggested procedure is as follows:[5]

1 For all treble voices, request the person to sing the alto part. For male voices, request the individual to sing either the bass or tenor part, depending upon the singer's vocal range and previous musical experience.

2 Provide the starting note and/or a short introduction. Accompany the singer, playing all the voice parts *except* the one he is requested to sing. (Omitting this part enables the director to determine more readily the extent to which a singer can carry a part without help from others in his section. This information is invaluable in assigning seating in an organization. "Followers" may be judiciously placed between "leaders," and from the reading standpoint the total effectiveness of the choral group will be enhanced.)

3 With some singers, because of their lack of experience, it may be necessary to provide occasionally some assistance with their parts. This procedure is justifiable, as the director really is desirous of determining just how quickly the individuals "catch on." In some instances, repeating the song a time or two (with less assistance each time) will enable the director to determine the singer's musical memory and his ability to adjust and profit from assistance provided during rehearsals.

[5] It is assumed that the individual has been oriented to the song through singing the melody during the previous part of the audition.

Following is a suggested list of other songs that might also be utilized for voice auditions. These selections may be located in most song books compiled for community singing.

All Through the Night (old Welch air)
Tell Me Why (college song)
My Homeland (from *Finlandia*)
Believe Me If All Those Endearing Young Charms
Annie Laurie
Fairest Lord Jesus (German folk song)
Juanita (Spanish air)
Jacob's Ladder (spiritual)

Many choral conductors have found it advantageous to maintain a permanent record of each choir member. Readily available information, included on personnel cards, can be helpful in administering the total choral music program. Figure 76 shows a sample card, which may be altered or adapted to suit individual tastes.

PERSONAL DATA

Name: _____

Address: _____

_____ Phone: _____

Previous musical experience: _____

Part(s) previously sung: S1, S2, A1, A2, T1, T2, B1, B2

Height:_____ Weight: _____ Chest Measurement: _____

Range:

Voice timbre: S. A. T. B.
Comments: _____
_____

Quality: 1 2 3 4 5   Part assigned: S1, S2, A1, A2

Intonation: 1 2 3 4 5   T1, T2, B1, B2

S. Reading: 1 2 3 4 5   Robe no. assigned: _____

FIGURE 76   *A sample personal data card. The vocal range in which the individual sings with comparative ease may be indicated in red; the undeveloped part of the vocal range may be indicated in blue.*

Seating Arrangements

Choral conductors generally have found, through experimentation, that certain seating arrangements are preferable to others. The type of arrangement selected usually depends upon several factors, including the number of voices assigned or available for each part, the comparative voice qualities of various members, and the relative musical experience of the singers. Plans 4–14 show several suggested seating arrangements for mixed voices, and the advantages of each are listed.

The advantages of the arrangement of Plan 4 are as follows:

PLAN 4

1 One of the problems confronting choral directors seems to be the development of tenor voices. When placed in the front of the choir, the tenors are more easily heard and may therefore sing in a more natural voice, thus improving the blend of the group.

2 At times the tenor part may need to be reinforced. If some of the second altos need to be utilized for this purpose, they will be close enough to effect a reasonably good blend.

3 The soprano and the bass sections are relatively close together. The proximity of these two sections, which are the outside two parts of the harmonic structure, can effect a stability to the chord and thus help to improve intonation.

4 The placement of a limited number of girls behind the boys can assist in the development of a better blend among the various sections. Choral blend is dependent to a great extent

upon the ability of the singers to hear adequately the other parts. This seating arrangement in which the treble voices literally surround the male section increases the latter's awareness of the treble parts and provides increased tonal support, which is especially desirable for unstable adolescent male voices.

Plan 5 shows another suggested arrangement that may be utilized effectively when the membership of boys is adequate from the standpoint of both quantity and quality. The advantages of this arrangement are as follows:

PLAN 5

Basses	Baritones	2nd Tenors	1st Tenors
1st Sopranos	2nd Sopranos	1st Altos	2nd Altos

1 With the taller students in each section standing toward the outside, a more uniform appearance is achieved—producing a total effect noticeably different from the first arrangement. The difference in height between boys and girls is not accentuated, as it would be were they placed in the same row.
2 Both choirs are reasonably close together and may function as separate units if necessary. (In terms of providing variety to a choral program, the inclusion of numbers arranged exclusively for male or female voices is highly desirable.)
3 In the event that the first tenor part needs to be reinforced with altos, the proximity of the second alto section would provide the maximum support and enable the singers to achieve a reasonably good blend.
4 The proximity of the soprano and bass sections effects a certain stability to the harmonic structure and assists in improving intonation.

The preceding arrangements have one advantage in common; that is, by grouping together the voices on the same part, a degree of security is provided the singers, particularly those in young choirs. However, with the security of singing next to others on the same part also goes the danger of some singers becoming overly dependent upon certain leaders within their section. If these leaders happen to be absent on a particular day, the effectiveness of the entire section is often hampered. It behooves the choral conductor, therefore, to seek ways to strengthen the aural sense of all the singers in his groups. The director's objective should be the development of individual security through vocal independence, not dependence. Seating arrangements may make their contribution to this end. After the choir members have had a certain minimal musical training, it is desirable for the director to experiment with different seating arrangements, in which each singer will be better able to hear himself and to evaluate his efforts properly.

One arrangement, used for a number of years, is the placement of choir members by quartets; that, SATB or any combination thereof, as shown in Plan 6.[6] The quartet seating

PLAN 6

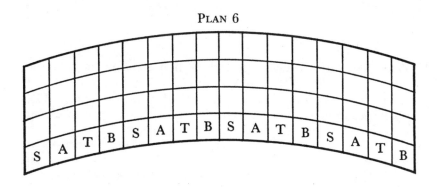

arrangement usually results in the achievement of better balance and blend. Although the voice parts are arranged in rows from the front to rear of the choir, each singer is nevertheless able to hear himself better as well as the other voice parts. Some conductors assign singers to quartets (or octets) on a continuing basis and utilize these groupings periodically for small ensemble practice. In school situations some con-

[6] Some directors utilize the arrangement of TSAB, whereas others prefer BSAT.

ductors, at intervals of about every six weeks, will request each quartet to sing a portion of selected music for evaluative purposes.

Another arrangement involves placing each singer as far as possible from another singing the same part, thus enabling him to hear his own voice better, and to evaluate his efforts toward improved tone quality, diction, balance and blend, and intonation. This arrangement, used by Robert Shaw, has been designated the "scrambled setup" by Louis Diercks. Plan 7 is for a choir of nine first sopranos, seven second sopranos, eight first altos, seven second altos, five first tenors, seven second tenors, eight baritones, and seven basses.[7]

PLAN 7

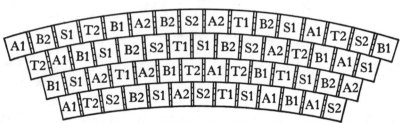

One of the most striking results that occurs through the use of this arrangement is that of improved balance and blend. The weaker singers are not in a position to affect the others in the section adversely, all singers can hear themselves better, and, with the sound of any particular part coming from all areas of the choir, there seems to result a better fusion of sound.[8]

As the voices in the front row are nearest to and the first to reach the audience, it is desirable, with this setup as well as with the quartet arrangement, to place the more selected singers in this position to serve as a "mask" to the choir.[9] Also,

[7] Louis H. Diercks, "The Individual in the Choral Situation," *The NATS Bulletin*, Vol. 17, No. 4, May 15, 1961, p. 7. Used by permission.
[8] Both the quartet arrangement and the "scrambled setup" are desirable for use primarily with music of a homophonic texture. When performing polyphonic music, the choir should utilize a traditional formation, as the beauty of polyphonic results from the interplay of the voice parts stemming from various sections of the choir.
[9] Diercks, *op. cit.*, p. 7.

when a sufficient number of choir risers are available, it is desirable to space the singers slightly farther apart than usual. This also contributes to the objectives of this arrangement.

Some conductors prefer to use either the quartet arrangement or the "scrambled setup" exclusively, even when introducing new music. Others prefer to use a more conventional setup until they feel that the singers possess at least a minimal understanding of, and ability to sing, their parts. For the latter group, Plan 8 is suggested. While the singers are learning the music in their respective sections, the voice parts are at least divided or arranged so as to achieve a somewhat better blend, or fusion of sound, than in some of the traditional arrangements.

PLAN 8

Basses	1st Tenors	Baritones	2nd Tenors
2nd Altos	1st Sopranos	1st Altos	2nd Sopranos

Directors of junior high school choirs often use SAB music arrangements because of a lack of well-developed tenor voices. Plan 9 is suggested for this voice combination. Because of the insecurity of the male voices of this age group, it is desirable to place them toward the front of the choir where they will be partially surrounded by the female voices. This will ensure their being heard more easily and will result in a better balance and blend. As the group progresses, and as the individual voices mature, it will become feasible to introduce some easy four-part (SATB) music. At this particular stage of development, the tenor voices are likely to be especially insecure, and perhaps fewer in number. Therefore, seating this group of voices in front of the baritones will also contribute to the balance and blend of the group.

PLAN 9

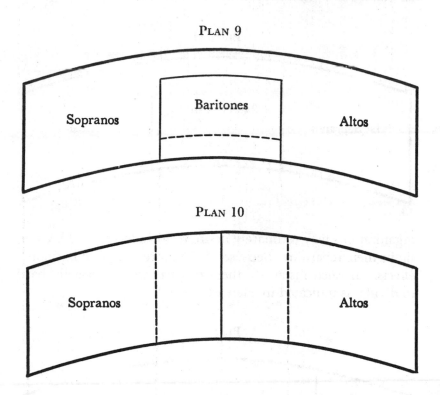

PLAN 10

For directors of treble voice choirs, the seating arrangements shown in Plans 10, 11, and 12 are suggested. Plan 10 is for grade school choirs comprised of selected fifth- and sixth-grade students. This plan allows for flexibility in rehearsing and programming a variety of music suitable for this age group. The repertoire will usually include a combination of two- and three-part music, some of which is learned in the general music class. When singing two-part music, the group placed in the center will sing their respective soprano or alto parts. When singing three-part music, they will sing the second soprano part. The group of students for this shifting, flexible role should be carefully selected through auditions held prior to the first rehearsal.

Plan 11 is suggested for use with girls' glee clubs in junior and senior high school, and for women's choruses on the college or adult level. Although a sufficient amount of three-part music is available for use with girls' glee clubs, the more proficient

PLAN 11

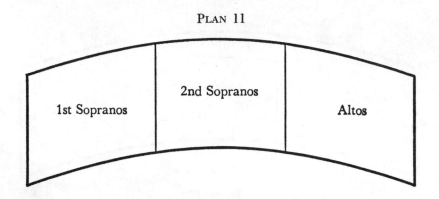

organizations may ultimately desire to include some SSAA music in their repertoire, because of the more complete harmonic effects. In such instances, the alto parts will necessarily have to divide, as indicated in Plan 12.

PLAN 12

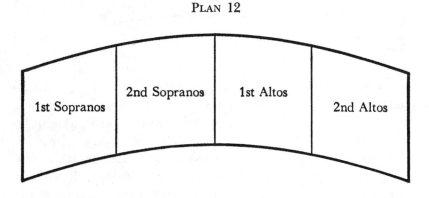

Since both SSA and SSAA arrangements may be utilized in a given program, both Plan 11 and Plan 12 will be found practical because of the adjacency of the second soprano and the alto parts. To achieve an adequate balance, it may be necessary, for example, to assign a few second sopranos, designated as "roving singers," to the first alto part. Or, in other instances, a few first altos may be used to bolster the second soprano part. These two seating arrangements allow for a flexible assignment of adjacent parts to meet the requirements of the music being performed.

Plans 13 and 14 are suitable for use with male glee clubs. The arrangement shown in Plan 13 generally will be found to

PLAN 13

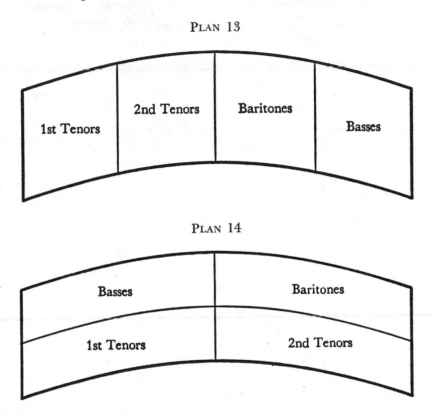

PLAN 14

be the more suitable, especially when an adequate number of boys is available to balance the parts. When, however, there occurs a definite lack of tenor voices, Plan 14 may provide an alternative solution. When the tenor voices are placed toward the front, they are more likely to be heard, and a more effective balance may be achieved.

In seating the students, it is advisable to place the stronger voices and some of the better readers toward the back of the group. In such a position they will be better able to assist the rest of the singers. It is also advisable to scatter some of the better readers throughout the choir, in order to stabilize the group.

In an effort to achieve the best choral blend, it is advisable to place singers with strident voices between singers with a more natural vocal production. Individuals are inclined to simulate or assume the voice qualities of the persons nearest them. When several singers of a similar voice quality are seated to-- gether, this particular quality is sometimes strengthened and the resultant tone becomes stronger and out of proportion to the number of singers with that particular quality. The same principle may also adversely affect intonation. When several chronic flatters (caused by faulty voice production) are seated together, intonation problems are sometimes magnified. By distributing these singers within the group, intonation prob- lems are usually lessened considerably.

Another factor to take into consideration is the height of the choir members. It is recommended that the taller indi- viduals be placed toward the outside and the back of the group. Especially when the singers are on choral risers, this arrange- ment will enable them to see better the conducting movements of the director and will result in greater security of the entire group.

Directors will find it highly profitable to experiment with a variety of seating arrangements. Given plans may be found more effective with certain groups than with others, and peri- odic changes in arrangements will sometimes contribute to the betterment of the choral organization.

The Choral Curriculum

The development of music education in America has been marked by different emphases during various periods or dec- ades. During the 1930s, for example, there was much empha- sis on the *a cappella* choir, and the choral literature of the time reflected this emphasis on unaccompanied singing. During the 1940s and the 1950s the emphasis was on diction and methods and means of improving choral tone. Concurrently during the 1950s, certain educators expounded upon the beauty and spiritual values of choral music as a means of fulfilling a basic human need. During the 1960s, and perhaps related to the effect of "Sputnik" upon the American educational system, music began to be considered as an "academic discipline." In a way, many subjects in the school curriculum needed to prove their worth and be justified, particularly in view of the continually increasing costs of education. During this period, and also during the 1970s, choral music has fulfilled the dual purpose of providing not only worthwhile aesthetic experiences, but (perhaps to keep pace with the other subject-matter areas) it has developed a definite subject-matter content of its own.

Fortunately, musicologists have provided the choral profession with considerable insight into the performance practices of music from various historical periods, while music theorists have developed college courses in musical styles (or analytical techniques) which develop the prospective teacher's capacities to analyze, create, and more thoroughly understand the music of particular composers, as well as the more generalized characteristics of the music of a different historical periods. Thus a sizable body of course content has developed for choral conductors, one that not only enhances the aesthetic experience, but provides students with insights and understanding of the stylistic aspects of music of various historical periods. Students also gain a comprehension of the ongoing social, economic, and political forces during the life of a particular composer and how these served as a "framework" for his creative output.

To develop student understanding of musical style and specific performance practices, the conductor need not resort to extensive lectures, as this might prove somewhat "deadly" and defeat his purposes. Rather, he should endeavor to relate, in a somewhat succinct manner, pertinent information as it applies to the performance of a particular musical selection. As a result, musical enjoyment can be increased, students gain a greater understanding of their musical heritage, and the artistic level of musical performances may be increased substantially. The conductor with adequate college preparation can achieve these goals without undue effort, providing he plans carefully for all his rehearsals.

Whereas dieticians and physicians speak of a balanced nutritional diet, musicians refer to a balanced musical diet—that is, the development of a choral curriculum that will provide students with some experience and comprehension of music of all types and styles, including music from the Renaissance, Baroque, Classical, Romantic, and Modern periods, folk music, and music of a popular, stylized nature. Often one particular choral group is unable to cover literature this broad in scope. Therefore, various groups are sometimes included in the choral curriculum, each with a slightly different focus, but all designed to meet the varied musical needs and interests of students.

In developing a balanced choral music program, the director may frequently ask himself the question "How many and what types of choral groups should I have?" Certainly the answer to this question depends upon the situation as it exists in a specific school. The size of the school and the existing need are both determining factors. The most successful school choral programs usually include a selected mixed choir or chorus with other junior groups utilized as "feeders" to the advanced group. This does not mean to suggest the exclusion of particular students from the advanced groups. Rather, it implies the necessity for choral experience commensurate with the level of each singer's musical development. The choral program should be based upon meeting the needs of all students and everyone with the desire should have the opportunity to participate in some choral group.

Students enter the junior high school with a variety of previous experiences and backgrounds. Although most of them have benefited from the general music program in the elementary school, certain pupils may have been fortunate enough to participate in grade school choruses comprised of selected fifth- and sixth-grade students. Figure 77 illustrates the type and variety of choral groups that the secondary school may endeavor to maintain. It also illustrates two alternative approaches in the basic pattern of organization. Both programs are predicated upon the philosophy of meeting the needs of all students,

FIGURE 77 *A junior-senior high school vocal music program.*

that is, providing an opportunity for all students who so desire it to participate in choral singing.

The general music class is usually required by most junior high schools. In some instances this class is required only of seventh-grade pupils, while being optional or elective for eighth-grade students. In general music classes, students are provided the opportunity for exploring special music areas of particular interest. Although some schools enroll seventh-grade students in selective choral groups, it is desirable to delay this particular experience until the eighth grade. At this point the music program usually becomes somewhat more selective, and students are encouraged to participate in some activity of special interest, whether it be choral or instrumental music, fine or industrial arts, home economics, or some other area.   In the late spring, before the close of school, seventh-grade students may be offered the opportunity of auditioning for the more selective eighth- and ninth-grade choral groups.

Junior High School Choral Groups

As indicated in Figure 77, the organization of special groups may follow one of several patterns.   Some schools organize a boys' and girls' glee club for eighth- and ninth-grade students. Where school enrollments are particularly large, separate boys' and girls' glee clubs are often maintained for *both* eighth- and ninth-grade students.   This plan of organization is predicated on the belief that during early adolescence boys and girls enjoy participating in activities with their own sex.   Another reason advanced is that the music composed or arranged for boys' and girls' glee clubs is more closely in line with their particular interests and musical tastes.   Advocates of this position advance the argument that these types of musical experience differ considerably from the standard choral literature for mixed voices, and should be an integral part of the junor high school students' background.

Administrators and music educators in other schools feel that boys and girls should have experiences that bring them together under socially desirable conditions; thus they advocate the *mixed chorus* as the most ideal plan of organization.   Still other schools, recognizing the values of both glee clubs and mixed groups, compromise between these two alternatives and thus capitalize upon the strong points of both plans of organization.   In such instances, the girls' glee club will rehearse during school hours on Monday and Wednesday, and the boys' glee club on Tuesday and Thursday.   Then on Friday the two groups are scheduled to meet together.[10] Thus, during their separate rehearsals the students have the opportunity to become better acquainted with the literature for either treble or male voices and also to rehearse separately their parts for the SATB (or SAB) music, which they will rehearse jointly on Friday of each week. For junior high schools this plan is advocated as the one that best meets the needs of the majority of students.

Senior High School Choral Groups

In the senior high school, the "combined" plan may also be followed for the "junior" groups, but owing to scheduling difficulties students generally participate in either a mixed chorus or a boys' or girls' glee club. (In certain schools, where the enrollment is exceptionally large, both types of organizations may be maintained.) It is desirable to schedule these groups for a minimum of three periods a week. In four-year high schools (grades 9–12) the membership in the mixed chorus (sometimes referred to as the junior choir) and the glee clubs is generally comprised of ninth- and tenth-grade students. In three-year high schools (grades 10–12), the membership in these organizations will consist primarily of tenth-grade students, plus a limited number of eleventh-grade students who were not accepted for membership in the advanced choir. Because of the greater variety and amount of literature available for mixed voices, and since in many cases it may be found more practical to schedule one organization than two, the mixed chorus is felt to be the most flexible arrangement. In addition, since all "senior" or advanced choral groups depend upon a "feeder" organization for their ultimate success, student experiences in

---

[10] Under this plan of organization, each student has the opportunity of participating in choral music activities for three periods a week, that is, either M.W.F. or T.Th.F. On alternate days he may be scheduled to participate in physical education, art, home economics, industrial arts, or some other class, depending upon the particular school situation.

singing music for mixed voices, prior to membership in the advanced choir, may contribute substantially to the degree of proficiency that the latter organization is able to achieve.

The "Concert Choir" or the "*A Cappella* Choir" are two names commonly given the selective choral group in the high school.[11] By maintaining a selective choral group, higher musical standards may be achieved and the participating singers will benefit from a higher quality of musical experiences. As the school's musical groups provide a "bridge of understanding" between the school and the community, it is highly desirable to develop and maintain a choral group that achieves and maintains high musical standards. The membership will usually consist of eleventh- and twelfth-grade students (juniors and seniors). A selective choral group, to achieve the maximum degree of musical proficiency, should rehearse at least five days a week, Monday through Friday. The most effective rehearsal time is during the morning, since students often become overly fatigued during the afternoon hours.

Small Vocal Ensembles

For particularly talented and interested students, experience in various small ensembles should also be provided. Participation in either an octet or a quartet will provide an outlet for boys who desire male companionship and the opportunity to explore the literature composed and arranged especially for male voices. Participation in a sextet or a triple trio will provide a similar opportunity for the especially talented girls in the school.

---

[11] Although the term *a cappella choir* is still used as a name for mixed choral groups in particular schools, it should be noted that the term is somewhat archaic and a "holdover" from several decades ago when the trend was to perform primarily music *a cappella* (without accompaniment) almost exclusively. Today, the practice is to choose the repertoire for its musical worth and, as a result, conductors generally achieve a reasonable balance between unaccompanied music and music with instrumental accompaniment—that is, with either piano, organ, string, wind, or percussion instruments, or an ensemble of instruments in various combinations.

The mixed ensemble, however, will provide perhaps an even more unique musical experience. Many schools organize a group of "madrigal singers," with a membership usually of about 12 to 16 voices. These groups generally devote themselves to a thorough study of madrigal singing and related types of choral literature. Other schools may organize a show choir, ranging from 16 to 24 voices, devoted to the study and performance of popular, stylized arrangements. Although the latter group is given various names, the title "The Modernaires" is descriptive of the choral music performed (see Chapter 5 on the jazz/show choir). Often the school enrollment and the degree of student interest necessitates the maintenance of both types of small mixed choral ensembles, that is, both a madrigal group and a "jazz" or "show" choir. If only enough students are available for one mixed ensemble, however, the group should study, rehearse, and perform a wider variety of choral literature, rather than devote itself to only one specific type or style of choral music.

Small vocal ensembles should rehearse at least twice weekly. In some cases the singers will find a "free" period during the day in which rehearsals can be scheduled. When this is not possible, rehearsals will necessarily have to be scheduled before or after school hours or during the noon period. The smaller ensembles, such as trios, quartets, sextets, and octets, may be encouraged to schedule, during the evening hours, an additional weekly rehearsal at one of the members' homes. Although the most desirable arrangement would have the director meet with the singers during every rehearsal, his busy schedule may not permit him to do so. Thus these evening rehearsals, if deemed necessary and desirable according to the local situation, may be conducted by one of the more talented student leaders. Such opportunity provides valuable experience for students who may eventually enter teacher training programs.

The Voice Class

The high school voice class is an adjunct of the choral program. It is usually taught by the choral director and may serve as a valuable training ground for student soloists in the advanced choir. Membership in the voice class should be selective and limited to those students who possess at least a reasonable degree of innate vocal and musical ability, and who display a keen interest in developing vocal proficiency. The particular value of the class approach to vocal training lies in the opportunity for singers to observe each other and discuss, as a group, common vocal difficulties. Although private vocal study is highly desirable, it may be financially prohibitive to many students; in addition, the opportunity for valuable group experience does not present itself. Therefore, by meeting the needs of a particularly interested and musically talented group, the high school voice class makes its unique contribution to the balanced vocal music curriculum.

The Music Budget

The cost of educating our children and running our schools has risen almost continually since World War II, and with continuing inflation, the problem is sure to become more and more acute. School administrators, therefore, must necessarily become more watchful of the amount of the budget allotted to each department. Departments not demonstrating a definite need for the funds allotted them are likely to suffer a decrease. Many music educators are especially concerned with the problem because, as their program develops and more students participate in it, additional funds are needed to purchase music and equipment necessary to provide the best musical education for the students. One bright spot, the more students enrolled, the lower the per capita cost.

Among administrators there seems to be a growing interest in a performance type of budget, where the emphasis is upon values received rather than upon only facts and figures. It might, therefore, prove most profitable for the music educator to discuss with his administrator the benefits of music study in terms of its aesthetic, expressive, cultural, personal, social, avocational, and vocational values. Although it will be found that most administrators are familiar with these benefits, it is nevertheless desirable for them to understand the music educator's particular point of view.

It is suggested that music educators demonstrate an interest in matters of budget. They should familiarize themselves with the proper procedures for requisitioning materials and keeping accounts and records. They should set up a system of filing and maintaining music materials, and should demonstrate knowledge of how to repair music. If administrators feel that the music educator is spending money wisely, and if they feel that materials are well cared for, they are more inclined to grant a request for an increase in the music department budget.

After careful planning and estimating of future choral department needs, the director should discuss the budget problem with his administrator, emphasizing the fact that the quality of instruction depends to a great extent upon adequate teaching materials and equipment. A long-term approach to departmental needs is highly recommended. The budget for the approaching school year might be divided into three categories: "Desirable and Helpful," "Highly Desirable," and "Essential and Necessary" for the operation of the program during the ensuing school year. Administrators are generally most appreciative of such a businesslike approach to the budget problem. (See Budget 1.)

Budget 1

CHORAL MUSIC DEPARTMENT

Proposed Budget for the Academic Year _____.

A. *Essential and Necessary Items**   *Amount*

    1. Octavo music (SATB, SSA, TTBB) ... $_____
    2. Music folders .... _____
    3. Music storage boxes .... _____
    4. Choir-robe maintenance and repairs ... _____
    5. Equipment maintenance .... _____
    6. Choral recordings and magnetic tapes .. _____

        Total .... $_____

B. *Highly Desirable Items†*

1. Additional storage cabinets .... $_____
2. Photographs (for publicity purposes) .. _____
3. Additional rehearsal-room risers .... _____
4. Additional chairs (for rehearsal room) _____
5. Additional standing risers (for concerts) _____
6. New bulletin board .... _____

Total .... $_____

C. *Desirable and Helpful Items‡*

1. Film rentals .... $_____
2. New tape-recording equipment .... _____
3. Stereophonic record player .... _____
4. Transportation expenses
   (festivals and contests) .... _____
5. Additional piano (for student practice) _____
6. Visiting conductors' fees .... _____

Total .... $_____

Grand Total .... $_____

* Essential and necessary for operation of the department or activity during the ensuing school year.
† Highly desirable for the future growth of the program.
‡ Desirable and helpful in terms of providing the best educational experiences for the students.

Another approach to the budget problem is simply to list the items under two rather than three categories. Under "Operating Expenses," list the items necessary for the efficient functioning of the department for the ensuing year. Under "Nonrecurring Expenses" (or "Capital Equipment Needs"), list the items that are important to the further development of the program. As the funds for special purchases are not likely to be available in any one year for the acquisition of all special needs, the items in this category should be listed in the order of importance. This will be of considerable assistance to the administrator in making his final budget allotments. Any items that the school is unable to acquire in a particular year may be included on the following year's budget request and perhaps ranked proportionately higher in their order of importance. Sample Budget 2 illustrates this idea.

Budget 2

CHORAL MUSIC DEPARTMENT

Proposed Budget for the Academic Year _____.

A. *Operating Expenses*   *Amount*

    1. Octavo music .... $_____
    2. Music folders .... _____
    3. Music storage boxes .... _____
    4. Choir-robe maintenance .... _____
    5. Equipment maintenance .... _____
    6. Choral recordings and magnetic tapes .. _____
    7. Photographs .... _____
    8. Film rentals .... _____
    9. Transportation expenses .... _____

         Total .... $_____

B. *Nonrecurring Expenses*

    1. Additional chairs (for rehearsal room) $_____
    2. Additional risers .... _____
    3. Additional piano .... _____
    4. Additional storage cabinets .... _____
    5. Choir robe replacements .... _____
    6. New tape-recording equipment .... _____
    7. Stereophonic record player .... _____

         Total .... $_____

         Grand Total .... $_____

Regardless of the type of form used, it has been found helpful to attach to the proposed budget a concise description of each item and the reasons for its need. This information will minimize questions of a general nature and thereby will facilitate the budget conference held between the choral director and the school administrator. Whenever conferences are held with administrators, a businesslike approach to the budget problem will be appreciated by the administrators and will be to the director's advantage. Choral directors should study carefully their groups' needs and be prepared to explain the importance of each item. They should be thoroughly familiar with the exact specifications of each requested item and be able to explain its desirability over other products of a similar nature but lower in cost.

Care of Choral Music

Indexing and Storing

A practical method of indexing and storing choral music has many advantages. It protects the music from unnecessary wear and tear, selections are more easily located, and a much neater appearance is usually created in the rehearsal or storage room. In general, choral directors find one of the following two methods most suitable for their particular situations. Some directors prefer to place each choral selection into a separate 9×12-inch manila filing envelope, and to file the music alphabetically by title in a metal filing cabinet. So that selections may be easily located, the title is placed in the upper left-hand corner of the envelope, along with other pertinent information such as the composer, arranger, voice arrangement, and the number of available copies. For easy reference, these data may also be kept on 3×5-inch cards and maintained in a metal file box.

Other music directors prefer to file their music in 7½×11-inch reinforced cardboard boxes and to place them on conveniently situated shelves. (Boxes are available in 1-, 2-, and 3-inch widths.) Each box is labeled and/or numbered so that selections may be easily located. Again, all pertinent information, as previously described, should be placed on 3×5-inch cards, along with the number of the box in which the music is stored. All cards are filed alphabetically by title in a file box in order that pertinent data or particular selections may be easily located. If so desired, a separate index by composers is oftentimes helpful in quickly locating certain sought selections. Although file boxes are slightly more expensive than manila envelopes, the latter system will be found to be less expensive to maintain. As the music library grows, it will be found slightly less expensive to build additonal shelves for storing music than to purchase additional filing cabinets.

Distribution

Choral directors distribute the music in various ways. Most find it a practical time-saver to insert the music in a folder of some type. Some use a plain 9×12-inch manila filing folder; others use a folder with cloth reinforced edges (8½×11-inch) with flaps that hold the music in place and prevent it from falling out. This type of folder, although a bit more expensive than manila folders, is well worth the investment; it is described in several music distributors' catalogs. Some directors utilize the services of student librarians to distribute the choral folders. Others file the music in a music cabinet near the door, so that each student may pick up a folder as he enters the room (cabinets may be constructed or purchased ready-made for this purpose). Choir members are instructed to leave the music in the same place when they leave the room. This procedure saves the director a great deal of time and energy and is a practice far superior to collecting music haphazardly left about the rehearsal room.

Repair

After choral selections have been removed from the folders and before they are filed, they should be examined carefully and repaired whenever necessary. A special tape, available in various widths and manufactured by the Minnesota Mining and Manufacturing Company, is particularly suitable for edging the backs of torn octavo publications. A special dispenser is available for applying this tape. The same company also manufactures a transparent, nondrying tape designed for use on torn music pages. All these items may be located in various music distributors' catalogs.

Many of the duties just described can be assigned to responsible students. In this way, not only can desirable training be provided younger persons, but also the director can be freed from many time-consuming chores and thus have more time to coordinate and develop the total choral music program.

Selecting Choir Robes

Just what are some of the reasons for wearing choir robes? In the first place, uniform appearance in any organization places emphasis upon the group rather than the individual. It helps to develop pride and a feeling of belonging—a feeling so essential to the success of any organization. Choir robes provide a comparatively cool garment, which may be donned with little effort and in a minimum amount of time. This advantage is especially important when program schedules allow only a limited amount of time for warming up and dressing. In this section we shall provide the directors of school and church choirs with information to facilitate the selection of choir robes.

Color

To obtain individuality, many school directors select robes and accessories in school colors. Two-tone color effects and pleasing color harmony may be achieved through the use of various accessories that can be worn with the choir robe. There are also robes now available that are constructed entirely in one material, but in a combination of two colors.

Many church choir directors purchase robes that blend with the interior decorations of the church. Some time ago, the Protestant church would not select choir robes in any color except black. However, today the trend is to use color in their choir apparel—color that is pleasing and that will blend with the interior of the church.

According to manufacturers, the most popular colors are shades of (1) blue, (2) gold, (3) green, (4) maroon and cardinal, and (5) black. White is sometimes used on special festive occasions such as Christmas and Easter, and also during the summer months. In addition to these colors, a wide range of delicate pastels is now available and is becoming increasingly popular. You may choose from such colors as Desert Gold, Spruce Green, Neptune, Malibu, and Monarch, to name a few.

Style

Styles are available to fit many individual tastes. There are robes designed specifically for children's, intermediate, and adult choirs. After the director determines his needs, he should consult various manufacturers' catalogs before any final decision is made. Upon request, manufacturers will provide detailed pictures, swatches of material, sample robes, and other pertinent information.

Also available are special robes for the director. The director's robe is altered by changing the sleeve construction; this is done by gathering the fullness of the sleeve at the wrist into a cuff. Robes designed in this manner allow the director greater hand visibility and more freedom in his conducting movements.

Fabric

In certain areas or sections of the country in which there is heavy industry, unless the material is specially treated, various chemical gases in the air will affect the robes, causing the color to fade. If one lives in such an area, great care should be taken to determine if the fabric has been treated to prevent fading. Question the manufacturer before making a purchase. The quality of the fabric will determine the price of any given style. The better fabrics wear longer, retain their shape, are more comfortable, have better draping qualities, do not fade, and are less subject to wrinkling. A "wash and wear" fabric for robes is not necessary or practical. Some of the new polyester materials are well-suited for robes; others are not. Check the quality carefully by examining samples.

Yoke

The foundation of any robe is the yoke, and the importance of its construction should not be overlooked. The yoke should be constructed of a substantial material so that it will hold its shape and prevent the body of the robe from drooping. It should be made of a strong, yet lightweight material—lightweight for comfort, but possessing strength so that the body will retain its shape. The yoke shouldn't shrink, and should lie flat when dry-cleaned.

Fluting

The fluting gathers the fullness of the robe over the shoulders and across the back, allowing the robe to hang in attractive folds. It is most desirable to purchase robes that have ample fullness so that large or small persons can wear them.

Size

Choir robes should be purchased in a range of sizes that will fit the average group. If money is available, a few extra robes should be bought, because it may not be possible to purchase the same material in future years to replace damaged robes or to increase the quantity. The mill that manufactures the fabric may discontinue it, and in dyeing new fabrics, it may not be possible to match the shade exactly. There should be at least two inches of hem at the bottom so that the robe may be lengthened if necessary.

Closures

Various companies recommend different kinds of closures. Here are some of the advantages and disadvantages of each: (a) zipper—faster and looks neater; care must be taken that clothes are not snagged; (b) hook and eye—hooks may pull out, causing some gapping; (c) snap placket—snaps may pull out if they are merely tacked on; however, if care is taken they are quite satisfactory; and (d) Velcro—sometimes difficult to align properly and not as serviceable as a zipper.

Care and Repair

When robes are purchased, it is wise to sew in a numeral near the label; robes can then be assigned by number, and choir members are more readily assured of locating their own robes. The director can maintain a list of all the choir members and the robe number that is assigned to each member.

All robes should be treated as one would treat fine clothes. To be protected against moths, they should be stored when not in actual use; they should be kept in a closet, away from light, since light will fade some robes as it will other fabrics. All robes should be dry-cleaned at least once a year, preferably by the same firm. If proper care is taken, choir robes should last at least ten years or more. Money spent for the proper maintenance and upkeep of robes is a wise way in which to protect one's investment.

Topics for Discussion

1 Endeavor to recall, if possible, your personal reactions to hearing an outstanding choral group from a neighboring community. In what way did this experience serve as a means of motivating your own music study?

2 What musical experiences or events in high school made the greatest impression upon you? In your opinion, why did these experiences make such a lasting impression?

3 Why are certain seating arrangements more effective with some choral groups than with others?

4 From a psychological basis, why it is more desirable to schedule music classes every day, rather than, for example, only twice a week?

5 Outline an instructional program in choral music designed to meet the musical and social needs of a specific school or church. What choral groups and ensembles would you organize, and what membership requirements would you specify?

6 In what way is the budget problem related to the scheduling problem?

7 Discuss the types of attire available for various choral groups. Discuss the appropriateness of attire in relation to various types of musical programs and in relation to particular occasions.

8 Utilizing the criteria of purpose, price or cost, and durability, discuss the strengths and weaknesses of essential musical equipment, such as pianos, risers, tape recorders, record players, directors' stands, music folders, music storage cabinets, choir robes (and storage cabinets), and other suitable attire.

9 What supplies and equipment do you consider basic to the effective operation of a balanced choral program?

Selected Readings

Andrews, Frances M., and Clara E. Cockerille, *Your School Music Program.* Englewood Cliffs, N.J.: Prentice-Hall, Inc., 1958, pp. 190–216 and Chapter 16.

Cain, Noble, *Choral Music and Its Practice*. New York: M. Witmark & Sons, 1942. (Chatpers 6, 7, and 8.)

Christy, Van A., *Glee Club and Chorus*. New York: G. Schirmer, Inc., 1940. (Chapters 2 and 3.)

Diercks, Louis H., "The Individual in the Choral Situation," *The NATS Bulletin*, Vol. 17, No. 4, May 15, 1961, p. 7.

Dykema, Peter W., and Karl W. Gehrkens, *The Teaching and Administration of High School Music*. Evanston, Ill.: Summy-Birchard Company, 1941. (Chapters 29 and 30.)

Garretson, Robert L., "Scheduling Choral Programs and Community Relations," *The Choral Journal*. Vol. XX, No. 2, October 1979, pp. 17–19.

Graham, Floyd F., *Public Relations in Music Education*. New York: Exposition Press, 1954. (Chapter 3.)

Klotman, Robert H., *Scheduling Music Classes*. Vienna, Va.: Music Educators National Conference, 1968.

Krone, Max T., *The Chorus and Its Conductor*. Chicago: Neil A. Kjos Music Co., 1945. (Chapters 1 and 2.)

Leeder, Joseph A., and William S. Haynie, *Music Education in the High School*. Englewood Cliffs, N.J.: Prentice-Hall, Inc., 1958 (Chapter 3 and pp. 214–222.)

MENC Committee on Music Rooms and Equipment, Elwyn Carter, Chairman, *Music Buildings, Rooms, and Equipment*. Revised and Enlarged Edition. Vienna, Va.: Music Educators National Conference, 1955.

Snyder, Keith D., *School Music Administration and Supervision*. Second Edition. Boston: Allyn and Bacon, Inc., 1965. (Chapters 7, 8, and 9.)

Sunderman, Lloyd F., *Choral Organization and Administration*. Rockville Centre, N.Y.: Belwin-Mills, Inc., 1954.

———, *Organization of the Church Choir*. Rockville Centre, N.Y.: Belwin-Mills, Inc., 1957. (Chapters 2 and 6.)

Van Bodegraven, Paul, and Harry R. Wilson, *The School Music Conductor*. Minneapolis: Schmitt, Hall & McCreary Co., 1942. (Chapters 10 and 12.)

Wilson, Harry R., *Artistic Choral Singing*. New York: G. Schirmer, Inc., 1959. (Chapter 10.)

———, and Jack L. Lyall, *Building a Church Choir*. Minneapolis: Schmitt, Hall & McCreary Co., 1957. (Chapter 5.)

Songs for Recreational Singing[12]

Introductory Songs

Chumbara (*Sing Again*, No. 103)

Hello! (*Lead a Song*, p. 37)

How D'ye Do (*Songs for Every Purpose*, p. 217)

Laugh Provoker, A (*Songs for Every Purpose*, p. 226)

More We Get Together, The (Tune—Did You Ever See a Lassie?)

Sweetly Sings the Donkey (*Sing Along*, No. 129)

Viva L'Amour (*Singing Time*, No. 79)

Action Songs

Alouette (*Sing Along*, No. 35)

Chiapanecas (*Sing Along*, No. 39)

Daisy Bell (*Sing Along*, No. 9)

Hokey Pokey (*Sing Again*, No. 96)

Little Tom Tinker (*Sing Along*, No. 130)

MacDonald's Farm (*Songs for Every Purpose*, p. 217)

Oh! Susanna (*Songs for Every Purpose*, p. 224)

Paw-Paw Patch (*Sing Again*, No. 100)

She'll Be Comin' Round the Mountain (*Sing Along*, No. 134)

Sweetly Sings the Donkey (*Sing Along*, No. 129)

Rounds and Canons

Alleluia (*Rounds and Canons*, No. 24)

Alphabet, The (*Rounds and Canons*, No. 41)

Are You Sleeping? (*Songs for Every Purpose*, p. 215)

At Summer Morn (*The Ditty Bag*, p. 123)

Bell Doth Toll, The (*Songs for Every Purpose*, p. 23)

Christmas Bells (*Sing Again*, No. 94)

De Bezem (The Broom) (*Songs for Every Purpose*, p. 105)

Dona Nobis Pacem (*Sing Along*, No. 78)

Down in the Valley (*Sing Along*, No. 84)

Early to Bed (*Silver Book*, p. 135)

[12] In organizing a "community sing," it is suggested that at least one song be selected from each of the categories listed.

French Cathedrals (*Sing Together*, p. 101)
Haste Thee Nymph (*Sing Together*, p. 101)
Ifca's Castle (Carl Fischer Octavo, No. 4708)
Kookaburra (*The Ditty Bag*, p. 143)
Like as a Father (Cherubini) (*Sing Again*, No. 69)
Little Tom Tinker (*Sing Along*, No. 130)
Lovely Evening (*Sing Along*, No. 128)
Make New Friends (*The Ditty Bag*, p. 33)
Merrily, Merrily (*Songs for Every Purpose*, p. 11)
Merry Lark, The (*Sing Together*, p. 110)
Morning Comes Stealing (*Sing Along*, No. 45)
Morning Is Come (*Sing Together*, p. 111)
Music Alone Shall Live (Old German) (*Sing Again*, No. 68)
Non Nobis, Domine (William Byrd) (*Sing Again*, No. 70)
Ol' Texas (*Sing Again*, No. 58)
Old Hungarian Round (*Sing Together*, p. 111)
Old King Cole (*Sing Together*, p. 96)
Orchestra, The (*Sing Again*, No. 101)
Reuben and Rachael (*Songs for Every Purpose*, p. 200)
Rise Up, O Flame (Praetorius) (*Sing Together*, p. 11)
Row, Row, Row Your Boat (*Sing Along*, No. 141)
Scotland's Burning (*Songs for Every Purpose*, p. 30)
Sing Together (*Sing Together*, p. 99)
Where Is John? (*The Ditty Bag*, p. 65)
White Coral Bells (*The Ditty Bag*, p. 31)
Willie, Willie Will (Brahms) (*The Ditty Bag*, p. 141)
Wise Old Owl (*Singing Time*, No. 142)

Combined Songs[13]

Are You Sleeping—Three Blind Mice (*Songs for Every Purpose*, pp. 215, 152)
Keep the Home Fires Burning—The Long, Long Trail (*Twice 55*, Nos. 177, 178)
Old Folks at Home—Humoresque (*Singing Time*, pp. 64, 75)
Solomon Levi—The Spanish Cavalier (*Songs for Every Purpose*, pp. 210, 211)
Tipperary—Pack up Your Troubles (Chappell & Co., Inc.)
Yankee Doodle—Dixie (*Songs for Every Purpose*, pp. 229, 238)

---

[13] For a variety of other combined songs, see Frederick Beckman, *Partner Songs*. Boston: Ginn & Company, 1958.

Songs for Harmonizing

All Through the Night (*Songs for Every Purpose*, p. 35)
Annie Laurie (*Sing Along*, No. 53)
Battle Hymn of the Republic (*Songs for Every Purpose*, p. 240)
Carry Me Back to Old Virginny (*Singing Time*, No. 27)
Clementine (*Sing Along*, No. 132)
Down by the Old Mill Stream (Forester Music Publishers)
Down in the Valley (*Sing Along*, No. 84)
Good-bye, My Lover, Good-bye (*Songs for Every Purpose*, p. 191)
Home on the Range (*Sing Along*, No. 30)
In the Evening by the Moonlight (*Singing Time*, No. 62)
I've Been Workin' on the Railroad (*Sing Along*, No. 133)
Jacob's Ladder (*Sing Along*, No. 89)
Little Annie Rooney (*Sing Along*, No. 10)
Lullaby (*The Ditty Bag*, p. 125)
My Bonnie (*Songs for Every Purpose*, p. 215)
Old Folks at Home (*Sing Along*, No. 20)
On Top of Old Smoky (*Mitch Miller Community Song Book*, p. 5)
Standin' in the Need of Prayer (*Singing Time*, No. 120)
Tell Me Why (*Sing Along*, No. 16)

Closing Songs

All Through the Night (*Songs for Every Purpose*, p. 35)
America (*Sing Along*, No. 138)
Auld Lang Syne (*Songs for Every Purpose*, p. 29)
Fare Thee Well (*Sing Together*, p. 12)
God Be with You (*Songs for Every Purpose*, No. 52)
God Bless America (Irving Berlin, Inc.)
Good Night (*Sing Together*, p. 49)
Good Night, Beloved (*Sing Together*, p. 58)
Good Night, Ladies (*Songs for Every Purpose*, p. 200)
Good Night to You All (*Rounds and Canons*, No. 60)
Jacob's Ladder (*Sing Along*, No. 89)
Now the Day Is Over (*Sing Along*, No. 66)
So Long, It's Been Good To Know Ya! (Folkway Music Publishers)

Softly Now the Light of Day (*Silver Book of Songs*, No. 170)
Taps (*Twice 55 Community Songs*, The Brown Book, No. 9)

Community Song Books

Abingdon Song Kit (by James F. Leisy). New York: Abingdon Press, 1957.

Choral Adventures (ed. Ruth Heller). Minneapolis: Schmitt, Hall & McCreary, 1951.

Christmas Caroler's Book in Song and Story (arr. Torstein O. Kramme). Minneapolis: Schmitt, Hall & McCreary, 1935.

Ditty Bag, The (by Janet E. Tobitt). Pleasantville, N.Y.: Janet E. Tobitt, 1946.

Fred Waring Song Book (comp. and ed. Hawley Ades). Delaware Water Gap, Pa.: Shawnee Press, Inc., 1962.

Golden Book of Favorite Songs, The. Minneapolis: Schmitt, Hall & McCreary, 1923.

Good Fellowship Songs. Delaware, Ohio: Cooperative Recreation Service.

Gray Book of Favorite Songs, The. Minneapolis: Schmitt, Hall & McCreary, 1924.

Mitch Miller Community Song Book (compiled and edited by Guy Freedman). New York: Remick Music Corp., 1962.

Noels (a collection of Christmas Carols by Marx and Anne Oberndorfer). Chicago: H. T. Fitzsimons, 1932.

Rounds and Canons (ed. Harry R. Wilson). Minneapolis: Schmitt, Hall & McCreary, 1943.

Silver Book of Songs. Minneapolis: Schmitt, Hall & McCreary, 1935.

Sing Again (arr. Harry R. Wilson). New York: J. J. Robbins, 1952.

Sing Along (arr. Harry R. Wilson). New York: J. J. Robbins, 1948.

Sing Around the Clock (arr. Howard Ross). New York: Charles Hansen Educational Music and Books, Inc., 1955.

Sing Together. New York: Girl Scouts of the U.S.A., 1957.

Singing Time (arr. Ruth Heller and Walter Goodell). Minneapolis: Schmitt, Hall & McCreary, 1952.

Songs for Every Purpose and Occasion. Minneapolis: Schmitt, Hall & McCreary, 1938 (includes 357 songs).

Songs of the Four Seasons (by Harry R. Wilson). New York: Consolidated Music Publishers, 1960.

Songs of the Gay Nineties (ed. Hugo Frey).   New York: J. J. Robbins, 1942.

Songs of Many Nations.   Delaware, Ohio: Cooperative Recreation Service, 1962.

Spirituals (arr. William Stickles).   New York: Charles Hansen Educational Music and Books, Inc., 1946.

Time to Sing: Folio of Community Songs for Every Occasion (arr. G. M. Compagno).   New York: Edw. B. Marks, 1938.

Twice 55 Community Songs (The Brown Book).   Chicago: Summy-Birchard Company, 1957.

Twice 55 Community Songs (The Green Book).   Chicago: Summy-Birchard Company, 1957.

Appendix:

Source Information

Choral Composers

This chronological list does not presume to be complete, but it does include most of the major contributors to choral literature from approximately 1400 to the present. Although some composers may be known as well or perhaps even better for compositions other than choral music, all have made contributions significant enough to justify inclusion herein. This list was developed primarily from the choral compositions listed in the Appendix. For representative compositions of these composers, see lists under sections titled Choral Octavo Publications, Choral Collections, and Extended Choral Works.

Pre-Renaissance (c. 1200–1400)

Perotin	b. France	c. 1183–c. 1238
(Perotinus Magnus)		
Adam de la Halle	b. Arras, France	c. 1240–1287
Guillaume de Machaut	b. France	c. 1304–1377

Renaissance Period (c. 1400–1600)

John Dunstable	b. Dunstable, England	c. 1370–1453
Gilles Binchois	b. Mons, Belgium	c. 1400–1460
Guillaume Dufay	b. Hainaut, Belgium	c. 1400–1474
Johannes Okeghem	b. East Flanders, Belgium	c. 1430–1495
Pierre de La Rue	b. Tournai, Belgium	c. 1430–1518
Heinrich Isaac	b. Brabant, Belgium	c. 1450–1517
Josquin Després	b. Hainaut, Belgium	c. 1450–1521
Jacob Obrecht	b. Berg-op-Zoom, Netherlands	c. 1452–1505
Loyset Compère	b. ?	c. 1455–1518
Jean Mouton	b. Haut-Wignes, France	c. 1470–1522
Antoine Brumel	b. Flanders	c. 1475–1520
Martin Luther	b. Eislenben, Germany	1483–1546
Clément Janequin	b. Châtellerault, France	c. 1485–1560
Ludwig Senfl	b. Zurich, Switzerland	c. 1490–c. 1543
Costanzo Festa	b. Rome, Italy	c. 1490–1545
Nicolas Gombert	b. Flanders	c. 1490–1556
Thomas Créquillon	b. Ghent, Belgium	?–1557
Claudin de Sermisy	b. France	c. 1490–1562
Passereau	Early 16th-century French composer	?–?
Adrian Willaert	b. Bruges, Belgium	c. 1490–1562
Robert Carver	b. Scotland	c. 1491–c. 1546
Johann Walther	b. Kahler, Thuringia	1496–1570
Cristóbal Morales	b. Seville, Spain	c. 1500–1553
Christopher Tye	b. England	c. 1500–c. 1572
Jacob Arcadelt	b. Liège, Belgium	c. 1505–1560

Claude Goudimel	b. Besançon, France	c. 1505–1572
Mattheus Le Maistre	b. near Liège, Belgium	c. 1505–1577
Thomas Tallis	b. Leicestershire (?), England	c. 1505–1585
Jacobus Clemens	b. Ypres, Belgium	c. 1510–1556
Antonio Scandello	b. Brescia, Italy	1517–1580
Noé Faignient	b. Flanders, Belgium	?–1595
Hubert Waelvant	b. Tongerloo, Belgium	c. 1517–1595
Andrea Gabrieli	b. Venice, Italy	c. 1520–1586
Philippe de Monte	b. Mons, Belgium	1521–1603
Fernando Franco	b. La Serena, Mexico	c. 1525–1585
Giovanni Pierluigi da Palestrina	b. Palestrina, Italy	c. 1525–1594
Claude Le Jeune	b. Valenciennes, France	1528–1600
Richard Farrant	b. England	c. 1530–1581
Guillaume Costeley	b. Pont-Audemer, France	1531–1606
Orlando di Lasso	b. Mons, Belgium	c. 1532–1594
Cornelius Freundt	b. Plauen, Germany	1535–1591
Giaches de Wert	b. Weert, Netherlands	c. 1535–1596
Andries Pevernage	b. Courtrai, Belgium	1543–1591
William Byrd	b. Lincolnshire (?), England	c. 1543–1623
Marco Antonio Ingegneri	b. Verona, Italy	1545–1592
Giovanni Maria Nanino	b. Tivoli, Italy	1545–1607
François-Eustache Du Caurroy	b. Beauvais, France	1549–1609
Tomás Luis de Victoria	b. Avila, Spain	c. 1549–1611
Francesco Suriano	b. Soriano, Italy	1549–c. 1621
Jacobus Gallus (Jacob Handl)	b. Reifnitz, Austria (now Yugoslavia)	1550–1591
Orazio Vecchi	b. Modena, Italy	c. 1550–1605
Giovanni Macque	b. Valenciennes, France	c. 1550–1614
Luca Marenzio	b. Coccaglio, Italy	1553–1599
Johannes Eccard	b. Mühlhausen, Germany	1553–1611
Bartholomeus Gesius	b. Müncheberg, Germany	c. 1555–1613
Sethus Calvisius	b. Gorsleben, Germany	1556–1615
Giovanni Gastoldi	b. Caravaggio, Italy	c. 1556–1622
Thomas Morley	b. England	1557–1602
Jacques Mauduit	b. Paris, France	1557–1627
Giovanni Croce	b. Chioggia, Italy	c. 1560–1609
Don Carlo Gesualdo	b. Naples, Italy	c. 1560–1613
Felice Anerio	b. Rome, Italy	c. 1560–1614
Melchior Vulpius	b. Wasungen, Germany	c. 1560–1615
Hieronymus Prateorius	b. Hamburg, Germany	1560–1629
Peter Philips	b. England	c. 1561–1628
Jacobo Peri	b. Florence, Italy	c. 1561–1633
Jan Pieterszoon Sweelinck	b. Deventer (or Amsterdam), Netherlands	1562–1621
John Dowland	b. Ireland, possibly in County Dublin	c. 1562–1626
John Bull	b. Somersetshire, England	c. 1562–1628

Francis Pilkington	b. England	c. 1562–1638
Gregor Aichinger	b. Regensburg, Germany	1564–1628
Ludocico da Viadana	b. Viadana, Italy	1564–1645
Michael Cavendish	b. England	c. 1565–1628
Adriano Banchieri	b. Bologna, Italy	1568–1634
Paul Peurl	b. Austria	c. 1570–1624
Thomas Tomkins	b. St. David's, England	c. 1572–1656
John Wilbye	b. Diss, England	1574–1638
Thomas Weelkes	b. England	c. 1575–1623
Melchior Franck	b. Zittau, Germany	c. 1579–1639
Michael East	b. London, England	c. 1580–c. 1648
Thomas Ford	b. England	c. 1580–1648
Orlando Gibbons	b. Oxford, England	1583–1625
Adrian Batten	b. London, England	c. 1585–1637

Baroque Period (c. 1600–1750)

Giulio Caccini	b. Rome, Italy	c. 1546–1618
Giovanni Gabrieli	b. Venice, Italy	c. 1557–1612
Hans Leo Hassler	b. Nuremberg, Germany	1564–1612
Claudio Monteverdi	b. Cremona, Italy	1567–1643
Michael Praetorius	b. Kreuzberg, Germany	c. 1571–1621
Richard Deering	b. Kent, England	c. 1580–c. 1630
Gregorio Allegri	b. Rome, Italy	1582–1652
Melchior Teschner	b. Fraustadt, Austria	1584–1635
Heinrich Schütz	b. Kostritz, Germany	1585–1672
Johann Hermann Schein	b. Grünhain, Germany	1586–1630
Salamone Rossi	b. Mantua, Italy	c. 1587–c. 1630
Samuel Scheidt	b. Halle, Germany	1587–1654
Thomas Ravenscroft	b. England	c. 1590–c. 1633
Johann Cruger	b. Grossbreece, Germany	1598–1662
Pier Francesco Cavalli	b. Crema, Italy	1602–1676
Orazio Benevoli	b. Rome, Italy	c. 1605–1672
Giacomo Carissimi	b. Marino, Italy	c. 1605–1674
Andreas Hammerschmidt	b. Brüx, Bohemia	1612–1675
Guillaume Bouzignac	Early 17th-century French composer	?–?
Franz Tunder	b. Burg auf Fehmarn, Germany	c. 1614–1667
Matthew Locke	b. Exeter, England	c. 1630–1677
George Jeffries	b. England	?–1685
Jean-Baptiste Lully	b. Florence, Italy	1632–1687
Marc-Antoine Charpentier	b. Paris, France	c. 1634–1704
Dietrich Buxtehude	b. Helsingør, Denmark	c. 1637–1707
Johann Christoph Bach	b. Erfurt, Germany	c. 1642–1703
Johann Wolfgang Franck	b. Unterschwaningen, Germany	1644–c. 1710
Pelham Humfrey	b. England	1647–1674
Michael Wise	b. Salisbury, England	c. 1648–1687
Johann Michael Bach	b. Arnstadt, Germany	c. 1648–1694
John Blow	b. Newark-on-Trent, England	1649–1708

Johann Pachelbel	b. Nuremberg, Germany	1653–1707
Philipp Heinrich Erlebach	b. Esens, Germany	1657–1714
Giuseppe Pitoni[1]	h. Rieti, Italy	1657–1743
Henry Purcell	b. London, England	1659–1695
Alessandro Scarlatti	b. Palermo, Italy	1660–1725
André Campra	b. Aix, France	1660–1744
Giacomo Antonio Perti	b. Crevalcore, Italy	1661–1756
Antonio Lotti	b. Venice, Italy	1667–1740
François Couperin	b. Paris, France	c. 1668–1733
Antonio Vivaldi	b. Venice, Italy	c. 1669–1741
Antonio Caldara	b. Venice, Italy	1670–1736
D. Pompeo Canniciari	b. Rome, Italy	c. 1670–1744
William Croft	b. Nether Ettington, England	c. 1678–1727
Jean-Philippe Rameau	b. Dijon, France	1683–1764
Bohuslav Cernohorsky	b. Nimburg, Czechoslovakia	1684–1742
Francesco Durante	b. Frattamaggiore, Italy	c. 1684–1755
Johann Sebastian Bach	b. Eisenach, Germany	1685–1750
George Friedrich Handel	b. Halle, Germany	1685–1759
Benedetto Marcello	b. Venice, Italy	c. 1686–1739
Niccola Antonio Porpora	b. Naples, Italy	1686–1768
Johan Helmich Roman	b. Stockholm, Sweden	c. 1694–1758
Georg Gottfried Wagner	b. Mühlberg, Germany	c. 1698–1756
Johann Ernst Eberlin	b. Jettingen, Germany	1702–1762
Karl Heinrich Graun	b. Wahrenbrück, Germany	c. 1704–1759
Giovanni Battista Pergolesi	b. Jesi, Italy	1710–1736
Thomas Arne	b. London, England	1710–1778

Classic Period (1750–1820)

Wilhelm Friedemann Bach	b. Weimar, Germany	1710–1784
Gottfried August Homilius	b. Rosenthal, Germany	1714–1785
Christoph Willibald Gluck	b. Erasbach, Germany	1714–1787
Karl Philipp Emanuel Bach	b. Weimar, Germany	c. 1714–1788
Johann Heinrich Rolle	b. Quedlinburg, Germany	1716–1785
Johann Christoph Altnikol	b. Bevna, Silesia	1719–1759
Johann Ernst Bach	b. Eisenach, Germany	1722–1777
Christian Friedrich Gregor	b. Dirsdorf, Germany	1723–1801
Johann Adam Hiller	b. Wendisch-Ossog, Germany	1728–1804
Johann C. Geisler	b. Germany	1729–1815
Johann C. F. Bach	b. Leipzig, Germany	1732–1795
Franz Joseph Haydn	b. Rohrau-on-the-Leitha, Austria	1732–1809
Michael Haydn	b. Rohrau, Austria	1737–1806
Carl Michael Bellman	b. Stockholm, Sweden	1740–1795
Quirino Gasparini	b. Bergamasco, Italy	?–1778
William Billings	b. Boston, Massachusetts	1746–1800

[1] Although Pitoni lived during the Baroque period, he was of the Roman school, which rejected the styles and forms of Baroque music and directed their efforts toward composing liturgical music in the style of Palestrina.

324 APPENDIX: SOURCE INFORMATION

Johann Friedrich Peter	b.	Heerendijk, Holland	1746–1813
Andrew Law	b.	Milford, Connecticut	1749–1821
Dimitri S. Bortniansky	b.	Glukhov, Russia	1751–1825
Jacob French		Early American composer	1754–18??
Wolfgang Amadeus Mozart	b.	Salzburg, Austria	1756–1791
Luigi Cherubini	b.	Florence, Italy	1760–1842
Joseph Eybler	b.	Schwechat (near Vienna), Austria	1764–1846
Thomas Attwood	b.	London, England	1765–1838
John Wall Callcott	b.	London, England	1766–1821
Ludwig van Beethoven	b.	Bonn, Germany	1770–1827

Romantic Period (1800–1900)

Ignaz von Seyfried	b.	Vienna, Austria	1776–1841
Johann Kaspar Aiblinger	b.	Wasserburg, Germany	1779–1867
Konradin Kreutzer	b.	Messkirch, Germany	1780–1849
Konrad Kocher	b.	Ditzinger, Germany	1786–1872
Gioacchino Rossini	b.	Pesaro, Italy	1792–1868
Franz Schubert	b.	Lichtenthal, Austria	1797–1828
Alexis F. Lvov	b.	Reval, Russia	1798–1870
Hector Berlioz	b.	Côte-Saint-André, France	1803–1869
Felix Mendelssohn	b.	Hamburg, Germany	1809–1847
Robert Schumann	b.	Zwickau, Germany	1810–1856
Samuel Sebastian Wesley	b.	London, England	1810–1876
Franz Liszt	b.	Raiding, Hungary	1811–1886
Richard Wagner	b.	Leipzig, Germany	1813–1883
Giuseppe Verdi	b.	Le Roncole, Italy	1813–1901
Robert Franz	b.	Halle, Germany	1815–1892
Charles François Gounod	b.	Paris, France	1818–1893
Jacques Offenbach	b.	Cologne, France	1819–1880
Franz Abt	b.	Eilenburg, Germany	1819–1885
Louis Lewandowski	b.	Wreschen (near Posen), Poland	1821–1904
César Franck	b.	Liège, Belgium	1822–1890
Peter Cornelius	b.	Mainz, Germany	1824–1874
Anton Bruckner	b.	Ansfelden, Austria	1824–1896
Johann Strauss (Jr.)	b.	Vienna, Austria	1825–1899
Stephen Collins Foster	b.	Pittsburgh, Pennsylvania	1826–1864
François Auguste Gevaert	b.	Huysse, Belgium	1828–1908
Johann von Herbeck	b.	Vienna, Austria	1831–1877
August Soderman	b.	Stockholm, Sweden	1832–1876
Alexander Borodin	b.	St. Petersburg, Russia	1833–1887
Johannes Brahms	b.	Hamburg, Germany	1833–1897
César Antonovitch Cui	b.	Vilna, Russia	1835–1918
Camille Saint-Saëns	b.	Paris, France	1835–1921
John Farmer	b.	Nottingham, England	1836–1901
Mily A. Balakirev	b.	Nizhny-Novgorod, Russia	1837–1910
Alfred Robert Gaul	b.	Norwich, England	1837–1913
Theodore Dubois	b.	Rosnay, France	1837–1924
Georges Bizet	b.	Paris, France	1838–1875

Modest P. Moussorgsky	b. Karevo, Russia	1839–1881
Peter Ilich Tchaikovsky	b. Kamsko-Votkinsk, Russia	1840–1893
John Stainer	b. London, England	1840–1901
Antonin Dvořák	b. Mühlhausen, Czechoslovakia	1841–1904
Arthur Sullivan	b. London, England	1842–1900
Edvard Grieg	b. Bergen, Norway	1843–1907
Herman Schroeder	b. Quedlinburg, Germany	1843–1909
Nikolai A. Rimsky-Korsakov	b. Tikhvin, Russia	1844–1908
Gabriel Urbain Fauré	b. Pamiers, France	1845–1924
Alexander Arkhangelsky	b. Penza, Russia	1846–1924
Gustav Schreck	b. Zeulenroda, Germany	1849–1918
Vincent D'Indy	b. Paris, France	1851–1931
Hugo Jungst	b. Dresden, Germany	1853–1923
Alexander A. Kopylov	b. St. Petersburg, Russia	1854–1911
Engelbert Humperdinck	b. Siegburg, Germany	1854–1921
Leos Janáček	b. Hukvaldy, Czechoslovakia	1854–1928
Stevan S. Mokranjac	b. Negotin, Yugoslavia	1855–1914
Sergei I. Taneyev	b. Vladimir, Russia	1856–1915
Alexander Kastalsky	b. Moscow, Russia	1856–1926
Edward Elgar	b. Broadheath, England	1857–1934
Reginald De Koven	b. Middletown, Connecticut	1859–1920
Mikhail M. Ippolitov-Ivanov	b. Gatchina, Russia	1859–1935
Edward MacDowell	b. New York, New York	1861–1908
Horatio Parker	b. Auburndale, Massachusetts	1863–1919
Pietro Mascagni	b. Leghorn, Italy	1863–1945
Richard Strauss	b. Munich, Germany	1864–1949
Alexander T. Gretchaninov	b. Moscow, Russia	1864–1956
Jean Sibelius	b. Tavastehus, Finland	1865–1957
Vassili S. Kalinnikov	b. Voin, Russia	1866–1901
Enrique Granados	b. Lérida, Spain	1867–1916
Granville Bantock	b. London, England	1868–1946
Franz Lehar	b. Komorn, Hungary	1870–1948
Henry Hadley	b. Somerville, Massachusetts	1871–1937
F. Melius Christiansen	b. Eidsvold, Norway	1871–1955
Max Reger	b. Brand, Germany	1873–1916
Sergei V. Rachmaninoff	b. Oneg, Russia	1873–1943
Hugh S. Roberton	b. Glasgow, Scotland	1874–1952
Samuel Coleridge-Taylor	b. London, England	1875–1912
Nikolai D. Leontovich	b. Monastirsh, Russia	1877–1921
Paul G. Tschesnokov	b. Vladimir, Russia	1877–1921
Jean-Baptiste Faure	b. Mouline, France	1800–1914

Modern Period (1890 to Present)

Claude Debussy	b. St. Germain-en-Laye, France	1862–1918
Frederick Delius	b. Bradford, England	1862–1934
Erik Satie	b. Honfleur, France	1866–1925
Ralph Vaughan Williams	b. Down Ampney, England	1872–1958

Gustav von Holst	b. Cheltenham, England	1874–1934
Arnold Schoenberg	b. Vienna, Austria	1874–1951
Paul Pierné	b. Metz, France	1874–1952
Charles Edward Ives	b. Danbury, Connecticut	1874–1954
Maurice Ravel	b. Ciboure, France	1875–1937
Martin Shaw	b. London, England	1875–1958
Ernest Bloch	b. Geneva, Switzerland	1880–1959
Healey Willan	b. Balham, England	1880–1968
Béla Bartók	b. Nagy Szent Miklós, Rumania	1881–1945
Zoltán Kodály	b. Kecskemet, Hungary	1882–1967
Igor Stravinsky	b. Oranienbaum, Russia	1882–1971
Anton Webern	b. Vienna, Austria	1883–1945
Marcel Dupré	b. Rouen, France	1886–1971
Konstantin N. Shvedov	b. Moscow, Russia	1886–
Norris Lindsay Norden	b. Philadelphia, Pennsylvania	1887–1956
Heitor Villa-Lobos	b. Rio de Janeiro, Brazil	1887–1959
Ernst Toch	b. Vienna, Austria	1887–1964
Božidar Sirola	b. Zakanj, Yugoslavia	1889–1956
Joseph W. Clokey	b. New Albany, Indiana	1890–1960
Heinrich Lemacher	b. Solingen, Germany	1891–1966
Arthur Honegger	b. Le Havre, France	1892–1955
Felix Labunski	b. Ksawerynów, Poland	1892–
Darius Milhaud	b. Aix-en-Provence, France	1892–1974
Carl F. Mueller	b. Sheboygan, Wisconsin	1892–
John Jacob Niles	b. Louisville, Kentucky	1892–
Bernard Rogers	b. New York, New York	1893–1968
Peter Warlock (Philip Heseltine)	b. London, England	1894–1930
Walter Piston	b. Rockland, Maine	1894–1976
Paul Hindemith	b. Hanau, Germany	1895–1963
Leo Sowerby	b. Grand Rapids, Michigan	1895–1968
Albert Hay Malotte	b. Philadelphia, Pennsylvania	1895–1964
Carl Orff	b. Munich, Germany	1895–
Richard Kountz	b. Pittsburgh, Pennsylvania	1896–1950
Howard Hanson	b. Wahoo, Nebraska	1896–
Virgil Thomson	b. Kansas City, Missouri	1896–
Henry Cowell	b. Menlo Park, California	1897–1965
Alexander Tansman	b. Lodz, Poland	1897–
Roy Harris	b. Lincoln County, Oklahoma	1898–1979
Hugh Ross	b. Langport, England	1898–
Francis Poulenc	b. Paris, France	1899–1963
Carlos Chávez	b. Mexico City, Mexico	1899–1978
Alexander Tcherepnin	b. St. Petersburg, Russia	1899–1977
Randall Thompson	b. New York, New York	1899–
George Antheil	b. Trenton, New Jersey	1900–1959
Aaron Copland	b. Brooklyn, New York	1900–
Otto Luening	b. Milwaukee, Wisconsin	1900–
Harry Robert Wilson	b. Salina, Kansas	1901–1968
Jean Berger	b. Hamm, Germany	1901–
Olaf C. Christiansen	b. Minneapolis, Minnesota	1901–

Edmund Rubbra	b. Northampton, England	1901–
Maurice Duruflé	b. Louviers, France	1902–
Jenö Takács	b. Siegendorf, Austria	1902–
William Walton	b. Oldham, England	1902–
Paul Creston	b. New York, New York	1906–
Normand Lockwood	b. New York, New York	1906–
Dmitri Shostakovitch	b. St. Petersburg, Russia	1906–1975
Miklos Rozsa	b. Budapest, Hungary	1907–
Hugo Distler	b. Nuremberg, Germany	1908–1942
Halsey Stevens	b. Scott, New York	c. 1908–
Samuel Barber	b. West Chester, Pennsylvania	1910–
Julius Chajes	b. Lwow, Poland	1910–
William Howard Schuman	b. New York, New York	1910–
Alan Hovhaness	b. Somerville, Massachusetts	1911–
Gian Carlo Menotti	b. Cadegliano, Italy	1911–
Franz Reizenstein	b. Nuremberg, Germany	1911–1968
Benjamin Britten	b. Lowestoft, England	1913–1976
Norman Dello Joio	b. New York, New York	1913–
Jan Meyerowitz	b. Breslau, Germany	1913–
Gardner Read	b. Evanston, Illinois	1913–
Irving Fine	b. Boston, Massachusetts	1914–1962
Cecil Effinger	b. Colorado Springs, Colorado	1914–
Knut Nystedt	b. Oslo, Norway	1915–
Vincent Persichetti	b. Philadelphia, Pennsylvania	1915–
Gordon Binkerd	b. Lynch, Nebraska	1916–
Houston Bright	b. Midland, Texas	1916–1970
Alberto Ginastera	b. Buenos Aires, Argentina	1916–
Scott Huston	b. Tacoma, Washington	1916–
Leonard Bernstein	b. Lawrence, Massachusetts	1918–
Vaclav Nelhybel	b. Czechoslovakia	1919–
Paul Fetler	b. Philadelphia, Pennsylvania	1920–
William Bergsma	b. Oakland, California	1921–
Lloyd Pfautsch	b. Washington, Missouri	1921–
Lukas Foss	b. Berlin, Germany	1922–
Anton Heiller	b. Vienna, Austria	1923–1979
Daniel Pinkham	b. Lynn, Massachusetts	1923–
Ned Rorem	b. Richmond, Indiana	1923–
Carlisle Floyd	b. Latta, South Carolina	1926–
Arnold Freed	b. New York, New York	1926–
Dominick Argento	b. York, Pennsylvania	1927–
Emma Lou Diemer	b. Kansas City, Missouri	1927–
Donald Erb	b. Youngstown, Ohio	1927–
Ron Nelson	b. Joliet, Illinois	1929–
Richard Felciano	b. Santa Rosa, California	1930–
Gilbert Trythall	b. Knoxville, Tennessee	1930–
Krzysztof Penderecki	b. Debiça, Poland	1933–
Nicolas Roussakis	b. Athens, Greece	1934–
Michael Hennigan	b. The Dalles, Oregon	1936–
James E. McCray	b. Kankakee, Illinois	1938–

Choral Octavo Publications

The octavo publications in this appendix have been included because they are particularly suitable for nonprofessional choral groups. SAB publications are included for junior high school choruses; also listed are SSA and TTBB publications that are particularly appropriate for high school as well as college glee clubs. SATB publications have been included for use with high school, college or university, church, and community choirs and choruses. In addition, there are listed selections that are appropriate for chorus and band and/or orchestra.

Because of the comparatively large number of publications included for use with mixed voices (SATB), all the music below is listed under various categories so that directors may easily locate certain sought selections. These categories are: "Christmas," "Easter and Lent," "Folk Songs and Spirituals," "Special Occasions," "General: Sacred and Secular," "Music with Electronic Tape," "Music with Nonconventional Notation," and "Music for Jazz/Show Choirs." For the other voice classifications (SAB, SSA, TTBB), publications are included under three categories: "Sacred," "Secular," and "Folk Songs and Spirituals."

Following the title, composer, and/or arranger, the publisher and catalog number are given. This information is provided to facilitate the ordering of music. Since the director will wish to know if the selection is to be performed *a cappella* or with accompaniment, this information is also provided. All publications have been graded according to difficulty, using the following terms: Easy, Moderately easy, Medium, Moderately difficult, and Difficult. Also indicated are those publications having incidental solos. Prices have not been included since they are subject to change. It is suggested that current prices be requested from local dealers immediately prior to placing an order; in this way, both billing and budgeting problems may be minimized. In selecting music, it is suggested that directors obtain for examination purposes single copies of particular octavo selections from the publisher or their local dealer, whichever is most convenient. The lists below provide a helpful starting point, but only through careful analysis of each selection in relation to the needs of a specific choral group will the most effective programming be achieved.

Publications for Mixed Voices (SATB)

Christmas (Sacred and Secular)

And the Trees Do Moan (Carol of the Mountain Whites)—arr. Gaul. Oliver Ditson No. 332. Optional accompaniment. Moderately easy.

Angelus Ad Pastores Ait—Gabrieli. C. F. Peters No. 5930. Two choirs—12 parts. Optional accompaniment. Difficult.

As Dew in Aprille (from *A Ceremony of Carols*)—Britten, arr. Harrison. Boosey & Hawkes No. 1829. Accompanied. Medium.

Behold a Star from Jacob Shining—Mendelssohn, arr. Davison. E. C. Schirmer No. 1683. Organ accompaniment. Medium.

Birds and the Christ Child, The (Czechoslovakian carol)—arr. Krone. Carl Fischer No. CM 4612. *A cappella.* Easy.

Born Today (Hodie Christus Natus Est)—Sweelinck. B. F. Wood No. 291. Accompanied. Moderately difficult.

Boy Was Born, A—Britten. Oxford No. X92. *A cappella.* Moderately easy.

Break Forth, O Beauteous Heavenly Light—J. S. Bach. Oliver Ditson No. 13744. Accompanied. Easy.

Carol of the Bells (Ukrainian carol; secular)—Leontovich, arr. Wilhousky. Carl Fischer No. CM 4604. *A cappella.* Easy.

Carol of the Birds (traditional French Christmas carol)—arr. Cain. Schmitt, Hall & McCreary No. 1507. Optional accompaniment. Moderately easy.

Carol of the Drum (Czech carol)—arr. Davis. B. F. Wood No. 568. Accompanied. Moderately easy.

Carol of the Italian Pipers (traditional carol)—arr. Zgodava. Shawnee Press No. A-967. Optional accompaniment. Moderately easy.

Carol of the Pifferari (old Neopolitan Christmas air)—arr. Christy. Belwin-Mills No. 2190. *A cappella.* Easy.

Carol of the Russian Children (White Russian carol)—arr. Gaul. G. Schirmer No. 6770. Optional accompaniment. Moderately easy.

Chocolate Burro, The (Mexican carol)—arr. Ringwald. Shawnee Press No. A-1318. Piano accompaniment. Moderately easy.

Christmas Carol, A (Hungarian traditional tune)—arr. Kodaly. Oxford No. 84.091. *A cappella.* Moderately easy.

Christmas Gift—Hairston. Bourne No. S1033. Piano accompaniment. Moderately easy.

Clear and Calm Was the Holy Night—Nikolsky, arr. Gnotov. Witmark No. 5-W2860. *A cappella.* Medium.

Fanfare for Christmas Day—Shaw. G. Schirmer No. 8745. Optional organ accompaniment. Moderately easy.

Fum, Fum, Fum (Catalonian carol)—arr. Parker and Shaw. G. Schirmer No. 10182. *A cappella.* Medium.

Gentle Mary and Her Child (Finnish folk melody)—arr. Lundquist. Elkan-Vogel No. 1152. *A cappella.* Easy.

Glory to God in the Highest—Pergolesi. Wood No. 289. Organ accompaniment. Moderately difficult.

Gloucestershire Wassail (traditional old English yule song)—arr. Scott. Shawnee Press No. A45. Accompanied. Bass or alto solo. Medium.

Go Tell it on the Mountain (Christmas spiritual)—arr. Work. Galaxy No. 1532. *A cappella.* Soprano and tenor solos. Medium.

God Rest You Merry, Gentlemen (old English Christmas carol)—arr. Stevens. Pro Art No. 1420. Accompanied. Easy.

Good Christian Men, Rejoice (traditional German)—arr. Parker and Shaw. G. Schirmer No. 10183. *A cappella.* Moderately easy.

Hawaiian Lullaby—Sargent. Oxford No. X85. *A cappella.* Medium.

He Is Born (Il est né)—arr. Roger Wagner. Lawson-Gould No. 663. *A cappella.* Easy.

330 APPENDIX: SOURCE INFORMATION

Here 'Mid the Cattle (Alsatian carol)—arr. Butler. Carl Fischer No. CM8065. Piano or organ accompaniment. Baritone solo. Moderately easy.

Holly and the Ivy, The (traditional English)—arr. Parker & Shaw. G. Schirmer No. 10187. *A cappella.* Moderately easy.

Holy Child, The (Puerto Rican carol)—arr. Hruby. Pro Art No. 2687. Accompanied. Easy.

How unto Bethlehem (traditional Italian)—arr. Parker and Shaw. G. Schirmer No. 10194. *A cappella.* Moderately easy.

I Heard An Angel—Krenek. Rongwen No. 3540. *A cappella.* Medium.

I Saw Three Ships (traditional English)—arr. Parker and Shaw. G. Schirmer No. 10188. *A cappella.* Moderately easy.

I Wonder As I Wander (Appalachian carol)—arr. Niles and Horton. G. Schirmer No. 8708. Optional accompaniment. Soprano or tenor solo. Medium.

In Fields Not Far from Bethlehem (Austrian carol)—arr. Ehret. Elkan-Vogel No. 362-03117. Accompanied. Moderately easy.

Infant Sweet and Gentle, An (Polish carol)—arr. Ehret. Presser No. 312-40765. Accompanied. Moderately easy.

Jesus Ahatonhia (Huron Indian carol)—arr. Schillio. G. Schirmer No. 12050. Piano accompaniment. Moderately easy.

Jesus' Christmas Lullaby (Bohemian folk song)—arr. Ehret. Elkan-Vogel No. 1140. Accompanied. Moderately easy.

Jesus, Jesus, Rest Your Head (Appalachian carol)—arr. Niles and Warrell. G. Schirmer No. 8302. *A cappella.* Moderately easy.

Joseph Dear, Oh Joseph Mild—Calvisius. Associated No. A-396. *A cappella.* Medium.

Let Heaven Rejoice and Sing (German carol)—arr. Ehret. Sam Fox No. CC7. Accompanied. Easy.

Lo, How a Rose E'er Blooming—Praetorius. G. Schirmer No. 2484. *A cappella.* Easy.

Lost in the Night (Finnish folk melody)—arr. F. M. Christiansen. Augsburg No. 119. *A cappella.* Soprano solo. Moderately difficult.

Mary Had a Baby—William L. Dawson. Tuskegee No. 118. *A cappella.* Soprano solo. Medium.

Masters in This Hall (traditional French)—arr. Parker and Shaw. G. Schirmer No. 10192. *A cappella.* Medium.

O Filii et Filiae—Leisring, arr. Row. R. D. Row No. 283. *A cappella.* Medium.

O Magnum Mysterium (O Wondrous Nativity)—Vittoria. G. Schirmer No. 7626. *A cappella.* Medium.

O Sanctissima (Sicilian folk melody)—arr. Parker and Shaw. G. Schirmer No. 10194. *A cappella.* Medium.

Old Polish Christmas Carol—arr. Liszniewski. Huntzinger No. 4049. *A cappella.* Easy.

Our Day of Joy Is Here Again (Swedish folk melody)—arr. Lundquist. Elkan-Vogel No. 1151. *A cappella.* Easy.

Quem Vidistis Pastores? (Shepherds, Tell Us Your Story)—arr. Felis. Edw. B. Marks No. 4491. Optional accompaniment. Medium.

Rocking (traditional Czech carol)—arr. Cashmore. Oxford No. X 33. *A cappella.* Medium.

Saviour Is Born, The (Austrian carol)—arr. Warner. Summy-Birchard No. 1578. Accompanied. Easy.

Shepherds All, and Shepherdesses (Allon, gay, gay)—Costeley. Oxford No. OCS 1667. *A cappella.* Medium.

Shepherds' Chorus (from *Amahl and the Night Visitors*)—Menotti. G. Schirmer No. 10801. Accompanied. Soprano and bass solos. Medium.

Silent Night—arr. Sargent. Oxford No. OCS 876. *A cappella.* Moderately easy.

Sleep in Peace, O Heavenly Child—Michael Haydn. G. Schirmer No. 11043. Accompanied. Moderately easy.

Slumber Song of the Infant Jesus, The—Gevaert. E. C. Schirmer No. 1163. *A cappella.* Easy.

So Blest a Sight (English traditional)—arr. Parker and Shaw. G. Schirmer No. 10196. *A cappella.* Moderately easy.

Songs of Praise the Angels Sang (Swedish folk melody)—arr. Lundquist. Elkan-Vogel No. 1145. *A cappella.* Easy.

Still, Still, Still—Luboff. Walton No. 3003. Accompanied. Easy.

Sweet Mary Tends Her New-Born Son (German carol)—arr. Ehret. Elkan-Vogel No. 362-03116. Accompanied. Medium.

There Shall a Star from Jacob—Mendelssohn. Carl Fischer No. CM 6228. Accompanied. Medium.

This Little Babe (from *A Ceremony of Carols*)—Britten, arr. Harrison. Boosey & Hawkes No. 1830. Harp or piano accompaniment. Moderately easy.

Three Far-Eastern Carols—Sargent. Oxford No. X73. *A cappella.* Moderately easy.

Three Kings, The—Willan. Carl Fischer No. OCS 718. *A cappella.* Medium.

Three Old English Carols—arr. Holst. Schmidt No. APS 15171. Accompanied. Moderately easy.

Two Folk Carols (Star in the South and Zither Carol)—arr. Sargent. Oxford No. X50. *A cappella.* Moderately easy.

We Wish You a Merry Christmas (English folk song; secular)—arr. the Krones. Kjos 4006. Accompanied. Easy.

What Child Is This? (old English)—arr. Parker and Shaw. G. Schirmer No. 10199. *A cappella.* Moderately difficult.

When Christ Was Born of Mary Free—Fissinger. World Library of Sacred Music No. AC-1523-8. Percussion accompaniment. Easy.

While by My Sheep (17th-century Christian hymn)—arr. Jungst. G. Schirmer No. 2532. *A cappella.* Easy.

Ye Watchers and Ye Holy Ones (17th-century German melody)—arr. Davison. E. C. Schirmer No. 1780. Accompanied. Moderately easy.

Easter and Lent

All Glory, Laud and Honor (Palm Sunday)—Teschner, arr. Cain. Flammer No. 81127. Accompanied. Easy.

Alleluia—Thompson. E. C. Schirmer No. 1786. *A cappella.* Moderately difficult.

Alleluia, Alleluia—Buxtehude. Presser No. 312-40668. Accompanied. Medium.

Ave Verum Corpus—Byrd. Associated No. NYPMA 7. *A cappella.*

Christ Is Arisen—Hassler. Edw. B. Marks No. 26. *A cappella.* Moderately easy.

Christ Is Arisen—Schubert. E. C. Schirmer No. 2686. *A cappella.* Moderately easy.

Crucifixus (from *Mass in B minor*)—J. S. Bach. E. C. Schirmer No. 1174. Accompanied. Medium.

Ecce, Quomodo Moritur—Jacobus Gallus (Jacob Handl). G. Schirmer No. 8424. *A cappella.* Moderately easy.

Four Chorales from the *Saint Matthew Passion*—J. S. Bach, ed. Ehret. Lawson-Gould No. 686. *A cappella.* Moderately easy.

Go to Dark Gethsemane—Noble. Gray No. CMR 501. *A cappella.* Medium.

God So Loved the World—Stainer. G. Schirmer No. 3798. *A cappella.* Easy.

He Never Said a Mumbalin' Word (spiritual)—arr. Wilson. Paull-Pioneer. *A cappella.* Moderately easy.

Hosanna (Palm Sunday)—F. M. Christiansen. Augsburg No. 57. *A cappella.* Difficult.

Lamb of God (Chorale 1540)—arr. F. M. Christiansen. Augsburg No. 133. *A cappella.* Easy.

Lamb of God—Hassler. Lawson-Gould No. 800. *A cappella.* Moderately easy.

Light Divine (scene and prayer from *Cavalleria Rusticana*)—Mascagni. G. Schirmer No. 5959. Accompanied. Moderately difficult.

Magdalena—Brahms. G. Schirmer No. 9953. *A cappella.* Medium.

My Savior Dear, What Woe of Soul—J. S. Bach, arr. Lundquist. Willis No. 5503. *A cappella.* Medium.

O Lamb of God—Kalinnikov, arr. Ehret. Pro Art No. 1513. *A cappella.* Moderately easy.

Palms, The (Palm Sunday)—Faure, arr. Howorth. Belwin-Mills No. 790. Accompanied. Medium.

Ride On! Ride On! (Palm Sunday)—Thompson. Gray No. CMR 1154. *A cappella.* Medium.

Sunrise Alleluia—Bright. Shawnee Press No. A-852. Accompanied. Moderately easy.

Surely, He Bore Our Sorrows (Lent)—Victoria. E. C. Schirmer No. 2217. *A cappella.* Medium.

Surely He Hath Borne Our Griefs (from *Messiah*)—Handel. G. Schirmer No. 6598. Accompanied. Medium.

Surrexit Pastor Bonus (The Shepherd Has Arisen)—Lasso. G. Schirmer No. 7685. *A cappella.* Medium.

This Is the Day Which the Lord Hath Made—Bortniansky. Bourne No. BL3041. *A cappella.* Medium.

Three Lenten Poems of Richard Crashaw—Pinkham. E. C. Schirmer No. 2693. Accompanied. Medium.

Tree of Sorrow—Chávez. Mercury No. MP-113. *A cappella.* Difficult.

Were You There? (Negro spiritual)—arr. Burleigh. Ricordi No. NY423. Optional accompaniment. Medium.

Folk Songs and Spirituals

Ain' a That Good News? (spiritual)—arr. Dawson. Music Press, Tuskegee Institute No. 103. *A cappella.* Moderately easy.

All My Trials, Lord (spiritual)—arr. Swenson. Galaxy No. 1.2824.1. Accompanied. Moderately easy.

Ash Grove, The (Welsh air)—arr. Jacob. Oxford No. F9. *A cappella.* Easy.

Black Is the Color of My True Love's Hair (Appalachian folk song)—arr. Churchill. Shawnee Press. Accompanied. Moderately easy.

Carmela (traditional Mexican song)—arr. Schillio. Presser No. 312-40740. Accompanied. Easy.

Charlottown (Southern folk song)—arr. Bryan. J. Fischer No. 8136. *A cappella.* Medium.

Chilly Waters (Negro spiritual)—arr. Roberton. Curwen No. 61420. *A cappella.* Easy.

Ching-A-Ring Chaw (minstrel song)—arr. Copland and Fine. Boosey & Hawkes No. 5024. Accompanied. Medium.

Cicirinella (Italian folk song)—arr. Krone. Witmark No. 5-W2592. Accompanied. Easy.

Cindy (American folk song)—arr. Ehret. Theodore Presser No. 312-41186. Accompanied. Easy.

Climbin' up the Mountain (spiritual)—arr. Smith. Kjos No. 1001. *A cappella.* Easy.

Czechoslovakian Dance Song—arr. Krone. Witmark No. 5-W2608. Optional accompaniment. Moderately easy.

Dance to Your Daddie (Scottish nursery song)—arr. Rubbra. Belwin-Mills No. 322. *A cappella.* Moderately easy.

Dark-Eyed Sailor, The (English folk song)—arr. Vaughan Williams. Galaxy No. 128. *A cappella.* Medium.

Deer Chase, The (American folk song)—arr. Luboff. Walton No. W3053. Accompanied. Moderately easy.

Didn't My Lord Deliver Daniel? (spiritual)—arr. Hunter. Lawson-Gould No. 957. Accompanied. Moderately easy.

Drei Volkslieder (Three folk Songs)—arr. Mendelssohn. European American No. EA 413. *A cappella.* Medium.

Drunken Sailor, The (sea chantey)—arr. Schumann and Erickson. Bourne No. C3004. *A cappella.* Medium.

Each Little Flower (Swedish folk melody)—arr. Lundquist. Elkan-Vogel No. 1150. *A cappella.* Easy.

Early One Morning (English folk song)—arr. Christy. Schmitt, Hall & McCreary No. 1115. *A cappella.* Moderately easy.

Elijah Rock (spiritual)—arr. Hairston. Bourne No. S 1017. Optional accompaniment. Medium.

Eriskay Love Lilt, An (Irish folk song)—arr. Roberton. G. Schirmer No. 8107. *A cappella.* Moderately easy.

Every Time I Feel de Spirit (Negro spiritual)—arr. Murray. Boosey & Hawkes No. 1737. Accompanied. Moderately easy.

Ezekiel Saw the Wheel (Negro spiritual)—arr. Simeone. Shawnee Press. Accompanied. Moderately difficult.

Farmer's Daughters, The (traditional English)—arr. Williams. G. Schirmer No. 8116. *A cappella.* Easy.

Fireflies (Russian)—arr. Clough and Leighter. E. C. Schirmer No. 1178. *A cappella.* Easy.

Frankie and Johnny (traditional)—arr. De Cormier. Lawson-Gould No. 52040. *A cappella.* Soprano, alto, tenor, and baritone solos. Medium.

Gay Fiesta (Mexican folk song)—arr. Riegger. Flammer No. 81149. Accompanied. Moderately easy.

Gently, Johnny, My Jingalo (English folk song)—arr. Parker and Shaw. Lawson-Gould No. 643. *A cappella*. Moderately easy.

Girl with the Buckles on Her Shoes, The (Irish traditional)—arr. Nelson. G. Schirmer No. 10968. Accompanied. Moderately easy.

Good Night (German folk song)—arr. Manney. B. F. Wood No. 292. Accompanied. Moderately easy.

Great Angelic Host, The (Norwegian folk song)—arr. Grieg. Carl Fischer No. CM530. *A cappella*. Medium.

Hawaiian Lullaby—arr. Sargent. Oxford No. X85. *A cappella*. Medium.

Ho-La-Hi (German folk song)—arr. Fiske. Oxford No. F53. *A cappella*. Easy.

How Good It Is (Hebrew folk song)—arr. Goldman. Lawson-Gould No. 51821. Accompanied. Moderately easy.

I Know My Love (Irish folk song)—arr. Parker and Shaw. Lawson-Gould No. 657. Accompanied. Moderately easy.

I Ride an Old Paint—arr. Bright. Shawnee A-661. *A cappella*. Moderately easy.

I Sowed the Seeds of Love (Hampshire folk song)—arr. Holst. G. Schirmer No. 11149. *A cappella*. Medium.

I Won't Kiss Katy (Yugoslavian folk song)—arr. Smith and Aschenbrenner. Carl Fischer No. CM4596. *A cappella*. Moderately difficult.

Ifca's Castle (Czechoslovakian folk song)—arr. Harley-Aschenbrenner. Carl Fischer No. CM 4708. *A cappella*. Easy.

I'm Goin' to Sing (spiritual)—arr. Parker and Shaw. Lawson-Gould No. 51101. *A cappella*. Moderately easy.

Island Sheiling Song, An (folksong from the Hebrides)—arr. Arch. Boosey & Hawkes No. 5669. *A cappella*. Moderately easy.

Jacob's Ladder (spiritual)—arr. Wilson. Ricordi No. NY1476. Optional accompaniment. Moderately easy.

Jesus on the Water Side (spiritual)—arr. Aschenbrenner. Fitzsimmons No. 1032. *A cappella*. Moderately difficult.

Just As the Tide Was Flowing (English folk song)—arr. Vaughan Williams. Galaxy No. 130. *A cappella*. Medium.

Keys of My Heart, The (North country traditional song)—arr. Warrell. G. Schirmer No. 8474. *A cappella*. Moderately easy.

Lark on the Morn, The (folk song from *Sommersetshire*)—arr. Thompson. E. C. Schirmer No. 1782. *A cappella*. Easy.

Linden Lea (old English folk song)—Vaughan Williams, arr. Salter. Boosey & Hawkes No. 1401. Accompanied. Moderately easy.

Little Duck in the Meadow (Russian folk song)—arr. Nikolsky. G. Schirmer No. 6669. *A cappella*. Moderately easy .

Marching to Pretoria (South African Veld song)—arr. Marais and Abbott. G. Schirmer No. 10423. Four-hand piano accompaniment. Easy.

Mary Had a Baby (spiritual)—arr. Dawson. Music Press, Tuskegee Institute No. T118. *A cappella*. Moderately easy.

Matthew, Mark, Luke and John (West country folk song)—arr. G. T. Holst. Schirmer No. 8548. *A cappella*. Moderately easy.

Mayday Carol (English folk song)—arr. Taylor. J. Fischer No. 4838. Accompanied. Moderately easy.

Miner's Lament (Tune: Lilly Dale)—arr. De Cormier. Lawson-Gould No. 51975. *A cappella*. Moderately easy.

Moan to the Moon (Estonian folk song)—arr. Hunter. Lawson-Gould No. 954. Accompanied. Moderately easy.

Morning Now Beckons (Czechoslovakian folk song)—arr. Manney. Wood No. 355. Accompanied. Easy.

My Lord, What a Mornin' (spiritual)—arr. Burleigh. Ricordi No. 412. *A cappella*. Medium.

My Pretty Little Pink (American folk song)—arr. Barthelson. Lawson-Gould No. 792. Accompanied. Moderately easy.

Nine Hundred Miles from Home (Appalachian Mountain folksong)—arr. Schillio. Associated No. A-712. Accompanied. Moderately easy.

Oh, Dear! What Can the Matter Be? (English folk song)—arr. Bantock. Joseph Williams, Ltd. No. 19. *A cappella*. Moderately easy.

Oh, What a Beautiful City (spiritual)—arr. Dawson. Music Press, Tuskegee Institute No. T 100. *A cappella*. Medium.

Old Woman and the Peddler, The (old English)—arr. Kinscella. G. Schirmer No. 7819. *A cappella*. Moderately easy.

Peasant and His Oxen (Yugoslavian folk song)—arr. Smith and Aschenbrenner. Carl Fischer No. 4595. *A cappella*. Medium.

Prince Charlie's Farewell (traditional English air)—arr. Robertson. G. Schirmer No. 8512. *A cappella*. Moderately easy.

Red, Red Rose, A (Scotch folk tune)—arr. Parker and Shaw. Lawson-Gould No. 645. *A cappella*. Tenor solo. Medium.

Ride the Chariot (spiritual)—arr. Smith. Kjos No. 1015. Optional accompaniment. Medium.

Rock-a My Soul (spiritual)—arr. De Vaux. Bourne No. 667. Accompanied. Moderately easy.

Russian Picnic (based on Russian folk tunes)—arr. Enders. G. Schirmer No. 9544. Accompanied. Moderately easy.

Sakura Sakura (Japanese folk song)—arr. Hairston. Bourne No. J1. Optional accompaniment. Moderately easy.

See the Gipsies (Hungarian folk song)—arr. Kodály. Oxford No. W61. *A cappella*. Medium.

She's like the Swallow (Newfoundland folk song)—arr. Chapman. Oxford No. X64. *A cappella*. Moderately easy.

Silver Moon Is Shining, The (Italian folk song)—arr. Davis. E. C. Schirmer No. 1754. *A cappella*. Moderately easy.

Soon-Ah Will Be Done (spiritual)—Dawson. Music Press, Tuskegee Institute No. 102. Optional accompaniment. Medium.

Spring of the Year, The (English folk song)—arr. Vaughan Williams. Galaxy No. 129. *A cappella*. Moderately easy.

Swiss Skiing Song—arr. Krone. Kjos No. 1200. *A cappella*. Moderately easy.

Tchum Bi-Ri Tchum (Israeli folk tune)—arr. Goldman. Lawson-Gould No. 51888. Accompanied. Moderately easy.

There Is a Balm in Gilead (spiritual)—arr. Dawson. Music Press, Tuskegee Institute No. 105. *A cappella*. Soprano solo. Medium.

There's a Lit'l' Wheel a-Turnin' in My Heart (spiritual)—arr. Dawson. Music Press, Tuskegee Institute No. T 121. *A cappella*. Medium.

Tomorrow Shall Be My Dancing Day (traditional English carol)—arr. Willcocks. Oxford No. 84.141. *A cappella*. Medium.

Turtle Dove, The (English folk song)—arr. Vaughan Williams. G. Schirmer No. 8105. *A cappella*. Baritone solo. Moderately easy.

Twenty Eighteen (English folk song)—arr. Taylor. J. Fischer No. 4846. Accompanied. Easy.

Two Macedonian Folk Songs—arr. Srebotnjak. G. Schirmer No. 11315. *A cappella*. Moderately easy.

Two Negro Spirituals (Deep River and Dig My Grave)—arr. Burleigh. G. Schirmer No. 5815. *A cappella*. Medium.

Wade in The Water (spiritual)—arr. Kirk. Carl Fischer No. CM 8022. *A cappella*. Solo. Easy.

Waltzing Matilda (Australian song)—arr. Wood. Oxford No. OCS 790. *A cappella*. Medium.

Waters Ripple and Flow (Czechoslovakian folk song)—arr. Taylor. J. Fischer No. 5675. Accompanied. Soprano and baritone solos. Moderately difficult.

Weep, O Willow (mountain tune)—arr. Lekberg. Summy-Birchard No. 5009. *A cappella*. Soprano solo. Medium.

Well-Beloved, The (Armenian folk song)—arr. Taylor. J. Fischer No. 4844. Accompanied. Soprano solo. Moderately easy.

When Love Is Kind (English folk song)—arr. Terri. Lawson-Gould No. 843. *A cappella*. Moderately easy.

Yarmouth Fair (English folk song)—arr. Warlock. Oxford No. X37. *A cappella*. Moderately easy.

Ya Ba Bom (Jewish folk tune)—arr. Goldman. Lawson-Gould No. 51814. Piano accompaniment, with optional string bass and drums. Medium.

Zum Gali (Israeli folk tune)—arr. Goldman. Lawson-Gould No. 52026. Accompanied. Medium.

Special Occasions (Commencement, Thanksgiving, Patriotic Holidays)

Battle Hymn of the Republic (patriotic)—Steffe, arr. Ringwald. Shawnee Press. Accompanied. Moderately easy.

Battle Hymn of the Republic (patriotic)—Steffe, arr. Wilhousky. Carl Fischer No. CM 4743. Accompanied. Medium.

Come, Let Us Sing to the Lord (Thanksgiving)—Schvedov, arr. Cain. Boosey & Hawkes No. 1800. *A cappella*. Difficult.

Give Me Your Tired, Your Poor (patriotic or commencement)—Berlin, arr. Ringwald. Shawnee Press. Accompanied. Medium.

Give Thanks (Thanksgiving)—Williams. Flammer No. 84191. Accompanied. Soprano solo. Easy.

In Solemn Silence (memorial anthem)—Ippolitov-Ivanov, arr. Wilhousky. Carl Fischer No. 635. *A cappella*. Medium.

Land of Hope and Glory (commencement)—Elgar. Boosey & Hawkes No. 1161. Accompanied. Moderately easy.

Let All Creatures of God His Praises Sing (Thanksgiving)—Kalinnikov, arr. Cain. Boosey & Hawkes No. 1801. *A cappella*. Medium.

Now Thank We All Our God (Thanksgiving)—Cruger, arr. Holst. Kjos No. 5138. Accompanied. Moderately easy.

Onward, Ye Peoples! (commencement)—Sibelius, arr. Lefebvre. Galaxy No. 938-10. Accompanied. Medium.

Prayer of Thanksgiving (Netherlands folk song; Thanksgiving)—arr. Kremser. G. Schirmer No. 4345. Accompanied. Easy.

Preludes to Eternity (commencement)—Liszt, arr. Reibold. Summy-Birchard No. 1442. Accompanied. Moderately difficult.

Recessional (Memorial Day)—DeKoven. Presser No. 322-35015. Accompanied. Moderately easy.

To Music (commencement)—Schubert, arr. Wilson. Schmitt, Hall & McCreary No. 1070. Accompanied. Moderately easy.

General: Sacred

Absalom—Tomkins. Chappell No. 6140. *A cappella*. Medium.

Adoramus Te—Corsi, arr. Greyson. Bourne No. ES15. *A cappella*. Moderately easy.

Adoramus Te—Gasparini. Belwin-Mills No. 2148. *A cappella*. Medium.

Adoramus Te—Lassus. Music Press No. MP-76. *A cappella*. Medium.

Adoramus Te—Mozart. G. Schirmer No. 9932. Optional accompaniment. Moderately easy.

Adoramus Te, Christe—Palestrina. Carl Fischer No. CM6578. *A cappella*. Easy.

Agnus Dei—Lotti. Edw. B. Marks. No. 4365. *A cappella*. Moderately easy.

Agnus Dei—Morley, arr. Greyson. Bourne No. ES36. *A cappella*. Medium.

Agnus Dei—Pergolesi. Mercury No. MC 147. Accompanied. Medium.

Agnus Dei (from *Deutsche Messe*)—Schubert. Piedmont No. 4449. Accompanied. Medium.

Agnus Dei—Victoria. Lawson-Gould No. 925. *A cappella*. Medium.

All Breathing Life (from the motet *Sing Ye to the Lord*)—J. S. Bach. G. Schirmer No. 7470. Optional accompaniment. Difficult.

All Glory Be to God on High (melody of Gregorian origin)—arr. Malin. Summy-Birchard No. 345. Accompanied. Moderately easy.

All Hail the Power—Vaughan Williams. Oxford. Accompanied. Moderately difficult.

All the Earth Doth Worship Thee—Handel. Ricordi No. NY2030. Accompanied. Moderately easy.

Alleluia (from the motet *Exultate, Jubilate*)—Mozart, arr. Rosenberg. Carl Fischer No. 541. Accompanied. Medium. (Soprano solo, difficult.)

Alleluia—Thompson. E. C. Schirmer No. 1786. *A cappella*. Moderately difficult.

Alleluja—J. S. Bach. C. F. Peters No. 6106a. Accompanied. Medium.

Almighty and Everlasting God—Gibbons. Bourne No. ES35. *A cappella*. Moderately easy.

Almighty God, Who Hast Me Brought—Ford. C. F. Peters No. 1558. *A cappella*. Moderately easy.

Amen—Scarlatti, arr. Ehret. European American No. EA 231. Organ or piano accompaniment. Moderately easy.

And Draw a Blessing Down (from *Theodora*)—Handel, arr. Malin. Edw. B. Marks No. 4535. Accompanied. Medium.

Angelic Greeting, The—Brahms, ed. Mattfeld. E. C. Schirmer No. 2477. *A cappella*. Medium.

Ave Christe, Immolate—Desprez. Editions Salabert No. MC 531. *A cappella.* Medium.

Ave Maria—Bach and Gounod, arr. Tolmadge. Staff No. 243. Accompanied. Easy.

Ave Maria—Brahms. C. F. Peters No. 66136. Accompanied. Medium.

Ave Maria—Bruckner. Edw. B. Marks No. 47. *A cappella.* Moderately easy.

Ave Maria—Franck, arr. Borucchia. McLaughlin & Reilly No. 1072. Organ accompaniment. Moderately easy.

Ave Maria—Mouton. Music Press No. DCS 40. *A cappella.* Moderately easy.

Ave Maria—Rachmaninoff. Oliver Ditson No. 332-14564. *A cappella.* Medium.

Ave Maria—Tchaikovsky. Boston Music Co. No. 1064. *A cappella.* Moderately easy.

Ave Maria—Verdi. C. F. Peters No. 4256a. *A cappella.* Moderately difficult.

Ave Maria—Victoria. Music Press No. MP-79. *A cappella.* Moderately easy.

Ave Maria, Gratia Plena—Desprez. Associated No. 28. *A cappella.* Medium.

Ave Maria No. 20—Villa-Lobos, new text by H. R. Wilson. Consolidated. *A cappella.* Medium.

Ave Maris Stella—Desprez. Associated No. 35. *A capella.* Medium.

Ave Maris Stella—Hassler. Kjos No. 5012. *A cappella.* Moderately easy.

Ave Regina Coelorum—Lassus. Associated No. A-406. *A cappella.* Medium.

Ave Regina Coelorum—Willaert. Ricordi No. NY1887. *A cappella.* Medium.

Ave Verum Corpus—Byrd. Bourne No. ES44. *A cappella.* Moderately easy.

Ave Verum Corpus—Mozart. G. Schirmer No. 5471. Organ accompaniment. Moderately easy.

Awake the Harp (from *The Creation*)—Haydn, ed. Neuen. Lawson-Gould No. 51982. Accompanied. Medium.

Be Joyful, Be Joyful—Homilius. Sam Fox No. MM5. Accompanied. Moderately easy.

Beautiful Savior (Silesian folk tune)—arr. F. M. Christiansen. Augsburg No. 51. *A cappella.* Medium.

Behold a Hallowed Day—Handl. Concordia No. 98-1690. *A cappella.* Medium.

Benedixisti (Thou Hast Been Gracious, Lord)—G. Gabrieli. G. Schirmer No. 7625. *A cappella.* Medium.

Best of Rooms, The—Thompson. E. C. Schirmer No. 2672. *A cappella.* Medium.

Bless the Lord for Ever and Ever—Mozart, arr. Hilton. Mercury No. 352-00459. Accompanied. Moderately difficult.

Blessed Are the Faithful—Schütz, ed. Shaw and Speer. G. Schirmer No. 10114. *A cappella.* Moderately difficult.

Blessed Savior, Our Lord Jesus—Hassler. G. Schirmer No. 7563. *A cappella.* Medium.

Blest Be the Lord—Haydn. McLaughlin & Reilly Co. No. 2217. Accompanied. Medium.

Brother James' Air (Marosa)—Jacob. Carl Fischer No. OCS763. *A cappella.* Easy.

Call to Mary—Brahms, ed. Mattfeld. E. C. Schirmer No. 2480. *A cappella.* Medium.

Call to Remembrance—Farrant, arr. Greyson. Bourne No. ES 17. *A cappella.* Moderately easy.

Cantantibus Organis—Marenzio. Available—World Library. *A cappella*. Moderately easy.

Cantate Domino—Pitoni. Bourne No. ES 5. *A cappella*. Moderately easy.

Cantate Domino—Schütz. Bourne No. ES 33. *A cappella*. Moderately difficult.

Cantique de Jean Racine—Fauré. Broude Bros. No. 801. Accompanied. Moderately easy.

Cherubic Hymn (Greek liturgy)—arr. Aliferis. Witmark No. 5-W3063. *A cappella*. Moderately difficult.

Cherubim Song—Gretchaninov, arr. Cain. Hoffmann No. 46012A. *A cappella*. Medium.

Cherubim Song No. 3—Tchaikovsky. G. Schirmer No. 2561. Piano or organ accompaniment. Moderately difficult.

Cherubim Song No. 7—Bortniansky, arr. Tchaikovsky. G. Schirmer No. 2560. *A cappella*. Easy.

Come, Blessed Rest—J. S. Bach. Kjos No. 2004. *A cappella*. Medium.

Come Let Us Start a Joyful Song—Hassler. Bourne No. ES 74. *A cappella*. Moderately easy.

Come, Then, O Holy Breath of God—Palestrina. Piedmont No. 4414. *A cappella*. Medium.

Come Thou, O Savior—J. S. Bach. Summy-Birchard No. 5203. *A cappella*. Moderately easy.

Comfort All Ye My People—Fauré, arr. Hopson. Carl Fischer No. CM8017. Piano or organ accompaniment. Moderately easy.

Contentment—Mozart. Lawson-Gould No. 937. Accompanied. Soprano solo. Moderately easy.

Corporis Mysterium (Sacrament of Priceless Worth)—Palestrina. Ricordi No. NY1852. *A cappella*. Moderately easy.

Create in Me, O God, a Pure Heart—Brahms, arr. Williamson. G. Schirmer No. 7504. *A cappella*. Moderately easy.

David's Lamentation—Billings. C. F. Peters No. 66336. Optional accompaniment. Moderately easy.

Day by Day We Magnify Thee—Handel. Lawson-Gould No. 797; Edw. B. Marks No. 4516. Accompanied. Medium.

De Profundis (Out of the Deep)—Thompson. Weintraub. *A cappella*. Moderately difficult.

Dies Irae (from *Requiem*)—Mozart. G. Schirmer No. 10016. Accompanied. Medium.

Ehre sei Dir, Christe (Christ, Be Thine the Glory!)—Schütz. G. Schirmer No. 10123. Optional accompaniment. Medium.

Et Misericordia—Vivaldi, arr. Kjelson. Belwin-Mills No. 2236. Accompanied. Moderately easy.

Every Thing You Do—Buxtehude. Sam Fox No. CM 19. Accompanied. Medium.

Exaltabo Te, Domine—Palestrina. G. Schirmer No. 7620. *A cappella*. Medium.

Exultate Deo (Sing and Praise Jehovah)—Palestrina. G. Schirmer No. 7672. *A cappella*. Medium.

Exultate Deo—Scarlatti. G. Schirmer No. 11001. *A cappella*. Medium.

Exultate Justi—Viadana, ed. Klein. G.I.A. No. G-2140. *A cappella*. Medium.

Gloria in Excelsis—Mozart. G. Schirmer No. 3515. Accompanied. Medium.

Gloria—Only Begotten Son—Gretchaninov, arr. Tellep. Boosey & Hawkes No. 5097. *A cappella*. Medium.

Gloria Patri (Glory to God)—Palestrina, arr. Greyson. Bourne No. ES46. *A cappella*. Easy.

Glory—Lotti. Edw. B. Marks No. 4366. *A cappella*. Moderately easy.

Glory and Honor Are Before Him—J. S. Bach. Kjos No. 5150. *A cappella*. Medium.

Glory and Worship—Purcell. E. C. Schirmer No. 1108. Organ accompaniment. Moderately easy.

Glory Be to God—Rachmaninoff, arr. Tkach. Kjos No. 6528. *A cappella*. Medium.

Glory to God—Bach, ed. Wilson. Ricordi No. NY1397. Optional accompaniment. Moderately difficult.

Glory to God—Bortniansky. Witmark No. 5-W2743. *A cappella*. Moderately easy.

Glory to God—Handel. Lawson-Gould No. 796. Accompanied. Medium.

Glory to God in the Highest—Thompson. E. C. Schirmer No. 2470. *A cappella*. Medium.

Gradual—Bruckner. G. Schirmer No. 12051. *A cappella*. Medium.

Graduale—Sancta Maria—Mozart. Broude Bros. No. 77. Accompanied. Medium.

Grant Unto Me the Joy of Thy Salvation—Brahms. G. Schirmer No. 7506. *A cappella*. Moderately difficult.

Great and Glorious—Haydn. Wood No. 316. Accompanied. Medium.

Haec Dies—Byrd. Oxford No. TCM 50. Optional accompaniment. Moderately difficult.

Hail, Thou Gladdening Light—Gretchaninov. Wood No. 594. *A cappella*. Moderately difficult.

Hail, Thou Holy One—Tchaikovsky, arr. Cain. Boosey & Hawkes No. 1979. *A cappella*. Medium.

Hallelujah (from *Mount of Olives*)—Beethoven. G. Schirmer No. 2215. Accompanied. Difficult.

Hallelujah, Amen (from *Judas Maccabaeus*)—Handel. Witmark No. 5-W3026. Optional accompaniment. Medium.

He Shall Rule from Sea to Sea—Rorem. Boosey & Hawkes No. 5651. Accompanied. Medium.

He Watching over Israel (from *Elijah*)—Mendelssohn. G. Schirmer No. 2498. Accompanied. Moderately difficult.

He Who with Weeping Soweth—Schütz. G. Schirmer No. 10115. Optional accompaniment. Moderately difficult.

Hear My Prayer—Kopylov. Boston Music No. 1294. *A cappella*. Medium.

Hear, O Lord, Hear My Prayer—Lasso, arr. Lundquist. Elkan-Vogel No. 1110. *A cappella*. Moderately easy.

Hear Our Supplication—Mozart, arr. Hilton. Mercury No. 352-00378. Accompanied. Medium.

Heavenly Light—Kopylov, arr. Wilhousky. Carl Fischer No. CM 497. *A cappella*. Moderately easy.

Heavens Are Declaring, The—Beethoven. G. Schirmer No. 3032. Accompanied. Easy.

Heavens Are Telling, The (from *The Creation*)—Haydn, arr. Phillips. Carl Fischer No. CM 127. Organ accompaniment. Moderately difficult.

Here Is Thy Footstool—Creston. G. Schirmer No. 11146. *A cappella*. Medium.

Hide Not Thy Face, O My Savior (Finnish folk melody)—arr. Lundquist. Willis No. 8469. *A cappella*. Moderately easy.

Hodie Nobis Coelorum Rex—Bright. Shawnee Press No. A-812. Accompanied. Medium.

Holy, Holy, Holy (Sanctus)—Lotti. E. C. Schirmer No. 2216. *A cappella*. Medium.

Holy, Holy, Holy—Scarlatti. Chappell No. 6141. *A cappella*. Medium.

Holy Is the Lord—Schubert. Presser No. 312-21416. Accompanied. Easy.

Honor and Glory—J. S. Bach. Plymouth No. SC10. Accompanied. Moderately easy.

Hosanna in Excelsis Deo—Gounod. Gentry No. G-136. Accompanied. Medium.

Hospodi Pomilui—von Lvov, ed. Wilhousky. Carl Fischer No. CM 6580. *A cappella*. Medium.

How Lovely Is Thy Dwelling Place—Brahms, ed. Wilson. Ricordi No. 1515. Accompanied. Moderately difficult.

Humility before Thee—C. P. E. Bach, arr. Ehret. Elkan-Vogel No. 1268. Piano or organ accompaniment. Medium.

Hundredth Psalm, The—Mendelssohn, ed. Hines. Concordia No. 98-2215. *A cappella*. Moderately difficult.

Hymn to Saint Peter—Britten. Boosey & Hawkes. Organ accompaniment. Soprano solo. Moderately difficult.

Hymn to the Trinity—Kopylov. Kjos No. 5337. *A cappella*. Easy.

If Ye Love Me, Keep My Commandments—Tallis. E. C. Schirmer No. 2269. *A cappella*. Medium.

I Will Clothe Thy Priests with Salvation—Peter, arr. Kroeger. Boosey & Hawkes No. 6004. Accompanied. Medium.

Incline Thine Ear, Oh Lord—Arkhangelsky. Witmark No. 5-W2689. *A cappella*. Medium.

In Excelsis Deo (from *Mass in C*)—Mozart. Theodore Presser No. 312-41198. Accompanied. Medium.

In Memoria Aeterna (from *Beatus Vir*)—Vivaldi, ed. McEwen. Hinshaw No. HMC-179. Accompanied. Medium.

In Omnem Terram—Campra, arr. Castle. B. F. Wood No. 44-964. Organ or piano accompaniment. Moderately difficult.

Iustorum Animae—Byrd. E. C. Schirmer No. 327. *A cappella*. Medium.

Jesu Dulcis Memoria—Victoria. G. Schirmer No. 5573. *A cappella*. Easy.

Jesu, Joy of Man's Desiring—J. S. Bach. E. C. Schirmer No. 317. Organ accompaniment. Moderately easy.

Jesus, Now to Thee I Turn Me—Cherubini, arr. Lundquist. Elkan-Vogel No. 1159. *A cappella*. Easy.

Jubilate Deo—Lassus. Mercury No. MP-80. *A cappella*. Moderately easy.

Jubilate Deo—Mozart. Pro Art No. 1007. *A cappella*. Moderately easy.

King of Glory—Mozart, ed. Ehret. Gentry No. G-345. Accompanied. Medium.

Kyrie—Mozart, ed. Landon. G. Schirmer No. 12067. Accompanied. Medium.

Kyrie Eleison—Durante. Pro Art No. 2279. *A cappella*. Moderately easy.

Kyrie Eleison—Haydn, arr. Ehret. Heritage No. H 94. Accompanied. Moderately easy.

Lacrymosa—Cherubini, ed. De Pietto. Lawson-Gould No. 51853. Accompanied. Medium.

Lacrymosa (from *Requiem*)—Mozart. G. Schirmer No. 10017. Accompanied. Medium.

Lasciatemi morire—Monteverdi. Ricordi No. NY841. *A cappella.* Moderately easy.

Last Words of David, The—Thompson. E. C. Schirmer No. 2294. Accompanied. Medium.

Laudate Pueri—Mozart. Lawson-Gould No. 51166; Associated No. A-683. Accompanied. Medium.

Lend Thine Ear to My Prayer—Arkhangelsky, arr. Wilhousky. Carl Fischer No. CM 613. *A cappella.* Moderately difficult.

Let All Mortal Flesh Keep Silence—Holst. Galaxy No. 3.2309.1. Accompanied. Medium.

Let Every Nation His Praises Sing—Franck. Sam Fox No. CM 20. *A cappella.* Medium.

Let My Prayer Come Up (Offertorium)—Purcell. Gray No. 1527; Mercury No. 352-00440. Accompanied. Moderately easy.

Let Nothing Ever Grieve Thee—Brahms. C. F. Peters No. 6093. Accompanied. Moderately easy.

Let Their Celestial Concerts All Unite (from *Samson*)—Handel. E. C. Schirmer No. 312. Accompanied. Moderately difficult.

Let Thy Holy Presence—Tchesnokov, arr. Cain. Summy-Birchard No. 12. *A cappella.* Medium.

Libera Me—Fauré. Belwin-Mills No. 2032. Accompanied. Medium.

Like As the Hart—Palestrina. G. Schirmer No. 3509. *A cappella.* Moderately easy.

Lo, I am The Voice of One Crying in the Wilderness—Schütz. G. Schirmer No. 10116. Optional accompaniment. Moderately difficult.

Lord Bless You and Keep You, The—Lutkin. Summy-Birchard No. 1089. *A cappella.* Easy.

Lord Christ, Son of God (Christe Dei Soboles)—Lasso. G. Schirmer No. 9414 *A cappella.* Medium.

Lord God, in Power and Glory—Haydn. Curwen No. 80782. Optional accompaniment. Moderately easy.

Lord, Have Mercy upon Us—Beethoven. Chappell No. 6145. Accompanied. Moderately easy.

Lord, Hear Our Prayer (from *Otello*)—Verdi, arr. Huguelet. Carl Fischer No. CM 616. Optional accompaniment. Medium.

Lord Is My Shepherd, The—Thompson. E. C. Schirmer No. 2688. Accompanied. Moderately easy.

Lord of Love, to Thee I Flee—Cornelius. Sam Fox No. MM 26. Accompanied. Medium.

Lord, Remember Not—Mendelssohn. Walton No. 6010. Optional accompaniment. Medium.

Lord Shall Be Unto Thee, The (from *Requiem*)—Thompson. E. C. Schirmer No. 2641. *A cappella.* Medium.

Lord, We Love the Place—Graun. Sam Fox No. MM 6. Accompanied. Medium.

Lovely Appear (from *The Redemption*)—Gounod. G. Schirmer No. 2013. Accompanied. Medium.

Magnificat—Gabrieli, Curwen No. 10565. *A cappella* Three choirs. Difficult.

Magnificat and Nunc Dimittis—Purcell. C. F. Peters No. 66266. Optional accompaniment. Medium.

Magnificat—My Soul Doth Magnify the Lord—Buxtehude. C. F. Peters No. 66288. Accompanied. Moderately difficult.

Mighty Fortress Is Our God, A—Luther. Witmark No. 5W2835. Optional accompaniment. Moderately easy.

Miserere Mei—Lotti. Boosey & Hawkes No. 1938. *A cappella*. Easy.

Miserere Mei—Pergolesi. Walton No. 6011. Accompanied. Medium.

My Heart Overflows—Harrer, ed. Frank. Sam Fox No. MM 1. Piano or organ accompaniment. Medium.

Ne Irascaris—Byrd. Alexander Broude No. 216-9. *A cappella*. Moderately difficult.

Now God Be Praised in Heav'n Above—Vulpius. E. C. Schirmer No. 1693. Optional accompaniment. Moderately easy.

Nunc Dimittis—Purcell. Summy-Birchard No. 5433. Accompanied. Moderately easy.

O Be Joyful! (Freut Euch, Freut Euch)—Mozart. Sam Fox No. MM 9. Accompanied. Medium.

O Blessed Lord—Tchaikovsky. Wallace Gillman No. 4001. Optional accompaniment. Moderately easy.

O Bone Jesu—Palestrina. Oliver Ditson No. 332-03070. *A cappella*. Easy.

O Cast Me Not Away from Thy Countenance—Brahms. G. Schirmer No. 7505. *A cappella*. Moderately difficult.

O Clap Your Hands—Vaughan Williams. Galaxy No. 222. Organ accompaniment. Moderately difficult.

O Divine Redeemer—Gounod, arr. Cain. Schmitt, Hall & McCreary No. 1602. Accompanied. Moderately easy.

O Glorious One—Gretchaninov, arr. Cain. Hoffman No. 46,339. *A cappella*. Moderately easy.

O God, I Thank Thee—Schumann, arr. Lundquist. Willis No. 8466. *A cappella*. Easy.

O Hear Me When I Call on Thee—Schubert. E. C. Schirmer No. 2684. Accompanied. Medium.

O Jesu, Salvator—Alberti, ed. Boyd. Lawson-Gould No. 51843. Accompanied. Medium.

O Lord, Hear Thou My Prayer—Schumann, arr. Goldman. Lawson-Gould No. 51968. Piano or organ accompaniment. Soprano solo. Medium.

O Lord, Have Mercy on Us (Kyrie Eleison)—Buxtehude. Sam Fox No. CM 6. Optional accompaniment. Medium.

O, Lord in Thee Have I Trusted—Handel. Kjos No. 5481 C. Accompanied. Medium.

O Lord Most Holy (Panis Angelicus)—Franck. Summy-Birchard No. 396. Accompanied. Medium.

O, Love Divine (from *Theodora*)—Handel, arr. Malin. Edw. B. Marks No. 4543. Accompanied. Moderately difficult.

O Magnum Mysterium—Rorem. Boosey & Hawkes No. 6006. *A cappella.* Medium.

O Rejoice, Ye Christians, Loudly—J. S. Bach. Carl Fischer No. CM 6600. *A cappella.* Moderately easy.

O Savior, Throw the Heavens Wide (Motet, Op. 74, No. 2)—Brahms. G. Schirmer No. 8545. *A cappella.* Moderately difficult.

O Sing unto the Lord—Hassler. G. Schirmer No. 10872. *A cappella.* Moderately easy.

O Sing unto the Lord—Purcell. E. C. Schirmer No. 1103. Organ accompaniment. Moderately easy.

O Sing unto the Lord a New Song—Piston. Associated No. A-640. Accompanied. Moderately difficult.

O Vos Omnes—Victoria. Ricordi No. NY1875. *A cappella.* Medium.

Oh, Blest Are They—Tchaikovsky, arr. Cain. Remick No. 3024. *A cappella.* Moderately difficult.

Omnipotence, The—Schubert. G. Schirmer No. 10146. Accompanied. Medium.

Once I Had Hoped from Thee—De Monte. Piedmont No. 4427. *A cappella.* Medium.

Onward, Ye Peoples!—Sibelius, arr. Lefebvre. Galaxy No. 938-10. Accompanied. Moderately easy.

Os Justi—Bruckner. G. Schirmer No. 8121. *A cappella.* Medium.

Our Father—Gretchaninov, English text by Kimball. Presser No. 332-13000. *A cappella.* Moderately difficult.

Our Soul Doth Wait upon the Lord—Antes, arr. Kroeger. Boosey & Hawkes No. 5941. Organ accompaniment. Medium.

Pater Noster—Stravinsky. Boosey & Hawkes No. 1833. *A cappella.* Medium.

Pater Noster (Our Father)—Tchaikovsky. G. Schirmer No. 5475. *A cappella.* Moderately easy.

Plorate Filii Israel (Lament, Ye Children of Israel)—Carissimi. Bourne No. ES 34; E. C. Schirmer No. 1172. Accompanied. Medium.

Praise Be to Thee—Palestrina, arr. Lundquist. Willis No. 5678. *A cappella.* Easy.

Praise Him, Praise Ye the Lord—Caldara, ed. Ehret. Elkan-Vogel No. 362-03145. Piano or organ accompaniment. Soprano, alto, tenor, and bass solos. Moderately easy.

Prayer and Chorale—Mendelssohn. Lawson-Gould No. 849. *A cappella.* Moderately easy.

Psallite—Praetorius, arr. Greyson. Bourne No. ES 21. *A cappella.* Easy.

Psalm 61—Hovhaness. C. F. Peters No. 6255. Organ accompaniment. Medium.

Psalm Ninety-two—Schubert, ed. Meyerowitz. Alexander Broude No. AB 823. *A cappella.* Baritone solo. Moderately difficult.

Psalm CL (Praise Ye the Lord)—Franck. Oliver Ditson No. 332-14082. Organ accompaniment. Medium.

Psalm 150 (Hallelujah, Praise Ye the Lord)—Lewandowski. Schmitt, Hall & McCreary No. 1640. Optional *a cappella.* Medium.

Quando Corpus (from *Stabat Mater*)—Rossini, ed. Van Camp. Music 70 No. 205. *A cappella.* Medium.

Rejoice in the Lord—Amram. Peters No. 66517. *A cappella.* Medium.

Religious Meditation—Berlioz, ed. Prussing. Tetra No. AB 833. Organ accompaniment. Medium.

Rejoice in the Lord Always—Purcell. Novello No. 1581. Accompanied. Moderately easy.

Requiescat—Schuman. G. Schirmer No. 8926. Accompanied. Medium.

Salvation Is Created—Tschesnokov, arr. Norden. J. Fischer No. 4129. *A cappella*. Medium.

Salve Regina—Lasso. Music Press No. MP-73. *A cappella*. Medium.

Sanctus (from *B Minor Mass*)—J. S. Bach. G. Schirmer No. 5654. Accompanied. Difficult.

Sanctus (from *C Major Mass*)—Beethoven. Walton No. 6014. Accompanied. Medium.

Sanctus (from *Requiem*)—Fauré. Fitzsimons No. 2119. Accompanied. Easy.

Sanctus (from *Mass VII*)—Lotti. G. Schirmer No. 9407. *A cappella*. Moderately easy.

Sanctus (from *16th Mass*)—Haydn, arr. Hilton. Mercury No. MC 399. Accompanied. Medium.

Sanctus—Rossini, ed. Ferguson. Lawson-Gould No. 51890. Accompanied. Moderately difficult.

Send Out Thy Light (Emitte Spiritum Tuum)—Schuetky. Carl Fischer No. CM 548. *A cappella*. Moderately easy.

Serve the Lord with Gladness—Handel. Lawson-Gould No. 794. Accompanied. Medium.

Sicut Moses Serpentem—Schütz. Associated No. A-412. Accompanied. Difficult.

Sing to the Lord (Gloria in Excelsis Deo)—Haydn. G. Schirmer No. 5414. Accompanied. Moderately easy.

Sing unto the Lord Most High—Pergolesi. Boosey & Hawkes. *A cappella*. Easy.

Sing We All Now with One Accord—Praetorius. G. Schirmer No. 7543. Accompanied. Moderately easy.

Sing with Gladness—Sweelinck, ed. Sateren. AMSI No. 337. *A cappella*. Moderately difficult.

Song of Galilee (El Yivneh Hagalil)—transcribed by Chajes. Transcontinental No. TCL 214. Accompanied. Medium.

Song of Repentance—J. S. Bach. Broude Bros. No. 65. *A cappella*. Medium.

Sound the Cymbal—Schubert. Schmitt, Hall & McCreary No. 1745. Accompanied. Medium.

Stabat Mater—Schubert. Belwin-Mills No. 2164. Accompanied. Moderately easy.

Surgens Jesus—di Lasso. Arista No. AE 309. *A cappella*. Medium.

Tarry Here and Watch—Pitoni, arr. Kingsbury. Tetra No. A.B. 757. *A cappella*. Medium.

Te Deum—Schuman. G. Schirmer No. 9453. *A cappella*. Medium.

This Is the Record of John—Gibbons, ed. Parker and Shaw. Lawson-Gould No. 550. Organ accompaniment. Tenor solo. Medium.

Thou Art the King of Glory—Handel. Kjos No. 5481A. Accompanied. Moderately easy.

Thou Art Worthy of Praise—Haydn. Sam Fox No. MM 13. *A cappella*. Moderately easy.

Thou Must Leave Thy Lowly Dwelling (from *Childhood of Christ*)—Berlioz. H. W. Gray No. 1898. Accompanied. Medium.

To Him Who Never Faileth—Altnikol, ed. Frank. Sam Fox No. MM 3. Accompanied. Moderately easy.

Tribulationes Civitatum—Thomson. Weintraub. *A cappella.* Moderately difficult.

Tribus Miraculis—Marenzio. Available—World Library. *A cappella.* Medium.

Tu Solus Qui Facis Mirabilla—Després. Mercury No. 352-00045. *A cappella.* Medium.

Turn Back, O Man—Holst. Galaxy No. 6. Accompanied. Medium.

Twenty-Third Psalm, The—Wilson. Bourne No. 703. *A cappella.* Medium.

Unto Thee I Lift My Spirit—Hiller. Sam Fox MM No. 7. Accompanied. Moderately easy.

Veni Jesu—Cherubini, arr. Riegger. Flammer No. 84189. Accompanied. Medium.

Veni Virgo Sacrata—Reutter, ed. Young. Broude Brothers No. MGC 21. Organ accompaniment. Medium.

Venite, Exsultemus Domino (O Come Let Us Sing)—Sweelinck. Summy-Birchard No. 5517. Optional accompaniment. Medium.

Von Himmel hoch (From Highest Heav'n)—J. S. Bach. Lawson-Gould No. 903. *A cappella.* Medium.

Vouchsafe, O Lord—Gretchaninov. Galaxy No. 1356. Optional accompaniment. Medium.

We Adore Thee (Adoramus Te)—Lotti. Chappell No. 6149. *A cappella.* Moderately easy.

We Have No Other Help—Arkhangelsky, arr. Gnotov. M. Witmark No. 5-W3005. *A cappella.* Moderately easy.

We Pledge You Forever (from *Cantata No. 208*)—J. S. Bach, ed. Malin. Belwin-Mills No. 2406. Accompanied. Moderately difficult.

We Praise and Bless Thee (from *Messe Solennelle*)—Gounod, arr. Witford. Oliver Ditson No. 332-40049. Accompanied. Moderately easy.

We Praise Thee—Gretchaninov, arr. Cain. Hoffman No. 46,335. *A cappella.* Easy.

We Will Rejoice in Thy Salvation—Handel, ed. Malin. Belwin-Mills No. 2407. Accompanied. Moderately difficult.

Who Shall Separate Us—Schuetz. Chantry Music Press. Organ or piano accompaniment. Medium.

Who With Grieving Soweth—Schein. Mercury No. 19. *A cappella.* Moderately difficult.

With a Voice of Singing—Shaw. G. Schirmer No. 8103. Accompanied. Moderately easy.

With Sorrow Shaken—C.P.E. Bach. Elkan-Vogel No. 362-01303. Piano or organ accompaniment. Alto solo. Moderately easy.

Ye Are Not of the Flesh (from the motet *Jesus meine Freude*)—Bach. Lawson-Gould No. 785. Accompanied. Difficult.

Your Voices Tune (from *Alexander's Feast*)—Handel, ed. Malin. Belwin-Mills No. 2408. Accompanied. Medium.

While As a Stone, Yet Living—Marenzio. Piedmont No. 4485. Optional accompaniment. Moderately easy.

General: Secular

Adieu, Sweet Amarillis—Wilbye, ed. Kaplan. Lawson-Gould No. 51865. *A cappella.* Medium.

Ah, Happy He Who Sees You!—Rossi. Piedmont No. 4484. *A cappella.* Moderately easy.

Ah, Love, To You I'm Crying—Hassler, ed. Ehret. Tetra No. A.B. 759. *A cappella.* Medium.

Anima Mia Perdona—Monteverdi, ed. Malin. Belwin-Mills No. 2380. *A cappella.* Medium.

Anthony O Daly—Barber. G. Schirmer No. 8909. *A cappella.* Medium.

April Is in Her Lovely Face—Morley. Ricordi No. 1398; E. C. Schirmer No. 1612. *A cappella.* Moderately easy.

As Long As Beauty Shall Remain—Brahms, arr. Christy. Schmitt, Hall & Mc-Creary No. 1172. *A cappella.* Easy.

As Torrents in Summer—Elgar, arr. Cain. Flammer No. 81068. *A cappella.* Moderately easy.

Ballad of Green Broom—Britten. Boosey & Hawkes No. 1875. *A cappella.* Moderately difficult.

Beggar's Canon (from *The Brigands*)—Offenbach. Broude Bros. No. 117. Accompanied. Medium.

Blow, Blow, Thou Winter Wind—Rutter. Oxford No. 52.024. Accompanied. Moderately easy.

Chanson on *Dessus le Marche d'Arras*—di Lasso. Associated No. NYPM 32. *A cappella.* Medium.

Choose Something like a Star—Thompson. E. C. Schirmer No. 2487. Accompanied. Moderately easy.

Come and Sing (from *Die Fledermaus*)—Strauss. Carl Fischer No. CM 4628. Accompanied. Moderately difficult.

Come, Let Your Hearts Be Singing—Gastoldi, arr. Greyson. Bourne No. ES 26. *A cappella.* Moderately easy.

Coolin, The—Barber. G. Schirmer No. 8910. *A cappella.* Moderately difficult.

Chorus of the Hebrew Captives (from *Nabucco*)—Verdi, ed. Serposs. Music 70 No. 224. Accompanied. Medium.

Chorus of the Office Clerks (from *Fortunio's Song*)—Offenbach. Broude Brothers No. 4066. Accompanied. Medium.

Dedication—Franz, arr. Riegger. Flammer No. 81043. *A cappella.* Medium.

Dirge for Two Veterans—Lockwood. Witmark No. 2879. *A cappella.* Soprano solo. Difficult.

Evening—Kodály. Boosey & Hawkes No. 1710. *A cappella.* Difficult.

Fa una canzone—Vecchi. Lawson-Gould No. 556. *A cappella.* Easy.

Fable, A—Dello Joio. Carl Fischer No. CM 6299. Accompanied. Moderately easy.

Face to Face (from *Ten Songs*)—Shostakovitch. G. Schirmer No. 12121. *A cappella.* Moderately difficult.

Fair Is the Crystal—di Lasso. Piedmont No. 4384. *A cappella.* Medium.

Fall, Leaves, Fall—Bright. Shawnee Press No. A-945. *A cappella.* Medium.

Farewell, The (Horch, der Wind klagt in den Zweigen)—Brahms. Sam Fox No. RC 2. Accompanied. Moderately easy.

Farmer's Wife Lost Her Cat—Mozart. Edw. B. Marks No. 1. *A cappella*. Moderately difficult.

From Grief to Glory (Verse II–Love in Grief)—F. M. Christiansen. Augsburg No. 175. *A cappella*. Difficult.

Geographical Fugue (speaking chorus)—Toch. Belwin-Mills No. 347. Difficult.

Glory (March from *Aida*)—Verdi. Willis No. 2892. Accompanied. Moderately difficult.

Happiness (O Seligkeit)—Schubert, ed. Freed. Sam Fox No. RC 4. Accompanied. Moderately easy.

Have Courage, Friends (from *Ten Songs*)—Shostakovitch. G. Schirmer No. 12118. *A cappella*. Medium.

Hear Me Now, Beloved—Marenzio. Piedmont No. 4334. *A cappella*. Medium.

How Still the Night (In stiller Nacht)—Brahms, arr. Track. World Library No. CE-2346. *A cappella*. Easy.

Hunting Song—Mendelssohn. Sam Fox No. RC 9. *A cappella*. Medium.

I Myself When Young Did Eagerly Frequent—Diemer. Boosey & Hawkes No. 5778. *A cappella*. Medium.

If All My Heartfelt Thinking—Brahms. Associated No. A-407. *A cappella*. Medium.

If I Should Part from You—Monteverdi. Presser No. 312-40939. *A cappella*. Moderately easy.

In Silent Night—Brahms. G. Schirmer No. 5848. *A cappella*. Easy.

In Swift Light Vessels Gliding (Opus 2)—Webern. Universal Edition No. E6643A. *A cappella*. Moderately difficult.

In the Quiet Night—Mennin. Carl Fischer No. CM6417. *A cappella*. Medium.

In These Delightful, Pleasant Groves—Purcell. Novello No. M. T. 1. *A cappella*. Medium.

In Winter—Hindemith. Associated No. AS 19432V. *A cappella*. Medium.

It Is Good to Be Merry—Berger. Kjos No. 5293. *A cappella*. Medium.

Je pleure (I Weep)—Le Jeune. Éditions Salabert No. 23-6. *A cappella*. Moderately easy.

Je serais enchanté (I Should Be Overjoyed)—Gounod. Alexander Broude No. 252-3. Accompanied. Moderately easy.

Jig for Voices—Rowley. Boosey & Hawkes No. 1699. Optional accompaniment. Medium.

Lady, So Fair Thou Seemest—de Wert. Belwin-Mills Music No. 60778. *A cappella*. Moderately easy.

Las Agachadas—Copland. Boosey & Hawkes. *A cappella*. For solo group and eight-part chorus. Moderately difficult.

Lebenslust (Joy of Living)—Schubert. Alexander Broude No. 258-6. Accompanied. Medium.

Lobster Quadrille, The—Fine. Witmark No. 5-W3180 I. Accompanied. Moderately easy.

Lonely Boat Drifts Slowly, A—Schumann. Broude Brothers No. 135. Soprano solo, flute, and horn. Medium.

Lost Youth (Verlorene Jugend)—Brahms. Presser No. 312-40946. *A cappella*. Medium.

Lotus Dust, The—Bright. Shawnee Press No. A-883. *A cappella*. Moderately easy.

Love Song—Brahms, arr. Wilson. Ricordi No. NY1475. Optional accompaniment. Moderately easy.

Lullaby (Weigenlied)—Mozart. Associated No. A-84. Accompanied. Soprano solo. Moderately easy.

Madrigal—Gesualdo. Edw. B. Marks No. 52. *A cappella.* Medium.

Matona, Lovely Maiden—Lasso. Carl Fischer No. CM 4637. *A cappella.* Moderately easy.

Modern Music—Billings. C. F. Peters No. 66340. *A cappella.* Medium.

Monotone—Lockwood. Kjos No. 8. *A cappella.* Medium.

Music the Comforter (Trösterin Music)—Bruckner. Sam Fox No. MM 12. Accompanied. Moderately easy.

My Love Dwelt in a Northern Land—Elgar. G. Schirmer No. 2366. *A cappella.* Moderately easy.

Neighbors' Chorus—Offenbach. Broude Bros. No. 130. Accompanied. Medium.

Nightingale, The—Mendelssohn, ed. Mason. Walton No. 7010. Optional accompaniment. Moderately easy.

Nuptial Chorus (from *The Guardsman*)—Tchaikovsky, ed. Malin. Belwin-Mills No. 2405. Accompanied. Medium.

O Care, Thou Wilt Despatch Me—Weelkes. Boston Music No. 13705. *A cappella.* Moderately easy.

O, Dearest Love of Mine (Herzlieb zu Dir allein)—Hassler. Boston Music No. 13703. *A cappella.* Medium.

O Lovely Mai (O Sussex Mai)—Brahms. Belwin-Mills No. 2174. *A cappella.* Moderately easy.

O voi che sospirate a migliore note—Marenzio. Dartmouth Publications No. A-977. *A cappella.* Medium.

O World, I Now Must Leave Thee (Innsbruck, ich muss dich lassen)—Isaac. Alexander Broude No. 251-3. *A cappella.* Medium.

Oh, When My Husband Comes Back Home—di Lasso. Pro Art No. 2365. *A cappella.* Moderately easy.

Old Abram Brown—Britten. Boosey & Hawkes No. 1786. Accompanied. Easy.

Old Joe Has Gone Fishing (from *Peter Grimes*)—Britten. Boosey & Hawkes No. 1784. Accompanied. Moderately difficult.

Old Man, The (Der Greis)—Haydn. Associated No. A-618. *A cappella.* Medium.

On the Way to My Sweetheart—Brahms, arr. Matesky. Gentry No. G-4007. Accompanied. Moderately easy.

Party of Lovers at Tea, A—Argento. Boosey & Hawkes No. 5712. *A cappella.* Medium.

Pavane pour une infante défunte—Ravel. Broude Bros. No. 100. Accompanied. Moderately difficult.

Placido e il mar (from *Idomeneo*)—Mozart. Lawson-Gould No. 841. Accompanied. Medium.

Pleasure Awaits Us (from *La Finta Giardiniera*)—Mozart. Belwin-Mills No. 2403. Accompanied. Medium.

Prelude—Schuman. G. Schirmer No. 8929. *A cappella.* Soprano solo. Moderately difficult.

Primrose, The (Die Primel)—Mendelssohn. Associated No. A-382. *A cappella.* Medium.

Promise of Living, The (from *The Tender Land*)—Copland. Boosey & Hawkes No. 5020. Piano duet accompaniment. Moderately difficult.

Rise Up, Oh Flame—Praetorius, arr. Harley and Aschenbrenner. Carl Fischer No. CM 4712. *A cappella.* Moderately easy.

Road Not Taken, The—Thompson. E. C. Schirmer No. 2485. Accompanied. Moderately easy.

Roses of the South—Strauss, arr. Gibb. Homeyer No. 437. Accompanied. Moderately easy.

See How Aurora Comes with Brow All Glowing—Marenzio. Piedmont No. 4438. *A cappella.* Medium.

Sigh Goes Stirring through the Wood, A—Brahms, ed. Richter. Associated No. A-379. *A cappella.* Medium.

Since All Is Passing—Hindemith. Schott No. AP 37. *A cappella.* Moderately easy.

Sing a Song of Sixpence—Bright. Shawnee Press No. A-851. *A cappella.* Medium.

Sing of Spring—Gershwin, ed. Smith. Lawson-Gould No. 51964. Accompanied. Medium.

Six Balletti—Gastoldi. C. F. Peters, Set I, No. 6877a. *A cappella.* Moderately easy. Set II, No. 6877b. *A cappella.* Medium.

Six Love Songs—Brahms. Summy-Birchard. Four-hand accompaniment. Moderately difficult.

Skylark's Song, The—Mendelssohn. Belwin-Mills No. 2181. Optional accompaniment. Moderately easy.

Song of the Lark (Lerchengesang)—Mendelssohn. Sam Fox No. RC 11. *A cappella.* Moderately easy.

Songs Filled My Heart—Dvořák. Presser No. 312-40813. Accompanied. Moderately easy.

Springtime—Hindemith. Schott No. 19432, IV. *A cappella.* Moderately difficult.

Stomp Your Foot (from *The Tender Land*)—Copland. Boosey & Hawkes No. 5019. Piano duet accompaniment. Moderately difficult.

Sunrise—Taneyev. G. Schirmer No. 2623. *A cappella.* Difficult.

Sure on This Shining Night—Barber. G. Schirmer No. 10864. Accompanied. Moderately easy.

Swan, A—Hindemith. Schott No. 19432, II. *A cappella.* Medium.

Sweet Day—McCray. J. Fischer No. 10132. *A cappella.* Moderately easy.

Talk Not to Me—Kaderavek. Westwood Press No. ESE-1497-8. *A cappella.* Medium.

These Are My Heartfelt Tears (madrigal)—Palestrina. Lawson-Gould No. 51029. *A cappella.* Moderately easy.

Thought Like Music, A—Brahms, arr. Suchoff. Plymouth No. A. S. 103. Accompanied. Moderately easy.

Three Nocturnes—Chávez. G. Schirmer No. 9522. *A cappella.* Moderately difficult.

To All Our Hearts Are Now Returning (from *Julius Caesar*)—Handel. Belwin-Mills No. 2404. Accompanied. Medium.

To All, To Each—Schuman. Presser No. 342-40013. *A cappella.* Medium.

To Music—Carter. Peer International. *A cappella.* Moderately difficult.

Trysting Placc, The—Brahms. E. C. Schirmer No. 391. Accompanied. Moderately easy.

Under the Willow Tree (from *Vanessa*)—Barber. G. Schirmer No. 10861. Accompanied. Soprano solo. Moderately difficult.

Up Sprang a Birch Tree Overnight—Dvořák. Mercury No. 312-40816. *A cappella.* Medium.

Voix Célestes (humming chorus)—Alcock. Chappell No. 2055. *A cappella.* Medium.

Walking on the Green Grass—Hennagin. Boosey & Hawkes No. 5443. *A cappella.* Medium.

Warm Was the Sun (Scaldava il sol)—Marenzio. Piedmont No. 4545. *A cappella.* Medium.

Warning—Diamond. Elkan-Vogel No. 362-03143. Accompaniment. Moderately difficult.

We Are Brave Matadors (from *La Traviata*)—Verdi. G. Schirmer No. 5435. Accompanied. Medium.

Welcome Sweet May (Wohl kommt der Mai)—de Lasso. Carl Fischer No. CM 7566. *A cappella.* Moderately easy.

When Evening Comes Chimes Fill the Forest—Dvořák. Mercury No. 312-40814. Accompanied. Medium.

When the Bright Sun—Byrd. Belwin-Mills No. A-202. *A cappella.* Moderately easy.

Whether Men Do Laugh or Weep—Vaughan Williams. Oxford No. X66. Accompanied. Medium.

Woman Is a Worthy Thing, A—Chávez. G. Schirmer No. 9611. *A cappella.* Medium.

Wonderful Life, A (Lebenslust)—Schubert. Sam Fox No. MM 8. Accompanied. Medium.

Younger Generation—Copland, arr. Swift. Boosey & Hawkes No. 1723. Accompanied. Moderately easy.

Publications for Mixed Voices (SAB)

Sacred

Alleluja (from the motet *Exultate, Jubilate*)—Mozart, arr. Riegger. Flammer No. 88522. Accompanied. Moderately difficult.

As Torrents in Summer—Elgar, arr. Cain. Flammer No. 88046. Optional *a cappella.* Easy.

Ave Maria—Gounod, arr. Downing. G. Schirmer No. 9450. Accompanied. Moderately easy.

Bless the Lord, O My Soul—Ippolitov-Ivanov, arr. Richardson. Boston Music No. 2801. *A cappella.* Moderately easy.

Blessing, Glory and Wisdom—J. S. Bach, arr. Ehret. Elkan-Vogel No. 362-03118. Optional accompaniment. Medium.

Cherubic Hymn, The (Opus 29)—Gretchaninov, arr. Howorth. Pro Art No. 1031. *A cappella.* Moderately easy.

Cherubim Song No. 7—Bortniansky, arr. Tchaikovsky. G. Schirmer No. 9753. Accompanied. Moderately easy.

Christus Resurgens (Christ Being Raised)—Viadana. Leeds No. L-441. Organ accompaniment. Moderately easy.

Come Souls, Behold Today—Bach, arr. Nelson. Augsburg No. 1171. *A cappella.* Moderately easy.

Dona Nobis Pacem (old German canon)—arr. Wilson. Schmitt, Hall & McCreary No. 5510. *A cappella.* Moderately easy.

For the Beauty of the Earth—Kocher, arr. Davis. Remick No. 4-R3231. Accompanied. Easy.

God So Loved the World—Stainer, arr. Martin. Schmitt, Hall & McCreary No. 5509. *A cappella.* Easy.

Heavens Are Declaring, The—Beethoven, arr. Kountz. Witmark No. 2565. Accompanied. Easy.

Heavens Are Declaring, The—Beethoven, arr. Mueller. G. Schirmer No. 10670. Accompanied. Easy.

Heavens Are Telling, The—Haydn, arr. Wilson. Lorenz No. 7020. Accompanied. Moderately easy.

Jesu, Joy of Man's Desiring (from Cantata No. 147)—J. S. Bach. G. Schirmer No. 10023; Remick No. R3279. Accompanied. Easy.

Jesu, Son of God (Ave Verum Corpus)—Mozart. Schmitt, Hall & McCreary 5502. Accompanied. Moderately easy.

Lead Me, O Lord—Wesley, arr. Pitcher. Willis No. 8493. Accompanied. Easy.

Legend, A (from the cycle *Songs for Young People*)—Tchaikovsky, arr. Deis. G. Schirmer No. 10035. Accompanied. Medium.

Let Our Gladness Know No End (old Bohemian Christmas carol)—arr. Ryg. Belwin-Mills No. 1761. *A cappella.* Moderately easy.

Lift Thine Eyes (from *Elijah*)—Mendelssohn, arr. Pitcher. Willis No. 8486. Optional accompaniment. Moderately easy.

Moon Shines Bright, The (old English carol)—arr. Wilson. Bourne No. T8. Accompanied. Moderately easy.

O Little Jesus (16th-century German carol)—arr. Gordon. Belwin-Mills. No. 1873. Accompanied. Easy.

O Lord Most Holy—Franck, arr. Pitcher. Willis No. 8489. Accompanied. Easy.

O Lord, Our God—Schvedov, arr. Wilson. Bourne No. T5. Optional accompaniment. Medium.

Praise the Almighty, My Soul, Adore Him—Zipp. Concordia No. CH 1086. *A cappella.* Moderately easy.

Praise Ye the Father—Gounod, arr. Pitcher. Willis No. 8482. Accompanied. Moderately easy.

Prayer for Peace, A (Panis Angelicus)—Franck, arr. Hoffman. Hoffman No. 46,107. Accompanied. Moderately easy.

Rocking (Czech carol)—arr. Ehret. Scholin No. 1076. Accompanied. Moderately easy.

Send Out Thy Light—Gounod, arr. Mueller. G. Schirmer No. 8695. Accompanied. Medium.

Shepherd of Eager Youth—Roff. Elkan-Vogel No. 507. Accompanied. Moderately easy.

To Realms of Glory—Schein, arr. Nelson. Augsburg No. 1169. *A cappella.* Easy.

Turn Thy Face from My Sins—Attwood, arr. Pitcher. Willis No. 8487. Accompanied. Easy.

Secular

Bells of St. Mary's—Adams, arr. Stickles. Chappell No. 7006. Accompanied. Easy.

Bells of the Sea—Solman, arr. Wilson. Sam Fox No. 542. Accompanied. Moderately easy.

Carol of the Bells (Ukrainian carol)—Leontovich, arr. Wilhousky. Carl Fischer No. 4747. Optional *a cappella.* Easy.

Danse Macabre—Saint-Saëns, arr Lorenz. Lorenz No. 7098. Accompanied. Moderately difficult.

Dedication—Franz, arr. Wilson. Paull-Pioneer. Accompanied. Moderately easy.

Down South—Myddleton, arr. High. Edw. B. Marks No. 403. Accompanied. Easy.

Green Cathedral—Hahn, arr. Montrose. Presser No. 322-35447. Accompanied. Easy.

Homing—Del Riego, arr. Stickles. Chappell No. 7007. Accompanied. Easy.

Kentucky Babe—Giebel, arr. Stickles. Edwin H. Morris No. 8003. Accompanied. Easy.

Ol' Man River—Kern, arr. Stickles. Chappell No. CR77. Accompanied. Moderately easy.

Pines of Home—Luvaas. Carl Fischer No. 6452. Optional *a cappella.* Moderately easy.

Prayer from *Hansel and Gretel*—Humperdinck, arr. Riegger. Flammer No. 88019. Accompanied. Easy.

Shortnin' Bread—Wolfe, arr. Riegger. Flammer No. 88088. Accompanied. Moderately easy.

Sing, Sing a Song for Me—Vecchi, arr. Greyson. Bourne No. ES 53C. Optional accompaniment. Moderately easy.

Three Madrigals from the XVIIth Century:
1. Your Shining Eyes—Bateson.
2. As Late in My Accounting—Weelkes.
3. Follow Me, Sweet Love—East.
J. Fischer No. 9455. *A cappella.* Medium.

Tickling Trio (Vadasi via di qua)—Martini. Witmark No. 4-W2750. *A cappella.* Moderately easy.

To Music—Schubert, arr. Wilson. Schmitt, Hall & McCreary No. 5011. Accompanied. Moderately easy.

Turn Ye to Me—Wilson, arr. Churchill. Belwin-Mills No. 1619. Accompanied. Moderately easy.

When Day Is Done—Katcher, arr. Koshetz. Harms, Inc. No. 614. Accompanied. Moderately easy.

Folk Songs and Spirituals

Certainly, Lord (Negro spiritual)—arr. Kirk. Pro Art No. 1834. Accompanied. Moderately easy.

Cindy (American folk song)—arr. Barthelson. Belwin-Mills No. 1984. Accompanied. Moderately easy.

Cindy (American folk song)—arr. Ehret. Theodore Presser No. 312-41185. Accompanied. Moderately easy.

Cowboy's Meditation, The (American folk song)—arr. Wilson. Paull-Pioneer. Accompanied. Moderately easy.

Ezekiel Saw de Wheel (spiritual)—arr. Cain. Belwin-Mills No. 1131. Accompanied. Medium.

From Lucerne to Weggis Fair (Swiss folk song)—arr. Harris. Pro Art No. 2369. Accompanied. Medium.

Go Down, Moses (Negro spiritual)—arr. Lorenz. Lorenz No. 7096. Accompanied. Easy.

Gonna Ride Up in the Chariot (spiritual)—arr. Richardson. Theodore Presser No. 312-41187. Accompanied. Easy.

He Never Said a Mumbalin' Word (spiritual)—arr. Wilson. Paull-Pioneer. Optional accompaniment. Moderately easy.

Hi, Ho, Sing Gaily! (Swiss folk tune)—arr. Luvaas. Summy-Birchard No. B1637. Accompanied. Moderately easy.

Ho La Li (Bavarian melody)—arr. Luvaas. Summy-Birchard No. B1613. Accompanied. Moderately easy.

I Ain't Gonna Grieve My Lord No More (Negro spiritual)—arr. Ehret. Belwin-Mills No. 1661. Accompanied. Medium.

I Got Shoes (Negro spiritual)—arr. Cain. Flammer No. 88047. Accompanied. Easy.

Jennie Jenkins (American dialogue song)—arr. Churchill. Belwin-Mills No. 1893. Accompanied. Easy.

John Anderson, My Jo (Scottish folk song)—arr. Gordon. Belwin-Mills No. 1494. Accompanied. Moderately easy.

Little David, Play on Your Harp (Negro spiritual)—arr. Cain. Flammer No. 88054. Accompanied. Moderately easy.

Night Herding Song (country folk ballad)—arr. Barker. Belwin-Mills No. 1828. Optional accompaniment. Moderately easy.

Oh, Vreneli (Swiss folk song)—arr. Larson. Summy-Birchard No. B1594. Accompanied. Moderately easy.

Rock-a My Soul (spiritual)—arr. Wilson. Bourne No. T 11. Accompanied. Moderately easy.

Rocking Carol (Czech carol)—arr. Graham. Presser No. 312-40698. Optional accompaniment. Moderately easy.

Russian Picnic (based on Russian folk tunes)—arr. Enders. G. Schirmer No. 9632. Accompanied. Medium.

Simple Gifts (American Shaker tune)—arr. Kirk. Pro Art No. 2662. Accompanied. Moderately easy.

Stodola Pumpa (Czech folk song)—arr. Wilson. Bourne No. T 12. Accompanied. Medium.

Turtle Dove, The (English folk song)—arr. Ahrold. Presser No. 312-40700. Accompanied. Moderately easy.

Vreneli (Swiss folk song)—arr. Ehret. Theodore Presser No. 312-41189. Accompanied. Easy.

Water Boy (Negro work song)—arr. Pitcher. Boston Music No. 2359, Accompanied. Baritone solo—melody in baritone. Easy.

Were You There (spiritual)—arr. Wilson. Bourne No. T 2. Accompanied. Medium.

Publications for Treble Voices (SSA)

Sacred

All Ye That Cried unto the Lord—Mendelssohn, arr. Gray. Pro Art No. 1839. Accompanied. Easy.

Alleluia—Mozart, arr. Riegger. Flammer No. 89024. Accompanied. Medium.

Angel Ever Bright—Handel, arr. Overby. Augsburg No. 1013. Optional accompaniment. Moderately easy.

Angels and the Shepherds—Kodály. Universal No. 312-40593. A cappella. Medium.

Angelus ad Pastores Ait and Hodie Christus Natus Est (from Sacrae Cantiunculae)—Monteverdi. Mercury Music No. 352-000-24. A cappella. Medium.

At the Gate of Heaven (Spanish folk song)—arr. Allen. Summy-Birchard No. 1570. Accompanied. Moderately easy.

Ave Maria—Arcadelt. Bourne No. ES 3. A cappela. Moderately easy.

Ave Maria—Kodály. Universal No. 312-40592. A cappella. Moderately easy.

Ave Verum—Desprès, arr. Greyson. Bourne No. ES 88A. A cappella. Moderately easy.

Away in a Manger (traditional carol)—arr. Terri. Lawson-Gould No. 666. A cappella. Moderately easy.

Bless Ye the Lord—Ippolitov-Ivanov, arr. Wilhousky. Carl Fischer No. 639. A cappella. Moderately easy.

Blest Is the Man—Lasso. Augsburg No. PS603. A cappella. Moderately easy.

Bring a Torch, Jeannette, Isabella (old French carol)—arr. Nunn. E. C. Schirmer No. 496. A cappella. Moderately easy.

Call of the Shepherds, The (French Noël)—arr. Malin. B. F. Wood No. 826. A cappella. Moderately easy.

Cantate Domino—Pitoni. Flammer No. 89181. A cappella. Moderately easy.

Carol of the Italian Pipers (traditional carol)—arr. Zgodava. Shawnee Press No. B-321. Accompanied. Moderately easy.

Crucifixus—A. Gabrieli, ed. Ehret. Edward B. Marks No. 4332. A cappella. Medium.

Cherubic Hymn—Musitcheskoo. Boosey & Hawkes No. 5026. Accompanied. Medium.

Christ Is Born (Ukrainian carol)—arr. Boberg. Carl Fischer No. 7455. A cappella. Moderately easy.

Christ Is Born in a Manger Bed (17th-century melody). World Library No. AC-596-3. A cappella. Easy.

Christmas Hymn (17th century)—arr. Jüngst. G. Schirmer No. 9890. A cappella. Moderately easy.

Come to Me—Beethoven, arr. Aslanoff. G. Schirmer No. 8711. Accompanied. Easy.

Come, Ye Gay Shepherds—Costeley, arr. Cramer. Edw. B. Marks No. 4482. Optional accompaniment. Moderately easy.

Come, Ye Lofty, Come, Ye Lowly (Breton carol)—arr. Malin. Summy-Birchard No. 1419. Accompanied. Moderately easy.

Coventry Carol (English carol)—arr. Stone. Belwin-Mills No. 2070. Accompanied. Moderately easy.

Glory to God in the Highest!—Pergolesi, arr. Riegger. Flammer No. 89041. Accompanied. Medium.

God of Abraham Praise, The (traditional Hebrew melody)—arr. Malmin. Augsburg No. 1238. Accompanied. Easy.

God Rest You Merry, Gentlemen (English carol)—arr. Scholin. Belwin-Mills No. 1625. Accompanied. Moderately easy.

Hear Our Supplication—Mozart, arr. Hilton. Mercury No. 352-00460. Accompanied. Moderately easy.

Holy Infant's Lullaby, The—Dello Joio. Edw. B. Marks No. 4392. Accompanied. Moderately easy.

How Far Is It to Bethlehem?—Chesterton. World Library No. AC-595-3. *A cappella.* Easy.

Hush My Babe—Rousseau-Stone. Belwin-Mills No. 2067. Accompanied. Easy.

Incline Thine Ear, O Lord—Arkhangelsky, arr. Krone. Witmark No. 3220. *A cappella.* Medium.

Jesu, Joy of Man's Desiring—Bach, arr. Treharne. G. Schirmer No. 8388. Accompanied. Easy.

Jesu, Priceless Treasure (from the motet *Jesu, meine Freude*)—J. S. Bach. Summy-Birchard No. 4204. Optional accompaniment. Easy.

Lacrymosa—Mozart. Carl Fischer No. CM 6945. Accompanied. Medium.

Legend, A—Tchaikovsky. Carl Fischer No. CM 6325. Accompanied. Moderately easy.

Lift Thine Eyes (from *Elijah*)—Mendelssohn. Willis No. 698. *A cappella.* Moderately easy.

Lo, A Voice to Heaven Sounding—Bortniansky, arr. Davis. E. C. Schirmer No. 1079. *A cappella.* Moderately easy.

Lord Is My Shepherd, The—Schubert, arr. Watson. Remick No. 2-G1646. Accompanied. Moderately difficult.

O Little Jesus (16th-century German carol)—arr. Gordon. Belwin-Mills No. 1874. Accompanied. Moderately easy.

Once in Royal David's City (Finnish folk melody)—arr. Lundquist. Elkan-Vogel No. 3079. *A cappella.* Easy.

Praise to the Lord (17th-century German tune)—arr. Whitehead. Gray No. 2095. Organ accompaniment. Moderately easy.

Praise Ye the Lord—J. S. Bach, arr. Trusler. Plymouth No. TR-103. Piano or organ accompaniment. Moderately easy.

Praise Ye the Lord of Hosts—Saint-Saëns. Belwin-Mills No. 698. Accompanied. Easy.

Prayer of Thanksgiving (old Dutch melody)—arr. Kremser. G. Schirmer No. 6812. Accompanied. Easy.

Puer Natus Est—Morales. Bourne No. ES 73. Optional accompaniment. Medium.

Rejoice All Men—Niles and Ross. Carl Fischer No. CM 6462. Accompanied. Medium.

Rejoice, Holy Mary (French carol)—arr. Malin. Belwin-Mills No. 693. Accompanied. Moderately easy.

Send Out Thy Light—Balakirev. Boosey & Hawkes No. 1924. *A cappella.* Medium.

Shepherd's Carol—Billings. H. W. Gray No. 3024. Accompanied. Moderately easy.

Sing a Gay Noel (Basque melody)—arr. Glaser. B. F. Wood No. 816. *A cappella.* Moderately easy.

Slumber of the Infant Jesus—Gevaert, arr. Davis. E. C. Schirmer No. 1088. *A cappella.* Medium.

This Little Babe (from *A Ceremony of Carols*)—Britten. Bossey & Hawkes No. 5138. Accompanied. Moderately easy.

To Our Little Town (French carol)—arr. Malin. Belwin-Mills No. 692. *A cappella.* Moderately easy.

To Us There Comes a Little Child (German melody)—arr. Malin. Belwin-Mills No. 704. Accompanied. Moderately easy.

Two Czech Carols—arr. Peloguin. McLaughlin & Reilly No. 2047. *A cappella.* Moderately easy.

Vere Languores Nostros—Lotti. Bourne No. ES 22. *A cappella.* Moderately easy.

While Shepherds Watched (17th-century melody)—arr. Tkach. Kjos No. 6044. Accompanied. Easy.

Whither Going, Shepherd? (Hungarian folk song)—arr. Taylor. J. Fischer No. 5054. Accompanied. Moderately easy.

Wolcum Yole! (from *A Ceremony of Carols*)—Britten. Boosey & Hawkes No. 1755B. Accompanied. Medium.

Ya Ba Bom (Jewish folk tune)—arr. Goldman. Lawson-Gould No. 51958. Piano and percussion accompaniment. Medium.

Secular

Adelaide—Beethoven. Boston Music No. 3045. Accompanied. Moderately easy.

Adieu, Mignonne, When You Are Gone—Dello Joio. Carl Fischer No. 6784. Accompanied. Moderately difficult.

Amarilli, Mia Bella—Caccini, arr. Taylor. J. Fischer No. 4375. Accompanied. Medium.

An Offering—Baldwin, arr. Watson. Witmark No. 5W3362. *A cappella.* Moderately easy.

As Fair As Morn—Wilbye. Edw. B. Marks No. 4331. *A cappella.* Moderately easy.

As from the Earth a Flower Grows—Monteverdi. Edw. B. Marks No. 45. *A cappella.* Moderately easy.

Bird Flew, A—Clokey. J. Fischer No. 5506. Accompanied. Medium.

Bois épais—Lully, arr. Taylor. J. Fischer No. 4562. Accompanied. Moderately easy.

Calm As the Night—Boehm, arr. Cain. Schmitt, Hall & McCreary No. 2016. Accompanied. Moderately easy.

Carol of the Bells (Christmas)—Leontovich, arr. Wilhousky. Carl Fischer No. 5276. Optional accompaniment. Medium.

Come, Let Us Start a Joyful Song—Hassler. Bourne No. ES 31. Optional accompaniment. Moderately easy.

Come, Sirrah Jack Ho—Weelkes. E. C. Schirmer No. 840. A cappella. Medium.

Come, You Maidens—Tchaikovsky. Boosey & Hawkes No. 5031. Accompanied. Moderately easy.

Danza, Danza—Durante, arr. Taylor. J. Fischer No. 4378. Accompanied. Medium.

Dreams—Wagner, arr. Shelley. Presser No. 10687. Accompanied. Medium.

Go 'Way from My Window—Niles, arr. Ross. G. Schirmer No. 9805. Accompanied. Soprano solo. Medium.

Hark! Hark! the Lark—Schubert, arr. Bliss. Willis No. 2338. Accompanied. Easy.

He Came to Me—Franz. Schmitt, Hall & McCreary No. 2127. Accompanied. Easy.

In Summer Fields—Brahms. Boston Music Co. No. 3044. Accompanied. Moderately easy.

In the Mill—Rebikoff, arr. Sammond. J. Fischer No. 5689. A cappella. Medium.

In These Delightful Pleasant Groves—Purcell. Bourne No. ES 28; Gray No. 519. A cappella. Moderately easy.

Invocation of Orpheus—Peri. Witmark No. W 2728. Accompanied. Medium.

Lass with the Delicate Air, The—Arne, arr. Chambers. Gray No. 515. Optional accompaniment. Moderately easy.

Let Us Sing—Rameau. Witmark No. 2-W 2988. Accompanied. Medium.

Linden Lea—Vaughan Williams, arr. Harrison. Boosey & Hawkes No. MFS 219. Accompanied. Moderately easy.

Little White Hen, A (Ein Hennelin weiss)—Scandello, arr. Greyson. Bourne No. ES 29A. Optional accompaniment. Medium.

Loafer—Bartók. Boosey & Hawkes No. 1671. Accompanied. Moderately easy.

Love Song—Brahms, arr. Gibb. Boston No. 3046. Accompanied. Moderately easy.

Marienwürmehen (My Lady Bird)—Schumann, arr. Robinson. G. Schirmer No. 10743. Accompanied. Medium.

Mocking of Youth—Bartók. Boosey & Hawkes No. 1955. A cappella. Medium.

Mother, I Will Have a Husband—Vautor. Bourne No. ES 11. Optional accompaniment. Moderately easy.

Musetta's Waltz Song (from La Bohème)—Puccini. Boosey & Hawkes No. 5120. Accompanied. Moderately easy.

Music When Soft Voices Die—Clokey, arr. Cain. Flammer No. 83121. A cappella. Easy.

Nightingale, The—Weelkes, arr. Leslie. E. C. Schirmer No. 1008; Gray No. 671. A cappella. Medium.

O Lovely Spring—Brahms, arr. Grant. Belwin-Mills No. 1839. Accompanied. Medium.

Over the Gods Love Holds His Sway—Arcadelt, ed. Malin. Belwin-Mills No. 2413. A cappella. Moderately easy.

Pat-a-Pan (Burgundian carol; Christmas)—arr. Davis. E. C. Schirmer No. 1052. A cappella. Medium.

Prayer from *Hansel and Gretel*—Humperdinck, arr. Riegger. Flammer No. 83087. Accompanied. Easy.

Pretense—Clokey. J. Fischer No. 7361. Accompanied. Moderately easy.

Robin Loves Me—De La Halle. Edition Musicus No. 014. Optional accompaniment. Easy.

Silent Strings—Bantock, arr. O'Shea. Boosey & Hawkes No. 1467. Accompanied. Moderately easy.

Silver Swan, The—Gibbons, arr. Greyson. Bourne No. ES 12A. *A cappella*. Moderately easy.

Slumber, Beloved One—Ravel, arr. Douty. Presser No. 21434. Accompanied. Moderately difficult.

Slumber Song—Gretchaninov. G. Schirmer No. 7510. Accompanied. Moderately easy.

Smith, The—Brahms. Presser No. 312-40035. Accompanied. Easy.

Song from Ossian's Fingal—Brahms. E. C. Schirmer No. 495. Horn and harp accompaniment. Medium.

Song of Sorrow—Schumann. Leeds Music No. L-423. Optional accompaniment. Moderately easy.

Songs My Mother Taught Me—Dvořák, arr. Cain. Flammer No. 83097. Accompanied. Moderately easy.

Spanish Serenata—Granados, arr. Harris. G. Schirmer No. 7814. Accompanied. Moderately difficult.

Sweet Day—Vaughan Williams, arr. Pasfield. Galaxy No. 695. Optional accompaniment. Moderately easy.

Tambourine, The—Schumann. Leeds Music No. L-428. Optional accompaniment. Medium.

Weep, O Mine Eyes—Wilbye. E. C. Schirmer No. 841. *A cappella*. Moderately easy.

While the Birds Are Singing—Boccherini, arr. Ambrose. Schmidt No. 747. Accompanied. Moderately difficult.

Who Is Sylvia?—Schubert. G. Schirmer No. 733. Accompanied. Moderately easy.

Within My Heart Breathes Music—Brahms, arr. Gibb. J. Fischer No. 9158. Accompanied. Moderately easy.

Younger Generation—Copland, arr. Swift. Boosey & Hawkes No. 1722. Accompanied. Medium.

Folk Songs and Spirituals

Ay, Ay, Ay!—Freire, arr. Malin. Piedmont No. 4372. Accompanied. Moderately easy.

Charlottown—Bryan. J. Fischer No. 7993. *A cappella*. Medium.

Chiapanecas (Mexican dance song)—arr. Marlowe. Huntzinger No. 2039. Accompanied. Moderately easy.

Czechoslovakian Dance Song—arr. Row. R. D. Row No. 234. *A cappella*. Easy.

Dancing-Song (traditional Hungarian)—Kodály. Oxford No. 54.942. *A cappella*. Medium.

Dove on the Lily Tree, The (Swedish folk song)—arr. Vené. Carl Fischer No. CM 6280. Accompanied. Easy.

Down by the Sally Gardens (old Irish air)—arr. Donovan. Galaxy No. 555. Accompanied. Moderately easy.

Early One Morning (old English folk song)—arr. Scott. Shawnee Press. Accompanied. Medium.

Eriskay Love Lilt, An (folk song from the Hebrides)—arr. Arch. Boosey & Hawkes No. 5665. Accompanied. Moderately easy.

Farewell (Austrian folk song)—arr. Kanitz. Carl Fischer No. CM 6397. Accompanied. Easy.

Goin' to Boston (Kentucky folk song)—arr. Davis. Summy-Birchard No. 1573. Accompanied. Medium.

Good Night (German folk song)—arr. Malin. B. F. Wood No. 830. Accompanied. Moderately easy.

Gute Nacht (German folk song)—arr. G. W. W. E. C. Schirmer No. 819. Accompanied. Medium.

Hi, Ho, Sing Gaily (Swiss folk tune)—arr. Luvaas. Summy-Birchard No. 1505. Accompanied. Moderately easy.

I Got Shoes (spiritual)—arr. Cain. Flammer No. 83206. Accompanied. Moderately easy.

I Live Not Where I Love (traditional English tune)—arr. Parry. Oxford No. W45. Accompanied. Easy.

Ifca's Castle (Czechoslovakian folk song)—arr. Harley and Aschenbrenner. Carl Fischer No. 5223. A cappella. Moderately easy.

Keel Row, The (Tyneside air)—arr. Fletcher. Curwen No. 71227. Optional accompaniment. Medium.

Linden Lea—Vaughan Williams. Boosey & Hawkes No. MFS 219. Accompanied. Moderately easy.

Little Bird (Mexican folk song)—arr. Grant. Belwin-Mills No. 1723. Accompanied. Moderately easy.

Little David, Play on Your Harp (spiritual)—arr. Cain. Flammer No. 83178. Accompanied. Easy.

Little Sandman, The (German folk song)—arr. Harley & Aschenbrenner. Carl Fischer No. CM 5280. A cappella. Easy.

Little White Hen, A—Scandello, arr. Greyson. Bourne No. ES 29A. Optional accompaniment. Moderately easy.

Lollytoodum (American folk song)—arr. Bell. Shawnee Press. Accompanied. Medium.

May Day Carol (English folk song)—arr. Taylor. J. Fischer No. 4872. Accompanied. Moderately easy.

Meadows, Grow Ye Greene (Austrian folk song)—arr. Kanitz. Carl Fischer No. CM 6395. Accompanied. Easy.

Memories (Irish folk tune)—arr. Luvaas. Summy-Birchard No. 374. A cappella. Easy.

Meneate, buena moza (Spanish folk song)—arr. Malin. Piedmont No. 4374. Accompanied. Moderately easy.

My Desert Flower (North African folk song)—arr. Marshall. Belwin-Mills No. 1821. Accompanied. Moderately easy.

O Can Ye Sew Cushions? (old Scottish cradle song)—arr. Mansfield. Belwin-Mills No. 711. Accompanied. Moderately easy.

O Little Star in the Sky (Swedish folk tune)—arr. Davis. E. C. Schirmer No. 1065. Accompanied. Medium.

O Mary, Don't You Weep (spiritual)—arr. Siegmaster and Ehret. Bourne No. 25. Accompanied. Medium.

Old Woman and the Pedlar, The (English air)—arr. Davis. E. C. Schirmer No. 1060. *A cappella.* Medium.

Rock-a My Soul (spiritual)—arr. De Vaux. Bourne No. 195. Accompanied. Medium.

Shy Love (Ukrainian folk song)—arr. Boberg. Kjos No. 6088. Accompanied. Easy.

Song of a Happy Heart (Ukrainian folk song)—arr. Boberg. Kjos No. 6091. Accompanied. Easy.

Swallow's Wooing, The (Hungarian children's song)—arr. Kodály. Oxford No. 542. *A cappella.* Medium.

Swing Low, Sweet Chariot (spiritual)—arr. Burleigh. Ricordi No. 116469. Accompanied. Moderately easy.

Three Highland Airs (traditional Scotch melodies)—arr. Best. Shawnee Press No. B-158. Accompanied. Moderately easy.

Three Hungarian Folks Songs—Bartók, arr. Suchoft. Boosey & Hawkes No. 5488. Accompanied. Medium. ·

Three Irish Songs—arr. Frackenpohl. Shawnee Press No. B-200. Accompanied. Moderately easy.

Three Songs from Sweden—arr. Hallstrom. Shawnee Press No. B-215. Accompanied. Moderately easy.

Vreneli (Swiss folk song)—arr. Lester. Belwin-Mills No. 1830. Accompanied. Moderately easy.

Wandering River (Korean folk song)—arr. Ritz. Westwood Press No. ESE-1432-2. Accompanied. Moderately easy.

Waters Ripple and Flow (Czechoslovak folk song)—arr. Taylor. J. Fischer No. 5065. Accompanied. Moderately difficult.

We Wish You a Merry Christmas (English folk song)—arr. Krone. Kjos No. 1211. Optional accompaniment. Medium.

When Love Is Kind (traditional English or Austrian)—arr. Trinkaus. Carl Fischer No. 6139. Accompanied. Moderately easy.

Publications for Male Voices (TTBB)

Sacred

Adoramus Te—Palestrina, arr. Greyson. Bourne No. ES 16. *A cappella.* Easy.

Adoramus Te, Christe—Corsi, arr. Cain. Choral Art No. R180. *A cappella.* Moderately easy.

All Glory Be to God on High (chorale melody of Gregorian origin)—arr. Malin. Summy-Birchard No. 1538. Accompanied. Moderately easy.

Alleluia—Handel, arr. Dawe. G. Schirmer No. 9412. Accompanied. Tenor solo. Moderately difficult.

At Sunset—Schubert, arr. Ringwald. Shawnee Press. Accompanied. Medium.

Ave Maria (Give Ear unto my Prayer)—Arcadelt, arr. Greyson. Bourne No. ES 4. Optional accompaniment. Moderately difficult.

Ave, Maria—Vittoria, arr. Cain. Choral Art No. R174. *A cappella.* Moderately easy.

Ave, Maris Stella (Hail, O Star; Christmas)—Grieg, arr. Pitcher. Summy-Birchard No. 881. *A cappella.* Moderately difficult.

Babe, So Tender, A (old Flemish carol)—arr. Manton. E. C. Schirmer No. 543. *A cappella.* Medium.

Beautiful Savior (Silesian folk tune)—arr. F. M. Christiansen and Wycisk. Augsburg No. 263. *A cappella.* Moderately easy.

Behold That Star (spiritual; Christmas)—arr. Cunkle. Shawnee Press No. 10. *A cappella.* Bass solo. Medium.

Cantate Domino—Hassler, arr. Beveridge. E. C. Schirmer No. 2194. *A cappella.* Medium.

Carol of the Russian Children (White Russian carol)—arr. Gaul. G. Schirmer No. 7363. Optional accompaniment. Medium.

Christ Is Born of Maiden Fair (ancient carol)—ed. H. Clough-Leighter. E. C. Schirmer No. 515. *A cappella.* Medium.

Christmas Hymn (17th century)—arr. Jüngst. G. Schirmer No. 1414. *A cappella.* Moderately easy.

Come, Sweet Death—Bach, arr. Reed. G. Schirmer No. 8956. *A cappella.* Moderately easy.

God Rest You Merry, Gentlemen (English carol)—arr. the Krones. Kjos No. 1117. Optional accompaniment. Moderately easy.

Hallelujah (from *Mount of Olives*)—Beethoven. G. Schirmer No. 10774. Accompanied. Moderately difficult.

Hallelujah, Amen—Handel, arr. Davison. E. C. Schirmer No. 38. Accompanied. Moderately difficult.

Heart Worships, The—Holst, arr. Duey. Boston Music No. 2952. Accompanied. Medium.

Heavenly Light—Kopylov, arr. Wilhousky. Carl Fischer No. CM 611. *A cappella.* Moderately difficult.

I Wonder As I Wander (Appalachian carol)—arr. Niles and Horton. G. Schirmer No. 9292. *A cappella.* Medium.

Jacob's Ladder (spiritual)—arr. Wilson. Ricordi No. NY1680. Optional accompaniment. Medium.

Jesus, Joy of My Endeavor (chorale from *Cantata No. 147*)—Bach, arr. Scott. Shawnee Press. Accompanied. Moderately easy.

Joseph, Dear One, Joseph Mine (German carol)—arr. Barrow. E. C. Schirmer No. 2158. *A cappella.* Moderately easy.

Joyous Christmas Song, A (Norwegian carol)—arr. Hokanson. Summy-Birchard No. 3142. *A cappella.* Moderately easy.

Let All Give Thanks to Thee—J. S. Bach, arr. Treharne. G. Schirmer No. 8342. *A cappella.* Moderately easy.

Let Nothing Ever Grieve Thee—Brahms. C. F. Peters No. 6009. Accompanied. Medium.

Let Thy Holy Presence—Tschesnokov, arr. Ehret. Boosey & Hawkes No. 5022. *A cappella.* Moderately easy.

Lullaby of the Christ Child (old French carol)—arr. Scott. Shawnee Press. *A cappella.* Incidental tenor solo. Medium.

Matthew, Mark, Luke, and John (West Country folk song)—arr. Holst. Curwen No. 50616. *A cappella.* Tenor solo. Moderately easy.

May Now Thy Spirit—Schuetky, arr. Treharne. Willis No. 5641. *A cappella.* Medium.

May Thy Blessed Spirit—Tschesnokov, arr. Cookson. Fitzsimons No. 4062. *A cappella.* Medium.

My Gracious Lord and Master—Schubert. Piedmont No. 4450. *A cappella.* Medium.

Nature's Praise of God—Beethoven. G. Schirmer No. 6566. Optional accompaniment. Moderately easy.

Noel, Noel—Gevaert, arr. Grayson. Kjos No. 5513. Accompanied. Easy.

Now Thank We All Our God—Cruger, harmonized by Mendelssohn. Boston Music No. 471. Organ accompaniment. Easy.

O Bone Jesu—Palestrina. Bourne No. ES 45. *A cappella.* Easy.

O Light Divine—Arkhangelsky, arr. Bement. Oliver Ditson No. 15182. *A cappella.* Medium.

O Lovely, Holy Night (Christmas)—Kremser, arr. Biedermann. J. Fischer No. 3344. *A cappella.* Medium.

Praise the Name of the Lord—Ivanoff, arr. McKinney. J. Fischer No. 9166. *A cappella.* Medium.

Requiem Aeternam—Cherubini. Edition Musicus No. 1013. *A cappella.* Moderately easy.

Sleep of the Child Jesus—Gevaert, arr. Lefebvre. Franco Colombo No. NY773. *A cappella.* Easy.

Stars, The—Schubert, arr. Larson. Summy-Birchard No. 5021. *A cappella.* Tenor solo. Medium.

Tell Me, Shepherds, Dear (Polish carol)—arr. H. G. M. E. C. Schirmer No. 2105. *A cappella.* Medium.

Thanks Be to Thee—Handel, arr. Lefebvre. Galaxy No. 1222. Accompanied. Tenor solo. Easy.

Then Round About the Starry Throne (from *Samson*)—Handel. E. C. Schirmer No. 907. Accompanied. Medium.

They Sang That Night in Bethlehem—Schubert, arr. Deis. G. Schirmer No. 8292. *A cappella.* Medium.

Thou Must Leave Thy Lowly Dwelling—Berlioz. Galaxy No. 2065. Accompanied. Medium.

Who Ne'er His Bread with Tears Did Eat—Schubert. Lawson-Gould No. 876. Accompanied. Medium.

With a Voice of Singing—Shaw. G. Schirmer No. 10454. Piano or organ accompaniment. Medium.

Ye Watchers and Ye Holy Ones (17th-century German melody)—arr. Davison. E. C. Schirmer No. 65. Piano or organ accompaniment. Medium.

Secular

Aura Lee—Poulton, arr. Hunter, Parker, and Shaw. Lawson-Gould No. 527. *A cappella.* Moderately easy.

Battle Hymn of the Republic—Steffe, arr. Ringwald. Shawnee Press. Four-hand piano accompaniment. Baritone solo. Medium.

Brothers, Sing On!—Grieg, arr. McKinney. J. Fischer No. 6927. *A cappella.* Medium.

By the Sea—Schubert, arr. Bantock. Belwin-Mills Music No. 1145. *A cappella.* Moderately easy.

Crown of Roses, The—Tchaikovsky, arr. Bell. Belwin-Mills Music No. 1085. *A cappella.* Medium.

Death Came Knocking—Floyd. Boosey & Hawkes No. 5368. Accompanied. Moderately difficult.

Dreams—Wagner, arr. Scherer. Gray No. 436. Accompanied. Medium.

Gambler's Lament, The—Niles. G. Schirmer No. 10305. Accompanied. Medium.

Good Fellows Be Merry—Bach, arr. Duey. Boston Music No. 2944. Accompanied. Difficult.

Holiday Song—Schuman. G. Schirmer No. 9866. Accompanied. Moderately easy.

Hunting Song (Jaglied)—Mendelssohn, arr. Mueller. G. Schirmer No. 12074. *A cappella.* Medium.

In the Doorways I Will Linger—Schubert, arr. Rider. Lawson-Gould No. 875. Accompanied. Medium.

Laura Lee—Foster, arr. Parker and Shaw. Lawson-Gould No. 874. *A cappella.* Moderately easy.

Love and Wine (Liebe und Wein)—Mendelssohn, arr. Mueller. S. Schirmer No. 12033. *A cappella.* Baritone solo. Medium.

Musical Trust, The—Hadley. G. Schirmer No. 5800. *A cappella.* Medium.

Night, The (Die Nacht)—Schubert. Lawson-Gould No. 786. *A cappella.* Medium.

Nocturne—Mendelssohn, arr. Treharne. Boston Music No. 2987. Accompanied. Moderately difficult.

Passing By—Purcell, arr. Parker-Shaw. Lawson-Gould No. 967. *A cappella.* Moderately easy.

Pilgrims' Chorus (from *Tannhauser*)—Wagner, arr. Dawson. Kjos No. 5490. *A cappella.* Medium.

Pilgrim's Song—Tchaikovsky, arr. Treharne. G. Schirmer No. 8802. Accompanied. Moderately difficult.

Rain Has Kissed the Rose, The—Schumann. G. Schirmer No. 412. *A cappella.* Moderately easy.

Rest (Du bist die Ruh)—Schubert, arr. Bantock. Belwin-Mills No. 1146. *A cappella.* Medium.

Rhapsodie—Brahms. Boston Music No. 229. Accompanied. Alto solo. Moderately difficult.

Serenade—Haydn, arr. Schultz. G. Schirmer No. 1087. *A cappella.* Easy.

Sophomoric Philosophy—Dvořák. Remick No. 9G 1108. *A cappella.* Moderately easy.

Stopwatch and an Ordinance Map, A—Barber. G. Schirmer No. 8799. Kettledrum accompaniment. Moderately difficult.

Stouthearted Men—Romberg, arr. Scotson. Harms, Inc., No. 9-H1184. Accompanied. Moderately easy.

Swan, The—Saint-Saëns, arr. Boyce. G. Schirmer No. 10527. Humming chorus with violin solo and piano accompaniment. Medium.

Sweet Love Doth Now Invite—Dowland. Bourne No. ES7. Optional accompaniment. Moderately easy.

To All You Ladies Now on Land—Callcott. E. C. Schirmer No. 533. *A cappella.* Moderately easy.

When Allen-A-Dale Went A-Hunting—Pearsall, arr. Shepherd. Modern Music Press No. 4152. *A cappella.* Medium.

Winter Song—Bullard. Oliver Ditson No. 10160. Accompanied. Moderately easy.

Woods So Dense—Lully, arr. Sodero. G. Schirmer No. 8568. *A cappella.* Moderately easy.

Folk Songs and Spirituals

Ain'-a That Good News (spiritual)—arr. Dawson. Music Press, Tuskegee Institute No. 104. *A cappella.* Medium.

All Through the Night (old Welsh song)—arr. Ringwald. Shawnee Press No. C-21. Optional accompaniment. Medium.

A-Roving (sea chantey)—arr. Wagner. Lawson-Gould No. 791. *A cappella.* Baritone solo. Medium.

Aura Lee—Poulton, arr. Parker-Shaw. Lawson-Gould No. 527. *A cappella.* Moderately easy.

Believe Me, If All Those Endearing Young Charms (old Irish air)—arr. Hunter, Parker, and Shaw. Lawson-Gould No. 528. *A cappella.* Medium.

Blow the Man Down (English sea chantey)—arr. Parker and Shaw. Lawson-Gould No. 51055. *A cappella.* Bass solo. Moderately difficult.

Boar's Head Carol, The (English secular carol)—arr. Parker and Shaw. G. Schirmer No. 10179. *A cappella.* Easy.

Carol of the Bells (Ukrainian carol; Christmas)—Leontovich, arr. Wilhousky. Carl Fischer No. CM 2270. *A cappella.* Moderately easy.

Climbin' up the Mountain (Negro spiritual)—arr. Smith. Kjos No. 1101. *A cappella.* Medium.

De Animals a-Coming' (Negro spiritual)—arr. Bartholomew. G. Schirmer No. 8046. *A cappella.* Medium.

Down Among the Dead Men (old English air)—arr. Vaughan Williams. Belwin-Mills No. 1142. *A cappella.* Medium.

Down in the Valley (Kentucky folk tune)—arr. Mead. Galaxy No. 1716. Accompanied. Moderately easy.

Drink to Me Only with Thine Eyes (old English air)—arr. Hunter, Parker, and Shaw. Lawson-Gould No. 530. *A cappella.* Moderately difficult.

Gloucestershire Wassail (traditional old English yule song)—arr. Scott. Words and Music. Accompanied. Baritone solo. Moderately difficult.

Go Tell It on the Mountain (Negro spiritual)—arr. Huntley. Fitzsimons No. 4067. *A cappella.* Easy.

Green Grow the Rushes O! (Scottish folk song)—arr. Roberton. R. D. Row No. 519. *A cappella.* Medium.

Hickory Stick, The (American folk song)—arr. Sheppard. Boston Music No. 13042. Optional accompaniment. Medium.

I Got Shoes (Negro spiritual)—arr. Bartholomew. G. Schirmer No. 7144. *A cappella.* Moderately easy.

John Peel (old English hunting song)—arr. Andrews. Gray No. 31. *A cappella.* Moderately easy.

Lincolnshire Poacher, The (English folk song)—arr. Bantock. Belwin-Mills. *A cappella.* Medium.

Little Innocent Lamb (Negro spiritual)—arr. Bartholomew. G. Schirmer No. 9907. *A cappella.* Moderately easy.

Lord Randall (British folk song)—arr. Duey. Boston Music No. 2954. *A cappella.* Baritone or tenor solo. Medium.

Marianina (Italian folk song)—arr. Parker and Shaw. Lawson-Gould No. 974. *A cappella.* Tenor solo. Medium.

My Johnny Was a Shoemaker (English folk song)—arr. Taylor. J. Fischer No. 4834. Accompanied. Medium.

My Lord, What a Mornin' (Negro spiritual)—arr. Burleigh. Franco Colombo No. NY1713. *A cappella.* Moderately easy.

Night Herding Song (cowboy song)—arr. Luboff. Walton No. 1006. Accompanied. Easy.

O Tannenbaum (traditional German)—arr. Parker and Shaw. G. Schirmer No. 10195. *A cappella.* Moderately easy.

Old Chisholm Trail, The (Western folk song)—arr. Cain. Pro Art No. 1483. Accompanied. Easy.

On Top of Old Smoky (American folk song)—arr. Stone. Pro Art No. 1347. Accompanied. Easy.

Over Here (Irish folk song)—arr. Roberton. Boosey & Hawkes No. 1987. *A cappella.* Moderately easy.

Poor Lonesome Cowboy (cowboy song)—arr. Luboff. Walton No. 1007. *A cappella.* Moderately easy.

Poor Man Lazrus (Negro spiritual)—arr. Hairston. Bourne No. S1022. *A cappella.* Medium.

Rantin' Rovin' Robin (Scottish folk song)—arr. Davison. E. C. Schirmer No. 84. Accompanied. Baritone solo. Moderately easy.

Rebel Soldier, The (American folk song)—arr. Sheppard. Boston Music No. 3081. *A cappella.* Moderately easy.

Ride the Chariot (Negro spiritual)—arr. Smith. Kjos No. 1102. *A cappella.* Tenor solo. Moderately easy.

Rio Grande (sea chantey)—arr. Dougherty. G. Schirmer No. 10414. Accompanied. Moderately easy.

Scissors-Grinder, The (Flemish folk song)—arr. Jungst. G. Schirmer No. 10414. Accompanied. Moderately easy.

Shenandoah (sea chantey)—arr. Wagner. Lawson-Gould No. 848. *A cappella.* Baritone solo. Moderately easy.

Sippin' Cider (American folk song)—arr. Sheppard. Summy-Birchard No. 1588. *A cappella.* Moderately easy.

Sister Mary Wore Three Lengths of Chain (Negro spiritual)—arr. Bartholomew. G. Schirmer No. 10243. *A cappella.* Medium.

Soon-Ah Will Be Done—Dawson. Tuskegee No. 101. *A cappella.* Moderately difficult.

Sourwood Mountain (Kentucky mountain song)—arr. Hall. G. Schirmer No. 8140. *A cappella.* Medium.

Swansea Town (Hampshire folk song)—arr. Holst. Curwen No. 50615. *A cappella.* Medium.

Turtle Dove, The (folk song)—arr. Vaughan Williams. Curwen No. 50570. Accompanied. Baritone or tenor solo. Medium.

We Wish You a Merry Christmas (English folk song; secular)—arr. the Krones. Kjos No. 1114. Optional accompaniment. Moderately easy.

What Shall We Do with a Drunken Sailor? (traditional sea chantey)—arr. Bartholomew. G. Schirmer No. 7422. Accompanied. Easy.

Publications for Two Parts (SA or TB)

Achieved Is the Glorious Work—Haydn, arr. Davies. Oxford No. E111. Accompanied. Medium.

Ah, Lovely Meadows (Czech folk song)—arr. Kjelson. Belwin-Mills No. 1901. Accompanied. Easy.

Ash Grove, The (Welsh folk song)—arr. Stone. Belwin-Mills No. 2199. Accompanied. Moderately easy.

At the Gates of Heaven (Basque folk song)—arr. Kjelson. Belwin-Mills No. 1903. Accompanied. Moderately easy.

Bright Star (Polish carol)—arr. Ehret. Edw. B. Marks No. 4407. Accompanied. Moderately easy.

Christ Is Born to You Today (German folk song)—arr. Ehret. Edw. B. Marks No. 4408. Accompanied. Moderately easy.

Cielito Lindo (Mexican folk song)—arr. Tate. Oxford No. T72. Accompanied. Medium.

Cindy (American folk song)—arr. Barthelson. Belwin-Mills No. 1746. Moderately easy.

Come, All Ye Lads and Lassies (old English melody)—arr. Howorth. Belwin-Mills No. 1874. Medium.

Coventry Carol (English carol)—arr. Stone. Belwin-Mills No. 2142. Accompanied. Moderately easy.

Cuckoo Cries, The—Möller, arr. Swift. Belwin-Mills No. 1436. With solo voices. Medium.

Cuckoo Song (German folk song)—arr. Keldermans. Greenwood Press No. ESE-1059-2. Accompanied. Easy.

Cuckoo, the Nightingale, and the Donkey, The—Mahler. Oxford No. T75. Accompanied. Medium.

De Gospel Train (spiritual), and There's Music in the Air (G. F. Root)—arr. Rhea. Bourne No. MD2. Easy.

Drill, Ye Tarriers, Drill (American ballad)—arr. Kjelson. Belwin-Mills No. 1904. Moderately easy.

Elephant and the Flea, The (nonsense song)—arr. Barthelson. Belwin-Mills No. 1747. Moderately easy.

Go Tell It on the Mountain (Christmas spiritual)—arr. Barthelson. Belwin-Mills No. 1833. Moderately easy.

He's Goin' Away (American folk song)—arr. Howorth. Belwin-Mills No. 1848. Moderately easy.

He's Got the Whole World in His Hands (spiritual)—arr. Howorth. Belwin-Mills No. 1777. Optional solo. Moderately easy.

368 APPENDIX: SOURCE INFORMATION

I Love Little Willie (Southern mountain song)—arr. Barthelson. Belwin-Mills No. 1748. Easy.

I'm Goin' Leave Old Texas Now (cowboy song)—arr. Pitcher. Belwin-Mills No. 1835. Easy.

Jesus Christ Our Savior Is Born (Lithuanian carol)—arr. Gordon. Belwin-Mills No. 1844. Moderately easy.

Kentucky Babe—Giebel, arr. Churchill. Belwin-Mills No. 1836. Easy.

Let Us Cheer the Weary Traveller (spiritual)—arr. Howorth. Belwin-Mills No. 1846. Medium.

Little Cradle Rocks Tonight in Glory, The (spiritual)—arr. Walker. Concordia No. 98-2139. Xylophone and percussion accompaniment. Moderately easy.

Loch Lomond (old Scotch air)—arr. Kirk. Belwin-Mills No. 1605. Easy.

Lolly Tu-Dum (American folk song)—arr. Churchill. Belwin-Mills No. 1630. Moderately easy.

My Heart Ever Faithful—J. S. Bach, arr. Bampton. Presser No. 312-40474. Accompanied. Moderately easy.

O Come, All Ye Children (German Christmas carol)—arr. Gordon. Belwin-Mills No. 1720. Easy.

Patapan (Burgundian carol)—arr. Jacques. Oxford No. T86. Accompanied. Easy.

Rocking (Christmas carol)—arr. Ehret. Scholin No. 2012. Medium.

Shenandoah (sea chantey)—arr. Stone. Belwin-Mills No. 2141. Accompanied. Moderately easy.

Sing Hallelujah, Praise the Lord (Moravian melody)—arr. Mueller. G. Schirmer No. 10754. Moderately easy.

Standin' in the Need of Prayer (Negro spiritual)—arr. Kjelson. Belwin-Mills No. 1902. With solo voice. Moderately easy.

Still, Still (German carol)—arr. Sumner. Scholin No. 2021. Easy.

Sweet Betsy from Pike (American folk song)—arr. Swift. Belwin-Mills No. 1622. Moderately easy.

There's a Little Wheel a-Turnin' (Negro spiritual)—arr. Vance. Belwin-Mills No. 1898. Optional third voice and solo. Medium.

Today with Loud Rejoicing—Mozart, arr. Heinrich. Boston No. 3117. Easy.

Viennese Lullaby (Viennese popular song)—arr. Wilson. Bourne No. HL 12. Easy.

Wandering River (Korean folk song)—arr. Papale. Westwood Press No. ESE-1413-2. Accompanied. Easy.

Wild Wind (Korean folk song)—arr. Papale. Westwood Press No. ESE-1415-2. Percussion accompaniment. Easy.

Publications for Combined Chorus and Band and/or Orchestra

All Glory, Laud and Honor—Teschner, arr. Cain. Flammer. SATB—for chorus and band; chorus and orchestra.

America—E. Williams. Morris. SSAATTBB—for chorus and band; chorus and orchestra; chorus, band, and orchestra.

Ave Maria—Bach and Gounod, arr. Tolmadge. Staff. SATB—for chorus and band.

Battle Hymn of the Republic—Steffe, arr. Ringwald. Shawnee Press. SATB; TTBB—for chorus and band; chorus and orchestra.

Battle Hymn of the Republic—Steffe, arr. Wilhousky. Carl Fischer. SSATTBB —for chorus and band; chorus and orchestra.

Beautiful Dreamer—Foster, arr. Frangkiser. Boosey & Hawkes. SATB; TTBB —for chorus and band.

Bells of St. Mary's—Adams, arr. Lucas and Clark. Chappell. SATB—for chorus and band.

Break Forth, O Beauteous Heavenly Light—Bach. G. Schirmer. SATB—for chorus and orchestra (orchestra parts available from publisher on rental only).

Brigadoon (choral selection)—Loewe, arr. Leidzen. Sam Fox. SATB—for chorus and band; chorus and orchestra.

Choral Prelude on Dundee—Whitney. Sam Fox. SATB—for chorus and band.

Choral Procession (Finale to Cantata *The Song of Man*)—Kountz, arr. Campbell and Watson. Witmark. SATB—for chorus and band.

Chorale: St. Antoni—Haydn and Brahms, arr. Tolmadge. Staff. SATB—for chorus and band.

Christmas Day—Holst. Gray. SATB—for chorus and orchestra (orchestral parts available from publisher on rental only).

Christmas Story, The—Yoder. Kjos. SATB—for chorus and band.

Come Let Us Sing (95th Psalm)—Mendelssohn. G. Schirmer. SATB—for chorus and orchestra (orchestral parts available from publisher on rental only).

Elsa Entering the Cathedral (from *Lohengrin*)—Wagner, arr. Duelzman. Carl Fischer. SSAATTBB—for chorus and orchestra (orchestral parts available from publisher on rental only).

Emperor Waltz—Strauss. Sam Fox. SATB—for chorus and orchestra (orchestral parts available in Fox Festival Series for Orchestra, Book 3, by Dykema and Reibold).

Fantasie on Christmas Carols—Vaughan Williams. Galaxy. SATB, with bar, solo—for chorus and orchestra (orchestral parts available from publishers on rental only).

Festival Finale—Maddy. Kjos. SATB—for chorus and band; chorus and orchestra; chorus, band and orchestra.

Festival Song of Praise—Mendelssohn, arr. Wilson and Harris. Bourne. SATB—for chorus and orchestra.

Gloria in Excelsis (from *Twelfth Mass*)—Mozart. Presser. SATB—for chorus and orchestra.

Glory—Rimsky-Korsakov. Witmark. SSAATTBB—for chorus and orchestra.

Glory and Honor—J. S. Bach, arr. Klein. Schmitt, Hall & McCreary. SATB— for chorus and band.

Glory and Triumph—Berlioz. Mercury. SATB—for chorus and band; chorus and orchestra.

Glory to God in the Highest—Pergolesi, arr. Houseknect. Kjos. SATB—for chorus and band.

God of Our Fathers—arr. Gearhart. Shawnee Press. SATB—for chorus, with three trumpets, percussion, four-hand piano and organ accompaniment.

Gypsy Songs (Zigeunerlieder)—Brahms. Carl Fischer. SATB; SSA; TTBB—for chorus and orchestra (orchestral score and parts available from publisher on rental only.

Hail, Glorious Day—Elgar, arr. Schaefer. Boosey & Hawkes. SATB—for chorus and band.

Hallelujah Chorus (from *Messiah*)—Handel. Carl Fischer. SATB—for chorus and orchestra; chorus and band.

Heavens Are Telling, The—Haydn. Carl Fischer. SATB—for chorus and orchestra.

Holy, Holy, Holy—arr. Ledizén. Bourne. SATB—for chorus and band.

How Lovely Is Thy Dwelling (from *Requiem*)—Brahms. G. Schirmer. SATB—for chorus and orchestra (orchestral parts available from publisher on rental only).

Hymn of Freedom—Brahms, arr. Tolmadge. Staff. SATB—for chorus and band.

Hymn of Praise—Mozart, arr. Tolmadge. Staff. SATB—for chorus and band.

Hymn to America—McKay. Schmitt, Hall & McCreary. SATB—for chorus and band.

Joshua—Moussorgsky. G. Schirmer. SAATTBB—for chorus and orchestra (orchestral parts available from publisher on rental only).

Joshua (a rhythmic novelty)—arr. Yoder. Kjos. SATB—for chorus and band.

Land of Hope and Glory—Elgar. Boosey & Hawkes. SATB; SSA—for chorus and band; chorus and orchestra.

Land of Our Fathers (ode to America)—Lavalle. Sam Fox. SATB—for chorus and band.

Land-Sighting—Grieg. G. Schirmer. SATB—for chorus and orchestra (orchestral parts available from publisher on rental only).

Largo from *New World Symphony* (choral parts: "Behold Our God")—Dvořák. Belwin-Mills. SATB—for chorus and band.

Let All Mortal Flesh Keep Silence—Holst. Galaxy. SATB—for chorus and orchestra.

Lift Up Your Heads—Coleridge-Taylor, arr. Buchtel. Kjos. SATB—for chorus and band.

Magnificat—Vaughan Williams. Oxford. SSA, with contralto solo—for chorus and orchestra (orchestral parts available from publisher on rental only).

Mannin Veen (Dear Isle of Man)—Wood. Boosey & Hawkes. SATB; SAB; SSA—for chorus and orchestra; chorus and band.

Message of the Bells (Prelude in C Minor)—Rachmaninoff, arr. Lester. Remick. SATB—for chorus and orchestra.

Mighty Fortress Is Our God, A—Luther, arr. Caillet. Boosey & Hawkes. SATB; TTBB—for chorus and band; chorus and orchestra.

Nation's Creed, The—Williams. Schmitt, Hall & McCreary. SATB—for chorus and band.

Nation's Prayer, The (Panis Angelicus)—Franck. Belwin-Mills. SATB; SSA; TTBB—for chorus and band; chorus and orchestra; chorus, band and orchestra.

O Clap Your Hands—Vaughan Williams. Galaxy. SATB—for chorus, brass choir and percussion.

Ode to America—Cain. Flammer. SATB; SAB; SSA—for chorus and band; chorus and orchestra; chorus, band and orchestra.

Old Black Joe—Foster, arr. Frangkiser. Boosey & Hawkes. SATB; TTBB—for chorus and band.

Omnipotence, The—Franz Schubert. G. Schirmer. SSAATTBB; TTBB; SSA—for chorus and orchestra (orchestral parts available from publisher on rental only).

One World—O'Hara, arr. Wilson and Leidzen. Bourne. SATB; TTBB; SSA—for chorus and band; chorus and orchestra.

Onward, Christian Soldiers—arr. Simeone. Shawnee Press. SATB; TTBB—for chorus and band; chorus and orchestra.

Onward, Ye Peoples—Sibelius, arr. Lefebvre. Galaxy. SATB; SSA; TTBB—for chorus and band; chorus and orchestra.

Pilgrims' Chorus, The (from *Tannhäuser*)—Wagner. G. Schirmer. SATB—for chorus and orchestra (orchestral parts available from publisher on rental only).

Prayer for United Nations—Moore. Gray. SATB—for chorus and orchestra (orchestral parts available from publisher on rental only).

Rhapsody in Blue (choral finale)—Gershwin, arr. Warnick. Harms, Inc. SSATTBB—for chorus and band; chorus and orchestra.

Romany Life—Herbert. Witmark. SATB; SA; SSA; SSAA; TTBB; with soprano solo—for chorus and orchestra; chorus and band.

Rose Marie (choral selections)—Friml and Stothart, arr. MacLean and Schoenfeld. Witmark. SATB—for chorus and band.

Soldiers' Chorus (from *Faust*)—Gounod. G. Schirmer. TTBB; SATB—for chorus and orchestra (orchestration available for either arrangement from publisher on rental only).

Spirit of Music—Bennett. Carl Fischer. SATB divided—for chorus and orchestra; chorus, band and orchestra.

To Music—Schubert, arr. Wilson. Schmitt, Hall & McCreary. SATB; SAB; SSA—for chorus and orchestra.

Turn Back, O Man—Holst. Galaxy. SATB—for chorus and orchestra (orchestral parts available from publisher on rental only).

Victor Herbert Favorites—arr. MacLean. Witmark. SATB; SSA; TTBB—for chorus and orchestra; chorus and band.

Voice of Freedom—Rubinstein, arr. Caillet. Boosey & Hawkes. SATB; TTBB—for chorus and band; chorus and orchestra.

With a Voice of Singing—Shaw. G. Schirmer. SATB—for chorus and orchestra (orchestral accompaniment available from publisher on rental only).

Yuletide Overture—Lang. Belwin-Mills. SATB—for chorus and band.

Choral Music with Electronic Tape

Alleluia, Acclamation and Carol—Daniel Pinkham. E. C. Schirmer Nos. 2954 and 2955. SATB, timpani, percussion, and electronic tape.

Amens—Daniel Pinkham. E. C. Schirmer No. 3016. SATB and electronic tape.

Call of Isaiah, The—Daniel Pinkham. E. C. Schirmer No. 2911. SATB with organ and electronic tape.

Collect—Leslie Bassett. World Library of Sacred Music No. CA2000-8. SATB, electronic tape.

Dialogue—Robert Karlén. A.M.S.I. No. AMS 175. SATB, tape recorder.

Evergreen—Daniel Pinkham. E. C. Schirmer No. 2962. Unison chorus, electronic tape, and optional instruments (autoharp, bells, harp, guitar, piano, and organ).

Hymn of the Universe—Richard Felciano. E. C. Schirmer No. 2944. SAB and electronic sounds.

I Saw an Angel—Daniel Pinkham. E. C. Schirmer No. 2973. SATB and electronic tape.

In the Beginning of Creation—Daniel Pinkham. E. C. Schirmer No. 2902. Mixed chorus, electronic tape.

In the Presence—Gilbert Trythall. Edw. B. Marks No. 4495. SATB, electronic tape.

Kyrie—Donald Erb. Merion No. 342-40026. SATB, piano, percussion, electronic tape.

Out of Sight—Richard Felciano. E. C. Schirmer No. 2909. SATB, organ, and electronic tape.

Pentecost Sunday—Richard Felciano. World Library Publications No. EMP-1532-1. Unison male chorus, organ, electronic tape.

Sic Transit—Richard Felciano. E. C. Schirmer No. 2903. SAB chorus, organ, electronic tape, light sources.

Signs—Richard Felciano. E. C. Schirmer No. 2927. SATB, electronic tape and one, two, or three film strip projectors.

Three-in-One-in-Three—Richard Felciano. E. C. Schirmer No. 2910. Chorus, organ, tape.

Time to Every Purpose, A—Gilbert Trythall. Edw. B. Marks No. 4586. SATB, electronic tape.

Two Public Pieces—Richard Felciano. E. C. Schirmer No. 2937. Unison voices and electronic sounds.

Words of St. Peter—Richard Felciano. World Library Publications No. CA-2093-8. Mixed voices, organ, and electronic tape.

Music with Nonconventional Notation

Aleatory Psalm—Gordon H. Lamb. World Library Publications No. CA-4003-8. SATB.

All the Ways of a Man—Knut Nystedt. Augsburg No. 11-9004. SATB.

Anabathmos I—J. D. Weinland. Walton No. M-116. Chorus of 10 singers, violin, viola, cello, windchimes, and tape.

Ave Maria—Kenneth Gaburo. World Library Publications No. MO-985-8. SATB, a cappella.

Bilogy, A (Non-Lullaby, Audiences We've Known and Loved)—Brock McElheran. Carl Fischer No. CM 7802. SATB.

Canticle—Harold Schramm. Cappella Music, Inc. SATB, an aleatory composition.

Emperor of Ice Cream, The—Roger Reynolds. C. F. Peters. Eight singers, piano, percussion, bass; multimedia.
Etude and Pattern—Brock McElheran. Oxford. SSAATBB unaccompanied.
Etude and Scherzo—Brock McElheran. Oxford. SSAATBB unaccompanied.
God Love You Now—Donald Erb. Merion No. 342-40099. SATB, speaker, assorted instruments, reverberation device.
Night Speech—Nicolas Roussakis. Continuo Music Press. Speech-chorus, two players of instruments.
Praise to God—Knut Nystedt. Associated No. A-597. Mixed voices, *a cappella*.
Praise Ye the Lord—Gardner Read. Lawson-Gould No. 51871.
Psalm 27 (Part III)—Robert Karlen. A.M.S.I. No. 160. SATB.
Pshelley's Psalm—Richard Felciano. E. C. Schirmer No. 2930. SATB.
Rising Sun, The—Frank Pooler & Brent Pierce. Somerset Press No. CE 4328. SATB.
Rondes—Folke Rabe. Edition Wilhelm Hansen (G. Schirmer). SATB.
Signposts—Eskil Hemberg. G. Schirmer No. 11842. SATB, *a cappella*.
Suoni—Knut Nystedt. Associated. SATB.
Toma—Alfred Janson. Walton No. M-115. Twelve-part mixed choir, organ, percussion, piano.
Two Moves and the Slow Scat—Dennis Kam. Belwin Mills No. 2282. SATB.

Music for Jazz/Show Choirs

Alexander's Ragtime Band—Berlin, arr. Simeone. Shawnee Press No. A-638. Piano accompaniment. Moderately easy.
All of Me—Simons-Marks, arr. K. Shaw. Hal Leonard No. 07852370. Piano, electric bass, and drums. Moderately easy.
Anything Goes—Porter, arr. Rizzo. Warner Bros. No. H2187. Piano accompaniment. Medium.
Aura Lee (traditional)—arr. K. Shaw. Hal Leonard No. 07248306. *A cappella*. Moderately easy.
Beautiful City (from *Godspell*)—Schwartz, arr. Lojeski. Hal Leonard No. 08200630. Piano, with optional percussion, guitar, and string bass. Moderately easy.
Blues Down to My Shoes—K. Shaw. Hal Leonard No. 07852435. Piano, bass, and drums. Moderately easy.
Brandy—Lurie, arr. Lojeski. Hal Leonard No. 08202500. Piano, guitar, electric bass, and percussion. Medium.
Can't Stop Dancin'—Stevens and Pritchard, arr. Simeone. Charles Hansen No. Sim 134. Piano, bass, and drums. Moderately easy.
Circles—Chapin, arr. Lojeski. Hal Leonard No. 08207200. Piano, guitar, electric bass, and percussion. Moderately easy.
Come Go With Me—Quick, arr. K. Shaw. Hal Leonard No. 0785330. Vocal solo, SATB, with piano, electric guitar, electric bass, and percussion. Tenor sax or instrumental solo. Medium.
Corner of the Sky (from *Pippin*)—Schwartz, arr. Cacavas. Belwin-Mills No. OCT 2288. Piano accompaniment. Moderately easy.

Crazy Rhythm—Meyer & Kahn, arr. Bretton. Warner Bros. No. H2210. Piano, guitar, and bass. Moderately easy.

Daybreak—Manilow, arr. F. Metis. Kamakazi Music Corp. No. 2672. Piano, with optional guitar, percussion, and electric or string bass. Moderately easy.

Day by Day—Cahn, Stordahl, and Weston, arr. K. Shaw. Hal Leonard No. 07853501. Piano, bass, and drums. Medium.

Doctor Jazz—K. Shaw. Hal Leonard No. 07852681. Piano, guitar, bass, and drums. Moderately difficult.

Don't Take Away the Music—Tawney, arr. Lojeski. Hal Leonard No. 08212800. Piano, guitar, percussion, and electric bass. Medium.

Ease on Down the Road (from *The Wiz*)—Small, arr. Beard. Shawnee Press No. A-1374. Piano accompaniment. Moderately easy.

Entertainer, The—Joplin, arr. Lojeski. Hal Leonard No. 08214000. Piano, with optional guitar, string bass, and drums. Moderately easy.

Everybody Be Dancin'—Blackman, arr. Lojeski. Hal Leonard No. 08214400. Piano, guitar, electric bass, and percussion. Moderately easy.

Everybody Rejoice (from *The Wiz*)—Vandross, arr. H. Ades. Shawnee Press No. A-1402. Piano accompaniment. Moderately easy.

Everybody's Boppin'—Hendricks, arr. Ward. Michael Kysar No. A130. Piano and bass. Medium.

52nd Street—Steve Allen, arr. K. Shaw. Hal Leonard No. 07248380. Piano with optional bass and drums, flute, trumpet, and alto saxophone. Moderately easy.

Gene Puerling Sound, The (Am I Blue, April in Paris, Autumn in New York, Dancing in the Dark, Indian Summer)—arr. G. Puerling. Shawnee Press No. A-1291. Optional piano accompaniment.

God Bless' the Child—Herzog and Holiday, arr. Kerr. Edward B. Marks No. MC4504. Piano and drums. Moderately easy.

Goodbye Love—Kraintz. Michael Kysar No. A 105. *A cappella*. Moderately easy.

Got to Get You into My Life—Lennon & McCartney, arr. Lojeski. Hal Leonard No. 08220100. Piano, guitar, percussion, and electric bass. Moderately easy.

Got to Get You into My Life—Lennon & McCartney, arr. Strommen. Alfred No. 6823z. Piano, with optional guitar, bass, and drums. Stage band accompaniment also available.

Grease Medley—Casey and Jacobs, arr. Simeone. Edwin H. Morris No. E9333. Piano, with optional guitar, bass, and drums. Moderately easy.

Here Comes That Rainy Day Feeling Again—Macaulay, Cook & Greenaway, arr. Lojeski. Hal Leonard No. 08223500. Piano, guitar, electric bass, and percussion. Easy.

Here's That Rainy Day—Burke & Van Heusen, arr. K. Shaw. Hal Leonard No. 07853801. Vocal solo. Piano, with optional guitar, bass, and drums. Medium.

Hold Tight-Hold Tight—Brandow, Miller & Spotswood, arr. Rutherford. Belwin-Mills No. 64406. Piano, with optional guitar, bass, and drums. Medium.

I Can't Give You Anything but Love—Fields & McHugh, arr. Rutherford. Belwin-Mills No. 64400. Piano, with optional guitar, bass, and drums. Moderately easy.

I Can't Stop Loving You—Gibson, arr. K. Shaw. Hal Leonard No. 07853870.
Piano, with optional instrumental accompaniment (trumpet, alto sax, trombone, guitar, electric bass, and drums). Medium.

I Hear Music—Lane, arr. Lapin. Warner Bros No. CH0926. Piano, with
optional guitar, bass, and drums. Medium.

I'll Never Smile Again—Lowe, arr. Kerr. MCA Music No. UC 725. Piano, with
optional guitar, bass guitar, and percussion. Moderately easy.

I'm Feeling Right—Kraintz. Michael Kysar No. A 104. Piano accompaniment.
Medium.

It Don't Mean a Thing—Ellington, arr. Rutherford. Belwin-Mills No. 64402.
Piano, with optional guitar, bass, and drums. Medium.

I've Got the World on a String—Arlen, arr. Rutherford. Belwin-Mills No.
64404. Piano, with optional guitar, bass, and drums. Medium.

I Won't Be Around—Kunz. Michael Kysar No. A 109. Piano accompaniment.
Moderately easy.

Jubilation—Anka and Harris, arr. K. Shaw. Hal Leonard No. 07981266. Piano,
electric bass, drums, trumpet, alto saxophone, and trombone. Medium.

Jumpin' with Symphony Sid—Young & Feyne, arr. K. Shaw. Hal Leonard No.
07854501. Piano, with optional guitar, electric bass, and drums. Medium.

Laughter in the Rain—Sedaka, arr. Cassey. Warner Bros. No. CHO791. Piano,
with optional acoustic guitar, electric guitar, and bass. Moderately easy.

Let Me Be the One—Nichols, arr. Lojeski. Hal Leonard No. 08237250. Piano
with optional guitar, percussion, and electric or string bass. Moderately
easy.

Let There Be Love—Rand, arr. K. Shaw. Hal Leonard No. 07855120. Piano,
guitar, electric bass, and drums. Medium.

London by Night—Coates, arr. Peurling. Shawnee Press No. A-1428. A cappella.
Moderately difficult.

Lonesome Road (traditional)—arr. K. Shaw. Hal Leonard No. 07248500. Piano,
guitar, bass, and drums. Moderately easy.

Lookin' for the Right Words—De Miero, arr. Kraintz. Michael Kysar No. A
126. Piano and bass. Moderately easy.

Love Is the Answer—Hannisian. Shawnee Press No. A-1382. Piano accompaniment. Moderately easy.

Love's the Coming Thing—Lojewski, arr. Lojeski. Hal Leonard No. 08238400.
Piano, guitar, electric bass, and percussion. Moderately easy.

Loving You—Kunz. Michael Kysar No. A 124. A cappella. Solo. Medium.

Magic to Do (from Pippin)—Schwartz, arr. Fisher. Belwin-Mills No. OCT 2302.
Piano, with optional bass, guitar, and drums. Moderately easy.

Mama Told Me Not to Come—Newman, arr. K. Shaw. Hal Leonard No.
07981501. Piano, trumpet, alto saxophone, trombone, electric guitar, electric bass, and drums. Medium.

Mercy, Mercy, Mercy—Zawinul, arr. Sechler. Shawnee Press No. A-1153. Piano,
with optional guitar, drums, and bass. Moderately easy.

Michelle—Lennon and McCartney, arr. Puerling. Shawnee Press No. A-1344.
A cappella. Soprano and tenor solo. Medium.

Mood Indigo—Ellington, arr. Rutherford. Belwin-Mills No. 64395. Piano with
optional guitar, bass, and drums. Medium.

My Funny Valentine—arr. D. Barduhn. Creative World Music Publications. *A cappella.* Medium.

My Sweet Lady—Denver, arr. Lojeski. Hal Leonard No. 08246000. Piano, with optional guitar, percussion, and string bass. Moderately easy.

Old-fashioned Love Song, An—Williams, arr. Beard. Shawnee Press No. A-1336. Four-hand piano accompaniment. Moderately easy.

Opus One—Oliver & Garris, arr. K. Shaw. Hal Leonard No. 07856451. Piano, guitar, electric bass, and drums. Medium.

Paddlin' Madelin' Home—Woods, arr. Grusin. Shapiro, Bernstein & Co. No. sb 7006. Piano accompaniment. Moderately easy.

People Need Love—Anderson and Ulvaeus, arr. Lojeski. Hal Leonard No. 08252800. Piano, electric bass, and percussion. Easy.

Pippin (choral medley)—Schwartz, arr. Cassey. Belwin-Mills No. SB 939. Piano, with optional bass, guitar, and drums. Medium.

Reach for the Stars—G. Fry. Belwin-Mills No. OCT 2427. Piano, with optional guitar, bass, and drums. Medium.

Rubber Band Man—Creed-Ball, arr. Lojeski. Hal Leonard No. 07981850. Piano, first and second trumpet, trombone, tenor saxophone, electric guitar, electric bass, drums, and Congo drums. Medium.

Rock around the Fifties (a montage)—arr. Andrews. Shawnee Press No. A-1342. Piano, with optional guitar, string bass, and drums. Medium.

Saturday—Carpenter, arr. Lojeski. Hal Leonard No. 08256000. Piano, with optional percussion, guitar, and electric or string bass. Moderately easy.

Sausalito Strut—Strommen. Alfred No. 6836F. Piano, with optional guitar, bass, and drums. Stage band accompaniment also available. Moderately easy.

Save All Your Lovin'—Kraintz. Hinshaw Music No. A 112. Piano and bass. Medium.

Save the Bones for Henry Jones—Barker-Lee-Jones, arr. K. Shaw. Hal Leonard No. 07248725. Piano, electric bass, and drums. Moderately easy.

Save the Country—Nyro, arr. Cassey. Warner Bros. No. WB183. Piano, with optional guitar and bass. Moderately easy.

Sentimental Journey thru the 40's, A (medley)—arr. Ades. Shawnee Press No. A-1357. Accompaniment options: (1) piano, (2) rhythm section, (3) jazz ensemble. Medium.

Side by Side—Woods, arr. Coates. Shawnee Press No. A-1389. Piano accompaniment. Moderately easy.

Solitude—Ellington, arr. Rutherford. Belwin-Mills No. 64401. Piano, guitar, bass, and percussion. Medium.

Smiles (a choral montage of songs, 1900–1920)—arr. H. Ades. Shawnee Press No. A-1322. Piano accompaniment. Moderately easy.

Sound of the Singers Unlimited, The (We've Only Just Begun, Try to Remember, On a Clear Day, Emily, My Ship, Where Is Love)—arr. G. Peurling. Shawnee Press No. A-1412. Instrumental accompaniment (trumpet, alto saxophone, electric piano, string bass, and drums) available for three of the arrangements. Medium.

Summer Nights (from *Grease*)—Casey & Jacobs, arr. Lojeski. Hal Leonard No. 08264480. Piano, with electric guitar, percussion, and electric bass. Moderately easy.

Summertime—Gershwin, arr. K. Shaw. Hal Leonard No. 07858401. Piano, electric bass, and drums. Medium.

Their Hearts Were Full of Spring—Troup, arr. K. Shaw. Hal Leonard No. 07857851. *A cappella.* Medium.

They Just Can't Stop It—Simmons, Hawes, & Jefferson, arr. Lojeski. Hal Leonard No. 08266950. Piano, guitar, percussion, and electric bass. Medium.

This is It!—David & Livingston, arr. Lapin. Warner Bros. No. CH0873. Piano, with optional bass and drums. Moderately easy.

That's When the Music Takes Me—Sedaka, arr. Polistina. Warner Bros. No. CH0880. Piano accompaniment. Moderately easy.

Ticket to Ride—Lennon, arr. Lojeski. Hal Leonard No. 08268000. Piano, guitar, electric or string bass, and percussion. Moderately easy.

To Be In Love—Kunz. Hal Leonard No. 07258001. *A cappella.* Medium.

Touch Me in the Morning—Masser, arr. Harding. Jobete Music No. 4738TC1. Piano accompaniment. Moderately easy.

Twentiana (a choral montage of songs of the 1920s)—arr. Ades. Shawnee Press No. A-1261. Piano, with optional string bass and drums. Moderately easy to medium.

You Are So Beautiful—Preston and Fischer, arr. Lojeski. Hal Leonard No. 08292500. Piano, guitar, percussion, and electric bass. Easy.

You Can't Dance—Ryan and Yeomans, arr. Lojeski. Hal Leonard No. 08293930. Piano, guitar, electric bass, and percussion. Moderately easy.

You Needed Me—Goodrum, arr. Lojeski. Hal Leonard No. 08293965. Piano, guitar, percussion, and electric or string bass. Moderately easy.

You've Got Your Troubles—Greenaway & Cook, arr. Rutherford. Belwin-Mills No. 64403. Piano, with optional guitar, bass, and drums. Moderately easy.

When I Fall in Love—Young, arr. Azelton. Hal Leonard No. 07259001. *A cappella.* Medium.

Wonderful Day Like Today, A—Bricusse and Newley, arr. Leyden. Musical Comedy Productions No. 57029. Piano accompaniment. Easy.

Woodchoppers' Ball—Merman & Bishop, arr. H. Brooks. Hal Leonard No. 07259071. Piano, bass, and drums. Medium.

Choral Collections

Whether or not to use choral collections has been a subject of some concern to conductors. One's criterion in arriving at a decision should simply be: Is it possible to use the majority of the selections in the collection? If so, the use of a collection may be a saving to the budget. When it is not feasible to use most of the selections, then it is a better practice to utilize separate octavo publications. Following are particular collections that the author has found useful, and that the conductor will want to examine to see if they meet the particular needs of his groups.

Collections for Mixed Voices (SATB, SAB)[2]

A Cappella Singer, The—edited by H. Clough-Leighter. E. C. Schirmer 1682.
A collection of 30 secular selections, primarily madrigals, from the choral
literature of the sixteenth and early seventeenth centuries. An excellent
basic book for madrigal groups.

Carols for Choirs—edited and arranged by Reginald Jacques and David Willcocks. Oxford University Press. A collection of 50 Christmas carols,
arranged mostly for mixed voices.

Choral Perspective—compiled by Don Malin. Marks Music Corp. A cross section of choral music from the Renaissance to the twentieth century, with
compositions representing 18 composers.

Concord Anthem Book, The—compiled and edited by Archibald T. Davison and
Henry Wilder Foote. E. C. Schirmer No. 13. (Clothbound.) Contains 40
anthems selected from the choral literature of the sixteenth through the
nineteenth centuries. Music varies in difficulty from easy to moderately
difficult.

First Motet Book, A—compiled and edited by Paul Thomas, Concordia Publishing House. Contains 17 motets in a variety of styles from the Renaissance to the twentieth century.

Five Centuries of Choral Music—compiled by a committee of teachers in the
Los Angeles City High Schools. William C. Hartshorn, Supervisor in
charge. G. Schirmer, Inc. A collection of 30 compositions representing
various types and styles from the Renaissance to the present.

Golden Age of the Madrigal, The—edited by Alfred Einstein. G. Schirmer, Inc.
Twelve Italian madrigals for five-part chorus of mixed voices.

Madrigals and Motets of Four Centuries. Associated Music Publishers. A
Choral songbook of 18 European classics.

Medieval Motet Book, A—compiled and edited by Hans Tischler. Associated
Music Publishers. A collection of thirteenth-century motets in various vocal
and instrumental combinations.

Rediscovered Madrigals—edited by Don Malin. Marks Music Corp. A collection
of sixteenth-century Italian madrigals and French chansons representing
seven composers.

Renaissance Choral Music—edited by Don Malin. Edward B. Marks Music
Corp. A collection of 14 secular choral works from the sixteenth century.
Music is by French, English, German, and Italian composers, with notes on
the background of each.

Renaissance to Baroque—edited by Lehman Engel. Harold Flammer. A collection, in seven volumes, of choral music from the Renaissance and Baroque
periods. Volume I, French–Netherland Music; Volume II, Italian Music;
Volume III, English Music; Volume IV, German Music; Volume V, Spanish
Music; Volume VI; English Music; Volume VII, French Music.

Second Concord Anthem Book, The—compiled and edited by Archibald T.
Davison and Henry Wilder Foote. E. C. Schirmer No. 1200. (Clothbound.)
Contains 40 additional anthems selected from the choral literature of the
sixteenth through the nineteenth centuries. Music varies in difficulty from
easy to moderately difficult.

[2] All collections are for SATB unless otherwise indicated.

3 to Make Music—Hawley Ades, and edited by Lara Hoggard. Shawnee Press. "Three-part songs for girls and boys." A collection of 32 songs—folk songs, spirituals, patriotic, faith and brotherhood, Christmas and general secular. Difficulty: easy to medium.

Collections for Treble Voices (SA, SSA, SSAA)

Choral Program Series (Books One and Two)—Harry R. Wilson. Silver Burdett. Each book contains representative selections from various styles of choral literature. Book One contains 17 two-part songs (SA) for girls' voices. Book Two contains 17 three- and four-part selections for girls' glee clubs (SSA and SSAA).

Christmas Carols for Treble Choirs—arranged and edited by Florence M. Martin. Schmitt, Hall & McCreary, Auditorium Series No. 56. (SA and SSA.) A collection of 15 Christmas carols. Difficulty: easy to medium.

Concert Songs for Girls—edited by M. Therese Armitage. Summy-Birchard. A collection of 106 selections in two, three, and four parts (SA, SSA, SSAA). Folk songs, songs by master composers as well as contemporary writers. For high school girls' glee clubs.

Glenn Glee Club Book for Girls—edited by Mabelle Glenn and Virginia French. Oliver Ditson. A collection of 42 songs for use in junior and senior high schools.

Presser Choral Collection; Sacred and Secular Literature—Past and Present—general editors, Geraldine Healy and William C. Hartshorn. Theodore Presser Company. A collection of 40 compositions for treble voices, representing various types and styles of choral music, compiled by a committee of choral music teachers in the Los Angeles City Public Schools.

Collections for Male Voices (TB, TTB, TTBB)

Birchard Choral Collection No. 1 (TTBB)—edited by J. Lilian Vandevere and Stuart B. Hopkin. Summy-Birchard. Fifty songs of various types—work songs, patriotic songs, classics, hymns, spirituals, and nonsense songs. Difficulty: easy to medium.

Choral Program Series (Book Three)—Harry R. Wilson. Silver Burdett. Contains a variety of types and styles of music. Seventeen selections for boys' glee clubs in two, three, and four parts (TB, TTB, and TTBB).

Christmas Carols for Male Voices—arranged and edited by George F. Strickling. Schmitt, Hall & McCreary, Auditorium Series No. 43. (TTBB.) Collection of 45 Christmas carols, some familiar, and other lesser-known carols from many countries. Difficulty: easy to medium.

Gentlemen Songsters—Livingston Gearhart, edited by Lara Hoggard. Shawnee Press. A collection of 42 songs for boys' glee clubs in two, three, and four parts (TB, TTB, and TTBB). Sea chanties, songs of the American Revolution, ballads, folk songs, classics, songs for Christmas and other special occasions, college songs and novelties, songs of faith and brotherhood, spirituals, and patriotic songs. Difficulty: easy to medium.

Extended Choral Works

All choral conductors should familiarize themselves with the extended choral works of various composers, for if a conductor is not familiar with major choral works, which in certain instances represent the crowning achievement of a composer, he has only an incomplete picture or concept of choral literature. Although the advanced high school choir could perform some of these works in their entirety, even an advanced choir could not perform certain others because of their overall difficulty. Conductors of college, university, and adult community choruses should examine all of these works for possible use by their groups.

Ahle, Johann Rudolf	
Be Not Afraid	Concordia
Antheil, George	
Cabeza de Vaca	Templeton Pub. Co.
Bach, Carl Philip Emanuel	
Holy Is God	Concordia
Magnificat	G. Schirmer
Bach, Johann Christoph	
Childhood of Christ, The	J. Fischer
Bach, Johann Sebastian	
Be Not Afraid (Motet IV)	C. F. Peters
Beautify Thyself, My Spirit (Cantata No. 180)	G. Schirmer
Christ Lay in Death's Dark Prison (Cantata No. 4)	Breitkopf & Härtel;
	G. Schirmer
Christmas Oratorio	G. Schirmer
Coffee Cantata, The (3-part chorus)	G. Schirmer
Come, Jesus, Come (Motet V)	H. W. Gray; C. F. Peters
Come, My Spirit, Come Exalt (Cantata No. 189)	Breitkopf & Härtel
Come, Thou Lovely Hour (Cantata No. 161)	E. C. Schirmer
Deck Thyself, My Soul, with Gladness (Cantata No. 180)	E. C. Schirmer
For As the Rain and Snow from Heaven Fall (Cantata No. 18)	G. Schirmer
For the Righteous, Wedding Cantata (No. 195)	Breitkopf & Härtel
For Us a Child Is Born (Cantata No. 142)	Galaxy
From Depths of Woe (Cantata No. 38)	E. C. Schirmer
Gerechten muss das Licht, Dem (Cantata No. 195)	Breitkopf & Härtel
Gloria in Excelsis Deo (Cantata No. 191)	G. Schirmer
God Is My King (Cantata No. 71)	Breitkopf & Härtel
God, the Lord Is Sun and Shield (Cantata No. 79)	G. Schirmer
God's Time Is the Best (Cantata No. 106)	G. Schirmer
Great David's Lord and Greater Son (Cantata No. 23)	E. C. Schirmer
Heavens Declare the Glory of God, The (Cantata No. 76)	Breitkopf & Härtel
Heavens Laugh, the Earth Exults, The (Cantata No. 31)	G. Schirmer

How Brightly Shines Yon Morning Star (Cantata No. 1)	E. C. Schirmer
I Suffered with Great Heaviness (Cantata No. 21)	G. Schirmer
If Thou Wilt Suffer God To Guide Thee (Cantata No. 93)	G. Schirmer
In God I Place My Faith and Trust (Cantata No. 188)	G. Schirmer
It Is Enough (Cantata No. 82)	Breitkopf & Härtel
Jesus, My Great Pleasure (Motet III)	C. F. Peters
Jesus, Thou My Constant Gladness (Cantata No. 147)	H. W. Gray
Jesus, Thou My Wearied Spirit (Cantata No. 78)	G. Schirmer
Kantate	Breitkopf & Härtel
King of Heaven, Come in Triumph (Cantata No. 182)	E. C. Schirmer
Kyrie in D Minor	G. Schirmer
Let Songs of Rejoicing Be Raised (Cantata No. 149)	H. W. Gray
Lord, Enter Not into Wrath (Cantata No. 105)	E. C. Schirmer
Magnificat	Breitkopf & Härtel; C. F. Peters; G. Schirmer
Mass in B Minor	G. Schirmer
Messe No. 4 in G Major	C. F. Peters
Missa Brevis in G	H. W. Gray
My Soul Doth Magnify the Lord (Cantata No. 10)	G. Schirmer
My Soul Exalts the Lord (Cantata No. 10)	E. C. Schirmer
New-Born Babe, The (Cantata No. 122)	G. Schirmer
Now Thank We All Our God (Cantata No. 192)	G. Schirmer
Nun ist das Heil und die Kraft (Cantata No. 50)	Breitkopf & Härtel
O Christ, My All in Living (Cantata No. 95)	Novello
O God, How Grievous (Cantata No. 3)	E. C. Schirmer
O Jesus Christ, My Life and Light (Cantata No. 118)	G. Schirmer
O Light Everlasting (Cantata No. 34) .	E. C. Schirmer
O Lord, Relent, I Pray (Cantata No. 135)	E. C. Schirmer
O Lord, This Grieving Spirit (Cantata No. 135)	G. Schirmer
O Praise the Lord for All His Mercies (Cantata No. 28)	H. W. Gray
Ode of Mourning (Cantata No. 198)	G. Schirmer
Out of Darkness Call I Lord to Thee (Cantata No. 131)	Breitkopf & Härtel
Passion According to St. John, The	Breitkopf & Härtel; G. Schirmer
Passion According to St. Matthew, The	Breitkopf & Härtel; G. Schirmer
Peasant Cantata, The	Paterson's Pub. Ltd.
Praise Him, the Lord, the Almighty King (Cantata No. 137)	Breitkopf & Härtel
Praise Our God in All His Splendor (Cantata No. 11)	G. Schirmer
Praise the Lord, All Ye Nations (Motet VI)	C. F. Peters
Sheep May Safely Graze (Cantata No. 208)	G. Schirmer
Sing Ye to the Lord (Motet I)	C. F. Peters
Sleepers, Wake! (Cantata No. 140)	H. W. Gray

Spirit Also Helpeth Us, The (Motet II)	H. W. Gray; C. F. Peters
Stronghold Sure, A (Cantata No. 80)	G. Schirmer
There Uprose a Great Strife (Cantata No. 19)	G. Schirmer
Thou Guide of Israel (Cantata No. 104)	H. W. Gray
Thou Very God and David's Son (Cantata No. 23)	G. Schirmer
To Us a Child Is Given (Cantata No. 142)	G. Schirmer
We Must Through Great Tribulations (Cantata No. 146)	G. Schirmer
Weeping, Crying, Sorrow, Sighing (Cantata No. 12)	G. Schirmer
When Will God Recall My Spirit? (Cantata No. 8)	E. C. Schirmer
Barber, Samuel	
Prayers of Kierkgaard	G. Schirmer
Bartók, Béla	
Cantata Profana	Boosey & Hawkes
Shepherd's Christmas Songs	Boosey & Hawkes
Beethoven, Ludwig van	
Cantata on the Death of Emperor Joseph II	G. Schirmer
Choral Fantasia	Edwin F. Kalmus
Choral Finale to the Ninth Symphony	H. W. Gray; G. Schirmer
Christ on the Mount of Olives	Edwin F. Kalmus
Mass in C Major	Edwin F. Kalmus
Mass in D	Novello
Missa Solemnis, Op. 123	G. Schirmer
Berger, Jean	
Brazilian Psalm	G. Schirmer
Fiery Furnace, The	G. Schirmer
Psalm 57	Presser
Vision of Peace	Broude Bros.
Berlioz, Hector	
Childhood of Christ	G. Schirmer
Childhood of Christ (abridged version)	H. W. Gray
Choral Suite from Benvenuto Cellini	Oxford
Grand Death Mass, Op. 5	Breitkopf & Härtel
Requiem	G. Schirmer
Te Deum	G. Schirmer
Bernstein, Leonard	
Chichester Psalms	G. Schirmer
Choruses from The Lark	G. Schirmer
Kaddish	G. Schirmer
Blitzstein, Marc	
Airborne, The (cantata)	Chappell
Bloch, Ernest	
Sacred Service	Broude Bros.
Boito, Arrigo	
Prologue in Heaven (from Mefistofele)	G. Schirmer
Borodin, Alex	
Polovetzian Dance and Chorus (from Prince Igor)	G. Schirmer
Brahms, Johannes	
Love-Song Waltzes (Liebeslieder Walzer)	Associated

Marienlieder	Breitkopf & Härtel;
	C. F. Peters;
	E. C. Schirmer
Motet from Psalm LI, Op. 29, No. 2	G. Schirmer
Nänie	G. Schirmer;
	E. C. Schirmer
Neue Liebeslieder	Lawson-Gould
Requiem, Op. 45	Edwin F. Kalmus;
	G. Schirmer
Schicksalslied (Song of Destiny)	H. W. Gray;
	E. C. Schirmer
Triumphal Hymn	G. Schirmer
Britten, Benjamin	
Ballad of Heroes	Boosey & Hawkes
Cantata Misericordium	Boosey & Hawkes
Ceremony of Carols, A (SATB; SSA)	Boosey & Hawkes
Festival Te Deum	Boosey & Hawkes
Hymn to St. Cecilia	Boosey & Hawkes
Rejoice in the Lamb	Boosey & Hawkes
Saint Nicolas	Boosey & Hawkes
Spring Symphony	Boosey & Hawkes
Voices for Today	G. Schirmer
War Requiem	Boosey & Hawkes
Wedding Anthem, A (Amo, ergo Sum)	Boosey & Hawkes
Bruckner, Anton	
Mass in E minor	Broude Bros.
Mass No. 1 in D minor	C. F. Peters
Mass No. 3 in F minor	C. F. Peters
Te Deum Laudamus	G. Schirmer
Buxtehude, Dietrich	
Aperite Mihi Portas Justitiae	
(Open to Me Gates of Justice)	C. F. Peters
Good Christian Men, with Joy Draw Near	Concordia
Jesu, Joy and Treasure	C. F. Peters
Laudia Sion Salvatorem	Chantry Music Press
Missa Brevis	Mercury
Open to Me Gates of Justice	C. F. Peters
Rejoice, Earth and Heaven	C. F. Peters
Sing to God the Lord	Concordia
What Is the World to Me	Concordia
Byrd, William	
Mass for 4 Voices	Galaxy: Stainer & Bell
Mass for 5 Voices	Galaxy: Stainer & Bell
Carissimi, Giacomo	
Jephte	Ricordi
Charpentier, Marc-Antoine	
Midnight Mass for Christmas	Elkan-Vogel
Venite ad Me	G. Schirmer

Cherubini, Luigi
  Requiem in D Minor   C. F. Peters
  Requiem Mass in C Minor   G. Schirmer
Coleridge-Taylor, Samuel
  Hiawatha's Wedding Feast   G. Schirmer
Comes, Juan Bautista
  Beatus Vir   G. Schirmer
  Lamentación   G. Schirmer
  Magnificat   G. Schirmer
Copland, Aaron
  In the Beginning   Boosey & Hawkes
Creston, Paul
  Celestial Vision, The   Shawnee Press
  Isaiah's Prophecy   Franco Colombo
  Missa Solemnis, Op. 44   Belwin-Mills
Debussy, Claude
  Blessed Damoiselle, The   G. Schirmer
  L'Enfant Prodigue   Elkan-Vogel
  Ode à la France   Elkan-Vogel
Delius, Frederick
  Appalachia   Boosey & Hawkes
  Mass of Life, A   Universal
  Sea Drift   Boosey & Hawkes
  Songs of Farewell   Boosey & Hawkes
Dello Joio, Norman
  Mystic Trumpeter, The   G. Schirmer
  Psalm of David, A   Carl Fischer
  Psalm of Peace   Edw. B. Marks
  Song of Affirmation   Carl Fischer
  Song of the Open Road   Carl Fischer
  To St. Cecilia   Carl Fischer
  Years of the Modern   Edw. B. Marks
Diamond, David
  This Sacred Ground   Southern Music
Dorati, Antal
  Missa Brevis   Belwin-Mills
Dubois, Theodore
  Seven Last Words of Christ, The   G. Schirmer
Duruflé, Maurice
  Requiem   Durand
Dvořák, Anton
  Stabat Mater, Op. 58   G. Schirmer
Effinger, Cecil
  Invisible Fire, The   H. W. Gray
  St. Luke Christmas Story, The   G. Schirmer
  Set of Three   Elkan-Vogel
Elgar, Edward
  Dream of Gerontius   Novello
  29th Psalm   Novello
  48th Psalm   Novello

Etler, Alvin
  Ode to Pothos · Associated
Fauré, Gabriel
  Requiem · H. T. FitzSimons
Fetler, Paul
  Now This Is the Story (SSA) · Carl Fischer
  Te Deum · Augsburg
Foss, Lukas
  Parable of Death, A · Carl Fischer
  Prairie, The · G. Schirmer
  Psalms · Carl Fischer
Franck, César
  Beatitudes, The (oratorio) · G. Schirmer
  Communion Service in A Major, Op. 12 · E. C. Schirmer
Gabrieli, Giovanni
  Jubilate Deo · Bourne; G. Schirmer
  Timor et Tremor · Annie Banks
Galuppi, Baldassare
  Kyrie · Lawson-Gould
Gesualdo, Carlo
  Illumina Nos · Boosey & Hawkes
  Tres Sacrae Cantiones · Boosey & Hawkes
Goudimel, Claude
  Messe Audi Filia · Éditions Salabert
Gounod, Charles
  Gallia · G. Schirmer
  Mass in C · G. Schirmer
  Messe Solennelle (St. Cecilia) · G. Schirmer
  Missa Choralis · E. C. Schirmer
  Missa Paschalis · E. C. Schirmer
Grieg, Edvard
  Choral Suite · Hinrichsen & Peters
  Psalms for Mixed Chorus · C. F. Peters
Hammerschmidt, Andreas
  Holy Is the Lord · Concordia
  How Then Shall We Find Bread? · Concordia
  Now Death Is Devoured · Concordia
Handel, George Frederick
  Acis and Galatea · Novello
  Alceste · Novello
  Autumn Day, An · Oxford
  Belshazzar · Associated
  Canticle of Praise · G. Schirmer
  Dettingen Te Deum · H. W. Gray
  Foundling Hospital Anthem · C. F. Peters
  Funeral Anthem for Queen Caroline · G. Schirmer
  Israel in Egypt · G. Schirmer
  Joshua · Novello
  Judas Maccabaeus · G. Schirmer
  King Shall Rejoice, The · Novello

Laudate Pueri Dominum (Psalm 112)	C. F. Peters
Messiah	G. Schirmer
O Sing unto the Lord (Psalm 96)	G. Schirmer
Samson	G. Schirmer
Saul	H. W. Gray
Sixth Chandos Anthem	G. Schirmer
Solomon	Breitkopf & Härtel;
	H. W. Gray
Te Deum Laudamus	Verlag Merseburger
Utrecht Jubilate, The	Breitkopf & Härtel
Utrecht Te Deum, The	G. Schirmer
Hanson, Howard	
Beat! Beat! Drums!	J. Fischer
Cherubic Hymn, The	Carl Fischer
Song of Democracy	Carl Fischer
Song of Human Rights	Carl Fischer
Songs from *Drum Taps*	J. Fischer
Harris, Roy	
Mass in C (for Male Voices and Organ)	Carl Fischer
Hassler, Hans Leo	
Mass No. 5	Concordia
Haydn, Joseph	
Creation, The	G. Schirmer
Mass in Time of War	G. Schirmer
Missa Brevis in F	Doblinger
Missa Solemnis	C. F. Peters
Seasons, The	G. Schirmer
Seven Last Words of Christ, The	G. Schirmer
Sixteenth Mass	H. W. Gray
Stabat Mater	G. Schirmer
Third Mass (The Imperial or Lord Nelson)	G. Schirmer
Haydn, Michael	
Laudate Populi	Breitkopf & Härtel
Timete Dominum (O Fear the Lord)	G. Schirmer
Hindemith, Paul	
Apparebit Repentina Dies	Schott
Four Songs	Schott
Messe	Schott
When Lilacs Last in the Door-Yard Bloom'd	Schott
Holst, Gustav	
Coming of Christ, The	G. Schirmer
Honegger, Arthur	
Cantate de Noël	Éditions Salabert
Danse des morts, La	Éditions Salabert
King David	E. C. Schirmer
Nicholas de Flue	E. C. Schirmer
Hovhaness, Alan	
Glory to God	C. F. Peters
In the Beginning Was the Word	C. F. Peters
Look Toward the Sea	C. F. Peters

Make a Joyful Noise	C. F. Peters
30th Ode of Solomon	C. F. Peters
Janequin, Clement	
Messe La Bataille	Éditions Salabert
Kodály, Zoltán	
Missa Brevis	Boosey & Hawkes
Psalmus Hungaricus	Universal
Te Deum	Universal
Kubik, Gail	
Litany and Prayer (TTBB)	Southern Music
Record of Our Time, A	MCA Music
Lasso, Orlando di	
Missa Puisque j'ay perdu	J. Fischer
Liszt, Franz	
XIIIth Psalm, The	G. Schirmer
Lockwood, Normand	
Ballad of the North and South, A	Associated
Carol Fantasy	Associated
Holy Birth, The	Choral Services
Lotti, Antonio	
Mass VII in the Doric Mode	E. C. Schirmer
Lully, Jean Baptiste	
Te Deum	Schott
Machaut, Guillaume	
Messe Notre-Dame	Éditions Salabert
Mahler, Gustav	
Waldmärchen (Forest Legend)	Belwin-Mills
Martirano, Salvatore	
O O O O That Shakespearian Rag	Schott
McDonald, Harl	
Pioneers, O Pioneers	Elkan-Vogel
Songs of Conquest	Elkan-Vogel
McKay, George F.	
Choral Rhapsody	J. Fischer
Mendelssohn, Felix	
As the Hart Pants (42nd Psalm)	G. Schirmer
Christus	G. Schirmer
Come Let Us Sing (95th Psalm)	G. Schirmer
Elijah (oratorio)	G. Schirmer
First Walpurgis Night, The, Op. 60	G. Schirmer
Hear My Prayer	G. Schirmer
Hymn of Praise	G. Schirmer
Kyrie	Oxford
114th Psalm	Novello
St. Paul (oratorio)	G. Schirmer
Mennin, Peter	
Christmas Story, The	Carl Fischer
Cycle, The (Symphony No. 4)	Carl Fischer
Menotti, Gian Carlo	
Death of the Bishop of Brindisi, The	G. Schirmer

Milhaud, Darius
Cantate pour louer le Seigneur .... Universal
Cantique du Rhône .... Elkan-Vogel
Château du Feu, Le .... Associated
Miracles of Faith .... G. Schirmer
Naissance de Vénus .... Heugel
Pan et Syrinx .... Éditions Salabert
Three Psalms of David .... Associated
Monteverdi, Claudio
Lagrime d'Amante al Sepolcro dill'Amata ... Lawson-Gould
Magnificat Primo .... Lawson-Gould
Mozart, Wolfgang A.
Davidde Penitente (K. 459) .... Broude Bros.
Glory, Praise and Power .... H. W. Gray
Grand Mass in C Minor .... G. Schirmer
Litania in E Flat (K. 243) .... Edwin F. Kalmus
Mass in C (K. 317, "Coronation") .... Breitkopf & Härtel;
                                         G. Schirmer
Misericordias Offertorium de Tempore ...... G. Schirmer
Missa Brevis in C (K. 220) .... Associated
Missa Brevis in D (K. 194) .... Edw. B. Marks
Missa Brevis in F Major (K. 192) .... G. Schirmer
Regina Coeli .... G. Schirmer
Requiem Mass .... H. W. Gray; C. F. Peters;
                                         G. Schirmer
Vesperae Solennes de Dominica (K. 321) .... E. C. Schirmer
Orff, Carl
Carmina Burana .... Schott
Catulli Carmina .... Schott
Trionfo di Afrodite .... Schott
Pachelbel, Johann
Deus in Adjutorium .... Edw. B. Marks
Herr ist König, Der .... Concordia
Jauchzet dem Herrn (Shout Forth to the Lord) ... Concordia
Magnificat in C .... Summy-Birchard
Palestrina, Giovanni
Assumpta est Maria .... Breitkopf & Härtel
Leichte Chore .... Breitkopf & Härtel
Missa Brevis .... Breitkopf & Härtel;
                                         G. Schirmer
Missa Iste Confessor .... Breitkopf & Härtel;
                                         Edw. B. Marks
Missa Papae Marcelli .... J. Fischer; G. Schirmer
Missa Tu es Petrus .... Breitkopf & Härtel
Pater Noster .... Breitkopf & Härtel
Stabat Mater .... Belwin-Mills; G. Schirmer
Penderecki, Krzysztof
Canticum Canticorum Salomonis (Song of Songs) ... Schott
Kosmogonia .... Schott
Passion According to St. Luke .... Belwin-Mills

Utrenja	
Entombment of Christ, The	Schott
Resurrection of Christ, The	
Pergolesi, Giovanni	
Magnificat, The	Walton Music
Persichetti, Vincent	
Celebrations	Elkan-Vogel
Mass	Elkan-Vogel
Pierné, Gabriel	
Children at Bethlehem, The	G. Schirmer
Pinkham, Daniel	
Ascension Cantata	E. C. Schirmer
Canticle of Praise	E. C. Schirmer
Easter Cantata	C. F. Peters
Emily Dickinson Mosaic, An (SSAA)	C. F. Peters
Jonah	E. C. Schirmer
Jubilate Deo	E. C. Schirmer
Mass of the Word of God	E. C. Schirmer
Requiem	C. F. Peters
Saint Mark Passion	C. F. Peters
Wedding Cantata	C. F. Peters
Poulenc, Francis	
Gloria	Éditions Salabert
Messe en sol majeur	Éditions Salabert
Stabat Mater	Éditions Salabert
Praetorius, Michael	
Canticum Trium Puerorum	Sam Fox
Prokofieff, Serge	
Alexander Nevsky	Leeds Music
Purcell, Henry	
Te Deum Laudamus and Jubilate Deo	G. Schirmer
Rachmaninoff, Sergei	
Springtide	G. Schirmer
Reizenstein, Franz	
Voices of Night	H. W. Gray
Respighi, Ottorino	
Laud to the Nativity	Franco Colombo
Rimsky-Korsakov, Nikolai	
Polonaise with Chorus	Boosey & Hawkes
Rogers, Bernard	
Letter from Pete, A	Southern Music
Prophet Isaiah, The	Southern Music
Rorem, Ned	
From an Unknown Past	Southern Music
Two Psalms and a Proverb	E. C. Schirmer
Rossini, Gioacchino	
Stabat Mater	G. Schirmer
Rozsa, Miklos	
To Everything There Is a Season	Broude Bros; Breitkopf & Härtel

Saint-Saëns, Camille	
Christmas Oratorio	G. Schirmer
Scarlatti, Alessandro	
Salve Regina	Walton
Te Deum Laudamus	Presser
Schoenberg, Arnold	
De Profundis (Psalm 150)	Leeds Music
Gurre-Lieder	Universal
Kol Nidre	Boelke-Bomart
Ode to Napoleon (for speaker and string orchestra)	G. Schirmer
Peace on Earth	Schott
Survivor of Warsaw, A	Boelke-Bomart
Schubert, Franz	
Gesang der Geister über den Wassern	
(for male voices)	Carl Fischer
Mass in A♭	Breitkopf & Härtel; Novello
Mass No. 3 in B♭	Arista
Mass in F	G. Schirmer
Mass in G	H. W. Gray; G. Schirmer
Miriam's Song of Triumph	G. Schirmer
Rosamunde	G. Schirmer
Schuman, William	
Free Song, A	G. Schirmer
This Is Our Time	Boosey & Hawkes
Schütz, Heinrich	
Annunciation According to St. Luke, The	J. Fischer; G. Schirmer
Christmas Story, The	G. Schirmer
Deutsches Magnificat	Bärenreiter-Ausgabe
84th Psalm	G. Schirmer
German Requiem, A	G. Schirmer
Magnificat	Breitkopf & Härtel
Mein Sohn, warum hast du uns das getan?	Oxford
Nativity	Bärenreiter
Passion According to St. John, The	Oxford
St. Luke Passion, The	Oxford
St. Matthew Passion, The	Augsburg; Breitkopf & Härtel; Oxford
Seven Last Words, The	Oxford; G. Schirmer; E. C. Schirmer
Symphonia Sacra No. 4	Oxford
Senfl, Ludwig	
Ave Maria, Gratia Plena	Associated
Ich stund an einem Morgen	Lawson-Gould
Shostakovich, Dimitri	
Song of the Forests (cantata)	Leeds
Sowerby, Leo	
Ark of the Covenant, The	H. W. Gray
Canticle of the Sun, The	H. W. Gray

Christ Reborn	H. W. Gray
Forsaken of Man	H. W. Gray
Great Is the Lord	H. W. Gray
Throne of God, The	H. W. Gray
Spohr, Louis	
Mass, Op. 54	Arista
Stainer, John	
Crucifixion, The	G. Schirmer
Daughter of Jairus, The (cantata)	G. Schirmer
Stravinsky, Igor	
Cantata	Boosey & Hawkes
Flood, The	Boosey & Hawkes
Mass	Boosey & Hawkes
Noces, Les	Boosey & Hawkes
Oedipus Rex	Boosey & Hawkes
Perséphone (ballet with chorus)	Boosey & Hawkes
Symphony of Psalms	Boosey & Hawkes
Threni	Boosey & Hawkes
Surinach, Carlos	
Cantata of St. John	Associated
Sweelinck, Jan Pieterszoon	
Psalm 150	E. C. Schirmer
Tallis, Thomas	
Lamentations (Parts I and II)	Oxford
Thompson, Randall	
Americana	E. C. Schirmer
Concord Cantata, A	E. C. Schirmer
Feast of Praise, A	E. C. Schirmer
Mass of the Holy Spirit	E. C. Schirmer
Nativity According to St. Luke	E. C. Schirmer
Ode to the Virginian Voyage	E. C. Schirmer
Passion According to St. Luke	E. C. Schirmer
Peaceable Kingdom, The	E. C. Schirmer
Place of the Best, The	E. C. Schirmer
Psalm of Thanksgiving, A	E. C. Schirmer
Requiem	E. C. Schirmer
Testament of Freedom	E. C. Schirmer
Thomson, Virgil	
Mass (unison)	G. Schirmer
Missa pro Defunctis	H. W. Gray
Vaughan Williams, Ralph	
Dona Nobis Pacem	Oxford
Epithalamion	Oxford
First Nowell, The	Oxford
Five Tudor Portraits	Oxford
Four Songs of the Four Seasons	Oxford
Hodie	Oxford
Mass in G Minor	G. Schirmer
Pilgrim's Journey	Oxford
Sancta Civitas	Oxford; G. Schirmer

Sea Symphony, A	Galaxy; Oxford; Stainer & Bell
Serenade to Music	Oxford
Song of Thanksgiving, A	Oxford
Thanksgiving for Victory	Oxford
This Day	Oxford
Vision of Aeroplanes, A (Motet)	Oxford
Verdi, Guiseppe	
Four Sacred Pieces	Franco Colombo
Requiem	G. Schirmer
Te Deum	C. F. Peters
Victoria, Tomas Luis de	
O Magnum Mysterium	Associated; J. Fischer & Bros.
Missa "O Quam Gloriosum"	Arista
Vierne, Louis	
Solemn Mass	Mark Foster
Vivaldi, Antonio	
Chamber Mass	Lawson-Gould
Gloria	Ricordi
Walton, William	
Belshazzar's Feast	Oxford
Coronation Te Deum	Oxford
Gloria	Oxford
In Honor of the City of London	Oxford
Weber, Carl Maria von	
Mass No. 1 in G	Lawson-Gould

Music Publishers

Abingdon Press, 201 Eighth Ave. South, Nashville, TN 37202
Addington Press (order from Hinshaw Music, Inc.)
Agape, 380 S. Main Place, Carol Stream, IL 60187
Alexandria House, PO Box 300, Alexandria, IN 46001
Alfred Publishing Co., PO Box 5964, Sherman Oaks, CA 91413
Almo Publications, 1312 N. La Brae, Hollywood, CA 90028
American Composers Alliance, 170 W. 74th St., New York, NY 10023
AMSI, 2614 Nicollet Ave., Minneapolis, MN 55408
Arista Music Co., Box 1596, Brooklyn, NY 11201
Associated Music Publishers, Inc., 866 Third Ave., New York, NY 10022
Augsburg Publishing House, 426 S. Fifth St., Minneapolis, MN 55415
Bärenreiter Music Publishers (order from European American Music Distributors Corp.)
Barry E. C. I., Argentina (order from Boosey & Hawkes, Inc.)
Beckenhorst Press, PO Box 14273, Columbus, OH 43214
Belmont Music Publishers, Box 49961, Los Angeles, CA 90049
Belwin-Mills Publishing Corp., 25 Deshon Dr., Melville, NY 11746
Irving Berlin Music Corp., 1290 Avenue of the Americas, New York, NY 10019

Big 3 Music Corporation, 729 Seventh Ave., New York, NY 10019
Blixt Publications, 413 Rutland Ave., San Jose, CA 95128
Boelke-Bomart, Inc., and Mobart Music Publications, Hillsdale, NY 12529
Joseph Boonin, Inc. (order from European American Music Distributors Corp.)
Boosey & Hawkes, Inc., PO Box 130, Oceanside, NY 11572
Boston Music Company, 116 Boylston St., Boston, MA 02116
Bourne Company, 1212 Avenue of the Americas, New York, NY 10036
Breitkopf & Härtel (order from Alexander Broude, Inc.)
Broadman Press, 127 Ninth Ave. North, Nashville, TN 37234
Alexander Broude, Inc., 225 W. 57th St., New York, NY 10019
Broude Brothers, Ltd., 56 W. 45th St., New York, NY 10036
Cambiata Press, PO Box 1151, Conway, AR 72032
Chantry Music Press, 32 N. Center St., PO Box 1101, Springfield, OH 45501
Chappell Music (order from Theodore Presser Co.)
Charter Publications, PO Box 850, Valley Forge, PA 19482
Cherry Lane Music Co., Inc., 50 Holly Hill Lane, PO Box 4247, Greenwich, CT
    06830
Choristers Guild, PO Box 38188, Dallas, TX 75238
John Church Company (order from Theodore Presser Co.)
Franco Colombo Publications (order from Belwin-Mills Publishing Corp.)
Concordia Publishing House, 3558 S. Jefferson Ave., St. Louis, MO 63118
Consolidated Music Publishers, Inc (order from Music Sales Corp.)
Continuo Music Press, Inc. (order from Alexander Broude, Inc.)
J. B. Cramer, London (order from Alexander Broude, Inc.)
Creative Jazz Composers, PO Box T, Bowie, MD 20715
Creative World Music Publications (order from Warner Bros. Publications, Inc.)
Criterion Music Corp. (order from Studio P/R, Inc.)
Curtis Music Press, PO Box 19320, Minneapolis, MN 55419
J. Curwen & Sons (order from G. Schirmer, Inc.)
Dartmouth Collegium Musicum (order from Shawnee Press, Inc.)
Roger Dean Publishing Company, 324 W. Jackson, Macomb, IL 61455
Oliver Ditson (order from Theodore Presser Co.)
Editio Musica, Budapest, Hungary (order from Boosey & Hawkes)
Edition Musicus, 198 Selleck St., PO Box 1341, Stamford, CT 06904
Éditions Salabert, Inc., 575 Madison Ave., New York, NY 10022
Edizione Suvini Zerboni, Milan, Italy (order from Boosey & Hawkes)
Elkan-Vogel, Inc. (order from Theodore Presser Co.)
European American Music Distributors Corp., 195 Allwood Rd., Clifton, NJ 07012
Fine Arts Music Press, PO Box 45144, Tulsa, OK 74145
Carl Fischer, Inc., 62 Cooper Sq., New York, NY 10003
J. Fischer & Bros. (order from Belwin-Mills Publishing Corp.)
H. T. Fitzsimons Co. Inc., 615 N. LaSalle St., Chicago, IL 60610
Harold Flammer, Inc. (order from Shawnee Press)
Fortress Press, 2900 Queen Lane, Philadelphia, PA 19129
Mark Foster Music Company, Box 4012, Champaign, IL 61820
Sam Fox Publishing Company, PO Box 850, Valley Forge, PA 19482
Frank Music Corp. (order from Hal Leonard)
Galaxy Music Corporation, 2121 Broadway, New York, NY 10023
Genesis III Music Corp., 17 W. 60th St., New York, NY 10023
Gentry Publications (order from Theodore Presser Co.)

G.I.A. Publications, 7404 S. Mason Ave., Chicago, IL 60638
H. W. Gray Company, Inc. (order from Belwin-Mills Publishing Corp.)
Hansen Publications, Inc., 1842 West Ave., Miami Beach, FL 33139, or 1860
    Broadway, New York, NY 10023
Harms, Inc. (order from Warner Bros. Publications)
T. B. Harms Co. (order from Belwin-Mills Publishing Corp.)
The Frederick Harris Music Co., Ltd., 529 Speers Blvd., Oakville, Ontario,
    Canada L6K 2G4
Heritage Music Press (order from Lorenz Industries)
Heugel and Cie (order from Theodore Presser Co.)
Highgate Press (order from Galaxy Music Corp.)
Hinrichsen & Peters (order from C. F. Peters Corp.)
Hinshaw Music, Inc., 400 W. Franklin St., Chapel Hill, NC 27514
Charles W. Homeyer & Co. (order from Carl Fischer, Inc.)
InterVarsity Press, Downers Grove, IL 60515
Ione Press (order from E. C. Schirmer)
Jenson Publications, Inc., 2880 S. 171st St., New Berlin, NY 53151
Kendor Music, Inc., Delevan, NY 14042
E. C. Kerby, Ltd., 198 Davenport Rd., Toronto, Ontario, Canada M54 1J2
Neil A. Kjos Music Company, 4382 Jutland Dr., San Diego, CA 92117
Michael Kysar, Publisher (order from Hinshaw Music, Inc.)
Lawson-Gould Music Publishers, Inc., 866 Third Ave., New York, NY 10022
Leeds Music (order from Belwin-Mills Publishing Corp.)
Hal Leonard Publishing Corp., 8112 W. Bluemound Rd., Milwaukee, WI 53213
Lorenz Industries, 501 E. Third St., Dayton, OH 45401
Manna Music, Inc., 2111 Kenmere Ave., Burbank, CA 91504
Margun Music, 168 Dudley Rd., Newton Centre, MA 01259
Edward B. Marks Publishing Corp. (order from Belwin-Mills Publishing Corp.)
McAfee Music Corporation (order from Lorenz Industries)
MCA Music (order from Belwin-Mills Publishing Corp.)
McLaughlin & Reilly Company (order from Summy-Birchard Co.)
Mercury Music Corporation (order from Theodore Presser Co.)
Merion Music, Inc. (order from Theodore Presser Co.)
Miller Music Corporation (order from Big 3 Music Corp.)
Edwin H. Morris & Co., Inc. (order from Hansen Publications, Inc.)
Music Press, Tuskegee Institute (order from Neil A. Kjos Music Company)
Music Sales Corporation, 33 W. 60th St., New York, NY 10023
Music 70, PO Box 850, Valley Forge, PA 19482
NMP Publications, PO Box 868, Tustin, CA 92680
Novello Publications, 145 Palisade St., Dobbs Ferry, NY 10522
Oxford University Press, 16-00 Pollitt Dr., Fair Lawn, NJ 07410
Patterson's Pub., Ltd. (order from Carl Fischer, Inc.)
Paull Pioneer Publications (order from Shawnee Press, Inc.)
C. F. Peters Corp., 373 Park Ave. South, New York, NY 10016
Plymouth Music Co., Inc., 170 NE 33rd St., Ft. Lauderdale, FL 33334
Theodore Presser Company, Presser Place, Bryn Mawr, PA 19010
Proclamation Productions, Inc., Orange Sq., Port Jervis, NY 12771
Pro-Art Publications (order from Belwin-Mills Publishing Corp.)
Remick Music Corporation (order from Warner Bros. Publications, Inc.)

Richmond Music Press, Inc., PO Box 475, Richmond, IN 47374
G. Ricordi & Company (order from Belwin-Mills Publishing Corp.)
Robbins Music Corporation (order from Music Sales Corporation)
Rongwen Music (order from Broude Brothers, Ltd.)
R. D. Row Music Co. (order from Carl Fischer, Inc.)
Sacred Music Press (order from Lorenz Industries)
E. C. Schirmer Music Company, 112 South St., Boston, MA 02111
G. Schirmer, Inc., 866 Third Ave., New York, NY 10022
Arthur P. Schmidt Company (order from Summy-Birchard Co.)
Schmitt Publications, 110 N. Fifth St., Minneapolis, MN 55403
Schott & Company, Ltd. (order from European American Music Distributors
    Corp.)
Scott Music Publications, PO Box 148, Hollywood, CA 90028
Shawnee Press, Inc., Delaware Water Gap, PA 18327
John Sheppard Music Press (order from European American Music Distributors
    Corp.)
Southern Music Company, 1100 Broadway, PO Box 329, San Antonio, TX 78292
Spratt Music Publishers (order from Plymouth Music Co.)
Staff Music Publishing Co., Inc., 170 NE 33rd St., Ft. Lauderdale, FL 33334
Stainer & Bell (order from Galaxy Music Corp.)
Studio P/R, Inc., 224 S. Lebanon St., Lebanon, IN 46052
Summa Publications (order from AMSI)
Summy-Birchard Co., 1834 Ridge Ave., Evanston, IL 60204
Tetra Music Corp. (order from Alexander Broude, Inc.)
Thomas House Publications (order from Roger Dean Publishing Company)
Gordon Thompson, Ltd., 29 Birch Ave., Toronto, Ontario, Canada
Transcontinental Music Publications, 838 Fifth Ave., New York, NY 10021
Triune Music, Inc., 824 19th Ave. South, Nashville, TN 37203
United Artist Music Co., Inc. (order from Big 3 Music Corp.)
Universal Editions (order from European American Music Distributors Corp.)
Volkwein Bros., Inc., 117 Sandusky St., Pittsburgh, PA 15212
Walton Music Corp. (order from Lorenz Industries)
Warner Bros. Publications, Inc., 75 Rockefeller Plaza, New York, NY 10019
Josef Weinberger, Ltd., London (order from Boosey & Hawkes)
Weintraub Music Co., 39 W. 60th St., New York, NY 10023
Willis Music Co., 7380 Industrial Rd., Florence, KY 41042
M. Witmark & Sons (order from Warner Bros. Publications, Inc.)
Word, Inc., PO Box 1790, Waco, TX 76703
World Library Publications, 2145 Central Parkway, Cincinnati, OH 45214
The Zondervan Corporation, 1415 Lake Drive SE, Grand Rapids, MI 49506

Educational Films

Choral directors will find educational sound films to be of considerable
value in broadening their singers' musical backgrounds, and increasing

motivation and the effectiveness of their teaching.   Specific films are included to aid the director in the following ways:

1 To provide information about fundamental vocal techniques.
2 To broaden and clarify the singers' concept of artistic choral singing.
3 To develop an understanding of historical eras, and the musical styles of various composers.
4 To increase the singers' understanding of the theoretical aspects of music.
5 To assist young singers in their exploration of music as a possible career.

Obtaining Films

Films are available from a variety of sources: (a) city libraries, audio-visual or media centers; (b) university audiovisual departments; (c) film producers; (d) regional and national film distributors.   School music teachers should work through the visual-aids representative of their schools.   This person usually has an adequate supply of visual-aids catalogs, and will be able to provide valuable information and assistance in securing appropriate films.   It is suggested that in seeking films, teachers explore the sources in the order indicated above.   If films are not available locally, directors should refer to the catalog of the nearest state university or a university that distributes films for educational purposes. Most school audiovisual or media centers will have a number of their catalogs available.   As a final resort, one should inquire directly of the producer, or the national or regional distributor, for information concerning the availability and location of specifically desired films.

Following each film title in this listing is an abbreviation of the producer's name.   The complete name and address will be found at the end of this section.[3]   Also following the film title is the length of the film in minutes, the year of the film's release, and a key to the age level for which the film would be most appropriate.   This key is as follows:

el—elementary school (grades 4–6)
jh—junior high school (grades 7–9)
sh—senior high school (grades 10–12)
 c—college or university level
ad—adult level

Unless otherwise indicated, films are available in black and white only.   Films available in color, or in either black and white (b & w) or color, are also indicated by each title.   Rental prices are not listed be-

[3] In instances where the producer's address is not readily available, the national film distributor's name and address are given. While distributors may be subject to change, their names and addresses, as well as those of the producers, are listed in *Index to 16 mm Educational Films, National Information Center for Educational Media* (NICEM), 6th edition, Los Angeles: University of Southern California, 1977. This valuable reference source will be found in many libraries and school media centers.

cause they vary slightly with various film outlets. For specific price information, refer to the catalogs of film distributors in your area.

Procedure in Using Films

Three distinct steps are necessary in the successful use of films for instructional purposes:

Preparation. If the group is to be adequately motivated to learn, and if it is to gain the maximum benefit from viewing the film, it is essential that the group be prepared for what it is going to see and hear. Before the film is shown, the instructor should preview it in order to have sufficient knowledge and understanding of its content to focus and direct the class discussion.

Presentation. In presenting the film, the instructor should pay careful attention to the focus of the projector lens and the volume of the sound. Attention to these important factors is vital and permits the group to gain maximum benefit from the film. Attention to adequate ventilation and lighting and the elimination of outside disrupting sounds are also essential.

Follow-up. Following the showing, a discussion should be held and the group should review the essential points illustrated in the film. The subject matter of the film should then be specifically related to the problems and subject-matter content with which the group has been working.

Choral Groups

Almost Angels (DISNEY) 93 min. Color. jh-sh-c-ad. 1965. Describes the activities of the Vienna Boys Choir including their training and travels.

America (OF) 10 min. Color. jh-sh-c-ad. 1972. An explanation and presentation of the song "America" by the Mormon Tabernacle Choir.

Behold a Child Is Born (WMALTV) 27 min. Color. jh-sh-c-ad. 1966. A biblical account of the nativity featuring the Maryland Montgomery County Oratorio Chorus performing selections from Handel's *Messiah*.

Choral Concert (NFBC) 10 min. sh-c-ad. 1948. A choral concert by the "Leslie Bell Singers," a girl's choir. The following selections are included: "Ay-Ay-Ay," "Echo Song," "Ouard J'etau Chez Mon Père," "I Couldn't Hear Nobody Pray," "I'se De Boy Dat Builds De Boat," and "Ave Maria."

Christmas Carols (CASTLE) 10 min. el-jh-sh-ad. 1945. The Castle Choir sings "The First Noel," "Hark the Herald Angels Sing," and "Adeste Fideles."

Easter Greeting, An (BELLTV) 60 min. Color. sh-c-ad. The Mormon Tabernacle Choir performs selections from *Messiah* by George Friedrich Handel (from the Bell Telephone Hour series).

Freedom Isn't Free (AIM) 25 min. Color. sh-c. Portrays how the young Americans of Sing-Out "Up With People" relate their musical and social objectives through a European tour.

Glasgow Orpheus Choir (BIS) 12 min jh-sh-c-ad. 1953. The Glasgow Orpheus Choir sings: Scots psalm tune—"Kedron," Scottish song—"Mice and Men," Highland song—"The Isle of Mull," faery chorus from "The Immortal Hour," choral dance—"The Dashing White Sergeant."

Hail Alma Mater (USA) 6 min. sh-c-ad. 1951. (Free loan.) The West Point Glee Club sings "Army Blue" and Hail Alma Mater." Scenes of the U.S. Military Academy at West Point are utilized as pictorial background.

Howard University Choir (WMALTV) 30 min. sh-c. A performance of the Howard University Choir.

International Choral Film Festival (PHENIX) 30 min. Color. sh-c-ad. 1973. A review of the Third International Choral Festival held in Lincoln Center in New York.

It's Fun to Sing (NFBC) 11 min. sh-c-ad. 1948. A chorus of 60 Toronto business women, under the direction of Leslie Bell, sings "Greensleeves," "Long Beach Sea," "Ah, Si Mon Moine," and Palestrina's "Sanctus." The selection "Dry Bones" is sung informally.

Let My People Live (NTBA) 15 min. jh-sh-c-ad. 1938. The Tuskegee Institute Choir sings three Negro spirituals and a portion of the "Hallelujah Chorus" from *Messiah* as a musical background to a film dealing primarily with the problem of tuberculosis.

Lord's Prayer, The (UWF) 4 min. el-jh-sh-c. 1950. The U.S. Air Force Singing Sergeants sing "The Lord's Prayer."

Naval Noel (USN) 4 min. each. Color. sh-c-ad. A series of eight films, each 4 minutes in length, with the U.S. Naval Academy Glee Club performing the following Christmas carols: "Angels We Have Heard on High," "Carol of the Bells," "Good Christian Men Rejoice," "I Saw Three Ships," "Joy to the World," "Lo, How a Rose E'er Blooming," "Noel," and "Silent Night." (Order each film by song title.)

On Wings of Song (AUSTME) 15 min. el-jh-sh-c-ad. 1955. The Vienna Boys Choir sings Schubert's "Horch, Horch" and "Serenade," Mozart's "Minuet in E Flat," Brahms' "Lullaby," and Herbeck's "Pueri Concinite." A description of the singers' daily lives is also included.

Selections from the Christmas Oratorio by J. S. Bach (NFBC) 14 min. jh-sh-c-ad. 1965. Selections from J. S. Bach's *Christmas Oratorio* are performed by the Montreal Bach Choir, under the direction of George Little.

Songs of Christmas, The (PORTA) 18½ min. Color. jh-sh-c-ad. 1957. A presentation of Roy Ringwald's "The Song of Christmas," in which the story of the Nativity is related in songs, carols, and selections from the Bible.

Songs of the Campus (MGHT) 15 min. jh-sh-c-ad. 1952. The University of Michigan Men's Glee Club sings familiar college songs representing various sections of the country. Activities at various colleges provide a visual background.

Time for Bach, A (FALKBG) 26 min. sh-c-ad. 1950. Includes a rehearsal of the Bach Aria Group, organized for the purpose of performing arias from little-known Bach cantatas. The music of Bach is integrated into the various inconsistent patterns of contemporary life.

Thing of Beauty, A (FISKU) 45 min. Color. sh-c-ad. 1966. A performance by the Jubilee Singers of Fisk University.

Voice of a Choir (PATHP) 24 min. sh-c-ad. 1952. A performance of the Bach Choir is included in this film produced for the U.S. Department of State.

Young Americans (IDEAL) 94 min. Color. jh-sh-c-ad. The Young Americans, a Los Angeles based choral group, under the direction of Milton C. Anderson, performing folk songs, pop and show tunes, and spirituals.

Youth and Music in Detroit (WSU) 24 min. Color. el-jh-sh-c-ad. 1956. Includes choral, instrumental, and modern dance numbers of the Detroit Cooley High School's annual spring festival.

Composers

American Composers (KOEDTV) 20 min. Color. sh-c. Describes the distinct characteristics of the music of Charles Ives, Aaron Copland, and George Gershwin and how they drew from American folk songs, jazz, and Latin American music.

Beethoven and His Music (CORF) 13½ min. Color. jh. 1954. Relates how the social upheavals of the latter part of the eighteenth century are reflected in the music of Beethoven. Describes the unique qualities of Beethoven's music, and how it served as a bridge of transition from the Classical to the Romantic era.

Brahms and His Music (CORF) 13 min. Color. el-jh-sh. 1957. The ideas of Brahms, where he lived, and the persons who influenced him are related within a framework of his selected compositions.

Finlandia (CBSTV) 30 min. jh-sh-c-ad. 1965. Describes some major events in the life of Jean Sibelius and features the Radio Symphony Orchestra of Finland and the University of Helsinki Chorus.

Great Waltz (MGM) 17 min. jh-sh-c-ad. Scenes from the life of Johann Strauss, the "Waltz King," are depicted and some of his music is heard. Adapted from the MGM feature film produced in 1938, and prepared in collaboration with the Music Educators National Conference.

Immortal Bizet (ALM) 20 min. jh-sh-c-ad. 1950. Scenes depicting the life of Georges Bizet are shown against a background of European cities. Music is performed by the Concerts du Conservatoire, an outstanding French orchestra.

Mozart and His Music (CORF) 13½ min. Color. jh. 1954. Selections composed by Mozart are performed, and the elegant, formal life of the eighteenth century is recreated.

Music Experiences—Bach Is Beautiful (STEVNS) 15 min. Color. jh-sh-c. 1971. Describes the life and music of Johann Sebastian Bach.

Music in Art of the Renaissance (LUTHER) 28 min. Color. sh-c. Portrays the art and the music of the Renaissance period.

Secular Music of the Renaissance (NET) 30 min. sh-c-ad. 1965. Discusses the music of Josquin Deprés with selected works performed by the New York Pro Musica.

Schubert (IBF) 27 min. Color. jh-sh-c-ad. 1974. Describes the composer, Franz Schubert, and focuses on some of his compositions.

Schumann Story (MGM) 30 min. jh-sh-c. Adapted from the feature film *Song of Love*, produced by MGM. Scenes are shown depicting the life of the composer Robert Schumann and his music.

Music Theory[4]

Music As a Language (NET) 13 films. 29 min. each. sh-c-ad. 1955. Produced by the University of Rochester. Individual titles are:

1 *Alphabet in Black.* Illustrates how the use of black keys of the piano are characteristic of a great deal of primitive music, and describes how this device has been used by certain modern composers.

2 *Alphabet in White.* The different colors and tonal qualities of the various white key scales are illustrated as a part of the composer's musical vocabulary.

3 *Colors in Music.* Describes the use of instrumental tone colors and groups of instruments as a means of achieving varied musical effects.

4 *Essay in Sound.* A symphonic score is analyzed and explained.

5 *Merry Mount.* Describes the techniques and devices that a composer uses to convey the mood of the music, and the characterizations of certain roles in an opera, to an audience.

6 *Meter and Rhythm.* Tempo, pulse, rhythm, meter, and accent are discussed and illustrated with various musical examples.

7 *Modern Music.* Illustrates the difference between the white key scale and the scales used by such composers as Debussy.

8 *Music and Emotion.* Illustrates how composers have used rhythm, harmony, tonal quality, volume, and dissonance as a means of evoking emotion in music.

9 *Music as Sound.* Discusses the "chord of nature" as it is used in the composition of certain types of music.

10 *Musical Words.* The use of various words is illustrated as a part of the composer's musical vocabulary.

11 *Narrative Music.* Discusses the similarity among various composers' uses of certain chords to describe specific moods in music.

12 *Romantic Symphony.* Analyzes the structure of a symphony and compares form in music to the form or structure of other related arts.

13 *Six Basic Categories.* The theory that most music may be placed into one of six different categories is discussed.

Vocal Techniques

Changing Voice, The (FLASU) 29 min. jh-c-ad. 1959. A demonstration showing that boys can continue to sing throughout adolescence.

Human Throat (BRAY) 12 min. sh-c-ad. 1947. The function of the pharynx and larynx is described from the anatomical viewpoint.

Improving Your Posture (CORF) 11 min. Color. el-jh-sh. 1949. Good posture is explained and demonstrated. Certain posture difficulties are demonstrated, and exercises for their improvement are discussed.

Mechanism of the Falsetto (UMAVEC) 19 min. Color. sh-c. Portrays the mechanisms of the larynx in producing the falsetto sound. Vocalists range from beginners to the highly trained.

Mechanisms of Breathing (EBF) 11 min. sh-c-ad. 1954. Illustrates the various components of the body involved in the breathing process.

---

[4] Choral conductors will find particular films on music theory more adaptable for use with choral groups than others. However, since the conductor's ultimate use may extend to a theory class, a listing of the entire series on this topic has been included.

Vocal Music (EBF) 10 min. jh-sh. 1950. The structure of the human vocal instrument and some of the basic techniques of singing are described, such as correct posture, breath control, relaxation, use of chest and head resonators, and clarity of diction. Certain faults common to inexperienced singers are included. Filmed at the Carl Schurz High School in Chicago, Ill.
Your Voice (EBF) 11 min. jh-sh-c-ad. 1949. The four phases of voice pro duction—respiration, phonation, resonance, and articulation—are explained. Photography of the vocal cords or folds shows them in operation. Examples of solo and group singing are included, and the importance of proper exercises for vocal improvement is stressed.

Producers and Distributors of Educational Films[5]

AIM	Associated Instructional Materials, 600 Madison Ave., New York, NY 10022
ALM	Almanac Films, Inc., 915 Broadway, New York, NY 10010
AUSTME	Austrian Ministry for Education, Vienna, Austria
BELLTV	Bell Telephone Labs, Inc., Mountain Ave., Murray Hill, NJ 07971
BIS	British Information Service, Film and Publication Division, 845 Third Ave., New York, NY 10020
BRAY	Bray Studios, Inc., 630 Ninth Ave., New York, NY 10036
CASTLE	Castle Films, A Division of United World Films, 404 Park Ave. S., New York, NY 10016
CBSTV	Columbia Broadcasting System, 383 Madison Ave., New York, NY 10017
CORF	Coronet Instructional Films, 65 E. South Water, Chicago, IL 60601
DISNEY	Walt Disney Productions, Educational Film Division, 500 S. Buena Vista Ave., Burbank, CA 91503
EBF	Encyclopaedia Britannica Films, 425 N. Michigan Ave., Chicago, IL 60611
FALKBG	Paul Falkenberg Films, 1600 Broadway, New York, NY 10019
FISKU	Fisk University, 17th Avenue N., Nashville, TN 37203
FLASU	Florida State University, Off-Campus Media Services, Talla-hassee, FL 32306
IDEAL	Ideal Pictures, Inc. (see MacMillan Films, Inc.)
IFB	International Film Bureau, 332 S. Michigan Ave., Chicago, IL 60604
KOEDTV	KOED-TV, Bay Area Educational TV (title distributed by Great Plains Instructional TV Library, University of Nebraska, PO Box 80669, Lincoln, NB 68501)

[5] This list is limited to the producers and distributors of films included in this publication. For addresses of firms not included, see the *Index to Producers and Distributors, National Information Center for Educational Media* (NICEM). Sixth Edition. Los Angeles: University of Southern California, 1977.

LUTHER	Luthern Film Association, 315 Park Ave., New York, NY 10010
MACMLF	MacMillan Films, Inc., 866 Third Ave., New York, NY 10022
MGHT	McGraw-Hill Films, 1221 Avenue of the Americas, New York, NY 10020
MGM	Metro-Goldwyn-Mayer, 1202 W. Washington Blvd., Culver City, CA 90230
NET	National Educational TV, Inc., Indiana University, Bloomington, IN 47401
NFBC	National Film Board of Canada, 1251 Avenue of the Americas, New York, NY 10020
NTBA	National Tuberculosis Assoc., 1790 Broadway, New York, NY 10019
OF	Oxford Films (Paramount-Oxford Films), 5451 Marathon St., Los Angeles, CA 90038
PATHP	Pathescope Productions (title distributed by Universal Educational and Visual Arts, 100 Universal City Plaza, Universal City, CA 91608)
PHENIX	Phoenix Films, 470 Park Ave. S., New York, NY 10016
PORTA	Portafilms, Inc., 4180 Dixie Hwy., Drayton Plains, MI 48020
STEVNS	J. P. Stevens and Company (title distributed by Aims Instructional Media Services, Inc., 626 Justin Ave., Glendale, CA 91201)
USA	U.S. Army, The Pentagon, Washington, D.C. 20310
UMAVEC	University of Michigan, Audio Visual Education Center, 416 Fourth St., Ann Arbor, MI 48103
USN	U.S. Navy Department, Office of Information, Pentagon Bldg., Washington, D.C. 20350
UWF	United World Films, Inc., 221 Park Ave. South, New York, NY 10003
WMALTV	WMAL-TV, Public Affairs Dept., 4461 Connecticut Ave., Washington, D.C. 20008
WSU	Wayne State University, CIT Productions Center, 5035 Woodward, Detroit, MI 48202

Manufacturers of Music Equipment

In general, choral directors will find that local dealers can meet their particular music equipment needs, especially as they pertain to audio-visual equipment, pianos, and storage cabinets. In the event that certain equipment is not available through local firms, directors should contact the manufacturer directly for general information, including exact specifications and prices, as well as the name and address of the nearest dealer or company representative. Upon request, most companies will send catalogs as well as other pertinent information. Manufacturers of choir apparel, in addition, will send swatches of materials. The names of various companies and their addresses are as follows:

Audiovisual Equipment

Microphones

AKG Acoustics, Philips Audio Video Systems Corp., Audio Division, 91 McKee Dr., Mahwah, NJ 07430

Altec-Lansing Corp., 1515 S. Manchester Ave., Anaheim, CA 92803

Electro-Voice, Inc., 600 Cecil St., Buchanan, MI 49107

Gotham Audio Corp., 741 Washington St., New York, NY 10014 and 1710 LaBrea Ave., Hollywood, CA 90046 (Neumann microphones)

Peavey Electronics Corp., PO Box 2898, Meridian, MS 39301

Shure Brothers, Inc., 222 Hartrey Ave., Evanston, IL 60204

Motion Picture Projectors (16 mm)

Bell & Howell Co., 7100 McCormick Rd., Chicago, IL 60645

Eastman Kodak Co., 343 State St., Rochester, NY 14604

Eiki International, Inc., 27882 Camino Capistrano, Laguna Niguel, CA 92677

Elmo Mfg. Corp., 70 New Hyde Park Rd., New Hyde Park, NY 11040

Kalart Victor Corp., PO Box 112, Hultenius St., Plainview, CT 06062

Singer Education Systems, 3750 Monroe Ave., Rochester, NY 14603

Record Players

Audiotronics Corp., PO Box 3997, 7428 Bellaire Ave., North Hollywood, CA 91609

Califone International, Inc., 5922 Bowcroft St., Los Angeles, CA 90016

Garrard Division, Plessey Consumer Products, 100 Commercial St., Plainview, NY 11803

Newcomb Audio Products, 12881 Bradley Ave., Sylmar, CA 91342

Tape Recorders

Ampex Corporation, 500 Rodier Dr., Glendale, CA 91201

Gotham Audio Corp., 741 Washington St., New York, NY and 1710 La Brea Ave., Hollywood, CA 90046

Otari Corp., 981 Industrial Rd., San Carlos, CA 94070

Studer Revox America, Inc., 1819 Broadway, Nashville, TN 37203

Superscope, Inc., 20525 Nordhoff St., Chatsworth, CA 91311

Tandberg of America, Inc., Labriola Court, Armonk, NY 10504

TEAC Corp. of America, PO Box 750, 7733 Telegraph Rd., Montebello, CA 90640

Telex Communications Inc., 9600 Aldrich Ave. S., Minneapolis, MN 55420 (Magnecord and Telex-Viking tape recorders)

3M Company, 3M Center, St. Paul, MN 55101 (Wollensak tape recorders)

Video Equipment

Ampex Corporation, Audio-Video Systems Division, 401 Broadway, Redwood City, CA 94063

JVC Industries, 1011 W. Artesia Blvd., Compton, CA 90220

Panasonic Co., Video Systems Division, Matsushita Electric Corp. of America, 1 Panasonic Way, Secaucus, NJ 07094

Sony Corp. of America, 9 W. 57th St., New York, NY 10019

Acoustical Shells

Concert Design, Inc., 19 S. Compo Rd., Westport, CT 06880
Stage Engineering & Supply Co., 325 Karen La., Colorado Springs, CO 80906
Wenger Corp., 555 Park Dr., Owatonna, MN 55060

Choir Apparel

Collegiate Cap and Gown Co., 1000 N. Market St., Champaign, IL 61820
De Moulin Bros. & Co., 1099 S. Fourth St., Greenville, IL 62246
Fechheimer Bros. Co., 4545 Malsbary Rd., Cincinnati, OH 45242
Ireland Needlecraft, Inc., 3661 San Fernando Rd., Glendale, CA 91204
Macmillan Ward Ostwald, Inc., New London, OH 44851
Mercury Distributing Co., 2627 S. Milwaukee, Denver, CO 80210
E. R. Moore Co., 7230 N. Caldwell Ave., Niles (Chicago), IL 60648

Choir Risers

Humes & Berg Mfg. Co., Inc., 4801 Railroad Ave., East Chicago, IN 46312
Mitchell Mfg. Co., 2740 S. 34th St., Milwaukee, WI 53246
Peery Products Co., Box 8156, Portland, OR 97207
Wenger Corp., 555 Park Dr., Owatonna, MN 55060

Music Stands

King Musical Instruments Corp., 33999 Curtis Blvd., Eastlake, OH 44094
Krauth & Benninghofen Corp., 3001 Symmes Rd., PO Box 927, Hamilton, OH 45012
Selmer Company, The, Box 310, Elkart, IN 46514
Wenger Corp., 555 Park Dr., Owatonna, MN 55060

Pianos

Baldwin Piano & Organ Co., 1801 Gilbert Ave., Cincinnati, OH 45202
Everett Piano Co., 900 Indiana Ave., South Haven, MI 49090
Steinway & Sons, Steinway Pl., Long Island City, NY 11105
Story & Clark Piano Co., 100 Fulton St., Grand Haven, MI 49417
Wurlitzer Co., 403 East Gerler Rd., DeKalb, IL 60115
Yamaha International Corp., 6600 Orangethorpe Ave., Buena Park, CA 90622

Safety Candles (Battery-Operated)

Gamble Music Co., 312 S. Wabash, Chicago, IL 60604

Storage Cabinets

All-Steel, Inc., Route 31 and Ashland Ave., Aurora, IL 60507
Humes and Berg Mfg. Co., Inc., 4801 Railroad Ave., East Chicago, IN 46312
Lyon Metal Products, Inc., Box 671, Aurora, IL 60507
Norren Mfg. Inc., 778 North Georgia Ave., Azusa, CA 91702
Wenger Corp., 555 Park Dr., Owatonna, MI 55060

Hand Signals for Television

Stand by. *Arm bent. Hand up and open.*

Cue for "on the air." *Arm bent. Full arm motion with forefinger pointing to speaker.*

Time signals: 1. One minute. *Upright extended forefinger.*

2. One-half minute. *Crooked forefinger.*

3. Stretch. *Motion of hands pulled apart.*

4. Speed up. *Extended fore-finger, spun around . . . slow or fast, accordingly.*

5. Time is up. *Clenched fist. Given at 10 seconds, to allow speaker to complete thought.*

Cut. *Slashing motion of hand across throat.*

"On the air" camera. *Arm fully extended, forefinger pointing to camera.*

Speak louder. *"Donald Duck" motion with hand being raised.*

Speak softer. *"Donald Duck" motion with hand being lowered.*

Move. *Hand motion in direction to move.*

Move closer together. *Both hands moved toward each other.*

Move closer to microphone. *Hand moved toward mouth. Space being indicated.*

Rise. *Hand, palm up, being raised.*

Sit down. *Hand, palm down, being lowered.*

On time. *Forefinger touched to tip of nose.*

Film. *Rotating motion of clenched hand, at side of head. Other hand perpendicular to middle of face on vertical line.*

Spot signal. *Forefinger pointed to palm of other hand.*

Station break. *Both hands clenched, with breaking motion.*

Repeat. *Windmill movement of entire arm. Used only for musical numbers.*

(*Note:* All time signals are indicated with the right hand. All other movements, etc., are indicated with the left hand.)